The Holocaust in French Postmodern Fiction
Aesthetics, Politics, Ethics

LEGENDA

LEGENDA is the Modern Humanities Research Association's book imprint for new research in the Humanities. Founded in 1995 by Malcolm Bowie and others within the University of Oxford, Legenda has always been a collaborative publishing enterprise, directly governed by scholars. The Modern Humanities Research Association (MHRA) joined this collaboration in 1998, became half-owner in 2004, in partnership with Maney Publishing and then Routledge, and has since 2016 been sole owner. Titles range from medieval texts to contemporary cinema and form a widely comparative view of the modern humanities, including works on Arabic, Catalan, English, French, German, Greek, Italian, Portuguese, Russian, Spanish, and Yiddish literature. Editorial boards and committees of more than 60 leading academic specialists work in collaboration with bodies such as the Society for French Studies, the British Comparative Literature Association and the Association of Hispanists of Great Britain & Ireland.

The MHRA encourages and promotes advanced study and research in the field of the modern humanities, especially modern European languages and literature, including English, and also cinema. It aims to break down the barriers between scholars working in different disciplines and to maintain the unity of humanistic scholarship. The Association fulfils this purpose through the publication of journals, bibliographies, monographs, critical editions, and the MHRA Style Guide, and by making grants in support of research. Membership is open to all who work in the Humanities, whether independent or in a University post, and the participation of younger colleagues entering the field is especially welcomed.

ALSO PUBLISHED BY THE ASSOCIATION

Critical Texts
Tudor and Stuart Translations • New Translations • European Translations
MHRA Library of Medieval Welsh Literature

MHRA Bibliographies
Publications of the Modern Humanities Research Association

The Annual Bibliography of English Language & Literature
Austrian Studies
Modern Language Review
Portuguese Studies
The Slavonic and East European Review
Working Papers in the Humanities
The Yearbook of English Studies

www.mhra.org.uk
www.legendabooks.com

RESEARCH MONOGRAPHS IN FRENCH STUDIES

The *Research Monographs in French Studies* (RMFS) are selected, edited and supported by the Society for French Studies. The series seeks to publish the best new work in all areas of the literature, language, thought, history, politics, culture and film of the French-speaking world and to cover the full chronological range from the medieval period to the present day. Proposals are accepted for monographs of up to 85,000 words, while proposals for 'short' monographs (50,000–60,000 words), a traditional strength of the series, are still welcomed.

Editorial Committee
Tom Baldwin, University of Sheffield (General Editor)
Robert Blackwood, University of Liverpool
Jane Gilbert, University College London
Katherine Ibbett, Trinity College, Oxford
Shirley Jordan, Newcastle University
Max Silverman, University of Leeds

Advisory Committee
Wendy Ayres-Bennett, Murray Edwards College, Cambridge
Celia Britton, University College London
Ann Jefferson, New College, Oxford
Sarah Kay, New York University
Michael Moriarty, University of Cambridge
Keith Reader, University of Glasgow

PUBLISHED IN THIS SERIES

35. *The Subversive Poetics of Alfred Jarry*, by Marieke Dubbelboer
36. *Echo's Voice: The Theatres of Sarraute, Duras, Cixous and Renaude*, by Mary Noonan
37. *Stendhal's Less Loved Heroines: Fiction, Freedom, and the Female*, by Maria C. Scott
38. *Marie NDiaye: Inhospitable Fictions*, by Shirley Jordan
39. *Dada as Text, Thought and Theory*, by Stephen Forcer
40. *Variation and Change in French Morphosyntax*, by Anna Tristram
41. *Postcolonial Criticism and Representations of African Dictatorship*, by Cécile Bishop
42. *Regarding Manneken Pis: Culture, Celebration and Conflict in Brussels*, by Catherine Emerson
43. *The French Art Novel 1900-1930*, by Katherine Shingler
44. *Accent, Rhythm and Meaning in French Verse*, by Roger Pensom
45. *Baudelaire and Photography: Finding the Painter of Modern Life*, by Timothy Raser
46. *Broken Glass, Broken World: Glass in French Culture in the Aftermath of 1870*, by Hannah Scott
47. *Southern Regional French*, by Damien Mooney
48. *Pascal Quignard: Towards the Vanishing Point*, by Léa Vuong
49. *France, Algeria and the Moving Image*, by Maria Flood
50. *Genet's Genres of Politics*, by Mairéad Hanrahan
51. *Jean-François Vilar: Theatres Of Crime*, by Margaret Atack
52. *Balzac's Love Letters: Correspondence and the Literary Imagination*, by Ewa Szypula
53. *Saints and Monsters in Medieval French and Occitan Literature*, by Huw Grange
54. *Laforgue, Philosophy, and Ideas of Otherness*, by Sam Bootle
55. *Theorizing Medieval Race: Saracen Representations in Old French Literature*, by Victoria Turner
56. *I Suffer, Therefore I Am: Engaging with Empathy in Contemporary French Women's Writing*, by Kathryn Robson
57. *Ying Chen's Fiction: An Aesthetics of Non-Belonging*, by Rosalind Silvester
58. *The Poetry of Céline Arnauld: From Dada to Ultra-Modern*, by Ruth Hemus
59. *The Philomena of Chrétien the Jew: The Semiotics of Evil*, by Peter Haidu, edited by Matilda Tomaryn Bruckner
60. *Louis-René des Forêts and Inner Autobiography*, by Ian Maclachlan
61. *Geometry and Jean Genet: Shaping the Subject*, by Joanne Brueton
62. *The Language of Disease: Writing Syphilis in Nineteenth-Century France*, by Steven Wilson
63. *The Living Death of Modernity: Balzac, Baudelaire, Zola*, by Dorothy Kelly
64. *The Holocaust in French Postmodern Fiction: Aesthetics, Politics, Ethics*, by Helena Duffy
65. *Contemporary French Poetry: Towards a Minor Poetics*, by Daisy Sainsbury
66. *Frantz Fanon: Literature and Invention*, by Jane Hiddleston
67. *Essay as Enabler in Yves Bonnefoy: Creating the Good Reader*, by Layla Roesler
68. *Zola's Painters*, by Robert Lethbridge

www.rmfs.mhra.org.uk

The Holocaust in French Postmodern Fiction

Aesthetics, Politics, Ethics

Helena Duffy

LEGENDA

Research Monographs in French Studies 64
Modern Humanities Research Association
2022

Published by Legenda
an imprint of the Modern Humanities Research Association
Salisbury House, Station Road, Cambridge CB1 2LA

ISBN 978-1-78188-818-6 (HB)
ISBN 978-1-78188-822-3 (PB)

First published 2022

All rights reserved. No part of this publication may be reproduced or disseminated or transmitted in any form or by any means, electronic, mechanical, photocopying, recording or otherwise, or stored in any retrieval system, or otherwise used in any manner whatsoever without written permission of the copyright owner, except in accordance with the provisions of the Copyright, Designs and Patents Act 1988, or under the terms of a licence permitting restricted copying issued in the UK by the Copyright Licensing Agency Ltd, Saffron House, 6–10 Kirby Street, London EC1N 8TS, England, or in the USA by the Copyright Clearance Center, 222 Rosewood Drive, Danvers MA 01923. Application for the written permission of the copyright owner to reproduce any part of this publication must be made by email to legenda@mhra.org.uk.

Disclaimer: Statements of fact and opinion contained in this book are those of the author and not of the editors or the Modern Humanities Research Association. The publisher makes no representation, express or implied, in respect of the accuracy of the material in this book and cannot accept any legal responsibility or liability for any errors or omissions that may be made.

Trademark notice: Product or corporate names may be trademarks or registered trademarks, and are used only for identification and explanation without intent to infringe.

© *Modern Humanities Research Association 2022*

Copy-Editor: Charlotte Wathey

CONTENTS

	Acknowledgements	ix
	Introduction	1
1	The Non-places of Memory: Postmodern Topography of the Holocaust in Patrick Modiano's *Dora Bruder*	25
2	'L'infinie gamme des gris': Pierre Assouline's Re-evaluation of the Dark Years in *La Cliente*	55
3	'Non, che ne feux pas': Soazig Aaron's *Le Non de Klara* and the Question of Post-Holocaust Identity	77
4	'Father, don't you see I'm burning?': Jonathan Littell's *Les Bienveillantes* as an Example of Traumatic Metafiction	111
5	'The Dog and the Wolf': Philippe Claudel's *Le Rapport de Brodeck* as a Postmodern Beast Fable	151
6	A Poor Pole Enters the Ghetto: Yannick Haenel's *Jan Karski* as a Witness to the Differend	183
	Conclusion	219
	Bibliography of Works Cited	223
	Index	255

ACKNOWLEDGEMENTS

This book would not have been possible without the generous support of the Marie Skłodowska-Curie Individual Fellowship (grant number 654786) and the intellectual support of my colleagues at the Holocaust Research Institute (HRI) at Royal Holloway, University of London. My very special thanks go to Robert Eaglestone, whose seminal exploration of the link between the Holocaust and postmodernism aroused my interest in French historiographic metafiction about the Nazi genocide and who later mentored the project that led to the publication of this book. I am also greatly indebted to the Director of HRI, Dan Stone, whose work sparked my interest in postmodern historiography of the Holocaust and illuminated my thinking about the challenges faced by the postmodern novel about the Nazi genocide. I also wish to thank Beata Baczyńska, the Director of the Institute of Romance Studies at the University of Wrocław, Poland, for granting me leave so that I could take up the Marie-Curie Fellowship, and to the Turku Institute of Advanced Studies in Finland, for the possibility of completing the book. I am grateful to the following people and institutions for providing a platform for the dissemination of my research on postmodern Holocaust fiction in French: Christine Schmidt at the Wiener Library of the Holocaust in London, Liran Razinsky at the Bar-Ilan University in Israel, Seán Hand and Pierre-Philippe Fraiture at the University of Warwick, Henry Ravenhall at Kings College London, Wojtek Rappak at the Polish University Abroad in London, and the Battersea and Wandsworth Libraries in London. Last but not least, I wish to thank the Royal Holloway librarian, Eva Dan, for procuring materials necessary for the completion of this project, and Avril Tynan for proofreading the manuscript.

Before my thoughts about postmodern French Holocaust literature found their articulation in the form of the present monograph, I had shared some of the ideas explored in Chapters Two, Four, and Five through journal articles and book chapters. An earlier version of Chapter Two appeared as '"Les années noires avaient été grises": A Metaethical Analysis of Pierre Assouline's Appropriation of Primo Levi's "Grey Zone"', *French Forum*, 44.1 (Spring 2019), 29–44. A shorter version of my analysis of Max Aue's nightmares, 'Shit, Blood and Vomit: The Dreams of a Nazi in Jonathan Littell's *The Kindly Ones*', which constitutes one section of Chapter Five, will be published in 2022 in *Dreams and Atrocity: The Oneiric in Representations of Trauma*, ed. by Emily-Rose Baker and Diane Otosaka (Manchester: Manchester University Press). Finally, my identification of *Le Rapport de Brodeck* as a parody of the fable can be also found in 'Philippe Claudel's *Le Rapport de Brodeck* as a Parody of the Fable or the Holocaust Universalized', *Holocaust Studies*, 24.4 (2018), 503–26. I dedicate the book to the memory of the once large and diverse Jewish diaspora in my native Poland and to the memory of my maternal grandmother, Zofia Barańska, whose stories kept this memory alive and who encouraged me to think, to read, and to write. I also dedicate it to my son, Max, and to my parents, Anna and Waldemar, whose love has sustained me throughout the project..

H.D., September 2022

INTRODUCTION

During the 1995 commemorations of the mass arrest of Jews in July 1942 known as the *grande rafle du Vel' d'hiv*, Jacques Chirac made a speech that many saw as marking a break with the Gaullist narrative of *résistancialisme*. While glorifying the French people's opposition to the Nazis, this narrative obfuscated the humiliating defeat of summer 1940, the occupation by the enemy, and the liberation by foreign armies. Having been maintained by every previous head of the French state, the dominant discourse on the country's wartime past also kept at bay the thorny question of France's collaboration with the occupying German forces, and especially of the role that the French state and society played in the arrest, interment, and deportation of some 76,000 of the Jews living on French territory. Without constituting an apology or implicating the French nation in the Holocaust, Chirac's address opened the way for further acknowledgments of responsibility and for the ensuing institutionalisation of Holocaust memory in France. It is no coincidence that barely two years after the French president's long-awaited gesture, Patrick Modiano published a narrative confronting his country's participation in the extermination of European Jewry and the protracted silence of the post-war administrations surrounding it. By piecing together the life of a Franco-Jewish teenager who, alongside her foreign-born parents, was arrested and deported by the French police, Modiano's *Dora Bruder* (1997) pays particular tribute to those Jews who, drawn by the republican ideals of *liberté, égalité, fraternité*, had sought a better life in France, but who, paradoxically, became the most vulnerable victims of Vichy's discriminatory policies. And, just as thirty years earlier Modiano's *La Place de l'étoile* (1968) had inaugurated the questioning of the resistantialist narrative by French novelists and film-makers known as *la mode rétro*, *Dora Bruder* can be credited with initiating, or at least with intensifying, a novelistic inquiry by French writers into the Jewish tragedy.[1]

Whereas much of French and francophone literature about the Holocaust and its aftershocks that has appeared since 1997 continues to abide by realist representational tastes, some of these recently published novels employ tropes and writing techniques that are characteristically postmodern.[2] More specifically, these novels embrace the model of 'historiographic metafiction', as in the late 1980s Linda Hutcheon called narratives that, driven by progressive values and manifestly aware of their own constructedness as texts, engage in a critical dialogue with history and in a parodic reworking of established representational models. By concentrating on how writing strategies such as metafictionality, parodic intertextuality, fragmentariness, nonlinearity, and openendedness serve to dramatise the Nazi genocide, *The Holocaust in French Postmodern Fiction* identifies, and is the first major study of, this new tendency in French literature. As well as the aesthetics of six formally innovative French-language novels which take the Holocaust as their subject, in the following chapters I consider the ethical and political implications of their postmodern narrative strategies for Holocaust memory and our understanding of more contemporary instances of discrimination. Along with Modiano's *Dora Bruder*, I analyse Pierre Assouline's *La Cliente* (1998), Soazig Aaron's *Le Non de Klara* (2002), Jonathan Littell's *Les Bienveillantes* (2006), Philippe Claudel's *Le Rapport de Brodeck* (2007), and Yannick Haenel's *Jan Karski* (2010). I argue that the six narratives adhere to the paradigm identified and theorised in *A Poetics of Postmodernism* (1998) wherein Hutcheon describes historiographic metafiction as a novel defined by self-referentiality and by a grounding in a historical world. In other words, historiographic metafiction combines 'the "argument by poetics" (metafiction) with the "argument by historicism" (historiographic)', yet, in contrast to traditional historical literature, its engagement with the past is neither nostalgic nor antiquarian.[3] Rather, its concern with historical topics is both critical and accompanied by a metafictional reflection on the knowability of history and on the cultural and political contingencies of the (re)construction of history in the present.[4] As other recognisable features of historiographic metafiction, Hutcheon identifies fragmentariness, discontinuity, and refusal of closure. Equally, if not more characteristic is parodic intertextuality which enables the postmodern novel simultaneously to revisit and subvert the texts of the past and established narrative genres. The ironic intertextuality symptomatises the inherent self-contradictoriness of historiographic metafiction, which, more broadly, is a sign of postmodernism's inscription and questioning of dominant concepts, ideologies, and discourses. Consequently, for Hutcheon, historiographic metafiction is programmatically committed to telling the stories of marginalised racial, social, and sexual identities which she calls 'ex-centric', and of its linked commitment to the ethics of alterity and alignment with progressive political agendas.[5]

Among the novels Hutcheon recognises as representative of the narrative model she has identified and examined are works originally written in English, German, Italian, and Spanish.[6] The conspicuous absence of French-language novels among her references suggests that by the late 1980s historiographic metafiction had not yet captured the imagination of French writers. Indeed, despite the fact that the French philosophy of Jean-François Lyotard, Michel Foucault, Jacques Derrida, Emmanuel Levinas, and Gilles Deleuze and Félix Guattari is widely recognised as a source of inspiration for anglophone postmodern theories and practices, postmodernism has admittedly had limited purchase in France. Antoine Compagnon explains that, viewed as an alien concept, postmodernism has been approached with scepticism by French writers and literary critics alike.[7] Marc Gontard in turn elucidates postmodernism's reduced popularity in France with its widespread association with ludic playfulness, pastiche, irony, and superficiality.[8] Finally, Dominique Viart believes postmodern aesthetics to be poorly suited to the French literary landscape, as it promotes 'une déhiérarchisation des choses; *anything goes* est le slogan des postmodernes. Et puis, il y a l'idée de prendre tout avec ironie, avec distance' [a dehierarchisation of things; *anything goes* is the slogan of the postmodernists. And then there is the idea of approaching everything with irony, with a distance].[9] That said, some regard the *nouveau roman* as the French variant of the postmodern novel, since it too was a response to the cataclysms of the mid-twentieth century and constituted a decisive break with realism.[10] Yet, despite its self-theorising tendency, confused chronological structure, and refusal to characterise its protagonists and settings, the *nouveau roman*'s resolutely a-historical and a-political stance and its lack of ethical investment separate it from postmodern literature, at least as defined by Hutcheon.[11]

Writing in 1997, the year of the publication of *Dora Bruder*, Johnnie Gratton still detects no examples of historiographic metafiction among French novels. He nonetheless interprets the recent threefold return of the subject, of ethics, and of narrative as a symptom of postmodernism's growing hold on French fiction.[12] It was only in 2014 that America-based French scholar, Philippe Carrard, noted the appearance of narratives that 'mobilize several of the strategies that have been identified in [historiographic metafictions] written in English'.[13] These narratives which all happen to be about World War II and the Holocaust, are identified by Carrard as Littell's *Les Bienveillantes*, Haenel's *Jan Karski*, and Laurent Binet's *HHhH* (2010). While I consider the first two works in this study, I have recoiled from including Binet's novel in my corpus. This is despite the fact that, due to its references to the persecution of Jews and its focus on Reinhard Heydrich who was one of the architects of the 'Final Solution', other critics have recognised *HHhH* as a Holocaust novel.[14] In my view, however, Binet's narrative, which retraces the assassination of Heydrich by two Czechoslovak resistance agents, fails to comply with the widely accepted definition of Holocaust literature as 'literary works for which the historical context of the Holocaust is of major significance'.[15] Moreover, *HHhH* decisively distances itself from fiction; instead, it categorises itself as an 'infra-roman' [infra-novel] which uses all the strategies proper to fiction except fictional invention.[16] In contrast, a narrative that should have found its way into this book, but came too late to my attention and will therefore be addressed in a separate publication, is Fabrice Humbert's *L'Origine de la violence* (2010).[17]

To demonstrate the belated influence of the Hutcheonean narrative model on French literature is, however, not the main ambition of the present book. Rather, I wish to probe the coincidence of the espousal by contemporary French writers of postmodern aesthetics with their concern with the Jewish tragedy. I then wish to investigate whether these strategies can prove productive in dramatising the persecution of Europe's Jews within the specific context of France's fraught relationship with Holocaust memory. More specifically, I am interested in how the narrative model outlined by Hutcheon can help to deal with the prolonged suppression and recent institutionalisation of the Jewish memory of the Occupation. A more general question posed by this book regards the deployment of postmodern tropes and narrative devices to represent the Nazi genocide as it recedes from living memory and potentially enters the continuum of history and becomes open to comparative approaches. My analyses additionally broach the role of postmodern writing techniques, and especially of metafictionality, in articulating 'the aporia of Auschwitz', as Giorgio Agamben termed the non-coincidence of knowing (verification) and understanding (comprehension).[18] In other words, can these techniques serve to voice — or even to resolve — the epistemological and representational dilemmas attached to the Nazi genocide which is often believed to be unimaginable except to its survivors and whose creative reconstructions have been subject to regulatory discourses? As I discuss later in this Introduction, some continue to regard the Holocaust as resistant to fictionalisations or at least to unconventional representational forms, including those recognised as postmodern. And, since postmodernism has been widely associated with unseriousness, irony, and moral relativism, while being accused of irrationality, of questioning foundational truths and the knowability of history, or even of being complicit with Holocaust denial, the deployment of postmodern narrative devices in Holocaust fiction is understandably controversial. My aim is therefore to address the tension between the morally sensitive topic of the Jewish catastrophe and postmodern aesthetics, and, as anticipated by this monograph's subtitle — *Aesthetics, Ethics, Politics* — to interrogate the ethical engagement and ideological agendas of the novels marked by this tension. Namely, I examine the potential import of French historiographic metafictions about the Holocaust for our understanding of both the historical event they thematise and the more contemporary instances of the oppression of marginalised otherness. This means that I am concerned with the investment of the six novels in the ethics of alterity and with their interconnected political positioning on mainstream interpretations of the Jewish tragedy and on the present-day events that they construe as analogous to the Holocaust.

French Holocaust Literature and Literary Criticism

The recent surge in interest in the Nazi genocide of Europe's Jews among French novelists, a surge of which the works scrutinised in this study are representative, is remarkable considering that, in contrast to many other cultural contexts, one can hardly speak of the canon of French Holocaust literature. This situation has complex reasons, one of which is the institutionalised repression of Jewish memory during the post-war decades. As well as by the effort to obfuscate France's collaborationist past, this repression was motivated by official endeavours to unite the deeply divided nation through the blurring of the grounds for deportation. The silence over the fate of Jewish deportees is exemplified by the absence of any mention of the Holocaust from Jean-Paul Sartre's study of anti-Semitism, *Réflexions sur la question juive* (1954). Likewise, Alain Resnais's *Nuit et brouillard* (1955), a documentary about the deportation commissioned to commemorate the tenth anniversary of the end of the war, makes few references to Jews.[19] Other reasons why Holocaust memory in France did not emerge until the late 1960s include the relatively small numbers of Jewish returnees by comparison with POWs and political prisoners.[20] One also has to mention the reluctance of the Jews themselves to draw attention to the specificity of their wartime experience, a reluctance provoked by their desire to be reintegrated into post-war French society and by their fear of renewed discrimination.[21] Max Silverman additionally lists the hegemony of the anti-fascist and anti-communist discourses that 'removed attention from the specificity of the Nazi crimes, the Holocaust and the annihilation of the Jews'.[22]

This situation finds reflection in post-war French literature which, when revisiting *les années noires*, tended to address the more general phenomenon of *l'univers concentrationnaire*.[23] This is emblematised by the works of former political deportees such as Robert Antelme, Jorge Semprún, Jean Cayrol, and Charlotte Delbo. However horrific and traumatogenic, their experience differed from the fate of the so-called racial deportees who had been earmarked for total annihilation.[24] Not only were the survival chances of political prisoners significantly higher, but, in contrast to the Jews whose return presented a threat of dispossession to the current occupants of Jewish property and to those who had filled the jobs once held by Jews, the returning political prisoners were greeted enthusiastically and their imprisonment was viewed as an extension of their wartime resistance activities.[25] The specific experience of racial deportees therefore found a limited representation in literature where the silence surrounding it was broken only by the isolated voices of André Schwarz-Bart, Roger Ikor, and Romain Gary.[26] We owe further representations of the Jewish tragedy to writers who immigrated to France after the war, but whose novels, being based on these authors' experience of the ghettos and camps located in eastern Europe, conveniently deflected attention from the role of the French state and society in the attempted annihilation of European Jewry.[27] The late 1960s saw the publication of works by the second and '1.5' generations, as Susan Rubin Suleiman calls those who had lived through the war themselves but were too young to have had an adult understanding of what was happening to them, or who were born immediately after the Liberation.[28] Often highly experimental in form, the narratives by Georges Perec, Henry Raczymow, Gérard Wajcman, Raymond Federman, and Patrick Modiano appeared in the context of the questioning of the sanitised memory of *les années noires*.[29] Namely, in May 1968 students were contesting a government that was honouring the resistance fighters at home but persecuting those in the colonies, and, equating the French riot police with the SS, were identifying themselves with German Jews.[30] In the meantime, writers such as Modiano and cinematographers such as Marcel Ophüls and Louis Malle began to review critically the dominant narrative on France's wartime past.[31]

The under-representation of the Nazi genocide of the Jews in twentieth-century French writing is matched by a relatively small number of French-language critical studies of Holocaust literature, while the porosity of this literature's boundaries finds reflection in the focus of the available analyses.[32] For Karla Grierson, the reticence of French scholars to delve into Holocaust literature is brought into sharp relief by, on the one hand, the extensiveness of American criticism in this area and, on the other, the interest that French writers and philosophers have shown in the topic.[33] To substantiate her point, Grierson notes that, with the exception of Michel Borwicz's *Écrits des condamnés à mort sous l'occupation nazie (1939–1945)* (1973), French-language studies of Holocaust fiction began appearing only in the mid-1980s.[34] Catherine Coquio nuances Grierson's criticism by pointing out that while French Holocaust studies may be less institutionalised than their anglophone counterpart, French scholars have addressed Holocaust literature as part of their investigation of 'concentrationary literature', 'deportation literature', or, to use Jean Cayrol's term, 'Lazarean literature'.[35] According to Grierson, however, one needs to distinguish sharply between 'écriture concentrationnaire' [concentrationary writing] and 'écriture génocidaire' [genocidal writing]. Unlike the former, the latter is cosmopolitan in character, a position endorsed by Georges Bensoussan who believes that French-language narratives cannot be considered outside a comparative perspective. Bensoussan's stand is embodied by the transcultural approach of many of the critical studies, including Charlotte Wardi's pioneering *Le Génocide dans la fiction romanesque* (1986).[36] More recently, Grierson's typology has been co-opted by Yannick Malgouzou who, while upholding the separation between 'événement génocidaire' [genocidal event] and 'événement concentrationnaire' [concentrationary event], nevertheless stresses the political and cultural contingency of these categories and their mutual influence and permeation.[37] In contrast to Wardi, Clara Lévy, and Myriam Ruszniewski-Dahan, whose studies all narrowly focus on works concerned with the Jewish experience of persecution, in her *La Littérature en suspens* (2014) Coquio considers not only works that belong to, to use her own terminology, 'la littérature de l'Holocauste' [Holocaust literature], but also those representing 'la littérature de déportation' [literature of deportation].[38] Likewise, Marie Bornand's *Témoignage et fictions* (2004) and Fransiska Louwagie's *Témoignage et littérature d'après Auschwitz* (2020) examine both concentrationary and genocidal writings, while Bornand additionally analyses narratives that do not directly address the Holocaust.

Since none of the cited works of literary criticism, including the more recent ones, considers the use of postmodern representational strategies in Holocaust literature, in the present book I pay only cursory attention to them. Instead, I rely mainly on anglophone theorisations of postmodernism, and especially on Hutcheon's conceptualisation of historiographic metafiction. I also draw on Robert Eaglestone's seminal study of the links between the postmodern and the Holocaust, and on Dan Stone's advocacy of the deployment of postmodern methodologies in Holocaust historiography. Since anglophone theories of postmodernism were originally inspired by French post-structuralism and deconstruction, my analyses will be informed in equal measure by the work of Derrida, Lyotard, and Levinas. Coincidentally, while the philosophy of Derrida and Lyotard derives its thrust from the cataclysmic events of the Holocaust, it has been argued that the Jewish tragedy is 'ubiquitously implicit' in Levinas's ethics.[39] Finally, in the six main chapters, I refer to a wide range of theoretical studies relevant to the foci of my readings. Among these are works on French memory politics, Holocaust history, trauma, postfeminism, animal rights, Polish-Jewish relations, and testimony.

To return to French criticism of Holocaust literature, without addressing postmodernism directly, some of its concerns resonate with Hutcheon's conceptualisation of historiographic metafiction. Central among these concerns are, firstly, the tension between fact and fiction underpinning post-Auschwitz literature and, secondly, this literature's inherently self-questioning character. Inherited from Aristotelian poetics, the perceived opposition between what happened (history) and what might happen (fiction) crystallised, as Hutcheon reminds us, in the nineteenth century; while Romantic artists conceived of their works as autonomous constructs, positivist historians put their trust in the ability of history to offer a faithful and objective representation of observable facts.[40] Historiographic metafiction has resolved — or at least has mitigated — this tension by showing 'history' and 'literature' to be historically determined terms, and by foregrounding the shared reliance of the two representational modes on narrative structures, verisimilitude, and intertexts.[41] In the specific case of Holocaust literature, the tension between the real and the possible can be mapped on to that between the narrative modes of testimony and fiction, which adhere to different reading contracts. According to Bornand, since the need for testimony will exist for as long as the aftershocks of the Holocaust continue to be felt, literature will gradually assume the testimonial role, while the witness category itself will be broadened to receivers of eyewitness accounts.[42] Similarly, according to Ruszniewski-Dahan, a Jewish post-Shoah writer must take on the role of a witness and, in an effort to undo the contamination of language by the Nazis' euphemistic parlance, reinvent the existing narrative forms and language.[43] In the following chapters, I demonstrate the pertinence of such a vision of Holocaust literature to postmodern novels which, while often styling themselves on testimonies, metafictionally question the nature and role of testimony, interrogate its reported distinctiveness from fiction, meditate on the capacity of language to express the inexpressible, and ponder the future of testimony in the post-witness era.

The testimonial role of post-Auschwitz writing has been most fully addressed by Coquio who believes that the Holocaust has endowed literature with the messianic mission to bear witness.[44] The 'Catastrophe', as Coquio prefers to call the Holocaust, has thus made literature reconnect with historicity and with *engagement*, and has provided it with a new *raison d'être*, after its viability was put into doubt by Theodor Adorno and Elie Wiesel.[45] What this means in practice is that literature challenges conventional generic categories or, should it inscribe them, does so through irony.[46] To capture the inherently transgeneric nature of Holocaust literature, Coquio borrows Claude Mouchard's concept of 'œuvres-témoignages' which denotes works narrating *l'univers concentrationnaire* regardless of the positionality of their authors in relation to the Holocaust.[47] Coquio's vision of post-Auschwitz writing therefore echoes Hutcheon's conception of postmodern fiction as a genre that embraces heterogeneity, multiplicity, and indeterminacy, including in relation to narrative genres, and that engages established narrative modes only to subject them to ironic reworkings.[48]

While destabilising traditional narrative genres, post-Holocaust literature interrogates its own existence and purpose, a process that, following Imre Kertész,

Coquio calls 'la mise en suspens'.⁴⁹ The suspension of which Kertész spoke during his Nobel lecture takes the form of:

> Une mise en crise ou une mise en doute de la 'littérature', de sa pertinence, de son contenu, de son héritage. Cette mise en doute, qui est aussi la question de sa poursuite, ou de sa relance, lui est désormais *constitutive*. La littérature ne peut plus officier sans questionner radicalement son office, sans concevoir son illégitimité ou plutôt sa dérision, alors même qu'elle s'était vue et se voit confirmée dans sa nécessité de fait, vitale et durable.⁵⁰

> [A throwing into a state of crisis or a calling into doubt of 'literature', of its relevance, its content, its heritage. This calling into doubt, which is also the questioning of its continuation or its revival, will henceforth be its *constitutive* feature. Literature can no longer officiate without radically questioning its own position, without coming to terms with its illegitimacy or rather its ridicule, although it used to and continues to take itself for granted and sees itself as indispensable and enduring.]

As part of its radical and ongoing self-questioning, literature rejects a cultural heritage contaminated by the Holocaust and instead seeks to appoint what Coquio terms 'une philologie critique non positivise' [a critical and non-positivist philology].⁵¹ The need for a new poetics and new idioms stems, as Wardi, Ruszniewski-Dahan, Malgouzou, and Bornand all postulate, from the impossibility of enclosing the unimaginably horrific events of the genocide within the confines of literary realism. Indeed, to try to render these events plausible would mean to distort them and to betray the memory of their victims. According to Wardi, 'Obéir à cette tendance naturelle revient à intégrer le génocide dans la vie quotidienne en l'interprétant non à partir de sa spécificité mais en fonction des idéologies, des croyances philosophiques et des sciences vulgarisées en vogue' [To obey this natural tendency is to integrate the genocide into everyday life, interpreting it not in terms of its specificity but according to ideologies, philosophical beliefs, and fashionable popularised scientific theories].⁵² It is not surprising therefore that several of the critics cited here invoke Roland Barthes's remarks regarding the stupefaction and impotence of literature in the face of the events of Auschwitz, of the Warsaw Ghetto, and of Buchenwald. Barthes goes on to identify literary realism as too timid to depict a world that escapes it and as particularly unsuitable to represent the Holocaust. He thus suggests replacing mimesis with semiosis, and the *finite* order of 'literature' with a 'text' which can figure the *infinite* of language.⁵³

Historiographic Metafiction and the Holocaust

Despite Barthes's view of realism as unable to represent Auschwitz and its ravages, the desire for realism and referentiality continues, according to Michael Rothberg, to be 'one of the defining features of the study of the Holocaust'.⁵⁴ Such a position is exemplified by Berel Lang's ardent defence of historical realism and of the chronicle as best suited to the unusual, not to say, unique character of the Nazi genocide.⁵⁵ Lang advanced this view in response to the calls of Hans Kellner, Robert Braun, and Dominick LaCapra for a renewal of methodological approaches in Holocaust research. These philosophers of history had been largely inspired by Hayden White's conception of history as subjective, reliant on narrative forms, politically positioned, and historically contingent, and of the related weakening of the direct connection between the past reality and the historian's interpretation of it.[56] More recently, in line with LaCapra's remark that 'nowhere more than with reference to the Holocaust do positivism and standard techniques of narrowly empirical-analytic inquiry seem wanting', Dan Stone has urged historians of the Nazi era to abandon epistemologies compromised by the very subject of their research.[57] What he means is that cognitive rationality and the notion of historical truth were the pillars of the science and culture that gave rise to Nazism.[58] Stone also dismisses the conception of the Holocaust as a static phenomenon and instead acknowledges its constructedness in the light of present concerns, including the political and social contingencies of its changing meaning. He therefore invites historians to take into account their own ideological positionality, since 'to construct the past is always to construct the past for a purpose'.[59] Equally important for Stone is the capacity of Holocaust history to capture the 'disruptive excess' which conventional discourses fail to accommodate or, to use Stone's own expression, which they 'domesticate'.[60] And even though the Holocaust does not present representational problems different from those of other historical events, 'its impact is terrifying visceral' and its implications for 'western society such as to give these philosophical questions greater urgency and weight'.[61]

Some literary scholars have shared the perception of realism as unqualified to represent the Holocaust, and this is not only because of its implication in the culture that gave rise to Nazism.[62] Realism has been criticised for its conventional generic and ethical norms and teleologies, for its will to make absent objects present and credible, and for its resulting affirmative and resurrective drive which, according to Rothberg, 'traduce[s] the unsurpassable negativity of the genocide'.[63] As part of his analysis of testimonial writings, James Young accuses realism of taming the violence inherent in the Holocaust experience and of depriving this experience of its particularity.[64] This contentiousness of realism in Holocaust writing is evidenced by the advent of new narrative modes, such as 'traumatic realism' which, as Rothberg puts it, 'entails a survival of the claims of realism into a discourse that would otherwise be identified as [...] modernist or even postmodernist'.[65] Other alternatives to realism are 'magic realism', the 'conflicted realism' of the counterfactual historical novel, and 'realism of exhaustion' which, by carrying the Balzacian model to the extreme, problematises the place of realism in the 'compromised epistemological and representational project of modernity'.[66]

While some of the novels examined in the present study could fall under the rubric of the mentioned generic alternatives to, or extensions of, the realist novel, I consider their conflicting relationship with realism mainly as symptomatic of their adherence to the model of historiographic metafiction. In fact, the realist novel is only one of the conventional forms that these novels, to use Hutcheon's terms, 'use and abuse', other narrative modes subjected to parodic treatment being the fable, the diary, and a genre that has been identified as born out of the Holocaust: the testimony.[67] More specifically, I interpret the simultaneous inscription and subversion of recognised narrative forms as part of a postmodern interrogation of what Hutcheon calls the dominants of our culture — 'History, the individual self, the relation of language to its referents' — which postmodernism cannot escape.[68] By transgressing generic borders, the novels studied in this book also join in the postmodern contestation of totalising and homogenising systems. More pertinently, I contend that the ironic relationship that the six narratives maintain with traditional literary genres translates their recognition of the failure of these genres to do justice to the Holocaust experience with its unusual temporality, underlying trauma, openendedness, and inherent ethical complexities.[69] Their generic undecidability is thus a sign that new narrative forms must be created if events that are thought to be beyond imagination and representation are to be creatively reimagined and represented. Finally, the defamiliarising effect of the innovative transgeneric forms championed by the six texts has the potential to counter the empathy fatigue engendered by the recent overrepresentation of the Jewish tragedy in the media and in cultural productions.

The six novels manifest their parodic relationship with the Western literary tradition mainly through their overt and intense intertextuality. While intertextuality has been listed by Hutcheon as a key characteristic of postmodern culture, it has also been identified as an inalienable ingredient of Holocaust fiction, postmodern or not.[70] However, what distinguishes the novels analysed in this study from formally conventional representations of the Nazi genocide is that they do not try to conceal the texts and documents that they have absorbed. Rather, they flaunt their reliance on external sources, both historical and cultural, and thus undermine their own unity and originality. Such a narrative approach not only embodies the position of the postmodern philosophy of history that the past is recoverable only through its textual traces in the present, but, more pertinently, acknowledges the impossibility of direct referentiality when it comes to representing the Holocaust from a generational distance. Indeed, the six writers whose work I consider in this book belong to the second or even third generation, and have only an affiliative or horizontal — to borrow Marianne Hirsch's terminology — relationship to the events they narrativise.[71] The explicit intertextuality of their novels therefore points to the source of their authority in other texts rather than in their direct experience of Nazi persecution, and draws attention to the fact that even autobiographically-inspired Holocaust narratives, including testimonies of first-hand witnesses, can be inflected by post-war theorisations and cultural representations of the genocide.[72]

Alongside its intertextuality, the postmodern novel's critical engagement with the texts and narrative genres of the past is laid bare through its characteristic self-reflexivity.[73] In the case of Holocaust fiction, the novel's simultaneous declaration of its status as a narrative construct and destruction of mimetic illusion can have important ethical implications. Holocaust fiction has been a morally vexed genre ever since Adorno's influential injunction against an art that elicits enjoyment of 'the sheer bodily pain of people beaten to the ground by rifle butts', that imputes meaning to the unthinkable fate of the victims, and that, by mitigating the horror, does injustice to those persecuted by the Nazis.[74] Since then, imaginary reconstructions of the Holocaust have been condemned by eminent figures such as Wiesel and Claude Lanzmann, so much so that Holocaust fiction may be considered, to put it in Sue Vice's words, as 'tantamount to making a fiction of the Holocaust' and hence as 'scandalous'.[75] Vice's observation is shared by Efraim Sicher who describes Holocaust fiction as 'an entangled battlefield, crisscrossed by ideological minefields and rhetorical quagmires'.[76] In an effort to understand the unease provoked by the genre, Matthew Boswell has contextualised it with the enduring hold of dialectics on our understanding of Holocaust writing where fiction is viewed as a poor relation of testimony and as guilty of 'spreading harmful falsehoods about the genocide'.[77] In the specifically French context, the association between the Holocaust and fiction has led to the spurious idea that the Nazi genocide 'may always already have been contaminated by fiction', an idea that constitutes 'a principal plank of *négationnisme*'.[78] One of the questions I ask in this study is whether the postmodern novel's self-awareness of its constructedness, limitations, and partiality could ease the anxieties surrounding Holocaust fiction, and whether its foregrounding of the narrative status and positionality of history could make Holocaust fiction a more palatable concept. To tackle this question, in the next six chapters I examine the role of postmodern self-reflexivity in mitigating the aesthetic pleasure and in undermining the sense of redemption, closure, and catharsis that we are accustomed to seek in literature, but that can be 'disquieting' when experienced by readers of Holocaust novels.[79] Correspondingly, I investigate the capacity of postmodern self-reflexivity to thwart readerly identification which, too, has been deemed an inappropriate mode of reception in Holocaust culture. LaCapra, for example, warns against the dangers of 'an unmediated fusion of self and other where the [...] alterity of the other is not recognized and respected'. He exemplifies such a scenario with Henri Raczymow's novel *Un cri sans voix* (1985) which stages the appropriation of the other's pain. He also invokes Steven Spielberg's blockbuster *Schindler's List* (1993) which denies trauma by 'prematurely (re)turning to the pleasure principle, harmonising events, and often recuperating the past in terms of uplifting messages or optimistic, self-serving scenarios'.[80]

Self-reflexivity is, however, not an exclusively postmodern concept.[81] This is evidenced, for example, by Patricia Waugh's study of modernist metafiction as a literature marked by the tension between 'the construction of fictional illusion (as in traditional realism) and the laying bare of that illusion'. Metafiction also 'breaks down the distinctions between "creation" and "criticism"', 'merg[ing] them into the concepts of "interpretation" and "deconstruction"'.[82] In contrast to modernist novels which, as Hutcheon notes, replace referentiality with textual materiality and display confidence that the act of writing can counter chaos, historiographic metafiction enlists self-reflexivity in the service of historicity and political engagement. By thus redefining the postmodern novel, Hutcheon counters the dominant view of postmodernism as lacking in political potential and in genuine interest in the past, and as nostalgically neoconservative.[83] In contrast to Terry Eagleton or Fredric Jameson, Hutcheon associates postmodern culture with left-wing political agendas which are achieved through the commitment of this culture to 'ex-centric' individuals and communities. Among these are 'women, blacks, gays, Native Peoples, and others who have made us aware of the politics of all — and not just postmodern — representations'.[84] Similarly, Elisabeth Wesseling hails the postmodern novel's endeavour to recover for our collective memory the stories of 'the losers of history', as she calls the 'subordinated or defeated peoples and social classes, who usually do not have access to the channels of official culture and rarely make the records'.[85]

Such an attempt to rehabilitate postmodern literature as a transformative force for social and political change undermines its frequent bundling with 'irresponsible, free-wheeling relativism and moral evasion' and with the 'demise of the ethical'.[86] It therefore tallies with the belief of Herbert Grabes and Vera Nünning in the strong ethical investment of the postmodern novel, which lies foremostly in its concern with otherness and in making us not only endure, but also find pleasure in a high degree of alterity. While Grabes hopes that this pleasure 'trickles through into ethical sensibility', Nünning, more cautious, praises postmodern fiction's insight into difference and appreciation of others.[87] In the anglophone context, Eaglestone has forthrightly identified postmodernism as 'an ethical response to exactly the idea of a "single pattern" that characterises western thought and the activity that stems from this "single pattern"'.[88] Without offering a new ethical system or reviving existing ones, postmodernism, according to Eaglestone, responds to what Simon Critchley calls 'primordial ethical experience', which means disrupting western metaphysics of comprehension through an encounter with otherness.[89]

One of the aims of this book is to test the positive perception of postmodernism as a politically and ethically committed enterprise. The very subject of the analysed novels, which is the Nazis' oppression of Europe's Jewish diaspora between 1933 and 1945, points to their 'ethico-political' investment through their concern with persecuted alterity.[90] Furthermore, these narratives tell stories that have been silenced by mainstream Holocaust history and culture, and that belong to, among other neglected groups, women whose gender-specific suffering was long subsumed within the supposedly gender-neutral but in fact male-oriented perspective. The analysed novels also throw light on the Porajmos (the extermination of the Romanies) and on the plight of persons with mixed ethnic origins whom the Nazis called *Mischlinge* (literally, 'mongrels') and to whom they imputed racial impurity and physical and mental degeneracy. The interest that the six narratives pay to the historically marginalised participants of the Holocaust goes in tandem with their questioning of the dominant interpretations of the Nazi genocide. For instance, they interrogate the perceived uniqueness of the Holocaust by reinserting it into an historical continuum and comparing it with other instances of interhuman violence as well as with our perennial abuse of nonhuman otherness. Other discourses the six novels take to task are those that attribute redemptive meaning to the Nuremberg trials, draw a neat line under the Holocaust with the liberation of the concentration camps, paint Holocaust victims as invariably morally virtuous, and represent bystanders, such as non-Jewish Poles, as uniquely complicit in the persecution of Jews.

The Holocaust and the Postmodern

The key argument of this book, which is that historiographic metafiction can be a suitable representational mode when it comes to writing about the Holocaust from a generational distance, goes against the widespread misgivings surrounding the application of postmodern epistemologies and representational strategies to the Nazi genocide. It is these misgivings that provide the starting-point for Alan Milchman and Alan Rosenberg's pioneering inquiry into the philosophical and historical links between the two phenomena.[91] Eaglestone's more recent study, *The Postmodern and the Holocaust* (2014), also opens with the discussion of postmodernism's association with 'playfulness, pastiche, irony [and] a superficiality beyond caring about truth and falsity'.[92] It additionally invokes the Nazi sympathies of Martin Heidegger who, without being a postmodern philosopher himself, exercised a powerful influence on Derrida's deconstruction.[93] Alongside Heidegger's membership of the Nazi party and his subsequent silence on Nazi atrocities, Milchman and Rosenberg cite revelations concerning the collaborationist past of Paul de Man whose deconstructionism is seen as concomitant with postmodernism.[94] They also mention the fact that similar charges were levelled at other precursors of postmodernism, including Maurice Blanchot, Georges Bataille, and Michel Foucault.[95]

Among the staunchest opponents of the juxtaposition of postmodernism and the Holocaust are Berel Lang and Gertrude Himmelfarb. While Lang is scandalised by the connection of the Jewish catastrophe to 'the bottomless ambiguities and sequence of ironies of postmodernist ethics', Himmelfarb accuses postmodernism of erasing the once solid border between history and historical fiction, of depriving the past 'of any reality' and history 'of any truth', and of unnecessarily pluralising, particularising, and fragmenting history by rewriting it from the perspective of race, gender, and class.[96] However, if Himmelfarb stops short of equating postmodernism with *négationnisme* when she accuses it of 'a denial of any objective truth', Michiko Kakutani links postmodernism's efforts to reinsert misinterpreted or ignored communities into history to 'an atmosphere in which Holocaust deniers can gain foothold in academia'.[97] Similarly, Deborah Lipstadt believes *négationnisme* to have been nurtured by deconstruction where 'no event, no aspect of history has any fixed meaning or content. Any truth can be retold. Any fact can be recast. There is no ultimate historical reality'.[98] Even more forthright has been David Patterson who equates postmodernism with godlessness, and therefore — as though god was a uniquely Jewish concept — with the desire to murder the Jews, to silence the last of their prayers, and to destroy every Torah scroll. In contrast to Zygmunt Bauman's location of the origins of the Nazi genocide in modernity, Patterson calls the Nazis' extermination programme 'the final, postmodern solution to the Jewish Question'. The Final Solution is '*post*modern because the modern thinking of the Age of Reason at least tried to find an absolute ground for the prohibition against murder, whereas the postmodern period has done away with all absolutes'.[99] Finally, while acknowledging the origins of the Nazis' racist policies in the modernist 'arrogance of self-certainty', Gregory Fried doubts postmodernism's ability to keep Holocaust deniers at bay. Postmodernism, Fried contends, provides us with no means of maintaining 'the truth as something given, as something impervious to the "abyssal" mythologisation and perverse manipulation'.[100]

The position represented by Fried and others has often been rebuffed with recourse to Lyotard's ground-breaking theorisation of the causal link between the seismic violence of the Holocaust and the rise of postmodern sensibility. In *Le Différent* (1983), which derives its thrust from Robert Faurisson's negationist claims, Lyotard demonstrates how empirical history based on the principle 'seeing is believing' can be harnessed to revisionist agendas. Consequently, he calls for new historical methodologies and representational modes to be elaborated, so that not only testimony but also its metareality may be articulated. This metareality consists in the impossibility of testimony resulting from the scarcity of survivors, from the deliberate destruction of documents, and from the inexpressibility of the survivor's experience with the available discursive means. Lyotard thus commands postmodern writers to 'allégue[r] l'irreprésentable dans la présentation elle-même' [pu[t] forward the unrepresentable in presentation itself], 'se refuse[r] à la consolation de bonnes formes, au consensus d'un goût qui permettrait d'éprouver en commun la nostalgie de l'impossible' [den[y] [themselves] the solace of good forms, the consensus of a taste which would make it possible to share collectively the nostalgia for the unattainable], and 's'enq[uérir] de présentations nouvelles, non pas pour en jouir, mais pour mieux faire sentir qu'il y a de l'irreprésentable' [search for new presentations, not in order to enjoy them but in order to impart a stronger sense of the unrepresentable].[101]

Lyotard's belief that to write sensitively about the Holocaust, archivally-based documentary realism needs to be exceeded is shared by both Stone and Eaglestone.[102] Opposing the view that postmodern relativism enabled the 'Final Solution', Stone argues that Nazism was anything but a form of relativism and instead evidenced the terrible consequences of efforts 'to impute one absolute meaning to History'. To ensure historical freedom, we therefore need to open ourselves to a multiplicity of interpretations.[103] Drawing on Lyotard's analogy between the Nazi genocide and an earthquake that has destroyed not only a physical reality but also the instruments used to record, evaluate, and represent the destruction, Eaglestone reimagines postmodernism as a set of tools conceptualised to 'measure and offer new perspectives on a range of issues in our understanding of the Holocaust and its aftermath'.[104] While acknowledging the awareness of postmodern thinkers of rationality's limits, he considers postmodernism as profoundly committed to rationality and deems absurd the suggestion that it may foster Holocaust denial. Eaglestone supports his claim with Derrida's concern with the Jewish tragedy and with his philosophy's potential for exposing deniers rather than spurring them on.[105] Countering Kakutani's accusations that postmodernism opens the door for revisionism, Derrida, for whom, as Judith Still notes, post-Auschwitz equals postmodern, asserts that 'il faudra sans relâche combattre les pires des révisionnismes ou des négationnismes' [there must be no let-up in the opposition to the worst revisionisms and negationisms] that are marked by 'perversité abyssale' [abyssal perversity].[106] Similarly, postmodern metahistorians such as White can help reveal what is and what is not history, and can enable us to unmask those who manipulate historical evidence for their own ill-willed ends.[107] Yet what for Eaglestone ultimately demonstrates the commitment of postmodernism to combatting revisionism is the fact that Lyotard's quintessentially postmodern treatise draws its impetus from Faurisson's denial of the existence of gas chambers.[108]

Structure of the Book

The outlined aesthetic, ethical, and political concerns arising from the combination of postmodern representational modes and Holocaust thematics are the focus of my readings throughout this book. The following six chapters, each of which is dedicated to one of the examined novels, have nevertheless different foci which are determined by the key themes of the analysed texts and by the main narrative devices they employ. The chapters follow the chronological order of the publication dates of the six novels. Such a structure of the book reflects my ambition to trace the development of the examined literary phenomenon between 1997 and 2010, and to foreground any dialogical relations among the analysed works.

In Chapter One, I centre my attention on Modiano's relationship with Parisian topography in his generically unstable narrative, *Dora Bruder*. I suggest that, unlike in his earlier and also postmodern novels, here Modiano refrains from parodying the reality effect through a proliferation of meaningless geographical references. In the hope of retracing the life of an anonymous Holocaust victim, Modiano puts his trust in what seems to be the empirical approach, even if this approach ultimately fails to provide unequivocal answers to his questions. As well as *Dora Bruder*'s self-contradictory and therefore typically postmodern engagement with the topographical and forensic methods, I consider its dual political goals and the role that Parisian addresses play in their achievement. These goals are to do with, on the one hand, the exposure of French complicity in the Nazis' exterminatory policies and of the protracted suppression of Jewish memory in post-war France. On the other hand, they relate to Modiano's efforts to identify his father and himself with Dora Bruder with a view to reconfiguring his father's and his own relationship with the memory of the Occupation. I conclude the chapter by examining the ethics of the author's identification with a Holocaust victim, which I frame with Levinas's extension of his conceptualisation of the self's encounter with alterity to the dead Other.

In Chapter Two, I analyse Assouline's untranslated debut novel, *La Cliente*, in which I recognise a rejoinder to Modiano's outright attack on French wartime and post-war authorities. More generally, Assouline takes to task the 'Vichy syndrome', as Henry Rousso called France's obsessive and Judeocentric preoccupation with its wartime past. My reading focuses on the ethics of Assouline's efforts to nuance the overwhelmingly negative understanding of the Occupation as *les années noires*. The vector for these efforts is the novel's eponymous protagonist who, while being responsible for Jewish deaths, is the victim of a betrayal by the French police and, later, of misguided *épuration*. I am particularly concerned with Assouline's mobilisation of Primo Levi's concept of the 'Grey Zone', which equates a French informer with the Jews who *in extremis* colluded with their oppressors. Equally unsettling is the novel's condemnation of the sexist and violent practice of *la tonte*, whose sole aim seems to be inciting readerly sympathy for a wartime informer. Finally, I ponder the ramifications of Assouline's self-conscious espousal of historiographic metafiction as a narrative model that, in contrast to historiography, biography, and traditional historical literature, his narrator judges capable of doing justice to morally complex historical realities. The chapter therefore examines the implications of Assouline's use of postmodern aesthetics in an ethically problematic narrative for Hutcheon's defence of postmodernism against attempts to associate it with neoconservative political agendas.

In Chapter Three, I scrutinise the only female-authored narrative considered in this book and, unsurprisingly, invested with a feminist sensibility. This sensibility manifests itself in the foregrounding by *Le Non de Klara* of the specifically female experience of Nazi persecution, including the corrosive and long-term effects of the Holocaust on Jewish motherhood. Aaron's debut novel subscribes not only to feminist but to postfeminist logic, where postfeminism is understood as an enterprise arisen from feminism's intersection with postmodernism's challenge to dichotomous thinking and to the perception of the subject as stable and cohesive. In this light, my analysis addresses Aaron's questioning of the viability of the construct of identity in the post-Auschwitz world and her interest in both the horizontal and transgenerational reach of Holocaust trauma. As well as to the grim, not to say nihilistic, outlook of *Le Non de Klara*, I give attention to the novel's simultaneous espousal and destabilisation of the diary form through the diary's focus on a person other than its author.

In Chapter Four, I revisit Littell's much debated retelling of the Holocaust from the point of view of a Nazi. Approaching the Franco-American novelist's narrative strategy from the original perspective of perpetrator trauma, I reposit *Les Bienveillantes* as an example of 'traumatic metafiction'. Analogically to historiographic metafiction, traumatic metafiction represents the effects and processes of trauma, while providing a metafictional commentary on the articulation of psychological injury. My reading of *Les Bienveillantes* revolves around Littell's reliance on images of Jewish agony in describing the symptomatology of Max Aue's mental wounding. To throw light on such a controversial narrative choice, I draw on Cathy Caruth's influential reconceptualisation of trauma as an ethical position of engagement with the wounded or dead Other, exemplified by Tancred's realisation of Clorinda's pain thanks to his own trauma. The analogy between the scenario from Tasso's epic and the revelation of Jewish suffering through Aue's psychological injury enables me to interpret Littell's focalisation of his novel through a post-traumatic perpetrator as a way of defamiliarising the ordeal of Jewish victims and of countering the Holocaust fatigue engendered by the proliferation of victim-focused cultural and media representations of the genocide.

In Chapter Five, I identify Claudel's *Le Rapport de Brodeck* as a postmodern parody of the fairy tale and the beast fable whose simplistic zoomorphic and anthropomorphic strategies are thus exposed as complicit in the domination, exploitation, and ill-treatment by humans of both the nonhumans and some subgroups of humanity. My focus rests on Claudel's endeavour to locate the sources of the Nazis' oppression of animalised humanity in the human-animal divide and in the linked notions of the moral superiority of humans and their consequent deservedness of greater moral rights. I am also interested in the novel's use of the Holocaust to raise animal rights awareness, and its resultant extension of Rothberg's concept of 'multidirectional memory' from various instances of interhuman violence to man's exploitative and cruel behaviour towards the animal world. The central question of my reading concerns the narrative means Claudel mobilises to negotiate the vexed analogy between the Nazi genocide of the Jews and what has become known as 'the animal Holocaust'. I ponder the ethics of this analogy which, despite being championed by Jewish thinkers and writers, including by Holocaust victims and their descendants, continues to be regarded as profoundly problematic.

Finally, in Chapter Six I turn to the parodic engagement of Haenel's *Jan Karski* with the testimonial genre, and to its meditation on the ontological status of the witness and on the future of Holocaust testimony in the face of the encroaching absence of survivors. The alignment of *Jan Karski* with the postmodern ethos can also be traced in the attention it pays to the historically neglected figure of the Polish messenger and in its correlated confrontation of mainstream interpretations of World War II and the Holocaust. While reminding us of Polish efforts to stop the Holocaust in its tracks, *Jan Karski* contests the general understanding of the end of the war as the Allies' triumph over Fascism and of the western Allies as morally superior to the Nazis. With the figure of Karski, Haenel's novel also challenges the increasingly dominant view of non-Jewish Poles as ardent anti-Semites. The postmodern outlook of Haenel's generically hybrid narrative is ultimately confirmed by its reframing of the tragedy of the Jews and of their Polish messenger with Lyotard's concept of the 'differend'. This means the inexpressibility of the unravelling genocide with the discourse of wartime politics, and, subsequently, the incompatibility of Karski's rescue mission with Lanzmann's view of the Poles as (passive) bystanders to the Holocaust and with his belief that the Jews could not have been saved. I question, however, both Haenel's romanticised view of Poland and the ethics of his evident ambition not only to voice the wrong (*le tort*) suffered by the Polish diplomat and resister, but also to resolve the differend resulting from Karski's lack of discursive power and the world's deafness to his pleas.

Notes to the Introduction

1. Modiano's *La Place de l'étoile* was shortly followed by Marcel Ophüls's documentary *Le Chagrin et la pitié* (1971), Louis Malle's feature film, *Lacombe Lucien* (1974), and the French translation of Robert O. Paxton's *Vichy France: Old Guard and New Order, 1940–1944* (New York: Knopf, 1972), published a year later as *La France de Vichy, 1940–1944*, trans. by Claude Bertrand (Paris: Seuil, 1973).
2. Among the more traditional recent Holocaust novels are Robert Bober's *Berg et Beck* (1999), Gilles Rozier's *Un amour sans résistance* (2003), Philippe Grimbert's *Un secret* (2004), Arnaud Rykner's *Le Wagon* (2010), Colombe Schneck's *La Réparation* (2012), and Valentine Goby's *Kinderzimmer* (2014). In the wider francophone context, the recently published novels include

Nathacha Appanach's *Le Dernier Frère* (2007) and Louis-Philippe Dalembert's *Avant que les ombres s'effacent* (2017).

3. Linda Hutcheon, *A Poetics of Postmodernism: History, Theory, Fiction* (New York: Routledge, 1988), p. 42.
4. Ibid., p. xii.
5. Linda Hutcheon, *The Politics of Postmodernism* (London: Routledge, 1989), p. 17.
6. As examples of historiographic metafiction Hutcheon quotes Günther Grass's *Die Blechtrommel* (1959), Gabriel García Márquez's *Cien años de soledad* (1967), E. L. Doctorow's *The Book of Daniel* (1971), Umberto Eco's *Il nome della rosa* (1980), Christa Wolf's *Cassandra* (1981), and Graham Swift's *Waterland* (1983).
7. Antoine Compagnon, *Les Cinq Paradoxes de la modernité* (Paris: Seuil, 1990), p. 146.
8. Marc Gontard, *Écrire la crise: l'esthétique postmoderne* (Rennes: Presses universitaires de Rennes, 2013), p. 8.
9. Radio interview with Matthieu Garrigou-Lagrange, *La Compagnie des auteurs*. 'Claude Simon: le travail de la mémoire', 27 February 2019 <https://www.franceculture.fr/emissions/la-compagnie-des-auteurs/claude-simon-34-le-travail-de-la-memoire> [accessed 4 April 2019].
10. Alan Wilde, 'Shooting for Smallness: Limits and Values in Some Recent American Fiction', *Boundary 2*, 13.2–3 (1985), 343–69; Christopher Butler, *After the Wake: An Essay on the Contemporary Avant-garde* (Oxford: Oxford University Press, 1980); David Lodge, *The Modes of Modern Writing: Metaphor, Metonymy, and the Typology of Modern Literature* (London: Edward Arnold, 1977); Edmund J. Smyth, 'The *Nouveau Roman*: Modernity and Postmodernity', in *Postmodernism and Contemporary Fiction*, ed. by Edmund J. Smyth (London: Batsford, 1991), pp. 54–73. *Cf.* Hutcheon, *A Poetics of Postmodernism*, p. 4. Analysing the specific case of Claude Simon's work, Fredric Jameson describes it as a pastiche of both the Faulknerian style and the new novel. Fredric Jameson, *Postmodernism, or the Cultural Logic of Late Capitalism* (Durham, NC: Duke University Press, 1991), pp. 131–53. What is postmodern about Simon's writing, according to Jameson, is 'the evident emptiness of [the authorial] subject beyond all phenomenology, its capacity to embrace another style as though it were another world' (p. 133). Jameson therefore places Simon's prose in the rubric of postmodernism which he disparagingly reduces to nostalgia, pastiche, kitsch, and absence of meaning.
11. By revisiting historical events such as the Spanish Civil War and World War II, Simon's work constitutes an exception.
12. Johnnie Gratton, 'Postmodern Fiction: Practice and Theory', in *The Cambridge Companion to the French Novel: From 1800 to the Present*, ed. by Timothy Unwin (Cambridge: Cambridge University Press, 1997), pp. 242–60. Apart from Modiano's novels, as examples of this phenomenon Gratton lists texts as temporarily and formally diverse as Georges Perec's *La Vie mode d'emploi* (1978), Michel Tournier's *Le Roi des Aulnes* (1979), Marguerite Duras's *L'Amant* (1980), Philippe Toussaint's *L'Appareil-photo* (1989), Jean Echenoz's *Nous trois* (1992), and Christian Oster's *Le Pont d'Arcueil* (1994).
13. Philippe Carrard, 'Historiographic Metafiction, French Style', *Style*, 48.2 (Summer 2014), 181–202 (p. 182).
14. Christine Berberich, '"I think I'm beginning to understand. What I'm writing is an infranovel": Laurent Binet, *HHhH* and the Problem of "Writing History"', *Holocaust Studies: A Journal of Culture and History*, 25.1–2 (2019), 74–87; Robert Eaglestone, *The Broken Voice: Reading Post-Holocaust Literature* (Oxford: Oxford University Press, 2018), p. 54; Joanne Pettitt, *Perpetrators in Holocaust Narratives: Encountering the Nazi Beast* (Basingstoke: Palgrave Macmillan, 2017).
15. Jenni Adams, 'Traces, Dis/Continuities, Complicities: An Introduction to Holocaust Literature', in *The Bloomsbury Companion to Holocaust Literature*, ed. by Jenni Adams (London: Bloomsbury, 2014), pp. 1–24 (p. 1). The following alternative definition has been offered by David Roskies and Naomi Diamant: 'Holocaust literature comprises all forms of writing [...] that have shaped the public memory of the Holocaust and been shaped by it': *Holocaust Literature: A History and Guide* (Waltham, MA: Brandeis University Press, 2012), p. 2.
16. Laurent Binet, *HHhH* (Paris: Livre de poche, 2009), p. 327; *HHhH*, trans. by Sam Taylor (London: Vintage, 2013), fragment 205 (the English edition has no pagination). For the

definition of the infra-novel, see Stéphanie Joly, 'Entretien avec Laurent Binet pour son ouvrage *HHhH*', *Le Site de Paris-ci la culture*, <http://www.pariscilaculture.fr/2011/07/entretien-avec-laurent-binet/> [accessed 9 April 2017].
17. See Helena Duffy, 'Postmémoire culturelle, paramémoire ou complicité traumatique? Une enquête sur la Shoah dans *L'Origine de la violence* de Fabrice Humbert', in *Enquêter sur la Shoah aujourd'hui* (= special issue of *Europe* (2022)), 123–33.
18. Giorgio Agamben, *Remnants of Auschwitz: The Witness and the Archive*, trans. by Daniel Heller-Roazen (New York: Zone Books, 1999), p. 12.
19. Maxim Silverman, *Facing Postmodernity: Contemporary French Thought* (London: Routledge, 1999), p. 10. Sartre's text was originally written in 1946.
20. Although Jews constituted nearly half of those deported from France, they were often deported straight to their deaths, while those who were imprisoned faced conditions radically worse than those experienced by political deportees. Rebecca Clifford, *Commemorating the Holocaust: The Dilemmas of Remembrance in France and Italy* (Oxford: Oxford University Press, 2013), pp. 31–2; Pieter Lagrou, 'Victims of Genocide and National Memory: Belgium, France and the Netherlands, 1945–1965', *Past and Present*, 154 (1997), 187–90. According to Renée Poznanski, sixty per cent of political prisoners and only three per cent of the deported Jews returned to France. Renée Poznanski, 'French Apprehensions, Jewish Expectations: From a Social Imaginary to a Political Practice', in *The Jews Are Coming Back: The Return of the Jews to Their Countries of Origin after WWII*, ed. by David Bankier (New York: Berghahn Books, 2005), pp. 25–57 (p. 25).
21. Clifford, *Commemorating the Holocaust*, p. 32.
22. Silverman, *Facing Postmodernity*, p. 11.
23. David Rousset, *L'Univers concentrationnaire* (Paris: Pavois, 1947).
24. Robert Antelme, *L'Espèce humaine* (1947); Jorge Semprún, *Le Grand Voyage* (1963); Charlotte Delbo, *Auschwitz et après* (1965); and Jean Cayrol, *Poèmes de la nuit et du bruillard* (1946).
25. Poznanski, 'French Apprehensions, Jewish Expectations', p. 26; Clifford, *Commemorating the Holocaust*, p. 36.
26. André Schwarz-Bart, *Le Dernier des Justes* (1959); Roger Ikor, *Les Fils d'Avrom* (1958); Romain Gary, *La Danse de Gengis Cohn* (1967).
27. Anna Langfus, *Le Sel et le soufre* (1960), *Saute, Barbara* (1965), and *Les Bagages de sable* (1962); Piotr Rawicz, *Le Sang du ciel* (1961); Elie Wiesel, *La Nuit* (1951).
28. See Susan Rubin Suleiman, 'The 1.5 Generation: Thinking about Child Survivors and the Holocaust', *American Imago*, 59.3 (Autumn 2002), 277–95.
29. Georges Perec, *W ou le souvenir d'enfance* (1975), Henry Raczymow, *Un cri sans voix* (1985), Gérard Wajcman, *L'Interdit* (1985), Raymond Federman, *The Voice in the Closet/ La Voix dans le cabinet de débarras* (1979), and Patrick Modiano, *La Place de l'étoile* (1968), *Ronde de nuit* (1969), *Boulevards de ceinture* (1972), and *Rue des Boutiques obscures* (1978).
30. The slogan 'Nous sommes tous des juifs allemands' [We are all German Jews] referred specifically to one of the leaders of the student movement of May '68, Daniel Cohn-Bendit, whose German-Jewish origins were exploited by the movement's opponents. See Clifford, *Commemorating the Holocaust*, p. 52.
31. Paxton, *La France de Vichy, 1940–1944*.
32. As well as the work discussed here, these studies include Alain Parrau's *Écrire les camps* (Paris: Belin, 1995) and Anny Dayan Rosenman's *Les Alphabets de la Shoah* (Paris: CNRS, 2007).
33. Karla Grierson, *Discours d'Auschwitz: littérature, représentation, symbolisation* (Paris: Honoré Champion, 2003), p. 59. Among the French philosophers and writers who have shown interest in the Holocaust Grierson lists Jean-François Lyotard, Sarah Kofman, Jacques Derrida, Georges Perec, Jean Cayrol, and Maurice Blanchot.
34. Ibid., pp. 69–71.
35. Catherine Coquio, *La Littérature en suspens. Écritures de la Shoah: le témoignage et les œuvres* (Paris: L'Arachnéen, 2015), pp. 73–75.
36. Georges Bensoussan, 'Éditorial', in *La Shoah dans la littérature française*, ed. by Myriam Ruszniewski-Dahan and Georges Bensoussan (= special issue of *Revue d'histoire de la Shoah: le monde juif*, 176 (September-December 2002)), 4–13 (p. 5).

37. Yannick Malgouzou, *Les Camps nazis: réflexions sur la réception littéraire française* (Paris: Classiques Garnier, 2012), pp. 20–21.
38. Clara Lévy, *Écriture de l'identité: les écrivains juifs après la Shoah* (Paris: Presses universitaires de France, 1998). Myriam Ruszniewski-Dahan, *Romanciers de la Shoah: si l'écho de leur voix faiblit* (Paris: L'Harmattan, 1999). *La Shoah dans la littérature française*, ed. by Ruszniewski-Dahan and Bensoussan.
39. Robert Eaglestone, 'Levinas and the Holocaust', in *The Oxford Handbook of Levinas*, ed. by Michael L. Morgan (Oxford: Oxford University Press, 2019), pp. 37–52.
40. Hutcheon, *A Poetics of Postmodernism*, p. 105.
41. Ibid., p. 105.
42. Marie Bornand, *Témoignage et fiction: les récits de rescapés dans la littérature de la langue française* (Geneva: Droz, 2004), pp. 55, 17.
43. Ruszniewski-Dahan, *Romanciers de la Shoah*, p. 30.
44. Coquio, *La Littérature en suspens*, p. 15.
45. 'To write a poem after Auschwitz is barbaric' and 'It has been impossible to write poetry today' are the two oft-cited statements made by Adorno. Theodor Adorno, 'Kulturkritik und Gesellschaft', in *Prismen: Kulturkritik und Gesellschaft* (Munich: Deutschen Taschenbuch Verlag, 1963), pp. 7–26 (p. 26). Wiesel has in turn proclaimed that 'a novel about Treblinka is either not a novel or not about Treblinka. A novel about Majdanek is a blasphemy'. Elie Wiesel, 'The Holocaust as Literary Inspiration', in *Dimensions of the Holocaust: A Series of Lectures Presented at Northwestern University*, ed by. Elie Wiesel and others (Evanston, IL: Northwestern University Press, 1977), pp. 5–19 (p. 7).
46. Coquio, *La Littérature en suspens*, pp. 16, 21.
47. Claude Mouchard, *Qui si je criais...? Œuvres-témoignages dans les tourments du XXe siècle* (Paris: Lawrence Teper, 2007).
48. Hutcheon, *A Poetics of Postmodernism*, p. 66.
49. Coquio, *La Littérature en suspens*, p. 13.
50. Quoted in ibid., p. 13. Unless stated otherwise, all translations are my own.
51. Ibid., p. 23.
52. Charlotte Wardi, *Le Génocide dans la fiction romanesque* (Paris: Presses universitaires de France, 1986), p. 22.
53. Roland Barthes, *Roland Barthes by Roland Barthes*, trans. by Richard Howard (Berkley: University of California Press, 1994), p. 119.
54. Michael Rothberg, *Traumatic Realism: The Demands of Holocaust Representation* (Minneapolis: University of Minnesota Press, 2000), p. 99.
55. Berel Lang, 'The Representation of Limits', in *Probing the Limits of Representation: Nazism and the 'Final Solution'*, ed. by Saul Friedländer (Cambridge, MA: Harvard University Press, 1992), pp. 300–17.
56. Hans Kellner, '"Never Again" Is Now', *History and Theory*, 33.2 (May 1994), 127–44; Robert Braun, 'The Holocaust and Problems of Historical Representation', *History and Theory*, 33.2 (May 1994), 172–97; Dominick LaCapra, 'Representing the Holocaust: Reflections on the Historians' Debate', in *Probing the Limits of Representation*, ed. by Friedländer, pp.108–27; Dan Stone, *Constructing the Holocaust: A Study in Historiography* (London: Vallentine Mitchell, 2003). Hayden White presented his views in *Metahistory: The Historical Imagination in 19th-Century Europe* [1973] (Baltimore, MD: Johns Hopkins University Press, 2014).
57. LaCapra, 'Representing the Holocaust', p. 111. Stone, *Constructing the Holocaust*, p. xiii.
58. Ibid., p. 22.
59. Ibid., pp. 20, 21.
60. Ibid., p. xii. Stone borrows the term 'disruptive excess' from Luce Irigaray, 'The Power of Discourse and the Subordination of the Feminine', in *The Irigaray Reader*, ed. by Margaret Whitford (Oxford: Blackwell, 1991), pp. 118–32 (p. 126).
61. Stone, *Constructing the Holocaust*, p. 21.
62. For an assessment of realism's compatibility with the Holocaust, see, for example, Jenni Adams, 'Relationships to Realism in Post-Holocaust Fiction: Conflicted Realism and the

Counterfactual Historical Novel', in *The Bloomsbury Companion to Holocaust Literature*, ed. by Adams, pp. 81–102. For a discussion of genres thought to be implicated in modernity, see Hayden White, 'Historical Emplotment and the Problem of Truth', in *Probing the Limits*, ed. by Friedländer, pp. 37–54.

63. Rothberg, *Traumatic Realism*, p. 99. Cf. Barbara Foley, 'Fact, Fiction, Fascism: Testimony and Mimesis in Holocaust Narratives', *Comparative Literature*, 34.4 (1982), 330–60.
64. James E. Young, *Writing and Rewriting the Holocaust: Narratives and Consequences of Interpretation* (Bloomington: Indiana University Press, 1988), p. 15.
65. Adams, 'Relationships to Realism in Post-Holocaust Fiction', p. 82. Rothberg, *Traumatic Realism*, p. 99.
66. Adams, 'Relationships to Realism in Post-Holocaust Fiction', p. 85.
67. Hutcheon, *A Poetics of Postmodernism*, p. 46. Wiesel, 'The Holocaust as Literary Inspiration', p. 7.
68. Hutcheon, *A Poetics of Postmodernism*, p. xii.
69. Berel Lang, *Holocaust Representation: Art within the Limits of History and Ethics* (Baltimore, MD: Johns Hopkins University Press, 2000), pp. 10, 35.
70. Sue Vice, *Holocaust Fiction* (London: Routledge, 2000), p. 2.
71. Marianne Hirsch, 'The Generation of Postmemory', *Poetics Today*, 29.1 (Spring 2008), 103–28.
72. Ibid., p. 112.
73. Hutcheon, *A Poetics of Postmodernism*, p. 40.
74. Theodor Adorno, 'On Commitment [Continued]', trans. by Francis McDonagh, *Performing Arts Journal*, 3.3 (Winter, 1979), 57–67 (p. 61).
75. Claude Lanzmann has called Holocaust fiction 'la transgression la plus grave' [the most serious transgression] and criticised it for enabling comforting identifications precluded by the very nature of the genocide: 'Le Lieu et la parole', in *Au sujet de 'Shoah'*, ed. by Michel Deguy (Paris: Belin, 1990), pp. 407–25 (p. 410). Vice, *Holocaust Fiction*, p. 1.
76. Efraim Sicher, *The Holocaust Novel* (London: Routledge, 2005), p. xiii.
77. Matthew Boswell, 'Beyond Autobiography: Hybrid Testimony and the Art of Witness', in *The Future of Testimony: Interdisciplinary Perspectives on Witnessing*, ed. by Jane Kilby and Antony Rowland (New York: Routledge, 2014), pp. 144–59
78. Jeffrey Mehlman, 'French Literature and the Holocaust', in *Literature and the Holocaust*, ed. Alan Rosen (Cambridge: Cambridge University Press, 2013), pp. 174–90 (p. 174).
79. Irving Howe, 'Writing and the Holocaust', in *A Voice Still Heard: Selected Essays of Irving Howe*, ed. by Nina Howe with Nicolas Howe Bukowski (New Haven, CT: Yale University Press, 2014), pp. 277–98 (p. 282). For the question of aesthetic pleasure in the reception of Holocaust culture, see Brett Ashley Kaplan, *Unwanted Beauty: Aesthetic Pleasure in Holocaust Representation* (Urbana: University of Illinois Press, 2007).
80. Dominick LaCapra, *Writing History, Writing Trauma* (Baltimore, MD, & London: Johns Hopkins University Press, 2001), p. 27, n. 31.
81. Hutcheon, *A Poetics of Postmodernism*, p. 52.
82. Patricia Waugh, *Metafiction: The Theory and Practice of Self-conscious Fiction* (London: Routledge, 1984), p. 6.
83. Jameson, *Postmodernism, or the Cultural Logic of Late Capitalism*; and Terry Eagleton, 'Capitalism, Modernism and Postmodernism', in *Modern Criticism and Theory: A Reader*, ed. by David Lodge (London: Longman, 1988), pp. 385–98. Hutcheon, *A Poetics of Postmodernism*, p. 46. Jürgen Habermas, 'Modernity Versus Postmodernity', *New German Critique*, 22 (Winter 1981), 3–14; Hal Foster, '(Post)Modern Polemics', *New German Critique*, 33 (Autumn 1984), 67–78.
84. Hutcheon, *The Politics of Postmodernism*, pp. 5, 17.
85. Elisabeth Wesseling, *Writing History as a Prophet: Postmodernist Innovations in a Historical Novel* (Amsterdam: John Benjamin's Publishing Company, 1991), p. 110.
86. Christina Kotte, *Ethical Dimensions in British Historiographic Metafiction: Julian Barnes, Graham Swift, Penelope Lively* (Freiburg: Wissenschaftlicher Verlag Trier, 2001), p. 2. Cf. Zygmunt Bauman, *Postmodern Ethics* (Oxford: Blackwell, 1993), p. 2.
87. Herbert Grabes, 'Ethics, Aesthetics, and Alterity', in *Ethics and Aesthetics: The Moral Turn of Postmodernism*, ed. by Gerhard Hoffman and Alfred Hornung (Heidelberg: Universitätsverlag C.

Winter, 1996), pp. 13–28 (p. 26). Vera Nünning, 'Ethics and Aesthetics in British Novels at the Beginning of the Twenty-First Century', in *Ethics in Culture: The Dissemination of Values through Literature and Other Media*, ed. by Astrid Erll, Herbert Grabes, and Ansgar Nünning (Berlin: Walter de Gruyter, 2008), pp. 360–91 (pp. 371–72).
88. Robert Eaglestone, 'Postmodernism and Ethics against the Metaphysics of Comprehension', in *The Cambridge Companion to Postmodernism*, ed. by Steven Connor (Cambridge: Cambridge University Press, 2005), pp. 182–95 (p. 183).
89. Simon Critchley, *The Ethics of Deconstruction: Derrida and Levinas* (Oxford: Blackwell, 1992), p. 3.
90. I borrow the term 'ethico-political' from Bat-Ami Bar On and Ann Ferguson, *Daring to Be Good: Essays in Feminist Ethico-politics* (London: Routledge, 1998).
91. *Postmodernism and the Holocaust*, ed. by Alan Milchman and Alan Rosenberg (Amsterdam: Rodopi, 1998).
92. Robert Eaglestone, *The Holocaust and the Postmodern* (Oxford: Oxford University Press, 2004), p. 3.
93. Victor Farías, *Heidegger and Nazism* (Philadelphia: Temple University Press, 1998).
94. De Man was posthumously identified as wartime contributor to the collaborationist Belgian newspaper with anti-Semitic content, *Le Soir*. See David H. Hirsch, *The Deconstruction of Literature: Criticism after Auschwitz* (Hanover, NH: University Press of New England, 1991), p. 73.
95. Blanchot was linked to Charles Maurras's extreme right movement Action française and Bataille was accused of anti-Semitism. Even Foucault, who was very young during the war, has been criticised for his 'screaming silence' on Auschwitz, while his condemnation of the repressive practices of liberal democracies has been interpreted as a sign of his admiration for fascism and approval of totalitarian regimes. Hirsch, *The Deconstruction of Literature*, p. 122.
96. Lang, *Holocaust Representation*, p. 142. Gertrude Himmelfarb, 'Telling It as You Like It: Postmodernist History and the Flight from the Fact', in *The Postmodern History Reader*, ed. by Keith Jenkins (London: Routledge, 1997), pp. 157–74 (pp. 165, 179).
97. Himmelfarb, 'Telling It as You Like It', p. 164. Elsewhere, however, Himmelfarb explicitly equates those who seek to deconstruct the history of the genocide of the Jews with 'revisionists who deny the reality of the Holocaust': *On Looking into the Abyss: Untimely Thoughts on Culture and Society* (New York: Alfred A. Knopf, 1994), p. xi. Michiko Kakutani, 'When History and Memory Are Casualties', *The New York Times*, 30 April 1993 <https://www.nytimes.com/1993/04/30/arts/critic-s-notebook-when-history-is-a-casualty.html> [accessed 15 April 2019].
98. Deborah Lipstadt, *Denying the Holocaust: The Growing Assault on Truth and Memory* (New York: Free Press, 1993), pp. 18–19. For a discussion of Lipstadt's arguments, see Robert Eaglestone, *Postmodernism and Holocaust Denial* (Cambridge: Icon Books, 2001), and Wayne Klein, 'Truth's Turning: History and the Holocaust', in *Postmodernism and the Holocaust*, ed. by Milchman and Rosenberg, pp. 53–84. Klein aptly condemns Lipstadt's word choice in the statement that deniers 'have distorted and *deconstructed* the definition of the Holocaust' and her comparison of Paul de Man to David Duke, a former official of the Ku Klux Klan and gubernatorial candidate in Louisiana (p. 56).
99. David Patterson, *Anti-semitism and its Metaphysical Origins* (New York: Cambridge University Press, 2015), p. 21.
100. Gregory Fried, '*Inhalt Unzulässig*: Late Mail from Łódź — A Meditation on Time and Truth', in *Postmodernism and the Holocaust*, ed. by Milchman and Rosenberg, pp. 23–52 (pp. 43, 44).
101. Jean-François Lyotard, 'Réponse à la question: qu'est-ce que le postmoderne?', *Critique*, 419 (1982), 357–67 (pp. 366–67); 'Appendix: Answering the Question: What is Postmodernism?', in *The Postmodern Condition: A Report on Knowledge*, trans. by Geoff Bennington and Brian Massumi (Manchester: Manchester University Press, 1984), pp. 71–84 (p. 81).
102. Stone, *Constructing the Holocaust*, p. 16; Eaglestone, *The Holocaust and the Postmodern*, pp. 225–46.
103. Ibid. Similarly, Paul Crosthwaite sees the Holocaust as the apotheosis of modernity which was premised on 'the inherently antagonistic character of the nation state; the dominance of instrumental rationality within modern bureaucratic, administrative, and logistical systems, and the consequent adaptability of such systems to mass reification, and ultimately extermination,

of human life; the capacity of political and military institutions to dominate, discipline, and control the natural environment and its human inhabitants; the propensity of scientific and technological expertise to be channelled into the production of highly efficient technologies of war and genocide; the co-construction of co-capitalism, imperialism, and militarism; the liability of western culture to objectify, oppress, and eliminate its ethnic and racial "others"; and the bloody futility of attempts to make over the world in the image of some grand, Utopian vision, whether of the right or of the left': *Trauma, Postmodernism and the Aftermath of World War II* (Basingstoke: Palgrave Macmillan, 2009), p. 15.
104. Eaglestone, *The Holocaust and the Postmodern*, p. 2.
105. David Michael Levin, 'Cinders, Traces, Shadows on the Page: The Holocaust in Derrida's Writing', in *Postmodernism and the Holocaust*, ed. by Milchman and Rosenberg, pp. 265–86 (p. 265); Eaglestone, *The Holocaust and the Postmodern*, p. 227.
106. Judith Still, *Derrida and Other Animals: The Boundaries of the Human* (Edinburgh: Edinburgh University Press, 2015), p. 23. Jacques Derrida, *Spectres de Marx* (Paris: Galilée, 1993), p. 172, n. 1; *Spectres of Marx: The State of the Debt, the Work of Mourning and the New International*, trans. by Peggy Kamuf (New York: Routledge, 1994), p. 185, n. 5. In the same footnote, Derrida accuses the likes of Kakutani of 'a symmetrical perversity that is no less threatening', and of abusing the memory of Holocaust victims and manipulating the term 'revisionism' to attack anyone positing philosophical or epistemological questions about history.
107. Eaglestone, *The Holocaust and the Postmodern*, p. 246.
108. Ibid., p. 225.

CHAPTER 1

The Non-places of Memory: Postmodern Topography of the Holocaust in Patrick Modiano's *Dora Bruder*

> The Nazis' aim was to make the Jewish universe shrink — from town to neighbourhood to street, from street to house, from house to room, from room to garret, from garret to cattle car, from cattle car to gas chamber. And they did the same to the individual — separated from his or her community, then from his or her family, then from his or her identity, eventually becoming a work permit, then a number, until the number itself was turned into ashes.
>
> — ELIE WIESEL, 'All Was Lost, Yet Something Was Preserved'[1]

Holocaust Landscapes and Postmodern Topography

In 1995, Simon Schama wrote that we are accustomed to think of the Holocaust as:

> Having no landscape — or at best one emptied of features and colour, shrouded in night and fog, blanketed by perpetual winter, collapsed into shades of dun and grey; the grey of smoke, of ash, of pulverized bones, of quick lime.[2]

More recently, Angeliki Tseti has asserted that 'despite historical specificity, the Holocaust is geographically non-specific; the event is marked by a notable placelessness'.[3] Such an understanding of the Nazi genocide was first challenged in the early 1990s by the topographical perspective in Holocaust studies. Its advent was part of the historians' wider interest in questions of landscape, palimpsest, panopticism, community, and territoriality, known as the spatial turn. Holocaust geographers argued that by repositing the Nazis' persecution of Europe's Jews as 'a place-making event that saw the creation of new places — ghetto and camp — as well as the reuse (and reimagining) of existing places — the house, the room, the cattle car',[4] they can guard the genocidal act from its reductive equation with Auschwitz and reveal the diversity and complexity of the experience of the victims.[5] Furthermore, according to the editors of *Geographies of the Holocaust* (2014), a study of the spaces affected by the genocide enables us to see it as part of the Nazis' overarching aim to separate Aryan from non-Aryan areas, which involved the confinement, removal and, ultimately, annihilation of undesirable populations:

> The Nazis violently imposed new rules that restructured daily lives for victims [...] by declaring — and enforcing — where people could and could not go,

where and how they could and could not live, all depending on the social category to which they were assigned.⁶

Needless to say, this economically and ideologically motivated 'geography of oppression' affected all scales of human experience, from the body to the continent, changing the lives of victims, bystanders, and perpetrators.⁷ Andrew Charlesworth additionally notes that the location and architecture of concentration camps can impart vital information about the men who designed them. This is illustrated by the Germans' decision to position KL Płaszów on the site of two Jewish cemeteries, or to plant quick-growing pines around similar installations, which, for Charlesworth, conveys the secrecy shrouding the industrialised murder of the Jews and the Nazis' cowardice.⁸ As a prime example of the attentiveness to spaces in Holocaust research, Charlesworth considers *Shoah* (1985) which Lanzmann himself has called 'un film de géographe, de topographe' [a geographer's, a topographer's film], and which demonstrates that 'the genocidal actions at the heart of Nazi racial policy occurred in ordinary landscapes'.⁹

Having initially focused on the sites where extermination happened, Holocaust geographers have progressively broadened the scope of their research to other locales. These include ghettos, trains used for transporting prisoners, urban hiding places, spaces repurposed for the internment of Jews, the roads that saw the death marches, and the forests which were either the theatre of mass executions, or provided Jews with refuge and the opportunity for active resistance.¹⁰ More recently, the topographical perspective has developed into the ecocritical approach, illustrated by the work of Eric Katz and by a special issue of the *Journal of Genocide Studies* (2020) which brings together studies of the environmental impact of the Holocaust and commemorative practices.¹¹ Jacek Małczyński, for example, has adopted Susan Schuppli's concept of the 'material witness', to interrogate the marks left by barbed wire on the trees growing around the former camp of Auschwitz and thus to determine the camp's original perimeter.¹²

While these innovative methodologies could also provide a productive theoretical lens for several of the novels addressed in this book, in this chapter, I extend the topographical perspective used by Holocaust historians to *Dora Bruder* whose efforts to reconstruct the wartime trajectory of the eponymous Franco-Jewish teenager heavily rely on Parisian addresses.¹³ By staying away from the sites that are readily associated with the Holocaust — the camps and ghettos of Eastern Europe — and that provide the setting for the canonical French Holocaust writings of Wiesel, Semprún, Rawicz, Delbo, and Anna Langfus, *Dora Bruder* supports Tim Cole's remark that 'the entire European landscape was the setting for the genocide'.¹⁴ In the terms of Sidra deKoven Ezrahi, Modiano's narrative counters the centripetal thrust towards a terminus with 'a centrifugal thrust that establishes the physical and symbolic centre as *point of departure*'.¹⁵ As we shall see, Modiano's topographical approach supports *Dora Bruder*'s ethico-political agenda which, as indicated in the Introduction, is to take French memory politics to task and to reconfigure Modiano's father's (and Modiano's own) relationship with the Vichy past.¹⁶

As well as to the penury of more traditional sources of information about Dora

Bruder, such as archival records and witness statements, Modiano's topographical approach must be attributed to the prominence of the Bruders' address in the small ad featured in a December copy of *Paris Soir*, which originally aroused the novelist's interest in the teenager.[17] Placed by a father searching for his missing daughter, the advertisement appeals for information about Dora to be addressed to Mr and Mrs Bruder at 41, boulevard Ornano in the eighteenth *arrondissement*. In the course of the novel, apart from the apartment block where Dora's family occupied a room with a kitchenette, its protagonist-narrator, whom I identify here with *Dora Bruder*'s author, visits other locations through which the family passed after arriving in Paris in the 1920s from Austria and Hungary.[18] Among these locations are the former site of the Catholic school Saint-Cœur-de-Marie which Dora attended and from which in December 1941 she ran away, the army barracks where the young woman was briefly interned, and the road followed by the convoys of prisoners from the Caserne des Tourelles to the transit camp of Drancy from which in September 1942 Dora was deported to Auschwitz. In the course of his inquiry, Modiano also inspects the cinema where Dora might have watched films and the square where she might have played as a child. Furthermore, the novel discusses locations that are less directly connected with Dora, such as Vienna where Dora's father was born and raised, and places in North Africa where he fought in the Foreign Legion. In Paris, Modiano walks down the rue des Jardins-Saint-Paul in the fourth *arrondissement*, where many Jews lived before the war and whose redevelopment becomes an illustration of what he sees as a deliberate obfuscation of Jewish memory by postwar French authorities.

Topographical precision has been a consistent feature of Modiano's writing and has already been the subject of academic scrutiny.[19] In contrast to the existing studies, my reading of *Dora Bruder* focuses on the potential incongruity between the novel's trust in the denotative power of geographical locations and its clearly postmodern outlook, manifest in its intense metafictionality, intertextuality, and generic hybridity.[20] Another hallmark of *Dora Bruder*'s postmodern ethos is its narrator whose fluid and heterogenous identity, sense of disorientation, and self-doubt make him identifiable with postmodern protagonists. Considering Modiano's overt dissociation from literary realism,[21] his narrative approach in *Dora Bruder* seems at odds with postmodernism's rejection of direct referentiality.[22] An alternative way for a postmodern narrative to engage with realism is, according to Hutcheon, to parody the conventional novel's confidence in its descriptive power and in the investment of geographical locations with denotative and connotative potential.[23] It is precisely this strategy that can be identified in Modiano's earlier writings which, as Akane Kawakami shows, by proliferating with inconsequential addresses and telephone numbers, parody mimetic and verisimilar literature.[24] The deictic rather than descriptive quality that Kawakami attaches to Modiano's topographical exactitude results in the failure of his writing to create the Barthesian 'effect de réel' [reality effect]. This is evidenced by the uncanny incongruity of the insistent catalogue of names, addresses, and telephone numbers with the glaring lack of verisimilitude, the pervading sense of confusion and uncertainty, and the unstable identities of Modiano's protagonists.²⁵ Camping in Parisian hotel rooms or borrowed apartments, these protagonists feel alienated from a city that appears more often unreal than familiar.²⁶ This is exemplified by Ambrose Guise in *Quartier perdu* (1984) who complains about 'le sentiment d'irréalité que j'éprouvais au milieu de cette ville fantôme' [the sense of unreality I felt in the midst of this ghostly city]. Having returned to Paris from abroad, Guise asks himself 'si je ne traversais pas une ville fantôme après un bombardement et l'exode de ses habitants' [if I was crossing a ghost city abandoned by its inhabitants after a bombardment].²⁷ Modiano's other protagonists counter their sense of estrangement by revisiting familiar places, as does Serge Alexandre in *Les Boulevards de ceinture*, who admits that 'au milieu de tant d'incertitudes, mes seuls points de repère, le seul terrain qui ne se dérobait pas, c'était les carrefours et les trottoirs de cette ville où je finirais sans doute par me retrouver seul' [in the midst of so much uncertainty, my only landmarks, the only ground that didn't shift beneath my feet, were the pavements and the junctions of this city, where, in the end, I would probably find myself alone].²⁸ This sense of unreality and malaise proceeds, for Kawakami, from 'the imbalance of sign and referent, the signs proliferating beyond all reasonable referential bounds'.²⁹ What it results in is a 'postmodern topography', a term Kawakami borrows from Jacques Guicharnaud to denote Modiano's self-conscious espousal and questioning of literary realism.³⁰

While sharing Kawakami's interpretation of *Quartier perdu* and *Les Boulevards de ceinture*, I consider *Dora Bruder* as a departure from Modiano's parodic relationship with realism. Instead, I see it as symptomatic of the author's renewed confidence in the symbolic and connotative value of referents, and therefore in their cognitive potential. My aim in the following pages is therefore to investigate whether *Dora Bruder* compromises Modiano's commitment to postmodern scepticism regarding the adequacy of the empirical recovery of the past. Alternatively, *Dora Bruder*'s relationship with referentiality might be regarded as self-contradictory and therefore as postmodern, if we consider that the novel's reliance on geographical locations for information about Dora is ultimately undercut by the failure of these locations to provide unequivocal answers to the narrator's questions regarding the teenager's trajectory, and especially her *fugues*.

The Hollow Trace of the (Dead) Other

Modiano's exploration of the Parisian addresses as places that, in Anna-Louise Milne's words, 'hold unsuspected potential, in the manner of an archive, if we understand by archive a repository of as-yet-unknown meanings', begins at 41 boulevard Ornano.³¹ Although it quickly transpires that details such as which room precisely the family occupied or which school Dora attended are impossible to establish, the cramped conditions in which the Bruders lived may explain Ernest and Cécile's decision to place their daughter in a boarding school. They may also provide a key to Dora's second *fugue* in the spring of 1942, this time from her parents' place. Furthermore, the exactitude of the details offered by the small ad provides an ironic contrast to the dearth of in-depth information concerning Dora, which Modiano metaphorises as 'la nuit, l'inconnu, l'oubli, le néant tout autour' [the night, the unknown, oblivion, nothingness all around] (*DB*, 53; *SW*, 48). Thus highlighted, this dearth of information is in itself an eloquent signifier of the wartime destruction of the Jewish community of Paris, as a consequence of which there are few witnesses to the Bruders' pre-war and wartime life. It is also an indicator of the family's social marginality resulting from their immigrant and working-class status:

> Ce sont des personnes qui laissent peu de traces derrière elles. Presque des anonymes. Elles ne se détachent pas de certaines rues de Paris, de certains paysages de banlieue [...]. Ce que l'on sait d'elles se résume souvent à une simple adresse. Et cette précision topographique contraste avec ce que l'on ignorera pour toujours de leur vie — ce blanc, ce bloc d'inconnu et de silence. (*DB*, 28)
>
> [They are the sort of people who leave few traces. Virtually anonymous. Inseparable from those Paris streets, those suburban landscapes [...]. Often what is known about them amounts to no more than a simple address. And such topographical precision contrasts with what will never be known about their life — this blank, this mute block of the unknown.] (*SW*, 23, translation modified)

The use of the term *trace* in the quoted passage invites me to read Modiano's quest for Dora through the prism of Levinas's ethics which some believe to have been shaped by the Jewish tragedy.[32] More specifically, the *trace* invokes the philosopher's conceptualisation of the self's encounter with the dead Other through its traces, a conceptualisation that extends Levinas's earlier and better known theorisation of the self's relationship with living alterity. Levinas's view that we should react responsibly to the interpellations of the Other has the power to illuminate the ethical dimension of Modiano's response to his belated cognisance of Dora's disappearance, including his identification with the adolescent. To summarise Levinas's argument, we are summoned into a non-identificatory and ethically-inflected relationship with alterity by the Other's face (*le visage*) which, as well as being the collection of features that is most readily available to sight and the most expressive part of our body, is, as Colin Davis puts it, 'an epiphany or revelation'. In the case of the *dead* Other, the encounter is enabled by the *trace* which, for Eaglestone, 'inaugurates the same ethical relation to the other in the past'.[33] In Levinas's own words, 'Le visage est dans la trace de l'Absent absolument révolu, absolument passé' [The face is in the trace of the absolutely completed, absolutely past Absent]. 'C'est dans la trace de l'Autre,' he continues, 'que luit le visage' [It is in the trace of the Other, that the face glows].[34] It needs adding that, just as in the encounter with the living other, the *trace* 'does not make the other present [...]; it instead offers a locus for the disruptive manifestation of their alterity, their lack of availability to our "grasping", coupled with a decentring awareness of the ethical obligation we bear them'.[35] Exemplified by animal spores, clues found by a detective, or relics of an ancient civilisation, the *trace* is distinct from the sign which is intentional and endowed with meaning, and which signifies what is only momentarily absent. Contrariwise, the *trace* is left unintentionally by something or someone who no longer exists, but whose existence persists into the present in the form of the *trace*. Notwithstanding this difference, some traces can become signs, as illustrated by the pertinent example of ashes. Normally but a trace of extinguished flames, in the context of the Holocaust, ashes, as demonstrated by Derrida's reading of Paul Celan's poetry, become a *sign* of racially inflamed hatred.[36]

Framed by Levinas's ethics, the missing person notice becomes a mnemonic trace of the Bruders, which has lasted into the present, soliciting its contemporary reader's ethical and affective response, and demanding to be transformed into a sign. Like the Levinasian *trace* which, as evidenced by the attempts to erase it, disturbs the order of things, the missing person notice disrupts the then still dominant Gaullist discourse of *résistancialisme*.[37] Placing emphasis on active resistance, which *Dora Bruder* exemplifies with the heroics of Missak Manouchian's group, *résistancialisme* downplayed the passive suffering of racial deportees such as the Jewish teenager and her parents. The disturbing quality of the small ad is corroborated by what Modiano deciphers as the resolve of wartime and post-war authorities to destroy all evidence of the disappearance of the Jews through, among other means, the redevelopment or demolition of the buildings these Jews once inhabited. In this sense, the endeavours of French postwar administrations to cover up their country's instrumentality in the Holocaust can be analogised to the murderer's effort to obliterate the evidence of her or his crime, which, for Levinas, constitutes a trace in itself: 'Celui qui a laissé des traces en effaçant ses traces n'a rien voulu dire ni faire par les traces qu'il laisse. Il a dérangé l'ordre d'une façon irréparable' [He who left traces in wiping out his trace did not mean to say or do anything by the trace he left. He disturbed the order in an irreparable way].[38]

Modiano's recourse to Parisian addresses in his search for Dora's traces can be further contextualised with his belief in an organic and reciprocal link between people and their habitat. Baptiste Roux's observation that there is a correspondence between the interior and exterior world of Modiano's protagonists who define themselves through the places they haunt, is illustrated by Ambrose Guise's sense of oneness with his urban environment: 'Je me confondais avec cette ville, j'étais le feuillage des arbres, les reflets de la pluie sur les trottoirs, le bourdonnement des voix, une poussière parmi les milliers de poussières des rues' [I merged into the city, I was the leaves of the trees, the gleam of rain on the pavements, the murmur of voices, a grain of dust among all the millions of grains of dust in the streets].[39] The sensation experienced by the protagonist of *Quartier perdu* is shared by the narrator of *Dora Bruder*, who recalls blending in with the cityscape while waiting for his girlfriend at a café near the Bruders' former home: 'Je n'étais rien, je me confondais avec ce crépuscule, ces rues' [I was non-existent. I blended into that twilight, into those streets] (*DB*, 8; *SW*, 5). Although apparently insignificant, the memory dating back to 1965 enables the author to imagine how Dora felt in the dark, cold, and increasingly hostile city. Despite the novelist's awareness of the triviality of his own predicament by comparison with that of Dora, the analogies between his own youth and that of the Jewish teenager remain the only way of accessing what is irretrievably lost. Modiano grafts on to Dora his own former sense of vulnerability, inconsequentiality, and anonymity, which he owed, on the one hand, to the lack of stability marking his childhood and, on the other, to his lack of sense of direction.[40] He does so in an effort to throw light on Dora's foolhardy escape from the school that provided her with some protection from the ever-worsening anti-Jewish measures. The perceived affinity between the situations of Modiano and Dora leads the author to hazard that, notwithstanding his unawareness of the teenager's existence, it was her and not his girlfriend that he was waiting for in 1965. This remark overrules the notion of chronology central to conventional history, instead tallying with the postmodern position that the past is always reconstructed in the light of our present knowledge. As well as with Hutcheon's concept of 'the presence of the past', such a view of the recovery of history chimes with Dora Apel's understanding of the postmodern approach to the Holocaust.[41] Placing the Nazi genocide 'in relation to the circumstances of its representation in the present', postmodern historiography recognises 'the altered ideological contexts of the present, the fragmented and conflicted nature of experience and subjectivity, and the difficulty of retrieving knowledge from the past'.[42] Thus contextualised, the sense of emptiness accompanying Modiano's peregrinations to the places inhabited by the Bruders can be explained by his awareness of the family's tragic end and, more broadly, of the destruction of the Jewish diaspora of Paris. This feeling of emptiness finds embodiment in Modiano's reconfiguration of the trace as a two-facetted construct:

> Empreinte: marque en creux ou en relief. Pour Ernest et Cécile Bruder, pour Dora, je dirai: en creux. J'ai ressenti une impression d'*absence* et de *vide* chaque fois que je me suis trouvé dans un endroit où ils avaient vécu. (*DB*, 28–29)
>
> [Stamp: an imprint, hollow or in relief. Hollow, I should say, in the case of Ernest and Cécile Bruder, of Dora. I have a sense of absence, of emptiness, whenever I find myself in a place where they have lived.] (*SW*, 24)

The 'Wandering Jew' and Transitopias

Modiano's sense of absence in the places associated with Dora and her parents proceeds, as he concludes, from the impermanence marking the Parisian lives of immigrant Jews. Throughout their stay in France, the Bruders lived in residential hotels, which means that they never rented an apartment, let alone owned one. This observation encourages Modiano to revisit critically the stereotype of the 'Wandering Jew' which had long been part of anti-Semitic ideology and which he addresses in, among other works, *La Place de l'étoile*. In his debut novel, Modiano exposes the derogatory stereotype by narrating the frenzied comings and goings of his main character, Raphaël Schlemilovitch.[43] In *Dora Bruder*, however, the tone is accusatory rather than playful, as Modiano mobilises the figure of the 'Wandering Jew' to indict French authorities for having let down Dora and her parents. Despite sacrificing his health during his service in the Foreign Legion, Ernest Bruder never received a disability pension, not to mention French citizenship. It was indeed his statelessness and reported lack of profession that, as Modiano believes, ultimately exposed him and his family to persecution. As Mary Jean Green aptly notes, the transient condition of Dora's father was eventually institutionalised through his internment in a *transit* camp: 'Born in a hostile foreign country, without nationality, without a fixed residence, without profession, Ernest Bruder was an easy target for ejection from the French scene'.[44]

The Bruders' lack of fixity can be deduced mainly from the addresses at which they lived. The boulevard de la Chapelle, where the family rented a room before moving to the boulevard Ornano, is located in a *quartier* punctuated by railway stations and resonating with the rattle of the overhead metro, and therefore described by Modiano as an area where 'personne ne devait se fixer longtemps' [nobody would stay [...] for long] (*DB*, 30; *SW*, 25, translation modified). As for the boulevard Ornano, not only has it been associated with subsequent waves of immigrants but it also leads to one of the exits from Paris, the Porte de Clignancourt.[45] In the terms of Peter Tame, the boulevard Ornano can be classified among the 'transitopias' that provide the setting for Modiano's novels and that include wastelands, railway lines, and ring roads. Zooming in on the two central characters of *Les Boulevards de ceinture*, Tame notes that Chalva Deyckecaire and his son, Serge Alexandre, are being pushed to the capital's limits by the city's mysterious centrifugal force. By stating that in Modiano's writing 'the identity of the characters proves to be just as mysterious and protean as that of places', Tame follows Green in connecting the wartime precarity of Modiano's Jewish protagonists to the liminality of the spaces they inhabit and haunt. He observes that the novelist systematically depicts these protagonists as disinherited human beings, moving in and out of properties, travelling from address to address, and thereby 'substantiat[ing] in ludic and highly ironic fashion the stereotype of the "rootless Jew", always on the move'.[46]

The transience marking the Bruders' life is echoed by the stories of diegetically peripheral characters who, like the Bruders themselves, are eastern or central European Jewish immigrants. Lacking the ludic and ironic aspect of Raphaël Schlemilovitch, these Parisian Jews are displaced figures who suffered or may have suffered racial persecution during the war and who now lead a liminal existence. The first of these figures is a travel-ware vendor who appears as part of Modiano's childhood memory of his weekend trips to the Saint-Ouen fleamarket located at the top of the boulevard Ornano. That this is a happy memory can be inferred from the rare presence of the writer's mother who otherwise features in his *œuvre* as an elusive and/or neglectful figure. Another telling detail is a photographer who out of the holiday season took snapshots of passers-by in the boulevard Ornano. Since in the summer the same photographer would set up his tripod in front of the 'Bar du Soleil' in the seaside resort of Deauville, his presence metonymically confers a sunny ambiance on a socially deprived Parisian quartier. The purpose of this reminiscence is to imagine Dora's childhood which, as Modiano's own memories of the area suggest, was modest but happy. As well as going shopping with her mother, Dora, as Modiano speculates, may have watched films at the nearby cinema 'Ornano 43' and played in the then still pastoral square de Clignancourt. The following description of the square deftly collapses the temporal distance between the author and the Jewish teenager, giving an impression that the two enjoyed its carefree ambiance simultaneously:

> Les soirs, les voisins disposaient des chaises sur les trottoirs et bavardaient entre eux. On allait boire une limonade à la terrasse d'un café. Quelquefois, des hommes, dont on ne savait pas si c'étaient de vrais chevriers ou des forains, passaient avec quelques chèvres et vendaient un grand verre de lait pour dix sous. La mousse vous faisait une moustache blanche. (*DB*, 34)
>
> [In the evenings, the neighbours would carry their tables outside and sit on the pavement for a chat. Or take a lemonade together on the café terrace. Sometimes men who could have been either real goatherds or else pedlars from the fairs would come by with a few goats and sell you tall glasses of milk for almost nothing. The froth gave you a white moustache.] (*SW*, 29)

Modiano's carefree memories of the area are, however, overshadowed by the appearance in the Saint-Ouen flea market of a vendor of second-hand suitcases whose lack of social and geographic fixity can be deduced from his Judeo-Polish origins and from the nature of the goods he sells: '[d]es valises luxueuses, en cuir, en crocodile, d'autres en carton bouilli, des sacs de voyage, des malles-cabines portant des étiquettes de compagnies transatlantiques' [luxury suitcases, in leather or crocodile skin, cardboard suitcases, travelling bags, cabin trunks labelled with the names of transatlantic companies] (*DB*, 11; *SW*, 7). As well as acting as a reminder of the Bruders' own rootlessness, the presence of the Polish Jew infuses the recurrent trope of travel with sinister overtones. Whereas Dora, possibly inspired by the resemblance of 'Ornano 43' to an ocean liner, may have dreamt of life-saving transatlantic travel or at least of a passage across the demarcation line, the pile of assorted suitcases on the vendor's stall invokes her final journey in a cattle train to Auschwitz.[47] The used suitcases unmistakably call to mind the luggage looted by the Nazis from their victims and now amassed at the Auschwitz-Birkenau Museum as a memorial to the enormity of the Nazis' crime.

Modiano's later memory stages an antique dealer whom he briefly knew in his twenties and who happens to be another Polish Jew. Considering that the *brocanteur* spent his youth near the Porte de Clignancourt, he may have known Dora Bruder. If the man's connection to the north of Paris establishes an affinity between him and the Jewish teenager, his narrow escape from deportation associates him with Modiano's father who was arrested on at least two occasions, but who each time managed to get away. By triangulating the *brocanteur*, Dora, and the author's father, Modiano foregrounds the endemic instability of Jewish lives during the Occupation and the resulting vulnerability of these Jews. Significantly, he repositions this instability as a consequence of anti-Semitism, rather than as an inherently Jewish trait, and thus drains the stereotype of the 'Wandering Jew' of its offensive resonance. Additionally, as I will argue later in this chapter, the parallels between various Jewish characters, including the author's father and the author himself, both mitigate Albert Modiano's moral ambiguity and extend Jewish wartime vulnerability and precarity to the second generation.

The Palimpsestic City

Modiano's superposition of his own memories of the boulevard Ornano on the sparsely sketched biography of the Jewish teenager results in a vision of Paris as a space holding different strata of memory where these strata exist in a non-chronological relation to each other. Such a palimpsestic view of an urban environment overrules the sequential temporality characteristic of conventional historiography, including biography. It also tallies with the postmodern conception of the past, which, according to Hutcheon, finds embodiment in Derrida's challenge to linear historical temporality: 'it offers a complex notion of repetition and change, iteration and alteration, operating together, a conceptual "chain" of history: "a 'monumental, stratified, contradictory' history, a history that also implies a new logic of *repetition and the trace*"'.[48] Modiano's efforts to bring historically disparate images and memories into dialogue is best exemplified by his representation of the boulevard Ornano as a single mnemonic space. While this strategy may have been suggested to him by the title of the column featuring the missing person notice — 'D'hier à aujourd'hui' [From Yesterday to Today] (*DB*, 7; *SW*, 3, translation modified) — it is definitely due to what Modiano sees as his unique gift of collapsing time:

> J'ai l'impression d'être le seul à faire le lien entre le Paris de ce temps-là et celui d'aujourd'hui, le seul à me souvenir de tous ces détails. Par moments, le lien s'amenuise et risque de se rompre, d'autres soirs la ville d'hier m'apparaît en reflets furtifs derrière celle d'aujourd'hui. (*DB*, 50–51)
>
> [I feel as if I am alone in making the link between Paris then and Paris now, alone in remembering all these details. There are moments when the link is stretched to breaking-point, and other evenings when the city of yesterday appears to me in fugitive gleams behind that of today.] (*SW*, 45)

The deconstruction of traditional sequentiality is further facilitated by the passage of time and the linked weakening of memory: 'Avec le recul des années, les perspectives se brouillent pour moi, les hivers se mêlent l'un à l'autre. Celui de 1965 et celui de 1942' [With the passage of time, I find, perspectives become blurred, one winter merging into another. That of 1965 and that of 1945] (*DB*, 10; *SW*, 6).

Apart from breathing life into Dora's story, the fusion of different temporal moments (1942, 1958, 1961, and 1996) has an ethico-political objective which is to insert Vichy's anti-Semitic measures into the long chain of racially motivated violence perpetrated by the French state. If Modiano's childhood memory of the boulevard Ornano is overshadowed by the then still fresh memory of the Holocaust, his later recollections of the area are dominated by images of colonial oppression: the riot police ready to supress demonstrations against the brutality of French soldiers in Algeria and the Clignancourt army barracks which, before opening their doors to French volunteers in the Waffen SS, had housed colonial troops. In these memories, the Algerian War becomes interwoven with the Occupation also through the detail of a Jaguar parked across the street from the café where Modiano would meet his girlfriend. Just as the luxury car jars with the deprived surroundings, the official memory of the war, encapsulated by the plaque affixed to the car's body, G.I.G. ('Grand Invalide de Guerre' [Disabled Ex-Serviceman]), clashes with France's amnesiac relationship with the former Jewish residents of the area (*DB*, 9; *SW*, 5).

Since the publication of *Dora Bruder*, efforts have been made to theorise the enmeshment of disparate histories borne out by the spaces that have witnessed them. Of particular note is Andrew Huyssen's concept of the 'urban palimpsest' which, drawing on an 'inherently literary' notion, captures 'configurations of urban spaces and their unfolding in time', and involves a reconstruction of history from 'traces of the past, erasures, losses, and heterotopias'. Huyssen explains that the fruitful interconnection of architecture and literature lies in the redeployment of 'techniques of reading historically, intertextually, constructively, and deconstructively' in order to understand 'the fundamental temporality of those human endeavours that pretend to transcend time through their material reality and relative durability'.[49] In *Dora Bruder* which, as a historiographic metafiction, softens generic boundaries between history and literary invention, the interconnections between urban spaces and literature are actualised through Modiano's decoding of the capital's past both historically and imaginatively, and through his bringing together of the city's historical and literary configurations. The encounter between history and fiction is emblematised by Modiano's hope that, like Jean Valjean and Causette in Victor Hugo's *Les Misérables*, Dora would have found a safe haven from her pursuers in the fictional *quartier* of Le Petit Picpus.

Since Huyssen's theorisation of the role played by urban spaces in creating historical memory, Max Silverman has engaged the figure of the palimpsest to examine the imbrications of the Holocaust and colonialism in the cultural representations of France's twentieth-century past.[50] Citing *Dora Bruder* as an illustration of palimpsestic memory, Silverman isolates the army barracks as 'a knotted cluster of meaning' where memories of two major crises in France's modern history meet and interact.[51] He exemplifies his observation with the analogy between the Caserne Clignancourt and the Caserne des Tourelles which housed colonial infantry before and after the war and which, in the meantime, served as an internment centre for communists, Jews, and 'Amis des Juifs' [Friends of the Jews], as were called those who showed solidarity with the stigmatised minority by wearing the yellow star. In *Dora Bruder*, the negative investment of the army barracks is amplified by Modiano's dread at the memory of his own military service: 'la perspective de vivre une vie de caserne comme je l'avais déjà vécue dans des pensionnats de onze à dix-sept ans me paraissait insurmountable' [the prospect of barrack-life such as I had already been leading in various boarding schools from the ages of eleven to seventeen seemed to me unendurable] (*DB*, 96; *SW*, 90). Significantly, Modiano's efforts to avoid conscription stemmed from his bad experience of structured life in boarding schools from which, like Dora, he repeatedly ran away. His efforts may also have been fuelled by his then still fresh memory of the Algerian War, and by his 'pre-memory' of the Occupation, as Johnnie Gratton designates the novelist's self-proclaimed ability to remember events preceding his birth.[52]

Richard Golsan and Alan Morris have both argued that, by binding together the memories of the Holocaust and colonial violence, *Dora Bruder* replicates the pattern established by Modiano's *œuvre* where *les années noires* routinely pass through 'the equally troubling memory of the Algerian War'.[53] Rather than construing *la guerre sans nom* as a simple echo of the Occupation, I am more inclined to follow Silverman's suggestion that Modiano posits history as an ironic and repetitive construct.[54] Such an interpretation is invited by the novelist's reconstruction of Ernest Bruder's engagement in the French Foreign Legion in the 1920s, which meant his enlistment in the perpetration of racialised violence of which he himself would later become a victim. For Silverman, the recurrent references to the barracks — Belfort, Nancy, Méknez, Fez, and Marrakesh — create a space for an analogy between French colonialism and the Nazis' empire-building project. It is noteworthy, however, that Modiano refrains from complicating the victimhood of Dora's father, instead using Ernest Bruder's sacrifice of his health to underscore the irony of the way that France treated him after he had settled in Paris. More broadly, as Silverman goes on to contend, Modiano connects Vichy and colonialism with a view to drawing out the generalised nature of institutionalised and dehumanising violence, which finds embodiment in 'les autorités d'occupation, le Dépôt, les casernes, les camps, l'Histoire, le temps' [the occupying authorities, the Dépôt, the barracks, the camps, history, time] (*DB*, 147; *SW*, 137).[55] In this sense, *Dora Bruder* could be read as a response to the ethical challenge of 'Lazarean art' which, as theorised by Jean Cayrol, reflects the disfigurement of humanity in the post-concentrationary era and invents a new literary style to render it.[56] In my view, the convergence of the disparate legacies of violence in *Dora Bruder* is intended primarily to cast wartime anti-Semitism as an extension of the violence of which Ernest Bruder was himself an unwitting agent before the war and which extended into the post-war period. My contention finds support in the coincidence of the publication of *Dora Bruder* with the trial of Maurice Papon, which revealed Papon's implication in both the wartime deportation of the Bordeaux Jews and the violent crackdown on the Front de libération nationale demonstration in 1961, which, according to some historians, resulted in between two and three hundred Algerian deaths. Without referencing the trial directly, *Dora Bruder*, too, connects wartime anti-Semitism and post-war racism, which it does with the aim of challenging the separation between the collaborationist État français and the Republic that at the time of the novel's writing, was still being upheld.

Memory under Erasure or the Non-places of Memory

On more than one occasion Modiano's palimpsestic exploration of Paris becomes frustrated by changes to the city's texture, which consist in the reconfiguration of streets and in the repurposing, redevelopment, or even demolition of buildings. This means that Brett Ashley Kaplan's observation that, with their natural tendency to reclaim and grow, the landscapes in which the genocide took place can be unreliable witnesses, may be extended to the urban context.[57] An example of the changing function of buildings is the cinema 'Ornano 43' which at the time of the writing of Dora Bruder served as a halal butcher's shop. Modiano's choice to single out a modernist building whose regrettable dilapidation during the post-war years pointed to the bankruptcy of the modernist confidence in science and progress, emblematised by the former cinema's gleamingly white façade styled on an ocean liner. In this light, it is only fitting that Modiano should resort to postmodern aesthetics in thematising a genocide that has been described as 'a characteristically modern phenomenon that cannot be understood out of the context of cultural tendencies and technical achievements of modernity'.[58]

Unlike the cinema building, which has only changed its function, other locations connected with the Bruders no longer exist. Together with the adjacent building, the residential hotel in the rue Bachelet, where Dora's parents once rented a room, has been redeveloped into a single apartment block. Likewise, the convent school that Dora attended has been razed and not even its plans seem to have survived. Still, Modiano's research into the layout and the surroundings of the school offers precious insights into the circumstances of Dora's *fugue*. Among the significant architectural elements are 'les faux rochers du monument funéraire' [the imitation grotto of the mausoleum] (*DB*, 46; *SW*, 41, translation modified) which the teenager must have passed daily in the school's courtyard. The monument's obvious morbidity aside, the epithet 'faux' [false] tacitly conveys the unease that a Jewish girl would have felt in a Catholic school and that may have contributed to her decision to run away. A telling element of the school's surroundings is the mass grave of the victims of the 1789 Revolution, which, had Dora been aware of its proximity, would have only amplified her anxiety. Significantly, both Hannah Arendt and some commentators of French literature observe a connection between the anti-aristocratic Terror and the anti-Jewish Holocaust. Jeffrey Mehlman notes that Arendt follows Tocqueville in analogising French people's hatred of the aristocracy, whose loss of influence was not accompanied by their loss of wealth, to the fulfilment of anti-Semitism in the Holocaust which coincided with the Jews' loss of power but not their fortunes.[59] That Modiano may have been influenced by this analogy transpires from his juxtaposition of the references to the Revolution and to the arrest of Jewish children carried out during a raid by the French police on institutions located near the mass grave.

As well as by her fear, Dora may have been driven to run away by the enticingly pastoral names of the surrounding streets: 'les Meuniers, la Brèche-aux-Loups, le sentier de Merisiers' (*DB*, 73).[60] Yet another factor may have been the closeness of the Gare de Lyon from which in Modiano's earlier novel Jews flee the Occupied Zone and which, together with other nearby railway stations, transforms the area into 'le quartier des départs' [a point of departure] (*DB*, 73; *SW*, 67).[61] Modiano also seeks explanation for Dora's *fugues* in the architecture of 'Ornano 43', which invokes transatlantic crossings, and in the romantic comedy screened by the cinema in 1941. Had Dora watched *Le Premier Rendez-vous*, it may have given her the idea to emulate the behaviour of its central character, a young woman who escapes from an orphanage into the arms of a handsome man. Watching the film fifty years later, Modiano realises that his reception is strongly inflected by his cognisance of the tragic fate of the film's erstwhile viewers. His impression that the reel has been impregnated with the anxious gaze of wartime spectators is a further indication of his awareness of history's inevitably subjective construction in the present.

According to Hutcheon, 'narrativized history, like fiction, reshapes any material (in this case, the past) in the light of the present issues and this interpretative process is precisely what historiographic metafiction calls to our attention'.[62]

As the narrative progresses, Modiano identifies architectural changes with the deliberate erasure by the post-war administrations of the memory of the deported Jews. As the novelist sees it, the authorities wished to draw a veil over the role of their wartime predecessors in the arrest, internment, and deportation of France's Jews. Modiano's accusatory position finds illustration in the passage dedicated to the rue des Jardins-Saint-Paul where in the 1960s a whole terrace gave way to nondescript and uniform buildings. In a gesture aimed at cohesion and control, in which one recognises the same totalising forces as those behind National Socialism, the plural meanings once evoked by the area have been reduced to the bureaucratic designator 'îlot 16' [bloc 16]: 'Les façades étaient rectilignes, les fenêtres carrées, le béton la couleur d'amnésie. Les lampadaires projetaient une lumière froide. [...] On avait tout anéanti pour construire une sorte de village suisse dont on ne pouvait plus mettre en doute la neutralité' [The facades are rectangular, the windows square, the cement the colour of amnesia. The street lamps throw out a cold light. [...] They have obliterated everything in order to build a sort of Swiss village, in order that nobody, ever again, would question its neutrality] (*DB*, 136; *SW*, 130). Modiano's frustration comes from the fact that the demolished buildings once housed, among their other tenants, French-born Jews of Dora's age. Like Dora, these young people were brutally wrenched by the French police from their habitat, even though their Parisian accent made them an organic part of the capital's townscape: 'ils se confondaient avec les façades des immeubles, les trottoirs, les infinis nuances de gris qui n'existent qu'à Paris' [they merged effortlessly into the façades, the apartment blocks, the pavements, the infinite shades of grey which belong to Paris alone] (*DB*, 139; *SW*, 132). Since the identity of the street's Jewish inhabitants has been reduced to names and addresses on the deportation lists, the reconfiguration of the house numbers has only added to the fading of their memory.

Continuing his journey in Dora's footsteps, Modiano follows the road leading to the former transit camp of Drancy. The post-war extension of the road to the Roissy airport indicates, for Modiano, the official wish to override the camp's negative connotations with the positive investment of the new departure point. Similarly, in the demolition of the buildings lining the road to Drancy the novelist recognises an effort to eradicate the nonhuman witnesses of the deportation: 'on a [...] bouleversé le paysage de cette banlieue nord-est pour la rendre, comme l'ancien îlot 16, aussi neutre que possible' [by transforming the landscape of this north-eastern suburb, they have rendered it, like the former Block 16, as neutral and grey as possible] (*DB*, 142; *SW*, 134). Among the few remaining 'material witnesses', to borrow Schuppli's term, to the Jewish convoys heading for the transit camp are the road signs 'Drancy' and 'Romainville' whose fortress, too, served as an internment camp. Modiano's attention is then caught by an old barn near the Porte de Bagnolet, whose side has been graffitied with the word 'Duremord'. Should the word's spelling be altered to 'du remord', the barn could be seen as a call for the French to express their remorse about their wartime persecution of Jews.

For Modiano, the survival of certain buildings into the present is as vexing as the redevelopment or demolition of other sites. For example, on visiting the Caserne des Tourelles, the novelist is appalled by the absence of a plaque commemorating those once imprisoned behind its walls.[63] He is even more outraged by the sign 'Zone militaire. Défense de filmer ou de photographier' [Military Zone. Filming or Photography Prohibited] (*DB*, 131; *SW*, 124) which he reads as meant to ward off the inquisitive gaze of visitors. Resorting to imagination, Modiano pictures a zone of emptiness and forgetting extending beyond the walls of the compound, which only adds to the already thick layer of institutionalised amnesia. Equally, if not more offensive, is the persistence of the building once housing the collaborationist Préfecture de Police where, during the war, Jews, communists, and resistance fighters were brutally interrogated. As if hoping that, by dint of analogy, the building might disintegrate before his very eyes, Modiano compares the Préfecture to the House of Usher in Edgar Allan Poe's eponymous short story. By extension, he implicitly fancies himself as Roderick Usher who suffers from hyperesthesia, a condition consisting in increased sense of smell, touch, taste, and sight. As if affected by Usher's condition, Modiano believes he can hear the cries of victims being tortured and the unanswered pleas of their relatives resonating within the corridors of the building. He also thinks to be able to pick up the scent of old leather and rotting tobacco exuded by the inspectors who tracked down and arrested Jews, even though the documents proving their guilt have all been methodically shredded.

Les Non-lieux de mémoire

Modiano's topographical approach to Dora's story can be likened to Lanzmann's strategy in *Shoah* which focuses on the 'non-lieux de mémoire' [non-places of memory], a term Lanzmann coined to capture the absence of Jewish life in post-Holocaust Poland.[64] The term extends the typology proposed by Pierre Nora as part of his seminal dichotomisation of history and memory.[65] Whereas the former is a 'reconstruction, always problematic and incomplete of what is no longer', and connected to the ideas of progression, continuity, and 'relation between things', the latter is an actual, perpetual phenomenon borne by living societies.[66] In the face of the absence of spontaneous memory which perished together with organic communities living in continuity with their past, and which, significantly, Nora exemplifies with the Jews of the diaspora, a need has arisen for 'lieux de mémoire' [places of memory] which take the shape of monuments, museums, famous authors, archives, anniversaries, celebrations, minutes of silence, veterans' reunions, and eulogies.[67]

While Modiano's efforts to retrace Dora's trajectory have been likened to the construction of a 'lieu de mémoire', I would argue that his writing simultaneously bewails the destruction of and attempts to revive what Nora calls the 'milieux de mémoire' [environments of memory].[68] That is to say, *Dora Bruder* is testimony to the erasure of a Jewish community that transmitted its cultural heritage from generation to generation through everyday gestures and rites. What is left of these environments of memory are non-places of memory, as Lanzmann calls a *shtetl* emptied of its Jewish inhabitants and resettled with non-Jewish Poles, or the Chełmno Castle which, during the war, served as a concentration camp and which Polish post-war authorities repurposed as a warehouse. Interestingly, Lanzmann also shares Modiano's dismay at the stubbornly unchanged appearance of other places, such as the railway station of Sobibór and the road sign 'Treblinka'. Shocked by the simultaneous ordinariness and immutability of these locations,[69] Lanzmann construes the decision of the Polish authorities not to rename the towns that were once the site of extermination camps as an insult to Jewish memory.[70] What distinguishes Lanzmann's quest for the lost Jewish world from that of Modiano is that *Shoah* dodges the question of France's involvement in the Nazis' genocidal project. This is despite the fact that, as Margaret Olin points out, 'French peasants could be held just as responsible as the Polish peasants'. Olin attributes the conspicuous absence of French witnesses from the film, an absence rendered even more perceptible by Lanzmann's use of French to interview some of his interlocutors and by his French accent in other languages, to the director's conviction that France would have never allowed for concentration camps to be located on its territory.[71] One can therefore speculate that it is, among other reasons, to expose Lanzmann's patriotically motivated blindness to the fate of French Jews and to France's role in the Holocaust that *Dora Bruder* focuses on the persecution suffered by a Jewish teenager in her Parisian habitat, rather than, as does Lanzmann, on the killing centres of Eastern Europe.[72] By the same token, Modiano's narrative shows that Paris, just like post-war Poland, has become a non-place of memory due to the destruction of its Jewish diaspora and to its subsequent deliberate forgetting. Their ideological differences aside, Lanzmann and Modiano share the conviction that the past can be reconstructed only from its remaining traces in the present, that inanimate objects can bear witness to historical events, and that imagination (or what Lanzmann calls 'hallucination') plays an important role in the reconstruction of history. In other words, whether their investigation deflects attention away from France or deliberately refocuses it closer to home, Modiano and Lanzmann both mobilise topographical locations as silent witnesses in their case against perpetrators, locally recruited collaborators, and indifferent, cowardly, or cruel bystanders.

The Self and the (Feminine) Other

Modiano's indictment of the French authorities at the time when France was beginning to confront its role in the Jewish tragedy is only one of *Dora Bruder*'s two key ethico-political objectives. The other one consists in the recasting of Modiano's father, Albert, who is usually staged in the novelist's work as a morally ambiguous or even murderous character, as victim of the Nazi persecution and, by extension, in reconfiguring his own relationship with the wartime past. Modiano achieves this goal by triangulating Dora Bruder, his father, and himself with the help of Parisian locations, and in particular of the chronotopic images of the police van and the hospital. As a way of preparing the ground for this three-way assimilation, he adopts the narrative model of the *récit de filiation* which Dominique Viart conceptualised around the time of *Dora Bruder*'s publication.[73] As well as with some of Modiano's own novels, Viart exemplifies the *récit de filiation* with Pierre Bergounioux's *L'Orphelin* (1992), Leïla Sebbar's *Je ne parle pas la langue de mon père* (2003), and Michel Séonnet's *La Marque du père* (2007).[74] Nourished by the wartime experience of the narrator's father, irrespective of his position as victim or perpetrator, these texts provide an opportunity for their narrators to probe their fathers' pasts, to gain a deeper understanding of themselves, and to speak openly about the Holocaust in France.[75] For Viart, the *récit de filiation* is therefore a product of the postmodern questioning of modernist metanarratives associated with the authority and language of the fathers' generation. Accordingly, while flaunting the subject's incapacity to know itself, the *récit de filiation* displays characteristically postmodern generic instability and disrespect for chronology, objectivity, and completeness.[76]

Following Viart's categorisation of Modiano's earlier novels as exemplars of the novelistic sub-genre he has delineated, I consider *Dora Bruder* as a *récit de filiation*, even if, rather than on its narrator's father, it focuses on a stranger. The departure from Viart's narrative model is mitigated, however, by Dora's gradual displacement of Modiano *père* from his ancestral position. We are programmed for this displacement by the scene describing Modiano's endeavours to procure Dora's birth certificate and by his indignation when a clerk at the registry office refuses to issue him with the required document on the grounds of his lack of kinship with the Jewish girl. As the narrative progresses, Modiano multiplies analogies between his father and Dora Bruder. Although separated by their age and gender, both Dora and Albert were second-generation Jewish immigrants who breached Vichy's anti-Semitic regulations: 'Si différents qu'ils aient été l'un et l'autre, on les avaient classés, cet hiver-là, dans la même catégorie de réprouvées' [Utterly different though they were, both, that winter, had found themselves in the same category, classed as outcasts] (*DB*, 63; *SW*, 58). To be more specific, Albert and Dora did not register with the police, nor did they wear the obligatory yellow star, which only deepened their social marginality: 'Ainsi, [mon père] n'avait-il plus aucune existence légale [...]. Désormais il était ailleurs. Un peu comme Dora après sa fugue' [And so [my father] had no legal existence [...]. Henceforth he was in limbo. A little like Dora after her escape] (*DB*, 63; *SW*, 58, translation modified).

As a result of their irregular legal situation, in 1942 Dora and Albert were arrested by the Police aux questions juives. The proximity of the dates of the two arrests and Albert Modiano's recollection of a young woman travelling with him in the police van invites the novelist to speculate that his father and Dora came across each other on that fateful day. Modiano does not conceal his hope that his father might have met the runaway teenager, yet, when it transpires that this was not the case, contents himself with uniting the two in the ostracism to which they were subjected as Jews living in occupied France. According to Mireille Hilsum, to imagine, however briefly, that his father and Dora shared the same contiguous space of the police van allows the author to bestow on Albert Dora's reported rebelliousness, illustrated by her defiance of Vichy's anti-Jewish legislation.[77] Indeed, Modiano equates the

Jewish adolescent with the writer and resistance fighter Albert Sciaky (also known as François Vernet), and with Manouchian's resistance group which carried out assassinations of Germans and bombed German targets. I therefore agree with Golsan who deciphers the episode of the arrest as Modiano's attempt to dissociate his father from his customary ambiguity and instead 'to sympathize, indeed, to empathize with him and all those among his contemporaries who suffered so terribly simply for being Jewish'.[78] Echoing Golsan, Dervila Cooke and Colin Nettelbeck argue that through the episode of the arrest Modiano extends to Albert the compassion that we feel for Dora.[79]

By amalgamating Albert Modiano with Dora Bruder, the arrest scene counterbalances the negligent and vindictive behaviour of the author's father towards his son in the 1960s. Importantly, the episode of Albert Modiano's denunciation of his son to the police for claiming overdue alimony payments also includes a police van whose design, as Modiano stresses, had remained almost unchanged since the Occupation. This detail serves to collapse the temporal distance separating his father's wartime arrest from the arrest of the father and son following their quarrel over alimony payments. Apart from restoring the father to his wartime victim position, the scene enables Modiano's own identification with persecuted Jews. Despite being conscious of the relative inconsequentiality of his own situation, he identifies with Dora whose arrest, like his own, had resulted from her father's contacting the police. The plausibility of such a reading increases in the intertextual light of *Les Boulevards de ceinture* in which, as the father and the son travel in a police van, the son fears they are being taken to Drancy.[80]

Albert's victimhood is consolidated through Modiano's memory of his vain attempt to visit his dying father at the Hôpital de la Pitié-Salpêtrière. It is noteworthy that Modiano dreads hospitals as much as penal institutions and boarding schools, describing them as places 'où l'on vous enfermait sans que vous sachiez si vous en sortiriez un jour' [where you were shut up, not knowing when or if you would be released] (*DB*, 41; *SW*, 36). The author's sentiment is illustrated by the metonymic reduction of the Hôpital Lariboisière to its black and interminable walls, and by the description of the surrounding area as 'la zone la plus obscure de Paris' [the darkest part of Paris] (*DB*, 29; *SW*, 24). As well as through the association of hospitals with confinement, readerly compassion for Albert Modiano is generated through the embedding of the hospital visit within the passage relating Modiano's efforts to obtain Dora's birth certificate in order to restore to the dead girl the legal identity her killers had denied her.[81] Modiano's unsuccessful search for his father in the labyrinthine corridors of the Pitié-Salpêtrière and his perambulations in the Palais de Justice are both figured as an Orphic quest for the dead (or the nearly dead) dwelling in the realm of anonymity and oblivion. The Jewish teenager and Modiano's father are further united through a reference to the history of the Pitié-Salpêtrière. Operating under the euphemistic name 'Hôpital Général', in the eighteenth century the compound served as a prison for undesirable young women who, like the heroine of the abbé Prévost's novel, *Manon Lescaut* (1731), were destined for deportation to the colonies. Hence, it is not only with Manon Lescaut who, having been banished as a prostitute to New Orleans, dies of exposure and exhaustion, that Modiano conflates his sick father, but also with Dora herself who, like Lescaut's heroine, was deported having been deemed undesirable. As for Modiano, he casts himself as Dora's avatar when he recalls his hospitalisation at a sanatorium that once served as a rehabilitation centre for delinquent girls.

As reimagined with the help of Parisian locations, Albert Modiano has little in common with the collaborating Jews populating Modiano's œuvre, who are patently modelled on the author's father. In contrast to Raphaël Schlemilovitch who is described as 'un juif collabo' [a collaborating Jew], and the similarly ambiguous Chalva Deyckecaire, the father character present in *Dora Bruder* is a defenceless victim of French anti-Semitism.[82] Mentioned only in passing, his shady black-market deals and even shadier connections with the French *gestapistes* are justified as an inevitable outcome of the social and professional exclusion to which Vichy France had condemned him. He is therefore put on a par with other persecuted Jews, such as a young woman called Hena, who, deprived of legitimate means of earning her living, resorted to theft and consequently was interned at Tourelles: 'Les ordonnances allemandes, les lois de Vichy, les articles de journaux ne leur accordaient que le statut de pestiférés et de droit commun, alors il était légitime qu'ils se conduisent comme des hors-la-loi afin de survivre' [According to German decrees, Vichy laws and articles in the press, they were no better than vermin or common criminals, so they felt justified in behaving like outlaws in order to survive] (*DB*, 117; *SW*, 111).

Modiano's re-presentation of his father as a victim is linked to his own detachment from the moral ambiguity he once believed he would have embraced had he been born earlier. Referring to the novelist's confession that he would have been 'un salaud' [a bastard], before becoming 'un martyre' [a martyr],[83] Morris describes Modiano as someone who feels himself to be 'à la fois victime et bourreau, Juif et antisémite, Français et étranger' [at the same time a victim and a victimiser, a Jew and an anti-Semite, a Frenchman and a foreigner].[84] In contrast, in *Dora Bruder* Modiano resolutely shifts towards the victim position through his identification with the Jewish girl. For instance, the author's meanderings through the tortuous structures of the Palais de Justice uncannily echo Dora's encounter with the arbitrary, anonymous, and ruthless authorities. And so, in Modiano's eyes, the security guard morphs into a policeman, the security check into a body search accompanying incarceration, and the objects he is requested to remove from his pockets into the shoelaces a convict must surrender at the gates of a prison. The intimidating omnipresence of begowned barristers adds to Modiano's sensation of helplessness, fear, and confinement in the face of, seemingly, the same power apparatus that Dora had to confront upon her arrest. Yet, as well as to identify with the Jewish teenager, Modiano uses this scene to bring attention to the complicity of post-war authorities with their wartime predecessors through their dogged denial of Vichy's crimes. This complicity is enacted, for example, through the clerk's obstruction of Modiano's effort to extricate Dora's birth certificate and is evident from the description of the clerk as 'l'une de ces sentinelles de l'oubli chargées de garder un secret honteux, et d'interdire à ceux qui le voulaient de retrouver la moindre trace de l'existence de quelqu'un' [one of these sentinels of oblivion whose role is to guard a shameful secret and to deny access to anybody seeking to uncover the least trace of a person's existence] (*DB*, 16; *SW*, 12).

There is, of course, nothing unusual in a biographer's identification with their subject, a novelist's identification with their protagonist, or a historian's identification with the participants of the studied event. But whereas in a conventional text this identification would be implicit rather than explicit, as a metafictionally present narrator of a postmodern novel, Modiano makes no secret of his emotional attachment to Dora. The perception of such an attachment changes, however, in the context of the Holocaust where it can raise serious ethical concerns. These have been dramatised, for example, by Emily Prager's novel *Eve's Tattoo* (1991) whose eponymous protagonist has the number of a woman murdered in Auschwitz tattooed on to her arm as a way of manifesting her solidarity with Holocaust victims. These ethical anxieties have also been embodied by Binjamin Wilkomirski's hoax memoir, *Bruchstücke: aus einer Kindheit 1939–1948* (1995), whose author, in retracing the survival of a Jewish boy in wartime Latvia, became convinced that he was that boy himself. For LaCapra, Wilkomirski's case demonstrates that unchecked identification may lead to the confusion of self and other, and 'bring an incorporation of the experience and voice of the victim and its reenactment or acting out'.[85] Identification is, LaCapra concedes, hard to avoid as 'there is something in the experience of the victim that has an almost compulsive power and should elicit our empathy'. That empathy may reach 'the point of fascination or extreme identification, wherein one becomes a kind of surrogate victim', is, for LaCapra, exemplified by Lanzmann's appropriative relationship with his interviewees.[86]

Like Lanzmann's relationship with Holocaust witnesses, that of Modiano with Dora Bruder has been subject to discussion. While some have spoken of the novelist's unhealthy obsession with the runaway teenager,[87] others have argued that 'the choice of Jewishness is a choice of marginalisation, of being on the side of the outsiders', and the novelist's way of fulfilling his *devoir de mémoire*.[88] Susan Rubin Suleiman has described Modiano's relationship with Dora as 'appropriative' and 'self-centred', yet not 'pathological'.[89] Appreciating the novelist's empathy, which 'involves both a recognition of kinship and an awareness of difference', Suleiman argues that a relationship such as his with Dora can productively lead to historical investigation, better social policies and jurisprudence, complex Holocaust fictions by 'nonsurvivors', and, as in Modiano's case, 'ethical consciousness and mourning'.[90] Both LaCapra's comments on the transferential historian–victim relation and Paul Ricœur's typology of identity (identity as sameness/ identity as continuity), which informs Suleiman's analysis, can illuminate Modiano's relationship with the murdered adolescent. Namely, the novelist's interest in Dora may come across as 'self-centred' and 'appropriative' in the sense that it is sparked by his recognition in the Jewish girl of a reflection of himself, his father, his absentee mother, and his prematurely deceased sibling, Rudi.[91] Like Dora, Modiano spent time in boarding schools and, like her, he was an insubordinate adolescent who, resenting discipline and confinement, repeatedly ran away. It appears therefore that Modiano brings Dora into his sphere of familiarity by grafting on to her his own feelings and experiences, which, seen in Levinasian terms, would amount to the assimilation of the Other as an object of *my* knowledge or of *my* experience, and would compromise the Other's alterity and hence the ethics of the Self's relationship to the Other.

As if wary of this danger, Modiano vacillates between assimilating Dora within his own and his father's experience and knowledge, and recognising and respecting her separateness and inscrutability. His recognition of Dora's difference is manifest, firstly, in his choice to write about a young woman rather than, as he had originally planned, two brothers whose 'mother didn't take much care of them'.[92] While Suleiman dismisses the significance of this fact and Kawakami insists on the sexlessness of Modiano's characters, I believe that, alongside her Jewishness, to which Modiano's claim through his absentee father is decidedly weaker than Dora's, the teenager's gender is what ensures her autonomy.[93] My contention is supported by Levinas's construction of the Self as implicitly male, and of the Other as feminine.[94] If, for Davis, femininity thus becomes reduced to 'qualities belonging to the most conventional gender stereotypes: a gentle, self-effacing, intimate, familiar presence at home', Tina Chanter reads Levinas's construction of femininity more sympathetically.[95] She identifies it with discretion and with what 'slip[s] away from the light', and, rather than accusing Levinas of reasserting the historical invisibility of women, she believes he 'makes of historical invisibility a philosophical positivity' by 'protest[ing] the virile world in which everything is "clear as day"'.[96] If Chanter's reading of Levinas can help to elucidate Modiano's association of Dora with inscrutability as related to her gender, the teenager's ontological independence from Modiano is ultimately ensured by the novelist's recognition of his failure to establish her reasons for running away and her whereabouts during her absences:

> J'ignorerai toujours à quoi elle passait ses journées, où elle se cachait, en compagnie de qui elle se trouvait pendant les mois d'hiver de sa première fugue et au cours des quelques semaines de printemps où elle s'est échappée à nouveau. C'est là son secret. Un pauvre et précieux secret que les bourreaux, les ordonnances, les autorités dites d'occupation, le Dépôt, les casernes, les camps, l'Histoire, le temps — tout ce qui vous souille et vous détruit — n'auront pas pu lui voler. (*DB* 144–45)
>
> [I shall never know how she spent her days, where she hid, in whose company she passed the winter months of her first escape, or the few weeks of spring when she escaped for the second time. That is her secret. A poor and precious secret which not even the executioners, the occupying authorities, the Dépôt, the barracks, the camps, history, time — everything that corrupts and destroys you — have been able to take away from her.] (*SW,* 177)

Notwithstanding Modiano's disappointment palpable in the quoted passage, *Dora Bruder*'s closing pages reframe his inability to answer his questions unequivocally as the young woman's triumph over all those who tried to curtail her freedom with discriminatory legislation. As evidenced by the generically hybrid form of Modiano's narrative, Dora Bruder has also triumphed over those who may try to impose on her story the completeness, coherence, and closure proper to traditional narrative patterns.

Conclusions

Modiano's self-acknowledged inability to reconstruct Dora's trajectory comprehensively suggests the limited effectiveness of the topographical approach. Recognised through Joseph Jurt's claim that 'le destin de Dora n'[est] pas saisissable à travers les lieux' [Dora's destiny is not graspable with the help of places], topography's failure to provide equivocal answers has been commented upon by the narrator of Modiano's *Un cirque qui passe* (1992), who confesses that 'les détails topographiques ont un drôle d'effet sur moi: loin de me rendre l'image du passé plus proche et plus claire, ils me causent une sensation déchirante de liens tranchés et de vide' [topographical details have a strange effect on me: instead of clarifying and sharpening images from the past, they give me a harrowing sensation of emptiness and severed relationships].[97] Regardless of the only partial success of Modiano's search, the novelist's reliance on Parisian streets and buildings as material witnesses to the Jewish girl's trajectory and tragedy makes *Dora Bruder* a beacon of the emergent topographical perspective in Holocaust studies. Modiano's regret over the capital's disfigurement resulting from the destruction of its Jewish community and over the efforts of post-war French governments to silence the memory of this community further testifies to the nascent intersection of these fields. At the same time, the paradoxical combination of Modiano's trust in the topographical approach and acknowledgement of its inefficacy bears witness to the adherence of *Dora Bruder* to the model of historiographic metafiction, which, according to Hutcheon, is stamped by self-contradiction. The postmodern quality of *Dora Bruder* is confirmed by its generic instability, intertextuality, and metafictional self-questioning. What further affiliates *Dora Bruder* with postmodern logic is its commitment to a historically insignificant figure, its linked distantiation from dominant historical discourses, such as that of *résistantialisme*, and its ethico-political engagement. To expose the emphasis of the Gaullist myth on the heroism of armed combat to the detriment of Jewish victimhood, Modiano recasts Dora's *fugues* as acts of resistance against Vichy's discriminatory legislation, and thus reinserts a neglected Jewish victim into the mainstream narrative of the war. *Dora Bruder* also challenges the official discourse on the Occupation through its conception of history as a process that is circular and cumulative, rather than logical and sequential, and as a construct akin to literature. As we have seen, this conception is supported by Modiano's re-presentation of the French capital as a palimpsest holding within its multiple folds both historical and literary layers of meaning. Such a textual vision of urban space is aimed, as I have shown, at linking France's colonial and anti-Semitic violence, and at connecting these violences to the post-war conspiracy of silence regarding them. The chronotopic images that enable the intersection of these apparently dissociated phenomena also serve to collapse the distance between a Holocaust victim, Modiano's morally dubious father, and Modiano himself. It is this identificatory drive that potentially compromises *Dora Bruder*'s postmodern ethics which manifests itself through Modiano's resolve to bring a Jewish victim out of anonymity and to expose the political mechanisms that caused her death and that made possible the forgetting of her and of her community. However, seen from a different angle, Modiano's narrative strategy can be deciphered as intended to lay bare the processes that are at work in conventional biographies, but that are obfuscated by the biographer's pretence of objectivity, emotional detachment, and scientific rigour. Consequently, rather than judging Modiano's internalisation of Dora's rebellious femininity, Jewishness, and victimhood as unethical, I construe it as one of the ways for his narrative to claim its alignment with postmodern ethics.

Notes to Chapter 1

1. Elie Wiesel, 'All Was Lost, Yet Something Was Preserved: A Review of the Chronicle of the Lodz Ghetto, 1941–1944', *The New York Times Books Review*, 19 August 1984, p. 1.
2. Simon Schama, *Landscape and Memory* (London: HarperCollins, 1995), p. 26.
3. Angeliki Tseti, 'In the Absence of Ruins: The "Non-sites of Memory" in Claude Lanzmann's *Shoah* and Daniel Mendelsohn's *Lost: A Search for Six of Six Million*', in *Ruins in the Literary and Cultural Imagination*, ed. by Efterpi Mitsi and others (Basingstoke: Palgrave Macmillan, 2019), pp. 213–28 (p. 214).
4. Tim Cole, 'Geographies of the Holocaust', in *A Companion to the Holocaust*, ed. by Simone Gigliotti and Hilary Earl (Hoboken, NJ: John Wiley, 2020), pp. 333–47 (p. 333).
5. Cheryl Hatt, 'Teaching the Holocaust through Geography', *Teaching Geography*, 36.3 (2011), 108–10. Andrew Charlesworth, 'The Topography of Genocide', in *The Historiography of the Holocaust*, ed. by Dan Stone (Basingstoke: Palgrave Macmillan, 2004), pp. 216–52 (p. 218).
6. Alberto Giordano, Anne Kelly Knowles, and Tim Cole, 'Geographies of the Holocaust', in *Geographies of the Holocaust*, ed. by Anne Kelly Knowles, Tim Coles, and Alberto Giordano (Bloomington: Indiana University Press, 2014), pp. 1–17 (p. 3).
7. Ibid., p. 3.
8. Charlesworth, 'The Topography of Genocide', pp. 218, 223. Cf. S. Lillian Kremer, *Women's Holocaust Writing: Memory and Imagination* (Lincoln: University of Nebraska Press, 1999), p. 40.
9. Claude Lanzmann, 'Les Non-lieux de la mémoire', in *Au sujet de 'Shoah'*, ed. by Deguy, pp. 385–406 (p. 398). Cf. Lanzmann, 'Le Lieu et la parole', p. 409. Charlesworth, 'The Topography of Genocide', p. 216.
10. Tim Cole, *Holocaust City: Making of a Jewish Ghetto* (New York: Routledge, 2003); *Traces of the Holocaust: Journeying In and Out of the Ghettos* (London: Bloomsbury, 2011). Simone Gigliotti, *The Train Journey: Transit, Captivity and Witnessing in the Holocaust* (New York: Berghahn Books, 2009). Gunnar S. Paulsson, *The Secret City: The Hidden Jews of Warsaw, 1940–1945* (New Haven, CT: Yale University Press, 2002). Martin Winstone, *The Holocaust Sites of Europe: An Historical Guide* (London: I. B. Tauris, 2010). Brett Ashley Kaplan, *Landscapes of Holocaust Postmemory* (New York: Routledge, 2011). Yehuda Merin and Jack Nusan Porter, 'Three Jewish Family Camps in the Forests of Volyn, Ukraine during the Holocaust', *Jewish Social Studies*, 46.1 (Winter 1984), 83–92. Suzanne Weiner Weber, 'Shedding City Life: Survival Mechanisms of Forest Fugitives during the Holocaust', *Holocaust Studies*, 18.1 (2012), 1–28. Katrin Reichelt, *Der Wald war unser letzter Ausweg: Hilfe für verfolgte Juden im Deutsch besetzen Weißrussland 1941–1944* (Berlin: Lukas, 2017). Tim Cole, '"Nature Was Helping Us": Forests, Trees and Environmental Histories of the Holocaust', *Environmental History* 19.4 (2019), 665–86.
11. Eric Katz, 'Nature's Healing Power, the Holocaust, and the Environment', *Judaism*, 46.1 (Winter 1997), 79–89; and *Anne Frank's Tree* (Cambridge: White Horse, 2015); Jacek Małczyński and others, 'The Environmental History of the Holocaust', *Journal of Genocide Studies*, 22.2 (2020), 183–96.
12. Susan Schuppli, *Material Witness: Media, Forensics, Evidence* (Cambridge, MA: MIT Press, 2020). Jacek Małczyński, 'Jak drzewa świadczą? W stronę nie-ludzkich figuracji świadka' [How Do Trees Testify? Towards a Nonhuman Figuration of the Witness], *Teksty Drugie*, 3 (2018), 373–85.
13. *La Cliente* maps Raul Hilberg's triangulation of Holocaust participants on to the constellation of Parisian businesses run by an informer, a survivor, and a bystander. Both Littell's *Les Bienveillantes*

and Claudel's *Le Rapport de Brodeck* invest sylvan landscapes with the symptomatology of human trauma, be it that of a perpetrator or survivor. They thus emphasise the inalienable human/ non-human dependency or, to use Stacy Alaimo's term, the 'trans-corporeal' character of the human experience, meaning that 'the human is always intermeshed with the more-than-human world', and that nature is more than an inert and empty background available to human exploits: *Bodily Natures: Science, Environment, and the Material Self* (Bloomington: Indiana University Press, 2010), p. 4. I have explored this question in 'Space of Trauma/ Space of Freedom: The Forest as a Posttraumatic Landscape in Holocaust Narratives', in *Interpreting Violence: Narrative, Ethics and Hermeneutics*, ed. by Cassandra Falke, Victoria Fareld, and Hanna Meretoja (New York: Routledge, forthcoming).

14. Tim Cole, 'Review Essay: Landscapes of Holocaust Memory', *Journal of Jewish Identities*, 4.2 (2011), 71–75 (p. 72).
15. Sidra deKoven Ezrahi, 'Representing Auschwitz', *History and Memory*, 7.1 (1996), 121–54 (p. 144)
16. For an analysis of France's reluctant acknowledgment of its role in the Holocaust, see Clifford, *Commemorating the Holocaust*.
17. The missing-person notice reads as follows: 'On recherche une jeune fille, Dora Bruder, 15 ans, 1 m. 55, visage ovale, yeux gris marron, manteaux sport gris, pull-over bordeaux, jupe et chapeau bleu marine, chaussures sport marron. Adresser toutes indications à M. et Mme Bruder, 41, boulevard Ornano. Paris' [Missing, a young girl, Dora Bruder, age 15, height 1 m 55, oval-shaped face, grey-brown eyes, grey sports coat, maroon pullover, navy blue skirt and hat, brown gym shoes. Address all information to Mr and Mrs Bruder, 41 Boulevard Ornano. Paris]. Patrick Modiano, *Dora Bruder* [1997] (Paris: Gallimard Folio, 2000), p. 7 (hereafter referenced as *DB* in the main text); *The Search Warrant*, trans. by Joanna Kilmartin (London: Harvill Secker, 2014), p. 3 (hereafter referenced as *SW* in the main text).
18. Here I follow a number of commentators of *Dora Bruder*. These include Marie Bronand who speaks of 'identité biographique du narrateur et de l'auteur' [the biographical identity of the narrator and the author]: *Témoignage et fiction*, p. 161.
19. Studies of topography in Modiano's writing include: France Grenaudier-Klijn, 'Street Names in Patrick Modiano's Work: *La Place de l'Étoile* and the Case of rue Lauriston', *Neohelicon*, 44 (2017), 217–27; Colin Davis, 'Disenchanted Places: Patrick Modiano's *Quartier perdu* and Recent French Fiction', in *Il senso del nonsense: scritti in memoria di Lynn Salkin Sbiroli*, ed. by M. S. Moretti, R. R. Cappelletti, and O. Martinez (Naples: Edizioni Scientifiche Italiane, 1995), pp. 663–76; Pierre Assouline, 'Modiano: lieux de mémoire', *Lire*, 176 (1990), 35–46; Régine Robin, 'Le Paris toujours déjà perdu de Patrick Modiano', *Cahiers de l'Herne: Patrick Modiano*, ed. by Maryline Heck and Raphaëlle Guidée (Paris: L'Herne, 2012), pp. 93–100; Luc Mary-Rabine, 'Les Lieux de Modiano', *Cahiers de l'Herne: Patrick Modiano*, ed. by Heck and Guidée, pp. 101–04; Ruth Malka, '"Paris of Days Gone By": The Quest for Memory in the Postwar Haunted City — A Case Study of Georges Perec's and Patrick Modiano's Novels', in *Shadows in the City of Light: Paris in Postwar French Jewish Writing*, ed. by Sara R. Horowitz, Amira Bojadzija-Dan, and Julia Creet (New York: State University of New York Press, 2021), pp. 123–37; and Maxime Decout, 'Patrick Modiano's *Dora Bruder*: Wandering Down Memory Lane', in *Shadows in the City of Light*, ed. by Horowitz, Bojadzija-Dan, and Creet, pp. 113–22.
20. For a discussion of *Dora Bruder*'s complex generic status, see Jeanne Bem, 'Dora Bruder ou la biographie déplacée de Modiano', *Cahiers de l'Association Internationale des études françaises*, 52 (2000), 221–32; Béatrice Damamme-Gilbert, 'The Question of Genre in Holocaust Narrative: The Case of Patrick Modiano's *Dora Bruder*', in *Genre Trajectories: Identifying, Mapping, Projecting*, ed. by Garin Dowd and Natalia Rulyova (Basingstoke: Palgrave Macmillan, 2015), pp. 45–65.
21. Gerhard Gerhardi, 'Topographie et histoire: Paris et l'Occupation dans l'œuvre de Patrick Modiano', in *Paris sous l'Occupation: Paris unter deutscher Besatzung*, ed. by Wolfgang Drost and others (Heidelberg: Universitätsverlag Carl Winter, 1995), pp. 114–21 (p. 114).
22. Hutcheon, *A Poetics of Postmodernism*, p. 52.
23. Ibid.
24. Akane Kawakami, *A Self-conscious Art: Patrick Modiano's Postmodern Fictions* (Liverpool: Liverpool University Press, 2000), p. 52.
25. Ibid., p. 55.

26. Isabelle Dangy, 'Hôtels, cafés et villas tristes: lieux privés et lieux publics dans les romans de Modiano', in *Lectures de Modiano*, ed. by Roger-Ives Roche (Nantes: Cécile Defaut, 2009), pp. 179–98 (p. 181).
27. Patrick Modiano, *Quartier perdu* (Paris: Gallimard, 1984), pp. 11, 9; *A Trace of Malice*, trans. by Anthea Bell (Henley-on-Thames: Aidan Ellis, 1988), pp. 10, 8.
28. Patrick Modiano, *Les Boulevards de ceinture* [1972] (Paris: Gallimard Folio, 1978), p. 96; *Ring Roads*, trans. by Frank Wynne, in *The Occupation Trilogy* (New York: Bloomsbury, 2015), pp. 218–324 (p. 271).
29. Kawakami, *A Self-conscious Art*, p. 53.
30. Ibid. Jacques Guicharnaud, 'De la Rive gauche à l'au-delà de la Concorde: remarques sur la topologie parisienne de Patrick Modiano', in *Dilemmes du roman: Essays in Honour of Georges May*, ed. by Catherine Lafarge (Saratoga, CA: Anma Libri, 1990), pp. 341–52 (p. 350).
31. Anna-Louise Milne, 'Introduction: The City as a Book', in *The Cambridge Companion to the Literature of Paris*, ed. by Anna-Louise Milne (Cambridge: Cambridge University Press, 2013), pp. 1–18 (p. 16).
32. Eaglestone, 'Levinas and the Holocaust'. This view is shared by Tina Chanter in *Time, Death and the Feminine* (Stanford, CA: Stanford University Press, 2011), p. 221, and by Michael Bernard-Donals in 'Theory and the Ethics of Holocaust Representation', in *The Bloomsbury Companion to Holocaust Literature*, ed. by Adams, pp. 103–19. Apart from the two articles by Levinas cited in this chapter, the concept of the 'trace' is discussed in *Autrement qu'être ou au-delà de l'essence* (1974) which Levinas dedicated to the six million Jewish victims of the Holocaust, including members of his own family.
33. Colin Davis, *Levinas: An Introduction* (Notre Dame, IN: University of Notre Dame Press, 1996), p. 46. Eaglestone, *The Postmodern and the Holocaust*, p. 285.
34. Emmanuel Levinas, 'La Signification et le sens', *Revue de métaphysique et de morale*, 2 (April-May, 1964), 126–56 (pp. 152, 155); 'Signification and Sense', in *Humanism of the Other*, trans. by Nidra Poller (Urbana: University of Illinois Press, 2006), pp. 9–44 (pp. 40, 44, the latter translation modified).
35. Adams, 'Traces, Dis/Continuities, Complicities', p. 3.
36. Jacques Derrida, 'Poetics and Politics of Witnessing', in *Sovereignties in Question: The Poetics of Paul Celan*, ed. by Thomas Dutoit and Outi Pasanen (New York: Fordham University Press, 2005), pp. 65–96 (p. 70). See also Levin, 'Cinders, Traces, Shadows on the Page', p. 271. Cf. Eaglestone's reading of Derrida's elaboration of Levinas's concept of the trace. Eaglestone, *The Postmodern and the Holocaust*, pp. 280–99.
37. Levinas, 'La Signification et le sens', p. 153; 'Signification and Sense', p. 41.
38. Emmanuel Levinas, 'La Trace de l'autre', *Tijdschrift voor Filosofie*, 3 (September 1963), 605–23 (p. 620); 'The Trace of the Other', trans. by A. Lingis, in *Deconstruction in Context: Literature and Philosophy*, ed. by Mark C. Taylor (Chicago: University of Chicago Press, 1986), pp. 345–59 (p. 357).
39. Baptiste Roux, *Figures de l'Occupation dans l'œuvre de Patrick Modiano* (Paris: L'Harmattan, 1999), p. 117. Modiano, *Quartier perdu*, p. 119; *A Trace of Malice*, p. 140.
40. Modiano's parents were Louisa Colpeyn, a travelling Flemish actress, and Albert Modiano, a Jewish wheeler-dealer with a shady past. Modiano spent much of his childhood in boarding schools and later dropped out of university.
41. Hutcheon, *A Poetics of Postmodernism*, p. 20.
42. Dora Apel, *Memory Effects: The Holocaust and the Art of Secondary Witnessing* (New Brunswick, NJ: Rutgers University Press, 2002), p. 7.
43. Edgar Knecht, 'Le Juif errant: éléments d'un mythe populaire', *Romantisme*, 9 (1975), 84–96. Modiano's exploration of the myth of the 'Wandering Jew' has been examined by Paul Gellings in *Poèsie et mythes dans l'œuvre de Patrick Modiano: le fardeau du nomade* (Paris: Minard, 2000), by Charles O'Keefe in 'Patrick Modiano's Raphaël Schlemilovitch and Homer's Odysseus Laertiades: Fit(ted) Companions', *Comparative Literature Studies*, 53.1 (2016), 28–56, and in *A Riffaterrean Reading of Patrick Modiano's 'La Place de l'étoile': Investigating the Family Crime* (Birmingham, AL: Summa Publications, 2005), pp. 39–41.

44. Mary Jean Green, 'People Who Leave No Trace: *Dora Bruder* and the French Immigrant Community', *Studies in 20th and 21st Century Literature*, 31.2 (2007), 434–49 (p. 443).
45. Bruno Blanckeman describes the eighteenth *arrondissement* as 'celui de toutes les immigrations' [one of all immigrant waves]: 'Droit de cité (un Paris de Patrick Modiano)', in *Lectures de Modiano*, ed. by Roche, pp. 163–78 (p. 168). Green notes that 'this neighbourhood still shelters immigrants (like Dora Bruder's parents) and their children, who (like Dora Bruder) have been born in France'. She rightly draws attention to the invisibility of these more recent immigrant communities in Modiano's text: 'People Who Leave No Trace', p. 435.
46. Peter Tame, 'Isotopias in Invented Autobiography: Four Novels on the Occupation by Patrick Modiano', in *Isotopias: Places and Spaces in French War Fiction of the Twentieth and Twenty-First Centuries* (Oxford: Peter Lang, 2015), pp. 475–508 (pp. 491, 489, 490).
47. In *Voyage de noces* (1990), which constitutes the fictional *avant-texte* of *Dora Bruder*, Modiano imagines that Ingrid Theyrsen escapes to the south of France and spends the war there with a man called Rigaud.
48. Hutcheon, *A Poetics of Postmodernism*, p. 97.
49. Andreas Huyssen, *Present Pasts: Urban Palimpsests and the Politics of Memory* (Stanford, CA: Stanford University Press, 2003), p. 7.
50. Max Silverman, *Palimpsestic Memory: The Holocaust and Colonialism in French and Francophone Fiction and Film* (New York: Berghahn Books, 2013). Silverman's study belongs to a wider and ongoing endeavour to (re)connect different traumatic memories. Rothberg has elaborated the paradigm of 'multidirectional memory' as a way of conceptualising the dynamics of the confrontation in the public sphere of different memories of extreme violence, including the Nazis' anti-Semitism, colonialism, slavery, and decolonisation. Michael Rothberg, *Multidirectional Memory: Remembering the Holocaust in the Age of Decolonisation* (Stanford, CA: Stanford University Press, 2009). Debarati Sanyal who, like Silverman, works in the francophone context, has proposed the notion of 'complicitous memory', where 'complicity' stands for our place in 'the folds that bring diverse histories into contact'. Although aware that such an approach can 'drive us to dangerous intersections, where difference is collapsed into sameness', Sanyal hopes that it can also productively trace not only 'the affinities between disparate legacies of violence and loss', but also 'the past's reverberations in the present': *Memory and Complicity: Migrations of Holocaust Remembrance* (New York: Fordham University Press, 2015), pp. 1–2.
51. Silverman, *Palimpsestic Memory*, p. 112.
52. Johnnie Gratton, 'Postmemory, Prememory, Paramemory: The Writing of Patrick Modiano', *French Studies*, 59.1 (2005), 39–45 (p. 42). In *Livret de famille*, Patrick Modiano states, 'J'étais sûr, par exemple, d'avoir vécu dans le Paris de l'Occupation puisque je me souvenais de certains personnages de cette époque et de détails intimes et troublants, de ceux qu'aucun livre d'histoire ne mentionne. [I was certain, for example, to have lived in Paris during the Occupation, since I could remember certain persons of that time and some intimate and troubling details, the likes of which no history manual mentions]: *Livret de famille* (Paris: Gallimard, 1977), p. 96.
53. Richard J. Golsan, *Vichy's Afterlife: History and Counterhistory in Postwar France* (Lincoln, NE: University of Nebraska Press, 2000), p. 46; Alan Morris, *Patrick Modiano* (Amsterdam: Rodopi, 2000), pp. 16–17. Cf. Richard J. Golsan, 'Modiano historien', *Studies in 20th and 21st Century Literature*, 31.2 (2007), 415–33 (p. 424)
54. Silverman, *Palimpsestic Memory*, p. 111.
55. Ibid., p. 113.
56. Max Silverman, 'Introduction: Lazarus and the Modern World', in *Concentrationary Art: Jean Cayrol, the Lazarean and the Everyday in Post-war Film, Literature, Music and the Visual Arts*, ed. by Griselda Pollock and Max Silverman (New York: Berghahn Books, 2019), pp. 1–28. For an analysis of *Dora Bruder* as an example of Lazarean art, see Anna Maziarczyk, 'Une inquiétante puissance du blanc: l'écriture lazaréenne dans *Dora Bruder* de Patrick Modiano', *Romanica Wratislaviensia*, 61 (2014), 109–20.
57. Kaplan, *Landscapes of Holocaust Postmemory*, p. 4.
58. Zygmunt Bauman, *Modernity and the Holocaust* (London: Polity Press, 1993 [1989]), p. xiii.
59. Hannah Arendt, *Antisemitism: Part One of the Origins of Totalitarianism* (New York: Harcourt Brace, 1951), p. 4.

60. Left in French in the English translation, these names could be rendered as 'The Millers', 'Wolves' Passage', and 'Cherry Tree Path'.
61. It is from the Gare de Lyon that in *Rue des Boutiques obscures* Jimmy Pedro Stern leaves Paris hoping to cross the border into Switzerland.
62. Hutcheon, *A Poetics of Postmodernism*, p. 137.
63. When visiting the site in 2017, I found a small commemorative plaque there.
64. Lanzmann, 'Le Lieu et la parole', p. 409.
65. Pierre Nora, *Les Lieux de mémoire*, 7 vols (Paris: Gallimard, 1984–94).
66. Pierre Nora, 'Between Memory and History: *Les Lieux de mémoire*', *Representations*, 26 (Spring 1989), 7–24 (pp. 8–9).
67. Nora calls Jews 'peoples of memory'. For to be Jewish is to remember that one is such and to be 'bound in daily devotion to the rituals and tradition': 'Between Memory and History', pp. 16, 8. Nora adds that, as Jewish tradition 'has no other history than its own memory', until recently it had no need for historians (p. 16).
68. Lynn Higgins has interpreted Modiano's narrative as an effort to create 'un lieu de mémoire vaste et varié' [a vast and varied place of memory]: 'Lieux de mémoire et géographie imaginaire dans *Dora Bruder*', in *Le Roman français au tournant du XXIe siècle*, ed. by Marc Dambre, Aline Mura-Brunel, and Bruno Blanckeman (Paris: Presses Sorbonne Nouvelle, 2004), pp. 394–405 (p. 404). Higgins notes that 'le narrateur de Dora se construit des monuments aux morts dans les endroits quotidiens et banals de Paris: dans les rues, les immeubles, même dans les endroits où "il ne reste plus rien"' [Dora's narrator constructs memorials in everyday and banal Parisian spaces: in the streets, buildings, even in places where 'there is nothing left'] (p. 404). Likewise, Green asserts that Modiano turns the Bruders' family life itself into such a place of memory: 'People Who Leave No Trace', p. 444.
69. Charlesworth, 'The Topography of Genocide', p. 216.
70. Lanzmann, 'Les Non-lieux de la mémoire', p. 399.
71. Margaret Olin, 'Lanzmann's *Shoah* and the Topography of the Holocaust Film', *Representations*, 57 (Winter 1997), 1–23 (pp. 6–7).
72. Shoshana Felman contextualises Lanzmann's approach with his French upbringing and his attunement 'to social and political French preoccupations and to contemporary philosophical concerns': 'The Return of the Voice: Claude Lanzmann's *Shoah*', in *Testimony: Crises of Witnessing in Literature, Psychoanalysis and History* (New York: Routledge, 1992), pp. 204–08 (p. 243). Olin notes in turn that Lanzmann's use of French language in the film draws attention to 'the blank on Lanzmann's map' which is France. Although French peasants could prove as callous as their Polish counterparts, they are conspicuously absent from the film, as are French Jews. For Olin, the glaring absence of France from *Shoah* implies that in Lanzmann's homeland 'the Holocaust could be experienced only vicariously, through translation': 'Lanzmann's *Shoah* and the Topography of the Holocaust Film', pp. 6–7.
73. Dominique Viart first proposed the term during the 1996 conference 'États du roman contemporain'. His presentation was subsequently published as 'Filiations littéraires', in *États du roman contemporain. Écritures contemporains 2: actes du colloque de Calaceite, Fondation Noésis, 6–13 juillet 1996*, ed. by Jan Baetens and Dominique Viart (Paris: Minard, 1999), pp. 115–39.
74. Dominique Viart, 'Le Silence des pères au principe du "récit de filiation"', *Études françaises*, 45.3 (2009), 95–112 (p. 96).
75. Ibid., pp. 96, 102.
76. 'Les écrivains remplac[ent] l'investigation de leur *intériorité* par celle de leur *antériorité* familiale. Père, mère, aïeux plus éloignés y sont les objets d'une recherche dont sans doute l'un des enjeux ultimes est une meilleure connaissance du narrateur lui-même à travers ce(ux) dont il hérite' [Writers replace the investigation of their *interiority* with that of their family *anteriority*. Father, mother, more distant ancestors are the object of research, one of whose ultimate challenges is a better knowledge of the narrator himself through the one/those from whom he is descended]. Ibid., p. 96.
77. Mireille Hilsum, 'L'Arrestation: poétique des transports chez Modiano', in *Lectures de Modiano*, ed. by Roche, pp. 137–48 (p. 143–44). Composed largely of immigrants and counting some sixty

members, the group began its activities in 1943. In 1944, twenty-four resisters were captured and twenty-two of them were executed. The Germans used this opportunity to vilify the Resistance through *L'Affige rouge* which is mentioned in *Dora Bruder*.
78. Golsan, *Vichy's Afterlife*, p. 44.
79. Dervila Cooke and Colin Nettelbeck, 'Modiano in the Feminine: À nous deux, madame la vie', *Nottingham French Studies*, 45.2 (Summer 2006), 39–53 (p. 42).
80. For a comparative analysis of these episodes, see Nelly Wolf, 'Figures de la fuite chez Patrick Modiano', in *Patrick Modiano*, ed. by John E. Flower (Amsterdam: Brill, 2007), pp. 211–22.
81. When Modiano first consulted Klarsfeld's *Mémoriel*, Dora's name figured over that of her father, without her date of birth.
82. Patrick Modiano, *La Place de l'étoile* (Paris: Gallimard, 1968), p. 114; *La Place de l'étoile*, trans. by Caroline Hillier, in *The Occupation Trilogy* (New York: Bloomsbury, 2015), pp. 1–116 (p. 62).
83. In a 1976 interview, Modiano confessed that he too might have occupied a similarly equivocal position: 'Je crois bien... franchement... que j'aurais été un salaud [...] et puis, j'aurais changé... après... comme les autres... j'aurais fini... non pas en héros... mais en martyre'. [I do believe... frankly... that I would have been a bastard [...] and then, I would have changed... afterwards... like the others... I would have wound up... not as a hero... but as a martyr]. Jean-Marie Magnan, 'Un apatride nommé Modiano', *Sud*, 19 (1976), 120, quoted by O'Keefe, 'Patrick Modiano's Raphaël Schlemilovitch and Homer's Odysseus Laertiades', p. 40 (the translation is by O'Keefe).
84. Morris, *Patrick Modiano*, p. 8.
85. LaCapra, *Writing History, Writing Trauma*, p. 40. Cf. Dominick LaCapra, *History in Transit: Experience, Identity, and Critical Theory* (Ithaca, NY: Cornell University Press, 2004), p. 81.
86. LaCapra, *Writing History, Writing Trauma*, p. 146.
87. Bem asserts that 'on voit que [Modiano] s'imagine avoir disparu sous l'Occupation' [one can see that [Modiano] imagines having perished during the Occupation]: 'Dora Bruder ou la biographie déplacée de Modiano', p. 225. Serge Klarsfeld suggested that Modiano was in love with his biographee. Denis Cosnard, 'Modiano-Klarsfeld: une correspondence autour de *Dora Bruder*' <http://lereseaumodiano.blogspot.com/2012/01/modiano-klarsfeld-une-correspondance.html> [accessed 12 September 2016].
88. Cooke and Nettelbeck, 'Modiano in the Feminine', p. 46. Similarly, Gratton ascribes the identificatory drive to Modiano's wish to break through the silence surrounding Holocaust victims in France: 'Postmemory, Prememory, Paramemory', p. 43. For Annelies Schulte Nordholt, Modiano's identification with Dora allows the author to see himself as his father's contemporary: '*Dora Bruder*: le témoignage par le biais de la fiction', in *Patrick Modiano*, ed. by Flower, pp. 75–87 (p. 79).
89. Susan Rubin Suleiman, '"Oneself as Another": Identification and Mourning in Patrick Modiano's *Dora Bruder*', *Studies in 20th and 21st Century Literature* 31.2 (2007), 325–50 (p. 331). As an example of pathological identification, Suleiman cites Henri Raczymow's novel, *Un cri sans voix* (1995). It tells the story of a French woman, Esther, who kills herself as a consequence of an identification with a Holocaust victim.
90. Suleiman, '"Oneself as Another"', p. 334. The term 'non-survivor' has been proposed by Gary Weissman in *Fantasies of Witnessing: Postwar Efforts to Experience the Holocaust* (Ithaca, NY: Cornell University Press, 2004), p. 5.
91. It has been pointed out that the German word *Bruder* means 'brother'. See Joseph Jurt, 'La Mémoire de la Shoah: *Dora Bruder*', in *Patrick Modiano*, ed. by Flower, pp. 89–108; Helge Vidar Holm, 'Chronotopes in Patrick Modiano's Fictional Writing of History', *Bergen Language and Linguistics Studies*, 7 (2017), 103–12 (p. 109); Cooke and Nettelbeck, 'Modiano in the Feminine', p. 48.
92. Modiano, letter to Serge Klarsfeld, 27 March, 1995, quoted by Suleiman, '"Oneself as Another"', p. 335.
93. Suleiman, '"Oneself as Another"', p. 335; Akane Kawakami, *Patrick Modiano* (Oxford: Oxford University Press, 2016), p. 152. Modiano's complex relationship with Jewishness has been discussed by Assouline, 'Modiano: lieux de mémoire', p. 42, and by Ora Avni, 'Patrick Modiano: A French Jew?', *Yale French Studies*, 85 (1994), 227–47.

94. Davis, *Levinas*, p. 61. Emmanuel Levinas, *Totalité et infini: essai sur l'extériorité* (The Hague: Martinus Nijhoff, 1971), p. 297.
95. Davis, *Levinas*, p. 60.
96. Tina Chanter, 'Feminism and the Other', in *The Provocation of Levinas: Rethinking the Other*, ed. by Robert Bernasconi and David Wood (London: Routledge, 2002), pp. 32–54 (pp. 37, 36).
97. Jurt, 'La Mémoire de la Shoah', p. 101. Patrick Modiano, *Un cirque qui passe* (Paris: Gallimard, 1992), p. 41; *After the Circus*, trans. by Mark Polizzotti (New Haven, CT: Yale University Press, 2015), p. 44.

CHAPTER 2

'L'infinie gamme des gris': Pierre Assouline's Re-evaluation of the Dark Years in *La Cliente*

> Only from the voices from the grey zone can we fully understand the Holocaust.
> — Susan L. Pentlin, 'Holocaust Victims of Privilege'[1]

'Ce passé qui ne passe pas'

Published in 1998, only a year after *Dora Bruder*, Pierre Assouline's debut novel clearly draws its inspiration and thrust from Modiano's forthright attack on French wartime and post-war authorities.[2] *La Cliente*'s polemic against *Dora Bruder* is part of its larger contestation of the obsession of French people — and especially of those without first-hand knowledge of wartime realities — with *les années noires*. The novel's opening reference to 'ce passé qui ne passe pas' [this past that doesn't pass away] points to its intended engagement with Henry Rousso and Éric Conan's 1994 study which developed Rousso's earlier identification of 'le syndrome de Vichy' [the Vichy syndrome] as France's unhealthy, guilt-ridden obsession with its lacklustre wartime past: the humiliating defeat of 1940, the collaboration with the Occupier, and the participation of the French state in the deportation of some seventy-six thousand Jews (C, 13).[3] In *Vichy: un passé qui ne passe pas*, Rousso and Conan took stock of the ways in which France had dealt with its wartime legacy, including through commemorative practices, trials of Vichy officials, and the institutionalisation of *le devoir de mémoire* [the obligation to remember] which reportedly deformed historical facts and compromised scholarly objectivity.[4] They also criticised the increasingly Judeocentric and, in their opinion, lamentably anachronistic, view of the Vichy period. Without denying the wartime persecution of Jews, Rousso and Conan noted that such Judeocentrism risked obfuscating the hardship of non-Jews and, more generally, the complexity of the realities of the Occupation. Correspondingly, the two authors recognised in the new generation's demands for more transparency about the Vichy years a desire for a black-and-white interpretation that serious scholarship is unable to offer. Finally, they interpreted young people's eagerness to judge their parents for having failed to oppose fascism in the 1930s and the 1940s as a symptom of their own anxiety about their inability to confront the problems faced by their generation.

As a rejoinder to Modiano's condemnation of the treatment of Jews by the Vichy regime and of the post-war obfuscation of France's role in the Holocaust, *La Cliente* explicitly sets out to nuance the allegedly simplistically negative evaluation of the wartime years. Its unnamed homodiegetic narrator who, like Assouline, is Jewish and of Sephardic origin, decides that, in order to do justice to the complexities of the Vichy period, he must abandon his usual toolkit of a journalist and biographer. Instead, he co-opts techniques of the historical novel and, more specifically, of historiographic metafiction. Indeed, *La Cliente* is intensely self-reflexive, explicitly intertextual, fragmented, and non-chronological. Set in Paris in the 1990s, Assouline's novel opens with its protagonist's research into the life of a crime writer, Désiré Simon, whose character seems to be based on one of Assouline's own subjects, Georges Simenon.[5] Before providing an unequivocal answer to the protagonist's question of whether Simon was denounced as a Jew during the war, the archival search yields a letter of denunciation that led to the arrest and deportation of the protagonist's own relatives. It does not take him long to establish the identity of the informer: Cécile Armand is a florist with a business in the rue de la Convention in the fifteenth *arrondissement*. Her shop is located opposite the fur shop of Henri Fechner who is the son and brother of those deported following Madame Armand's tip-off to the Commissariat général aux affaires juives. In an effort to understand the informer's motives for denouncing the Fechners and to make her assume responsibility for her odious deed, the protagonist begins to stalk her; he sends her anonymous death threats, bombards her with late-night telephone calls, orders flowers from her shop to be delivered to the Fechners' empty tomb, and has a Holocaust survivor bare his tattoo in front of her. He also consults the local archives and interviews those who knew the florist during the war, which is how he learns that, on the Liberation of Paris, Armand was briefly arrested and interrogated on account of her betrayal of the Fechners. The arrest aroused popular suspicion against her, which in turn led to her being accused of *collaboration horizonatale*. The public *tonte* (head-shaving) that followed took a toll on Armand's family life and mental health; having cleared her apartment of all the mirrors except a cheval glass which, coincidentally, is called in French *le psyché* [the psyche], the florist repeatedly hurled herself at its surface and then, having smashed it, tried to cut her wrists with its shards. This incident resulted in the break-up of Armand's marriage and left her with a lasting dread of mirrors. Unfortunately, as well as unveiling a more nuanced picture of wartime realities, the search undertaken by Assouline's protagonist provokes the florist's death. It thus occasions a paradoxical reversal of roles, turning a wartime informer into a victim, and a relative of those who perished in the Holocaust into a perpetrator.

Unlike the other novels considered in this study, *La Cliente* has not yet been translated into English and, in contrast to the other five narratives, has attracted little critical or scholarly attention.[6] This is somewhat surprising given the fact that in France novels about the Occupation usually do not pass unnoticed, and that, as journalist and biographer, Assouline has a prominent presence on the French literary scene. Among the subjects of his biographies are several controversial figures mired in collaboration, a topic that clearly interests Assouline.[7] Apart from Simenon, these figures include Jean Jardin, who was the right hand of the head of the collaborationist government, Pierre Laval;[8] Gaston Gallimard, who is remembered for his strict adherence to Vichy's anti-Semitic laws, illustrated by his description of his press as 'aryenne à capitaux aryens' [Aryan with Aryan capital];[9] Hergé, who published in the collaborationist newspaper, *Le Soir*; and Lucien Combelle, who was a member of the far-right monarchist movement, Action française, a contributor to the collaborationist weekly, *La Gerbe*, and the founder and editor-in-chief of the mouthpiece of the Vichy regime, *Révolution nationale*.[10] Combelle also served as the private secretary of the collaborationist novelist, Drieu La Rochelle, and was an admirer of Céline. Taking a sympathetic approach to his life-long friend, Assouline presents *Le Fleuve Combelle* as an answer to the film *Lacombe Lucien* (1974) which, written jointly by Modiano and Louis Malle, examined the collaboration of ordinary French people.

Assouline's preoccupation with the complexities of *les années noires* is also reflected in his fiction. *Lutetia* (2002), for example, follows the fortunes of the eponymous Parisian hotel which throughout the war housed, fed, and entertained the officers of the *Abwehr* (counter-espionage). On the Liberation, Lutetia was turned into a reception centre for returning POWs, displaced persons, and inmates of Nazi concentration camps. Even more recently, in *Sigmaringen* (2014), Assouline zooms in on the Hohenzollern castle in southern Germany where Hitler's crumbling regime harboured France's collaborationist government between September 1944 and July 1945.[11]

While being representative of Assouline's œuvre, both fictional and nonfictional, *La Cliente* is a less typical example of Holocaust fiction, which has so far paid scant attention to bystanders and collaborators. And yet it is believed these days that it is their passivity or support for the occupying German forces that 'allowed the Holocaust to occur on a scale that would have been impossible were only Germans involved'.[12] *La Cliente*'s ethico-political investment, which will be my central concern in this chapter, could therefore be located in its interest in the historically neglected figure of the collaborator. Such a strategy could be regarded not only as characteristic of the postmodern attentiveness to alterity, but also as productive in the same way as has been the engagement of some Holocaust writers with perpetrators. In her study of Jews who colluded with the Nazis in exchange for a more advantageous position in ghettos and concentration camps, Susan Pentlin asserts that by 'approach[ing] taboo topics which have been supressed' we can arrive at a fuller understanding of the Nazi genocide.[13] The taboo topic that Assouline's novel throws light on is the historically and culturally under-represented phenomenon of wartime denunciation, referred to in French as *la délation*.[14] Defined as 'dénonciation intéressée et méprisable' [mercenary and despicable denunciation] and distinguished from *la dénonciation* which serves to inform authorities of a crime that has been committed and which is generally regarded in positive terms, *la délation* is seen as motivated by the informer's desire to harm the person they denounce, and/or by personal gain.[15] While the exact extent of wartime *délation* is impossible to ascertain, it is estimated that between three and five million denunciation letters were dispatched.[16] Apart from Jews, these letters targeted critics of the Germans or of the collaborationist French authorities, or simply men and women against whom the informer bore a grudge.

The story of Madame Armand also enables Assouline to address the phenomenon of *la tonte* which is another under-researched aspect of the Occupation and which not only took the form of head shaving, but also of tattooing and marking with tar. Alain Brossat's designation of *la tonte* as the blind spot in French history of the Vichy period is due to the fact that, despite having affected some twenty thousand women, the punishment of *la collaboration horizontale* has so far found limited reflection in both the historiography and the cultural productions of the Liberation.[17] The very recent studies of the phenomenon have identified the *tondues* as victims of 'implicitly sexualised but muted corporeal violence'[18] and have linked *la tonte* itself to the crisis of masculinity engendered by the inability of French men to protect their country during the war.[19]

Finally, the ethical weight of *La Cliente* must be located in its ambition to nuance the dominant binary perception of *les années noires* (the dark, or literally black, years).[20] By rebranding the Occupation as 'les années grises' [the grey years], Assouline's novel appears to be partaking in the postmodern rejection of strongly valorised dichotomies in favour of complexities and hybridity (C, 62). The 'grey years' are personified by a wartime informer who denounces her Jewish neighbours under duress and, having been betrayed by the French police herself, is unfairly punished for a transgression she has most likely not committed. While Assouline's ethico-political agenda theoretically tallies with postmodern attentiveness to 'ex-centric' subject positions and commitment to antitotalisation and indeterminacy, in this chapter I question the ethics of the narrative strategies that the novelist employs in order to reach a more complex representation of the Occupation, and in particular of the role that the French state and populace played in the Nazis' attempted annihilation of the Jewish people. These strategies include Assouline's re-appropriation of Primo Levi's concept of the 'Grey Zone' and recourse to Christian imagery. My contention will be that, by equating a wartime informer with the so-called privileged Jews who occupy the centre stage of Levi's meditation on the figure of the prisoner-functionary, and with a Christian martyr, these strategies risk muddling the moral landscape of Assouline's novel or even dangerously inverting the positions of victim and perpetrator. My reading of *La Cliente* will therefore ask whether the representational techniques that Hutcheon associates with historiographic metafiction, and the postmodern provisionality and pluralising attitude to the discourse of history that she so praises can be placed in the service of political agendas other than the progressive ones that she believes to be championed by postmodern culture.

The 'Grey Zone': Readings, Re-readings, and Over-readings

To contextualise Asssouline's redeployment of the 'Grey Zone', it is necessary to recapitulate the main points of Primo Levi's study of the moral ambiguity reigning in the concentration camps. It is also helpful to survey the existing extensions of Levi's concept to other phenomena and to outline arguments for restricting its use to Auschwitz. Levi's momentous essay 'The Grey Zone' opens with criticism of those who, when trying to understand the dynamics of *l'univers concentrationnaire*, reduce the complex network of human relationships to the mutually opposing categories of evil tormentors and saintly victims. Reflected in Christ's gesture on Judgment day — 'here the righteous, over there the reprobates' — such dualistic thinking fails, according to Levi, in relation to Auschwitz whose horror consisted in, among its other aspects, its *indecipherability*.[21] Namely, some of the victims were dragged into defiling complicity with their oppressors, thus entering an area so 'incredibly complicated [in] its internal structure' that it 'confuse[s] our need to judge'.[22] The Nazi practice of granting privileges to some concentration camp inmates was intended to blur the clear-cut prisoner-guard divide and, consequently, to undermine the solidarity of the victims and implicate them in their own persecution. Within the intricate hierarchy of the 'Grey Zone', the Italian writer-survivor locates all kinds of prisoner-functionaries (*Funktionshäflinge*), beginning with kettle washers, bed smoothers, checkers for lice, and interpreters, and ending with the members of the *Sonderkommando*.[23] Recruited mainly among Jewish prisoners, the members of this euphemistically called 'Special Squad' were responsible for herding their fellow Jews to the gas chambers, disposing of the victims' bodies, and sorting their possessions (clothing, hair, and gold teeth), all this under the threat of instant death and in exchange for a few small privileges. Considered as *Geheimnisträger* (the depositories of secrets), the *Sonderkommando* members were routinely executed, their average life expectancy in the camp being three months. As well as prisoner-functionaries, Levi places in the 'Grey Zone' the controversial leader of the Lódź Ghetto, Chaim Rumkowski, or even SS Erich Muhsfeldt who briefly showed pity to a young survivor of gassing. Giving him the benefit of the doubt, Levi speculates that, under different circumstances, Muhsfeldt could have been a decent man.[24] However, in contrast to the 'privileged' Jews who ought to benefit from the suspension of our moral judgement, the oppressors of these Jews should not be forgiven.[25] Levi's intransigent stance is exemplified by his unequivocal endorsement of the death sentence meted out to Muhsfeldt by the Polish Supreme National Tribunal.[26]

Since the publication of Levi's essay in 1986, critics have debated the identity of the legitimate residents of the 'Grey Zone'. While some are convinced that the area of moral uncertainty should coincide with the physical space of Nazi concentration camps, others have employed it as a universal figure of enforced complicity with one's oppressor. Jonathan Petropoulos and John Roth, for example, contend that even if 'Levi spoke of the grey zone in the singular', 'his analysis made clear that this region was multi-faceted and multi-layered. It was not confined to one time and place'.[27] Based on this premise, Petropoulos and Roth's edited volume comprises examinations of subjects as diverse as:

> Ambiguity and compromise in writing and depicting Holocaust history; issues of identity, gender, and sexuality during and after the Third Reich; inquiries about 'gray spaces' — those regions of geography, imagination, and psychology that reflect the Holocaust's impact then and now; and dilemmas that have haunted the pursuit of justice, ethics, and religion during and after the Holocaust.[28]

Among other well-known attempts at extending Levi's concept is Tzvetan Todorov's assertion that the mechanics proper to the 'Grey Zone' can be found in all totalitarian regimes.[29] Gian Paolo Biasin goes even further by insisting on Levi's wish to approach Auschwitz from the standpoint of 'our human condition: not the Jewish condition, or the anti-fascist situation, or Italian nationality'.[30] Finally, Omer Bartov sees Auschwitz as a springboard for 'a rumination on the condition of humanity itself, on its capacity for endless evil and its moments of altruism and nobility'.[31] Yet, perhaps the best known attempt to impute universal applicability to the 'Grey Zone' is Giorgio Agamben's hotly contested deployment of Levi's concept as a paradigm for post-Auschwitz ethics. Positioning all human beings within this morally murky space, Agamben states that 'Auschwitz has never ceased to take place; it is always already repeating itself'.[32] Others still have reapplied Levi's term to bystanders, collaborators, and resisters, as well as to Holocaust-unrelated situations.[33]

It needs noting that, through his intertextual references, Levi himself expands the reach of the 'Grey Zone' beyond the boundaries of *l'univers concentrationnaire*. For instance, he analogises the members of the *Sonderkommando* to the collectors of corpses in Alessandro Manzoni's novel *I promesi sposi* (1827), or likens Muhsfeldt's brief hesitation to the single good deed of an old woman in Fyodor Dostoevsky's *The Brothers Karamazov* (1880). More directly, Levi inscribes into the area of moral unclarity, where dichotomies of evil and goodness are no longer operational, various collaborating governments, including Vichy. He also assimilates the 'Grey Zone' with the Soviet *gulag* and compares the Nazis' strategy of burdening their victims with guilt to the practices of the Italian Mafia. Finally, when dwelling on the culpability of the leader of the Łódź Ghetto, Levi appears to broaden the 'Grey Zone' to all humanity: 'We are all mirrored in Rumkowski, his ambiguity is ours, it is our second nature, we hybrids moulded from clay and spirit [...]. [H]is fever is ours [...]. Like Rumkowski, we too are so dazzled by power and prestige as to forget our essential fragility'.[34]

Notwithstanding Levi's wider references, his writings constantly remind us of the historical specificity of Auschwitz, exemplified by his repeated observation that the behaviour of deportees cannot be judged by today's moral standards: 'The mental mechanisms of the *Häftlinge* were different from ours; curiously and in parallel, different also were their physiology and pathology'.[35] This is because inmates of concentration camps had been demoralised by 'years of segregation, humiliations, maltreatments, forced migrations, the laceration of family ties, the rupture of contact with the rest of the world'.[36] Sensitive to these remarks, Adam Brown, who has written extensively and imaginatively on the 'Grey Zone', strongly believes in the term's historical and topographical specificity.[37] He stresses the physical isolation of the universe analysed by Levi, whose distinctiveness and internal cohesion are signalled by its domination in the Italian writer's work by the colour grey.[38] These two facts invite Brown to postulate that the 'Grey Zone' is inextricably linked to 'the unprecedented circumstances *and* environments [of Auschwitz]'.[39] Brown's position is shared by Debarati Sanyal who points to Levi's repeated insistence on the singularity of the prisoner's physical and emotional experience of the camp.[40] In the same vein, while allowing for the portability of the 'Grey Zone' beyond the limits of Auschwitz, so long as its dwellers are victims and not perpetrators or bystanders, Sander Lee considers it as reserved for Jews and other groups chosen for extermination. It is the lack of agency that he identifies as the decisive factor when defining the contours of this space of moral ambiguity.[41]

Lee's insistence on restricting the morally complex terrain described by Levi to victims takes me back to Agamben's (over)interpretation of Levi's essay, which is highly relevant to my examination of Assouline's choice to place a collaborator inside the 'Grey Zone'. It is noteworthy that Levi himself came under attack for allegedly conflating victims with victimisers when he parenthetically discussed Muhsfeldt's pity over a victim of gassing or defined the 'Grey Zone' as a space 'with ill-defined outlines which both separate and join the two camps of masters and servants'.[42] It is on the grounds of this definition that Agamben has reconceptualised the 'Grey Zone' as a space where 'victims become executioners and executioners become victims'.[43] Outraged by the Italian philosopher's overreading of Levi's work, Berel Lang reminds us that, for Levi, 'there is an objective line between good and evil'.[44] In an interview, Levi indeed finds David Rousset's statement that 'victim and executioner are equally ignoble' to be 'frightening', even if he concedes that there may be an element of truth in it. He adds that, however much the complicated hierarchy blurred the line between the two categories, 'the executioner is the executioner and the victim the victim'.[45] And, while acknowledging that both the oppressed and the oppressors had been dehumanised, Levi is unequivocal about the fact that for the former dehumanisation was imposed, whereas for the latter it was 'more or less chosen'.[46] He confirms his position by asserting that 'to confuse perpetrators with the victims is a moral disease or an aesthetic affectation or a sinister sign of complicity; above all, it is a precious service rendered (intentionally or not) to the negators of truth'.[47] Elsewhere, he states that 'the prisoners' errors and weaknesses are not enough to rank them with their custodians', and that, even if victims and their torturers were all 'made from the same cloth' and found themselves in 'the same trap', 'it is the oppressor and he alone, who has prepared and activated it'.[48] Consequently, victim and victimiser are not interchangeable: 'the former is to be punished and execrated [...], the latter to be pitied and helped'.[49]

'L'infinie gamme des gris'

Without directly referencing Levi's work, *La Cliente* repeatedly alludes to the concept of the 'Grey Zone'. For instance, its narrator metaphorises the generic undecidability of historical literature, including of his own writing, as 'une zone grise' [a grey zone] and mentions the colour grey as part of his argument against the binary conception of the war. Furthermore, the narrator's aphoristic statement 'Celui qui n'y est pas allé n'y pénétrera jamais, celui qui y est allé n'en sortira jamais, car la maison des morts est hors du monde' [the one who has not gone to the house of the dead will never enter it, the one who has gone there will never return from it, for it lies beyond this world] (*C*, 74) — unmistakably calls to mind Levi's aporetic remark in 'Shame' regarding the impossibility of bearing witness to the Holocaust:

> We, the survivors, are not the true witnesses. [...] we survivors are those who by their prevarications or abilities or good luck did not touch the bottom. Those who did so, those who saw the Gorgon, have not returned to tell about it or have returned mute.[50]

It is these indirect references to Levi's concept of the 'Grey Zone' that invite the reader to analogise Cécile Armand to the 'privileged' Jews, and, consequently, to share the narrator's indulgent attitude towards the florist and, by extension, to wartime collaboration in France.

To prepare us for a reconsideration of Armand's denunciation of a Jewish family, Assouline's novel outlines the ambiguities of the Occupation through the cameo story of Désiré Simon. To the narrator, the crime writer was neither a resister nor an outright collaborator, but an opportunist; regardless of the wartime shortage of paper, Simon managed to have his voluminous works published and had them adapted for the screen.[51] At the same time, if the protagonist is to trust Simon's diaries, the writer was denounced as a Jew without, as it ultimately transpires, being Jewish. The intricacies of Simon's position are meant to undermine the overwhelmingly negative evaluation of *les années noires*, which had dominated public discourse in France since the 1970s. The narrator's disapproval of the way the French have viewed their wartime past can be inferred from his perception of France as a country that, caught in the grip of *le devoir de mémoire*, 'éprouve une certaine volupté à se piétiner. [...] ne cesse de se déplorer. Un vieux pays [...] soumis à la dictature du souvenir, résigné à la tyrannie de la commémoration' [experiences a certain pleasure in self-beratement. [...] doesn't cease to pity itself. An age-old country [...] oppressed by memory, resigned to the tyranny of commemoration] (*C*, 30).

That said, when attempting to settle the question of Simon's denunciation with an archival search, the protagonist of *La Cliente* himself becomes carried away by the obsession with what he now calls 'cette période maudite' [this accursed time] (*C*, 23). He forms this view as a result of the barrage of administrative obstacles that he encounters when trying to gain access to the then still classified documents. Echoing the narrator of *Dora Bruder*, whose quest for the Jewish teenager's birth certificate was similarly frustrated, Assouline's protagonist vociferates against France's stubborn denial of its collaborationist past. Having finally accessed the archives thanks to his connections, he becomes profoundly affected — both physically and psychologically — by the abhorrent content and euphemistic language of the denunciation letters. Writing on Christmas Eve and, ironically, using the back of a page torn out of a teen magazine, one informer called for the deportation of Jewish children together with their parents. Others began their letters with the formula 'J'ai l'honneur de vous signaler les faits suivants' [I have the honour to bring to your attention the following facts] (C, 29) and ended with 'Un honnête citoyen' [An honest citizen] (C, 91). In view of the inherently dishonourable nature of *la délation* and the dishonesty attached to anonymous correspondence, these *formules de politesse* appear deeply ironic. Livid with rage and repulsion, the protagonist vomits in the lavatories of the archives, whose marble surfaces suddenly take on in his eyes the morbid quality of tombstones.

However, not even the venom of the denunciation letters can stop Assouline's protagonist from appreciating their duality: 'Le pire y côtoyait le meilleur, et des injustes les Justes' [The worst rubbed shoulders with the best, and the reprobates with the Righteous] (C, 25). Between the two extremes to which the Occupation has been routinely and regrettably reduced, he detects all shades of compromise and complicity which the programme of National Revolution had turned into French values:

> Celui qui est fier de servir son pays et celui qui balance avec l'air de ne pas y toucher. Celui qui n'ose pas et le fait quand même et celui qui trouve le gouvernement encore trop timoré sur la question. Celui qui se sent naître une vocation d'auxiliaire de police et celui qui est encore disponible si on a besoin de lui. Celui qui est prêt à consigner son acte sur un livre d'or et celui qui préférerait qu'on l'oublie. (C, 25)
>
> [The one who is proud to serve his country, and the one who hesitates, giving the impression of being far from it. The one who doesn't dare but does it all the same, and the one who finds the government too fainthearted on the issue. The one who senses a vocation of a police auxiliary rise within him, and the one who remains available should his services be needed. The one who is ready to sign the guest book, and the one who would rather his deed was forgotten.]

Although triggered by the protagonist's cognisance of the extent and nature of *la délation*, his obsession with wartime France manifests itself, surprisingly, through his critique of its Judeocentric memory rather than of the collaborators. This is suggested by the episode in which the protagonist returns on a bus from the archives and which is likely meant as a pastiche of Modiano's memory of his journey in a *panier à salade*. Like the police van that enables Modiano's assimilation with persecuted Jews, for Assouline's protagonist the bus becomes a means of reliving the realities of the Occupation. Looking out of the window, he interprets a sign reading '**NN' — 'nouvelle norme', the classification of a hotel — as the acronym of the operation *Nacht und Nebel* [Night and Fog] which targeted Hitler's opponents in German-occupied Europe, including France. Then, evidently imitating Modiano's description of the building formerly occupied by the collaborationist Préfecture de Police, Assouline's narrator claims to hear the screams of victims being tortured by the French *gestapistes* in the rue Lauriston. Modiano's palimpsestic vision of

French history, which finds embodiment in the layers of wallpaper covering the walls in the half-demolished houses once inhabited by Parisian Jews, is in turn parodied through the protagonist's comment on a half-detached poster pasted on a *colonne Morris*. It is noteworthy that an advertising column is a prime reification of palimpsestic memory which Silverman defines as 'the superimposition and productive interaction of different inscriptions and the spatialisation of time central to the work of memory'.[52] In *La Cliente*, the deported Jews whose obliteration Modiano bemoans, are displaced with the image of a benevolent elderly gentleman bearing an uncanny resemblance to the head of the collaborationist government, Marshal Philippe Pétain. As if to dispel any doubt as to the intended resonance of the image, the retirement homes advertised by the poster are called 'Maréchal'. Furthermore, fixing the protagonist with an insistent gaze, an elderly passenger mumbles under his breath the very question that was printed on the wartime posters that cast Pétain as a model of Frenchness and patriotism: 'Et vous, êtes-vous plus français que lui?' [And you, are you more French than him?] (*C*, 36). The passenger then abruptly changes seats, which Assouline's protagonist interprets as a sign of the man's unwillingness to share his space with a Jew. The bus is therefore cast as a mnemonic echo of wartime buses which, before being requisitioned by the French police for the rounding up of Jews, transported collaborators and profiteers. That little has changed since the war is corroborated by a later episode in which a fellow passenger threatens the protagonist with expulsion and legal action for publicly questioning Madame Armand about the motives of her denunciation of the Fechners. The reader is meant to conclude that, while Jews continue to be vilified and brutalised, former collaborators incite sympathy and protection.

At this stage, it is still unclear whether *La Cliente* exposes and laments the persistence of wartime attitudes in contemporary France or, conversely, ridicules its protagonist's growing paranoia. It is similarly uncertain whether we are to assimilate the narrator with his fellow Jews or to read his description of a family gathering as a critique of the entrenchment of his relatives in resentment and self-pity. Is the novel using the lingering anti-Semitism of the French to justify the position of the Jewish community or does it lampoon their enduring fear of persecution? That the latter is the case is suggested by the narrator's division of his fellow Jews into 'ceux qui mettaient l'horreur concentrationnaire à toutes les sauces' [those who spiced all dishes with concentrationary horror] and 'ceux qui la tenaient pour un événement unique dans l'histoire de l'humanité' [those who considered it a unique event in the history of humanity] (*C*, 69). To illustrate his view of French Jews the protagonist relates a conversation with his relatives. While an uncle talks of his plans to buy a house in the 'free zone' in case of the return of wartime conditions, others swap notes on the German products they continue to boycott. To expose the absurdity of their attitude and simultaneously to draw attention to France's embroilment in the execution of Germany's anti-Semitic policies, the narrator produces a long list of French goods and services which, as Jews, his relatives should also avoid. The list includes Renault cars, the French police, the novels of Drieu La Rochelle, and the plays of Sacha Guitry. The narrator also cites Photomaton, a company that runs coin-operated photo booths and that in 1941 put its machines at the disposal of the authorities so that they could photograph the interned Jews. It is hard to tell, however, whether the narrator's tone is ironic or whether he genuinely resents France for its wartime betrayal of its Jews.

A Collaborator as Incarnation of the 'Grey Zone'

Situated approximately half-way through the novel, the scene of the family dinner marks a juncture in the narrator's ideological positioning with respect to the Occupation and its memory. In practical terms, his condemnation of informers gives way to a more indulgent attitude, combined with a critique of the morose introspection, paranoid obsession, and rancorous disposition of certain Jews. The narrator's change of heart can be mapped on to his judgement of Madame Armand who, in his perception, gradually transforms from an embodiment of France's collaborationist past into a victim of the regime's blackmail and betrayal, and, later, of injudicious and misogynistic popular rage. The protagonist's original perception of the florist is based on her letter of denunciation which testifies to its author's wholehearted devotion to the Vichy regime and virulent anti-Semitism.[53] When challenged fifty years later, Armand firmly upholds her views and shows no remorse regarding her wartime deed. For example, when the narrator orders flowers from her shop to be sent to the Fechners' grave, she says disrespectfully, 'Je les croyais morts en déportation, *ceux-là*' [I thought *those ones* died in deportation] (C, 112, my emphasis). On another occasion, she shamelessly blames the tragedy of her neighbours on their own imprudence, and minimalises Jewish suffering by putting it on a par with the food shortages suffered by the non-Jewish French during the war. She thus repeatedly proves unrepentant about her betrayal, as well as self-serving, conceited, aggressive, and hateful.

The modification of the narrator's stand is occasioned by his uncovering of the circumstances of Madame Armand's act. Namely, he learns that she traded the address of the Fechners' hiding place against the promise of her brother's release from German captivity where he was held as a POW. The protagonist also discovers that at the Liberation Armand was publicly shamed and that her *tonte* had a devastating effect on her mental health and her marriage. As a result, in the protagonist's eyes, Armand grows to symbolise the ambiguity marking the Occupation, before becoming an outright victim. To encourage us to share its narrator's increasingly non-judgmental position in regard to Armand and, by implication, to other collaborators, *La Cliente* analogises the florist's situation to that of the 'privileged' Jews. Later in the novel, the narrator additionally recasts her as a Christian martyr and, by referencing St Paul's reputedly ambiguous dictum 'per speculum in aenigmate' (1 Corinthians 13:12), calls for our forbearance in the absence of complete knowledge of the past events.

By establishing a causal link between the promise of her brother's release and Armand's denunciation of her Jewish neighbours, *La Cliente* in a way replicates the conditions of what Levi termed an 'ill-defined area of ambiguity and compromise [...] born out of political coercion'.[54] The situation the florist is placed in by the

French police is indeed evocative of the 'choiceless choices', as Lawrence Langer has called the impossible moral decisions that the Jews were forced to make in extremis. These decisions, as Langer explains, 'did not reflect options between life and death, but between one form of "abnormal" response and another, both imposed by a situation that was in no way of the victim's own choosing'.[55] In other words, in camps and ghettos Jews colluded with their oppressors either under the threat of death or in hope of prolonging their life or that of their relatives. Although the blackmail and betrayal of which Armand was a victim theoretically make it possible to analogise her situation to that of the 'privileged' Jews whose actions may have been immoral, but who, in Levi's view, do not deserve our condemnation, several significant details separate the florist from a prisoner-functionary or even from Chaim Rumkowski. Firstly, wartime Paris cannot be compared to the ghettos or the camps, which were the stage for the demoralisation of the Jews by their oppressors. Secondly, as a non-Jewish French woman Armand cannot be equated with those who, having been marked out for total destruction, were subject to deliberate and systematic dehumanisation through starvation, backbreaking labour, lack of sanitary facilities, beatings, torture, random executions, and selections for gas chambers. According to Levi, the division of concentration camp inmates into ordinary and 'privileged' ones only added to the collapse of all moral standards they had experienced as a result of persecution.[56] Thirdly and finally, even if, in betraying the Fechners, Armand acted under duress, her rabid anti-Semitism renders the analogy between her and the 'privileged' Jews deeply problematic.

Considering that the character of Cécile Armand is meant as a synecdoche for Vichy France, *La Cliente* extends the concept of the 'Grey Zone' to the whole country. Although Levi himself may briefly include Europe's collaborating regimes, including Pétain's administration, within the 'Grey Zone', Brown judges this both inaccurate and morally flawed. In line with the Hungarian-Jewish lawyer, Rudolf Kasztner, who, speaking shortly after the war, deemed the analogy between the *Judenräte* (Jewish Councils operating in ghettos) and 'the ordinary Quislings and collaborationists' as 'entirely out of place', Brown reminds us of the immeasurable difference in the level of coercion, or indeed the lack of coercion in the case of some collaborating nations.[57] In the specific case of Vichy France, the deeply entrenched anti-Semitism, of which Assouline's novel itself provides ample evidence, 'disqualifies any comparison with the forced collaboration of the Jewish leaders and crematorium workers'.[58]

What renders Assouline's insertion of the florist into the 'Grey Zone' additionally suspect is his choice to thematise Levi's concept through the figure of a Catholic woman and thus to de-Judaise it. Although Levi himself at times brings Gentiles into the sphere of moral undecidability, Jews are unquestionably the main focus of his attention.[59] To throw more light on this particular point, *La Cliente* can be compared to William Styron's controversial novel, *Sophie's Choice* (1979), which has also been considered critically as a restaging of the 'Grey Zone'.[60] The novel is centred around the 'choiceless choice' that its eponymous character has to make upon her arrival at Auschwitz: to decide which of her two children will live. Unlike Olga Lengyel, whose Holocaust memoir *Five Chimneys* (1947) served as inspiration for Styron's novel, Sophie Zawistowski is a Catholic and, without perhaps sharing her father's position, is the daughter of a viciously anti-Jewish apologist for the Nazi regime.[61] If Styron places a Gentile at the centre of an agonising moral crisis, Assouline additionally reterritorialises the 'Grey Zone' by setting this crisis away from the ghettos and concentration camps of Nazi-occupied Poland. Furthermore, in contrast to *Sophie's Choice*, *La Cliente* places firm emphasis on its character's Catholicism and even likens Armand to a Christian martyr. Assouline achieves this with the episode in which, having followed the florist into a church, the protagonist watches her pause in front of a plaque listing her brother's name. His realisation that her brother died in captivity after all makes him assimilate her with St George who is represented by one of the stained-glass windows of the church. The narrator's analogy is based on the fact that the panel featuring the saint's face is missing, a detail that reminds him of Armand's urge to separate herself from her image following her *tonte* and that invokes his own efforts to unmask the florist as a wartime informer. However, the parallel between a collaborator and a Roman soldier killed for his Christian faith and then venerated for centuries across cultures seems misplaced, especially considering that martyrs are witnesses to the faith who 'die for their beliefs because they consciously refuse to compromise on the doctrines they consider absolute'.[62] Choosing to ignore this fact, the narrator suddenly sees the church as a space where 'on [...] bagnait dans une lueur d'une infinie pureté' [one bathed in the glow of infinite purity] and Madame Armand herself as deserving of his sympathy: 'Il y avait en elle autant de péché que de souffrance' [there was as much sin as suffering in her] (*C*, 149).

Even if at this stage Madame Armand is still surrounded by an aura of ambiguity, the protagonist's discovery of the brutal treatment to which she was subjected at the Liberation tips the balance in favour of her victimhood. The mental pain the florist suffered as a result of her *tonte* makes the narrator figure her once again as a martyr or even — as intimated by the likening of her psychological wounds to stigmata — as Christ himself. Similarly disturbing is the affinity the novel sets up between Armand who would cover her shorn head with a scarf, and the Jewish women who, during the war, used scarves to dissimulate the yellow stars that stigmatised, scapegoated, and banished them to the margins of society: 'son foulard désignait la pestiférée comme une coupable aux yeux du monde aussi sûrement que, plusieurs mois avant, ces écharpes posées nonchalamment des deux côtés du cou par de jeunes Juives soucieuses de dissimuler leur étoile jaune' [in everyone's eyes her scarf designated the pariah as a culprit, just as surely as several months earlier had done the scarves nonchalantly placed on both sides of the neck by young Jewish women eager to cover their yellow star] (*C*, 180). While this parallel is supposedly based on the fact that, like Jews during the Occupation, shorn women were brandished and ostracised at the Liberation, a discriminatory measure paving the way for mass extermination of an entire ethnic group cannot possibly be equated with the punishment meted out to Madame Armand. We must remember that, however heavy in consequences, the florist's *tonte* ensued from her earlier arrest and was therefore an indirect outcome of her denunciation of the Fechners.

'Per speculum in aenigmate'

Assouline's reliance on Christian imagery continues through his mobilisation of the trope of the mirror. Traditionally associated with self-awareness, inversion of reality, and the figure of the double, in *La Cliente* the mirror occupies an ambiguous position. While serving as a reminder of Madame Armand's public shaming, the mirror, when contextualised with St Paul's dictum 'per speculum in aenigmate', becomes instrumental in complicating the binary conception of the Occupation. Considering the novel's dialogue with Rousso's work, it is also possible to link the motif of the looking-glass to the phase of 'le miroir brisé' [the broken mirror], as Rousso designates the years of 1971–74, 'which were marked by an awakening of memory, the disintegration of the narrative of the heroic Resistance, and the emergence of new countermyths'.[63] In other words, having happily gazed into a flattering mirror fashioned from official memories of the war, French people suddenly had to confront the repressed truths about the Vichy period, including those related to France's role in the Holocaust. According to Ursula Hennigfeld, Armand's attempted suicide is indeed an attempt to undermine the prevalent heroic image of the Occupation:

> By plunging into the mirror, Madame Armand [...] wants to erase herself as well as the mirror which symbolizes these myths. The literary character represents France's confrontation with its own suppressed past and by looking into the mirror, she metaphorically reaches self-awareness.[64]

A less sympathetic reading could suggest that, rather than of her betrayal of her Jewish neighbours, mirrors remind Armand of her *tonte*. Such an interpretation of Armand's attempted suicide and subsequent dread of reflective surfaces is confirmed by her unabashed anti-Semitism and indifference to the tragedy of the Fechners, whose professional services she continues to use. It is therefore safe to assume that the mental health crisis Armand experienced after her public shaming was mainly to do with her self-image as a woman who had been unjustly disgraced in the eyes of her husband and her community.

And yet, it is a mirror — this time a little pocket one — that Assouline's protagonist uses to torment the florist in hope of awaking her conscience regarding her denunciation of his family. The reflections of light he sends into Armand's face from the Fechners' shop across the street blind the florist momentarily and cause her to injure her hand with scissors. As well as being a diminished echo of Armand's suicide attempt, this scene anticipates her death at the end of the novel. Blinded by sunlight refracted in the mirrored glasses of a passer-by and terrified of a new showdown with her pursuer, Armand falls under the wheels of a bus, that is of a vehicle that earlier in the novel enables the protagonist's imaginative return to Vichy France and is the stage for his attempt to confront the florist. The centrality of the mirror and the bus in this episode makes it possible to read Armand's death as a punishment for her wartime betrayal. However, the revelations yielded by the protagonist's investigation complicate our perception of such an ending of the novel. While the florist's guilt is mitigated by the circumstances of her decision to turn in the Fechners, her *tonte* places her in the position of a victim of gender-based violence whose purpose was to separate women from their sexuality and to brandish and stigmatise them until they could be reintegrated into a patriarchal society as reproductive and obedient bodies. Armand's death is therefore intended as a warning against the binary and narrowly Judeocentric interpretation of wartime realities which require a more careful consideration, especially beyond the reductive framework of anti-Semitism.

The mirror thus gradually morphs from a tool of potentially harmful exposures into one capable of complicating a simplistic understanding of a complex historical situation. Assouline achieves this with the character of Monsieur Adret, a mirror maker with a business located in the same street as Madame Armand and the Fechners. Acting as a passive bystander to the tragedy of the furriers and, later, to the florist's *tonte*, Adret nuances the dualistic view of Vichy France as populated uniquely by French collaborators and victimised Jews. Adret's observer position can be gathered from the nature of the goods he fashions and sells, and from his habit of speaking in quotations, which endows his speech with a reflective quality. Furthermore, in the photograph of Armand's *tonte,* Adret keeps at a distance from the nucleus of the scene. Finally and perhaps most importantly, it is the details provided by the mirror maker that overturn the protagonist's negative judgment of Armand. As the two men converse by the pond in the Parc Monceau, Adret troubles the reflective surface of the water with a pebble. His gesture inspires the protagonist to reframe the florist's story with St Paul's call for love and charity in the face of the provisional absence of full knowledge: 'Aujourd'hui nous voyons au moyen d'un miroir, d'une manière confuse, mais alors, nous verrons face à face; aujourd'hui je connais partiellement, mais alors je connaîtrai comme j'ai été connu' [Now we see in the mirror dimly, but then face to face. Now I know in part; then I shall know fully even as I have been fully known].[65] The mirror — broken or not — thus risks offering a confused image of the past, which can in turn lead to hasty and harsh judgements, such as the protagonist's condemnation of Madame Armand based on her letter of denunciation. However, clearly dissatisfied with the possibility of merely complicating the florist's guilt, the protagonist distorts the Pauline dictum in such a way as to reposit her as a victim and himself as a victimiser: 'nous voyons toute chose à l'envers. [...] Le miroir reflète la vie dans un tout autre sens' [we see everything upside down. [...] The mirror reflects life in a completely different way] (C, 185). It is François Fechner, the grandson of the deportees, who warns the protagonist against such a risky reversal of subject positions: 'Il ne faudrait pas que la culpabilité change de camp [...]. Sinon, on n'en finira vraiment jamais avec cette histoire' [we mustn't shift the blame to the opposite side [...]. Otherwise we'll never really put an end to this story] (C, 188).

The Grey Zone of Writing

To do justice to Madame Armand, the protagonist of *La Cliente* decides to tell her story in writing. However, instead of producing a newspaper article, as he originally planned, he decides to write a historical novel which would free him from the constraints of impartiality, chronology, causality, and reliance on hard evidence. These were indeed the principles guiding the protagonist's work as biographer; in other words, he adhered to his mentor's creed that 'les archives sont le sel de la recherche' [the archives are the salt of research] (C, 20). In Giulia Bassi's words, in traditional historiography 'each statement must be strictly (and positivistically) documented, "tested" according to the criteria of the reconstruction of a past which is "certain", "static", "given", "immutable"'. The historian's task is therefore 'to restore facts or, better, to *make the facts spontaneously emerge from the data*'.[66] The change in the protagonist's approach proceeds from his encounter with the *œuvre* of Simon, whose non-fictional and fictional writings prove difficult to separate. For example, it is impossible to ascertain whether Simon was actually denounced or the denunciation was the work of his imagination. Unable to resolve this question, the narrator makes the following confession: 'Je flottais dans un épais brouillard, incapable de faire la part de la fiction et celle de la réalité, écartelé entre une exigence officielle d'exactitude et une secrète attirance pour la vérité' [I was floating in a thick fog, unable to tell fiction from reality, torn between professional scrupulousness and a secret longing for truth] (C, 18). The impossibility of establishing historical truth leads Assouline's protagonist to deem traditional methodologies and representational modes as inadequate when it comes to complex historical phenomena such as *la délation*: 'Jamais un historien ne pourra donner la vraie mesure du phénomène. Seul un romancier y parviendrait' [Never will a historian be able to represent fully the phenomenon. Only a novelist could do it] (C, 29). Consequently, the protagonist follows Simon and ventures into 'une zone grise où les frontières s'estompaient' [a grey zone where borders were being blurred] (C, 19), transforming from a biographer into a historical novelist. More specifically, judging by his rejection of developmental continuity, he becomes a historical 'metafictionalist' who, as Patricia Waugh puts it, is wary of history's totalising and synthesising teleologies, and its ambition to produce unequivocal truths.[67]

The narrator of *La Cliente* further justifies his newfound narrative strategy by contrasting history's drive towards totalisation with historical (meta)fiction's capacity for individualising the past and exploring its nuances and ambiguities: 'Pour un historien, le détail ne signifiait rien. Pour moi, cela représentait beaucoup' [For a historian, a detail meant nothing. For me, it meant a lot] (C, 41). Furthermore, as opposed to a historian, a novelist is free to fill in the missing information with conjecture. This is illustrated by the protagonist's creative reconstruction of the arrest of the Fechners and by his imaginative portrait of the inspector who tracked them down. For the narrator, historiography and historical (meta)fiction are additionally separated by their relationship with chronology, continuity, and causality. Having accidentally disturbed the chronological order of the Fechners' file, which the novel compares to the emplotment of a Greek tragedy or of a realist novel, the narrator retells the events in the order in which he retrieved them. Alongside Madame Armand's story, he is thus able to retrace the progression of his own cognisance of the facts and, correspondingly, the development of his understanding of *les années noires*. Finally, the protagonist's refusal to heed the advice of François Fechner indicates his preference for historical (meta)fiction with its rejection of teleological closure which characterises the genres of history, biography, and conventional historical novel.

Conclusions

Through its simultaneous espousal of narrative strategies characteristic of historiographic metafiction and contestation of the dominant narrative on the Vichy period, *La Cliente* could be construed as an example of the representational model isolated and theorised by Hutcheon. Assouline's novel additionally throws light on under-represented aspects of the Occupation and of the Liberation, and on the overlooked subject position of the collaborator. Through the figure of a wartime informer who is later subjected to the practice of *la tonte*, *La Cliente* brings to the attention of its readers the phenomena of denunciation and of the punishment of female collaboration. Although Assouline's own writing has given much space to wartime collaborators, in contrast to his essays and biographies concerned with well-known public figures, *La Cliente* stages an ordinary woman.[68]

Regrettably, the exposure of these neglected phenomena does not seem to be the key objective of Assouline's debut novel. Rather, *La Cliente* tells the story of Madame Armand's betrayal and punishment with the intention of mitigating our condemnation of wartime collaboration and of deflecting our attention from France's persecution of its Jewish citizens and residents. Put differently, Assouline instrumentalises the illegitimate, sexist, and traumatogenic practice of public brandishing of women to counter a perception of Vichy France that is uniquely negative and Holocaust-focused. Yet more questionable is the novel's mobilisation of the concept of the 'Grey Zone' and its linked invitation to extend to French collaborators the stance of *impotentia judicandi* which Levi invites in relation to the 'privileged Jews'. As I have demonstrated, in co-opting Levi's paradigm, Assouline glosses over the insurmountable differences between the circumstances of the decision thematised by his novel and *l'univers concentrationnaire* which Langer has aptly described as 'beyond good and evil' and as marked by 'non-morality'.[69] What renders the analogies between Armand and the prisoner-functionaries even more offensive to the memory of the Jews who, when in extremis, were forced to collude with their own oppressors, is Assouline's relocation of the 'Grey Zone' to a country with a long history of both official and grassroots anti-Semitism. *La Cliente* further de-Judaises the 'Grey Zone' by spelling out Armand's Catholicism and anti-Jewish sentiment. Indeed, by likening the florist to a Christian martyr and by intertextually engaging with St Paul's call for unreserved love of Christ in the absence of our full knowledge of his goodness, *La Cliente* reiterates its demand that we suspend our judgment of collaborators until we fully understand the motives of their conduct. Finally, capitalising on the mirror's reversal of left and right, Assouline's narrator overinterprets St Paul's dictum 'per speculum in aenigmate' in order to invert the subject positions of victim and victimiser. This inversion suggests that while a collaborator may deserve our consideration or even compassion, the ongoing investigation of wartime crimes against Jews can harm those whose guilt is far from equivocal.

The ideological agenda of Assouline's novel which explicitly adopts narrative techniques and espouses values attached to postmodernism seems therefore at odds with Hutcheon's positive conception of the political engagement of historiographic metafiction. It appears that *La Cliente* takes advantage of, among other postmodern strategies, indeterminacy and challenge to strongly valorised binaries so that it may offer an ethically muddled tale that treads dangerously close to a rehabilitation of an informer with Jewish blood on her hands, and to a vilification of Jewish survivors and their descendants. To the confusion of the novel's ethical position is added its narrator who wavers between indignation at French anti-Semitism and exasperation with his fellow Jews' self-victimisation. Equally morally problematic are the means by which Assouline pursues his ideological goals, and which include a repeated amalgamation of distinct subject positions. That the analogy between Armand and the inhabitants of the 'Grey Zone' is indeed deliberate is confirmed by the parallels the novel establishes between the florist and Jewish women dissimulating their yellow stars. In the same vein, the novel likens Armand's anonymous letter of denunciation to the unsigned note scrawled by François Fechner, still reeling from his discovery of the identity of the person responsible for the deportation of his family. Consequently, *La Cliente* risks supporting Lee's association between misuses of the 'Grey Zone' and what he calls 'postmodern relativism'.[70] This relativism means that we limit ourselves to understanding wrongdoers without judging them, a situation that, as Lee believes, must be countered by ethics. While, as I claim throughout this book, ethics is something to which French historiographic metafictions about the Holocaust are normally strongly committed, there are clearly exceptions. In fact, Hutcheon herself allows the possibility that postmodern culture may articulate agendas other than progressive ones, when she observes that 'art can as easily confirm as trouble received codes, no matter how radical its surface transgressions'. Coincidentally, as an example of a writer whose works 'dismantle meaning and the unified humanist subject in the name of right-wing irrationalism [rather than] left-wing defamiliarizing critique', Hutcheon quotes another French author, Louis-Ferdinand Céline.[71]

Notes to Chapter 2

1. Susan L Pentlin, 'Holocaust Victims of Privilege', in *Problems Unique to the Holocaust*, ed. by Harry James Cargas (Lexington: University Press of Kentucky, 1999), pp. 25–42 (p. 39).
2. Pierre Assouline, *La Cliente* (Paris: Gallimard, 1998), p. 151 (hereafter referenced as *C* in the main text).
3. Henry Rousso, *Le Syndrome de Vichy: de 1944 à nos jours* (Paris: Seuil, 1987).
4. Henry Rousso and Éric Conan, *Vichy: un passé qui ne passe pas* (Paris: Fayard, 1994).
5. Pierre Assouline, *Simenon: biographie* (Paris: Julliard, 1992).

6. The only study of *La Cliente* published to date is Benn E. Williams, 'Varying Shades of Grey: Pierre Assouline at the Frontier of Fact and Fiction', in *Re-examining the Holocaust through Literature*, ed. by Aukje Kluge and Benn E. Williams (Cambridge: Cambridge Scholars Publishing, 2009), pp. 111–30. Ursula Hennigfeld and Richard Golsan have addressed *La Cliente* in a comparative perspective. Ursula Hennigfeld, 'Le Mirroir brisé: Reassessing the Occupation (1940–44) in Novels by Modiano, Assouline and Rozier', *Anuari de Filologia: Literatures Contemporànies*, 8 (2018), 137–58; Golsan, *Vichy's Afterlife*, pp. 183–84.
7. Assouline has worked with major newspapers (*France-Soir*), magazines (*Le Nouvel Observateur*, *L'Histoire*), and radio stations (France Culture, RTL, France Inter).
8. Pierre Assouline, *Jean Jardin: une éminence grise* (Paris: Gallimard, 1986). Without naming Assouline directly, the grandson of Jean Jardin, Alexandre Jardin, denounced the biography as one 'that sought to whitewash [his] grandfather': 'The Cry of my Conscience about my Family's Collaboration', *Guardian*, 12 January 2011 <https://www.theguardian.com/commentisfree/2011/jan/12/french-crime-collaboration-nazi> [accessed 12 October 2016].
9. Pierre Assouline, *Un demi-siècle d'édition française* (Paris: Balland, 1984), p. 352.
10. Pierre Assouline, *Hergé* (Paris: Plon, 1996); and *Le Fleuve Combelle* (Paris: Calmann-Levy, 1997).
11. Pierre Assouline, *Lutetia* (Paris: Gallimard, 2002); *Sigmaringen* (Paris: Gallimard, 2014).
12. Dan Stone, *Histories of the Holocaust* (Oxford: Oxford University Press, 2010), p. 15.
13. Pentlin, 'Holocaust Victims of Privilege', p. 26.
14. Prior to the publication of *La Cliente*, there existed only one comprehensive study of *la délation*, which is André Halimi, *La Délation sous l'Occupation* (Paris: Alain Moreau, 1983). Since 1998, the phenomenon has received further scrutiny: see *La Délation dans la France des années noires*, ed. by Laurent Joly (Paris: Perrin, 2012); and Laurent Joly, *Dénoncer les juifs sous l'Occupation* (Paris : CNRS, 2017). *La Cliente*'s narrator himself acknowledges the absence of research on *la délation* (C, 30).
15. Laurent Joly, 'Introduction', in *La Délation dans la France des années noires*, ed. by Joly, pp. 17–69 (p. 17). André Halimi defines *la délation* as 'la volonté de supprimer l'autre, de le tuer, pour atteindre son propre accomplissement' [the wish to suppress the other, to kill them, for the sake of one's own advancement]: *La Délation sous l'Occupation*, p. 14. Joly further elaborates on the distinction between the two notions in his more recent monograph: *Dénoncer les juifs sous l'Occupation*, pp. 28–30.
16. Halimi, *La Délation sous l'Occupation*, p. 24. See also Joly, *Dénoncer les juifs sous l'Occupation*, p. 29.
17. Alain Brossat, *Les Tondues: un carnaval moche* (Paris: Manya, 1992). Since the publication of Brossat's monograph, further studies on the topic have appeared. See Fabrice Virgili, *La France 'virile': les femmes tondues à la Libération* (Paris: Payot, 2000); *Shorn Women: Gender and Punishment in Liberation France*, trans. by John Flower (Oxford: Berg, 2002). See also Julie Desmarais, *Femmes tondues: France-Libération. Coupables, amoureuses, victimes* (Montreal: Presses de l'Université Laval, 2010); Alison M. Moore, 'History, Memory and Trauma in Photography of the *Tondues*: Visuality of the Vichy Past through the Silent Image of Women', *Gender and History*, 17.3 (2005), 657–81. Among the cultural representations of *la tonte* are Paul Éluard's poem 'Comprenne qui voudra' (1944), Marguerite Duras's screenplay for Alain Resnais's film *Hiroshima, mon amour* (1959), and Soazig Aaron's *Le Non de Klara* (2002). For a discussion of literary representations of the phenomenon, see Brossat, *Les Tondues*, pp. 48–52.
18. Moore, 'History, Memory and Trauma in Photography of the *Tondues*', p. 657.
19. Virgili, *Shorn Women*, pp. 237–38. Moore notes that France has frequently been constructed as a feminine body: 'History, Memory and Trauma in Photography of the *Tondues*', pp. 659–60. Cf. Leah D. Hewitt, 'Vichy's Female Icons: Chabrol's *Story of Women*', in *Gender and Fascism in Modern France*, ed. by Melanie Hawthorne and Richard J. Golsan (Hanover, NH: University of New England Press, 1997), pp. 156–74 (p. 161).
20. This less frequent translation of *les années noires* can be found in Richard J. Golsan, 'History and the "Duty of Memory" in Postwar France: The Pitfalls of Remembrance', in *What Happens to History: The Renewal of Ethics in Contemporary Thought*, ed. by Howard Marchitello (New York: Routledge, 2001), pp. 23–40.
21. Primo Levi, 'The Grey Zone', in *The Drowned and the Saved*, trans. by Raymond Rosenthal (London: Michael Joseph, 1988), pp. 22–51 (p. 22).

22. Ibid., p. 27.
23. Ibid., p. 29.
24. Ibid., p. 40.
25. Primo Levi, 'Primo Levi's Heartbreaking, Heroic Answers to the Most Common Questions He Was Asked about *Survival in Auschwitz*', trans. by Ruth Feldman, *The New Republic*, 17 February 1986 <https://newrepublic.com/article/119959/interview-primo-levi-survival-auschwitz> [accessed 8 April 2017]. Elsewhere, Levi stated, 'I'm not inclined to forgive, I never forgave our enemies of that time [...] because I know no human act that can erase a crime': 'The Intellectual in Auschwitz', in *The Drowned and the Saved*, pp. 102–20 (p. 110).
26. Levi, *The Drowned and the Saved*, p. 37.
27. Jonathan Petropoulos and John K. Roth, 'Prologue: The Gray Zones of the Holocaust', in *Gray Zones: Ambiguities and Compromise in the Holocaust and its Aftermath*, ed. by Jonathan Petropoulos and John K. Roth (New York: Berghahn Books, 2005), pp. xv–xxii (p. xviii).
28. Ibid., p. xix.
29. Tzvetan Todorov, 'The Enjoyment of Power', in *Facing the Extreme: Moral Life in Concentration Camps*, trans. by Arthur Denner and Abigail Pollack (New York: Metropolitan Books, 1995), pp. 179–94 (pp. 182–83).
30. Gian Paolo Biasin, 'Till My Ghastly Tale Is Told: Levi's Moral Discourse from *Se questo è un uomo* to *I sommersi e i salvati*', in *Reason and Light: Essays on Primo Levi*, ed. by Susan Tarrow (Ithaca, NY: Cornell University Press, 1990), pp. 127–41 (p. 128).
31. Omer Bartov, 'Introduction', in *The Holocaust: Origins, Implementation, Aftermath*, ed. by Omer Bartov (London: Routledge, 2000), pp. 1–18 (p. 10).
32. Agamben, *Remnants of Auschwitz*, p. 101. For a discussion of Agamben's expansion of the 'Grey Zone', see Sanyal, *Memory and Complicity*, pp. 23–55; Dominick LaCapra, 'Approaching Limit Events: Siting Agamben', in *History in Transit*, pp. 144–94; and Ruth Leys, *From Guilt to Shame: Auschwitz and After* (Princeton, NJ: Princeton University Press), pp. 157–74. While Sanyal states that 'Agamben's appropriation of Levi's voice when discussing a different order of violence altogether is a ventriloquism that disregards the survivor's explicit warning against conflating the camp and civilian life' (*Memory and Complicity*, p. 34), LaCapra notes that Agamben 'generalizes the gray zone in a manner that threatens to undo significant distinctions and to eventuate in a view of all existence in terms of the limit event or situation as a state of exception, if not emergency or crisis, in which the exception becomes the rule': *History in Transit*, p. 180.
33. Adam Brown lists studies that have redeployed Levi's term in alien contexts, such as patriarchal repression or psychiatric care. Adam Brown, *Judging 'Privileged' Jews: Holocaust Ethics, Representation, and the 'Grey Zone'* (New York: Berghahn Books, 2013), p. 71, n. 61. Other extensions include Claudia Card's critique of patriarchy and capitalism, where she argues that 'misogynous environments are routinely maintained by women': 'Groping Through Gray Zones', in *On Feminist Ethics and Politics*, ed. by Claudia Card (Lawrence: University Press of Kansas, 1999), pp. 3–26 (p. 5). Simona Forti claims that 'the gray zone, present in every human society, from the totalitarian regime to a "big, industrial factory", is the armature on which power props itself up': *New Demons: Rethinking Power and Evil Today*, trans. by Zakiya Hanafi (Stanford, CA: Stanford University Press, 2015).
34. Levi, *The Drowned and the Saved*, pp. 39, 40, 27, 27–28, 50.
35. Primo Levi, 'Shame', in *The Drowned and the Saved*, pp. 52–67 (p. 65).
36. Ibid., pp. 58, 61. Levi warns against judging 'distant epochs and places with the yardstick that prevails in the here and now: an error all the more difficult to avoid as the distance in space and time increases': 'Stereotypes', in *The Drowned and the Saved*, pp. 121–36 (p. 135).
37. Brown, *Judging 'Privileged' Jews*, p. 52.
38. Brown points out that in his novels *If This is a Man* (1947) and *Truce* (1963) Levi links greyness to various aspects of the Auschwitz environment, including the bread, the clouds, the sky, the fog, the dawn, and the inmates themselves. In *If This is a Man*, he writes, 'Everything is grey around us and we are grey': *Judging 'Privileged' Jews*, p. 52.
39. Ibid., pp. 52–53.
40. Sanyal, *Memory and Complicity*, p. 34.

41. Sander H. Lee, 'Primo Levi's *Gray Zone*: Implication for Post-Holocaust Ethics', *Holocaust and Genocide Studies*, 30.2 (Autumn 2016), 276–97 (p. 285). As examples of appropriate expansions of the 'Grey Zone', Lee quotes Christopher Browning's analysis of the Camp of Starachowice, or Robert Melson's study of the case of Jews living on the 'Aryan side' on false papers. Christopher R. Browning, '"Alleviation" and "Compliance": The Survival Strategies of the Jewish Leadership in the Wierzbnik Ghetto and Starachowice Factory Slave Labour Camps', in *Gray Zones*, ed. by Petropoulos and Roth, pp. 26–36; Robert Melson, 'Choiceless Choices: Surviving on False Papers on the "Aryan" Side', in *Gray Zones*, ed. by Petropoulos and Roth, pp. 97–106.
42. Levi, *The Drowned and the Saved*, p. 27.
43. Agamben, *Remnants of Auschwitz*, p. 17.
44. Berel Lang, *Primo Levi: The Matter of a Life* (New Haven, CT: Yale University Press, 2013), p. 125.
45. Primo Levi and Marco Vigevali, 'Words, Memory, Hope', in *The Voice of Memory: Interviews 1961–1987*, ed. by Marco Belpoliti and Robert Gordon, trans. by Robert Gordon (New York: Polity Press, 2001), pp. 250–57 (p. 253).
46. Ibid., p. 253.
47. Levi, *The Drowned and the Saved*, p. 33.
48. Primo Levi, 'The Memory of the Offence', in *The Drowned and the Saved*, pp. 11–21 (p. 12).
49. Ibid., p. 13.
50. Levi, *The Drowned and the Saved*, p. 64.
51. After the war, Simenon, on whom the character of Simon is based, was accused of having been close to the Vichy government and other collaborators, and of having written for collaborationist presses. Even if no charges were pressed against him, in 1945 Simenon left France for the United States.
52. Silverman, *Palimpsestic Memory*, p. 4.
53. In an interview, Pierre Assouline admits that, unable to transcribe an actual document ad verbatim, he composed Madame Armand's letter by collating sentences drawn from several such letters: 'Rencontre avec Pierre Assouline à l'occasion de la parution de *La Cliente* (1998)' <http://www.gallimard.fr/catalog/entretiens/01035681.htm> [accessed 12 February 2018].
54. Levi, *The Drowned and the Saved*, p. 49.
55. Lawrence Langer, 'The Dilemma of Choice in the Deathcamps', *Centerpoint*, 4 (Autumn 1980), 222–31 (p. 224).
56. Levi, *The Drowned and the Saved*, p. 24.
57. Brown, *Judging 'Privileged' Jews*, p. 73, n. 85. Kasztner's words must, however, be seen in the context of his own dubious stance during the war. Although he helped to smuggle persecuted Jews into Hungary and then, after German invasion, out of Hungary, he was accused by the Israeli court of collaboration and was assassinated in 1957. Jennifer Ring, *The Political Consequences of Thinking: Judaism in the Work of Hannah Arendt* (New York: State University of New York Press, 1997), p. 80.
58. Brown, *Judging 'Privileged' Jews*, p. 54.
59. Cf. ibid., p. 51.
60. For criticism of *Sophie's Choice*, see Alvin Rosenfeld, 'The Holocaust According to William Styron', *Midstream*, 25.10 (December 1979), 43–49; and Sylvie Mathé, 'The "Grey Zone" in William Styron's *Sophie's Choice*', *Études anglaises*, 4 (2004), 453–66. Mathé, 'The "Grey Zone" in William Styron's *Sophie's Choice*'.
61. To Styron's credit, it needs to be stated that, though Jewish, as a girl Lengyel went to a Catholic school and her memoir is punctuated by references to Christian doctrine. See Carmelle Stephens, 'Saints and Martyrs: Popular Maternal Tropes in Holocaust Memoir', *Journal of Holocaust Research*, 34.2 (April 2020), pp. 95–110.
62. Oren Baruch Stier, *Holocaust Icons: Symbolizing the Shoah in History and Memory* (New Brunswick, NJ: Rutgers University Press, 2015), p. 148.
63. Lynn A. Higgins, 'Unfinished Business: Reflections on the Occupation and May '68', *L'Esprit Créateur*, 33.1 (Spring 1993), 105–10 (p. 105).
64. Hennigfeld, 'Le Miroir brisé', p. 154.

65. The French translation quoted here is 'La Colombe'. The English translation comes from the Standard English Version of the Bible. In the King James Version we read, 'Now we see through a glass, darkly', while the New English Bible offers 'Now we see puzzling reflections in the mirror'. As Régis Burnet explains, St Paul's reference to seeing in a mirror darkly can be elucidated by the poor quality of ancient mirrors: 'Du miroir au face-à-face: voir comme Dieu voit dans le Nouveau Testament', *Pallas: Revue d'Études Antiques*, 92 (2013), para. 16 <https://journals.openedition.org/pallas/266> [accessed 1 June 2022].
66. Giulia Bassi, 'Against Historical Positivism: Some Skeptical Reflections about the Archival Fetishism', *Mnemoscape*, 1 (2015) <https://www.mnemoscape.org/single-post/2014/09/08/Against-Historiographical-Positivism-Some-Skeptical-Reflections-about-the-Archival-Fetishism---by-Giulia-Bassi> [accessed 6 April 2019].
67. Waugh, *Metafiction*, p. 3.
68. See, for example, Pierre Assouline, *L'Épuration des intellectuels 1944–1945* (Brussels: Édition Complexe, 1996).
69. Lawrence Langer, *Versions of Survival: The Holocaust and the Human Spirit* (Albany: State University of New York Press, 1982), p. 146.
70. Lee, 'Primo Levi's Grey Zone', p. 276.
71. Hutcheon, *A Poetics of Postmodernism*, p. 198.

CHAPTER 3

'Non, che ne feux pas': Soazig Aaron's *Le Non de Klara* and the Question of Post-Holocaust Identity

Les femmes, c'est à la chirurgie qu'on les stérilise. Et qu'importe? Puisque aucun d'eux ne doit revenir. Puisque aucun de nous ne reviendra.

[Women are sterilised in the surgical ward. What difference does it make? Since none of them will return. Since none of us will return.]

— CHARLOTTE DELBO, *Auschwitz, et après I*

'I'm your mother', she said, though she should have said: 'I'm the one who survived'. But that would be a line from a modern American novel.

— HANNA KRALL, 'The Woman from Hamburg'

Introduction: The Woman from Berlin

Charlotte Delbo's memoir, *Auschwitz et après*, and Hanna Krall's less known short story, 'Ta z Hamburga' [The Woman from Hamburg], are examples of Holocaust narratives that, authored by women writers, thematise specifically female experiences of the Holocaust. If both excerpts cited in the epigraph hint at the protracted ramifications of women's suffering under Nazi persecution, the lines from the Polish writer's story additionally touch on the dilemmas associated with Holocaust motherhood and with the articulation of these dilemmas in ways that avoid hackneyed narrative patterns, sentimentalisation, and stereotypical images of Jewish mothers in extremis.[1] Based on a true story, 'The Woman from Hamburg' casts a Holocaust survivor, Regina, who refuses to reconnect with her now grown-up daughter, Helusia. This is because, having been conceived and born when the protagonist was in hiding with a non-Jewish Polish couple in Lwów, Helusia reminds Regina of her wartime ordeal. These issues, including representational conundrums, are confronted also by the narrative addressed in the present chapter, which happens to be the only example of women's Holocaust literature included in this study. *Le Non de Klara* is the debut novel by Soazig Aaron, an author who, without apparently being Jewish, writes under a pen name incongruously uniting a Jewish-sounding surname and a female Breton first name.[2] Having studied history and run a bookstore, Aaron began writing in her early fifties and, since *Le Non de*

Klara, has so far published only one further novel.³ Her first narrative achieves its female focus by staging a young German-Jewish survivor of Auschwitz-Birkenau, who feels, like Regina in Krall's short story, unable to bond with her daughter. The novel opens with Klara Schwarz-Roth's belated return from captivity to Paris, where, on the eve of World War II, she and her husband, Rainer, found refuge from the anti-Semitic persecution they had faced in their native Germany. During her stay with her sister-in-law, Angélika, and Angélika's partner, Alban, Klara gradually divulges her unfathomably horrific experience of deportation. Cast as Angélika's diary, Aaron's novel frames Klara's reminiscences with the narrator's metafictional ruminations, intertextual asides, flashbacks, and reflections about the disturbing impact of her sister-in-law's testimony upon herself and Alban. *Le Non de Klara* thus addresses not only the horrors of the Nazi genocide and their long-lasting and intergenerational ramifications, but also the role of vicarious witnesses in memorialising the Shoah and the potential risk of secondary traumatisation. More importantly, the diary becomes a stage for Angélika's reflections on Klara's puzzling Holocaust-induced metamorphosis; apart from her refusal to resume the charge of her now three-year-old daughter, Victoire, Klara will not mourn her husband, who died as a *résistant*, or reconnect with any of her former acquaintances, including her closest friend, Agathe. Having disposed of all her property, Klara departs for the United States, her choice of destination being motivated by the fact that American soil and language have not been tainted by the Holocaust. She pledges never to return to the blood-soaked continent of Europe, or even to contact her friends and relatives, and plans to adopt a common English name and work as a photographer.

Le Non de Klara has had considerable critical success, winning several literary awards.⁴ These include the highly prestigious Geschwister-Scholl-Preis that in the past had been bestowed on prominent figures such as Holocaust historian Raul Hilberg and human rights activist Anna Politkovskaya. According to its website, the prize is conferred upon works that demonstrate 'spiritual independence', 'further the cause of civic freedom and intellectual courage', and 'are instrumental in providing impulses towards a responsible view of the present'.⁵ Aaron's novel has also been repeatedly adapted for the stage, has been translated into several languages, and has enjoyed many positive reviews.⁶ Among the critics who have applauded *Le Non de Klara* is Holocaust writer-survivor Jorge Semprún who called Aaron's novel 'don du ciel, merveille de l'écriture' [gift from heaven, marvel of writing].⁷ Semprún especially praised the novel's authenticity and central character's plausibility, and compared Klara's testimony to a story he had himself heard in Buchenwald from a member of the *Sonderkommando*. In contrast to the novel's original critical reception, academic criticism has been less positive. Lucille Cairns, Timo Obergöker, Danièle Sabbah, Anne-Berenike Binder, and Bruno Chaouat have raised concerns about Aaron's gentilisation and universalisation of the Holocaust, problematisation of Jewish victimhood, excessively violent representation of the Shoah, and blatant anachronism. Notably, the novel has been criticised for incorporating perspectives on the Nazi genocide that had not emerged by 1945, and in particular for articulating contemporary French anti-Israel sentiments.⁸

While my analysis will recontextualise some of the novel's purported ethical and historical shortcomings with its author's ostensible commitment to postmodern deconstructive thinking and representational modalities the chapter's main focus is the protagonist's steadfast position of refusal. I will read this refusal as a sign of postmodernism's critique and negation of modernity, including the notion of a stable and cohesive identity, which the Nazi ideology exploited to its murderous ends.[9] Klara's polyvalent 'no' can, of course, be deciphered as a symptom of the incurable trauma that she fears she may transmit to her daughter in a postmemorial process famously illustrated by Art Spiegelman's graphic memoir *Maus* (1980–91).[10] Yet, in keeping with the present book's ambition to trace postmodern tropes and narrative techniques in contemporary French Holocaust fiction, I will construe Klara's negation of her femininity, ethnicity, nationality, and linguistic identity, as well as of the institutions of marriage, motherhood, and the nation-state, as a postfeminist gesture. I hasten to add that postfeminism — a term fraught with contradictions — is understood here as an 'amorphous, critical, fluid and deconstructive' movement.[11] In other words, I define it as an enterprise arising from feminism's engagement with the postmodern questioning of dichotomous thinking and of the subject's integrity and stability that had underpinned Western ontology since the Enlightenment. By applying postmodern doubt and plurality to the formerly solid category of 'woman', which had been implicitly associated with white, middle-class, and heterosexual women, postfeminist thinkers have been able to locate oppression beyond patriarchy. As well as identifying imperialism, racism, and heteronormativity as sources of women's social marginalisation, they have connected the diversity of women's agendas to their ethnicity, religion, and sexuality.

If feminist theory would certainly provide a suitable lens for an examination of a novel addressing the gender-related specificity of women's suffering during and after the Holocaust, a postfeminist reading of *Le Non de Klara* can additionally throw light on the violent reduction of the eponymous protagonist's harmoniously plural self to the essentialist labels of 'Jew' and 'woman'. Such a reading can also foreground the novel's intention to interconnect patriarchy and racism, and, as exemplified by the undoing of the unity and solidarity of its female inmates, to reposition the concentration camp as the site of the entanglement and enactment of these two oppressive forces. Finally, the postfeminist approach promises to bring out some of the ideological inconsistencies of *Le Non de Klara* and its deconstructive drive which potentially jeopardises all efforts at reconstructing identity, including a feminine one, in the post-Holocaust world.

As well as with postfeminist theory, the following discussion of Klara's rejection of femininity, marriage, female friendship, and motherhood will be contextualised with historical studies of the Nazis' assault on Jewish women as mothers. I will also engage Derrida's deconstruction of binaries undergirding Western thinking and LaCapra's development of Derridean thought in relation to the victim-perpetrator binary, which has the power to illuminate Klara's hybrid gender and ethnic identity. Attributed by the novel to its protagonist's contamination by her oppressors' violence, Klara's post-Auschwitz self finds expression through her carefully cultivated androgyny and the name 'Sarah Adler' she assumes upon her return from deportation. Indeed, I will pay particular attention to the protagonist's choice of a name that, combining a typically Jewish and, as we shall see, negatively connoted first name with the surname of Klara's Nazi father, may be intended to complicate (Jewish) victimhood. More broadly, the protagonist's new name may signify her denunciation of the strictures of dichotomous thinking and of stable subject positions, or even her condemnation of a Jewishness that exploits the Holocaust to justify Israel's belligerence and its discriminatory policies towards the Palestinian minority. Since Aaron's novel identifies language as instrumental in defining oppressive identities from without, my discussion will also concern the role of language in Klara's metamorphosis and the protagonist's aversion to her native tongue. This part of my analysis of the novel will be informed by Foucault's view of bodies as constituted within the nexus of power and discourse, and by John Clammer's expansion of Judith Butler's theory of the performative power of language in determining ontologies to the categories of ethnicity and race. The chapter will close with my examination of the potential implications of Aaron's deconstructive impulse for our image of Holocaust survival and, more generally, of post-Holocaust selfhood. Namely, I ask whether the pessimism — not to say nihilism — marking *Le Non de Klara* leaves any room for reconstructive attempts in relation to post-Holocaust (feminine) identity.

Postfeminism and the Feminist Perspective in Holocaust Studies and Literature

Before examining *Le Non de Klara*, I will clarify my understanding of postfeminism and further justify my choice of this critical tool by outlining the protracted liminalisation of the female perspective on the Holocaust. Postfeminism has been conceptualised in two main and very different ways which could be designated as 'popular' and 'intellectual'.[12] Appropriated by the media and related to popular culture, 'popular' postfeminism has been used to denote a reactionary backlash against feminism in the face of the apparent achievement of the equality of the sexes, or even as a pernicious undoing of the gains of feminism through phenomena such as chick lit and the Spice Girls. More sympathetically, popular postfeminism has been interpreted as a space where tensions between feminism and femininity can be negotiated, and where questions about new directions in women's emancipation can be asked.[13] In academic writing in turn, postfeminism has been conceptualised as a discourse located at the intersection of feminism and other anti-foundationalist movements, such as postcolonialism, poststructuralism, and postmodernism. According to Ann Brooks, intellectual postfeminism:

> Represents a dynamic movement capable of challenging modernist, patriarchal and imperialist frameworks. In the process postfeminism facilitates a broad-based, pluralistic conception of the application of feminism, and addresses the demands of marginalized, diasporic and colonized cultures for a non-hegemonic feminism capable of giving voice to local, indigenous and postcolonial feminisms.[14]

The prefix 'post-' does not therefore indicate anti-feminism, but, analogically to postmodernism which Hutcheon describes as 'neither a simple and radical break from [modernity] nor a straightforward continuity with it', marks 'a process of ongoing transformation and change' in relation to feminism.[15] Following Brooks, I conceive of postfeminism as feminism's maturity in the sense of it being a continuing critique of patriarchal discourses and of feminism itself.[16] It is this critical self-consciousness that, despite some theorists' misgivings about feminism's and postmodernism's contradictory premises and politics, establishes a bridge between the two movements.[17] According to Pamela June, the overlap between feminism and postmodernism can be detected in their shared 'rigorous challenge to authority and convention'.[18] Patricia Waugh in turn regards the two enterprises as united in their espousal of the popular, rejection of the formalism of modernism, celebration of liminality, and confounding of the traditional markers of difference.[19] Waugh thereby concurs with Huyssen's view that feminism contributed to postmodern theory its 'recuperation of buried and mutilated traditions', emphasis on 'exploring forms of gender- and race-based subjectivity', and 'refusal to be limited to standard canonisations'.[20] More pertinently to my reading of Aaron's novel, postfeminism forsakes feminism's essentialist conception of 'woman' as a unified and unifying category. Instead, it embraces, as Stéphanie Genz and Benjamin Brabon put it, 'the postmodern notion of the dispersed and unstable subject' and pays attention to the multiplicity of marginalised or persecuted female subjectivities whose oppression stems from their class, ethnicity, religion, political allegiances, disability, or sexuality.[21]

Understood as a mix of postmodern and feminist theories, postfeminism presents itself as an appropriate theoretical framework within which to examine a novel that, as we will see, carries such hallmarks of historiographic metafiction as self-reflexivity, intertextual reliance on external discourses, self-contradictoriness, playfulness, fragmentariness, and anachronism. What also aligns *Le Non de Klara* with a postmodern ethos, while simultaneously placing it within (post)feminist logic, is its re-examination of a major historical event from a marginalised perspective. This perspective belongs to a *Mischling*, as the Nazis pejoratively designated those with mixed Christian-Jewish heritage. As Cathy Gelbin notes, the plight of the *Mischlinge* has been under-researched and the *Mischlinge* themselves have been a neglected subcategory of survivors.[22] The liminality of Klara's perspective is amplified by her gender, for, regardless of the steady growth of women's Holocaust studies since the late 1980s, a feminist approach to the Nazi genocide remains peripheral in relation to mainstream research.[23] Such a situation may seem paradoxical considering Myrna Goldberg's remark that 'the concentration camp is an ultimate expression of the extreme masculinity and misogyny that undergirded Nazi ideology' or the calls of prominent scholars such as Yehuda Bauer for a gender-related agenda in Holocaust studies.[24] And yet, until the later 1980s, women's lives had been, in Joan Ringelheim's words, 'neutralized into a so-called "human perspective", which on examination turns out to be a masculine one'.[25] Writing in 1985, Ringelheim stated that, since 'the similarity among Jewish victims of the Nazi policy of destruction has been considered more important than any differentiation', 'the experiences and perceptions of Jewish women have been obscured or absorbed into the descriptions of men's lives'.[26] The prolonged domination of the male-focused perspective may at least partially explain the scepticism, not to say outright hostility, with which the belated advent of gender-based Holocaust scholarship was greeted. Feminist critics were accused of de-Judaising and trivialising the Holocaust and of unnecessarily shifting the focus from anti-Semitism to misogyny. Their critics argued that 'rape, abortion, sexual exploitation, and pregnancy are always potentially part of a woman's life', and that 'discussions of sexuality desecrate the memory of the dead [...] or the Holocaust itself'.[27] Notwithstanding the dissenting voices, recent years have seen the arrival of a new generation of feminist Holocaust scholars. While continuing to investigate the specificity of women's experience of anti-Semitic persecution, researchers such as Zoë Waxman and Anna Hardman have been questioning some of the earlier assumptions about female victims.[28] For example, they have been arguing against the homogenisation of women's experience and identities, the representation of all women as intrinsically maternal, the myth of 'camp sisterhood', the valorisation of women's self-sacrifice for their offspring, and the linked condemnation of women's self-preservation.[29] Other feminist critics have gone further by warning against treating women as a monolithic group for fear that a gendered approach may lead to women's further marginalisation.[30] Others still have been exploring formerly proscribed topics such as rape, forced sterilisation, abortion, sexual barter, infanticide, and prostitution.[31]

Reflecting mainstream historiography's neglect of the specific questions arising from the Nazi persecution of Jewish women, Holocaust literature has been, including in France, dominated by male voices, a situation reflected in the corpus of the present study.[32] Despite the existence of works by Ida Fink, Ilona Karmel, Isabella Leitner, Olga Lengyel, Anna Langfus, and Chava Rosenfarb, to name but a few, literary Holocaust scholarship has largely focused on the writings of male authors.[33] Cynthia Ozick and Charlotte Delbo are the only two women who have enjoyed the stature afforded to Elie Wiesel, Primo Levi, Robert Antelme, Jean Améry, Jerzy Kosinski, Paul Celan, and Tadeusz Borowski. As a result, few studies of women's Holocaust literature have appeared to date, which means in turn that the way women suffered from anti-Semitic measures and coped with them remains underrepresented.[34] In other words, gender-specific issues such as pregnancy, giving birth, looking after small children, sexual barter, rape, menstruation, and the fear of infertility attached to amenorrhea have so far found limited expression. This is because, with rare exceptions, male-authored works ignore or minimise the hardships faced by female victims, whom they tend to cast as minor figures and/or reduce to stereotypes of passivity and vulnerability.[35] An apt example of this paradigm is Spiegelman's *Maus*, in which Anja Spiegelman's experience is mediated by the narratives first of her husband and then of her son. Although it is a well-documented fact that the conditions in the women's camp of Birkenau where Anja was held were considerably worse than in Auschwitz, Anja's husband Vladek dismisses the possibility of any differentiation between his own and his wife's experiences: '[Anja] went through the same what me: terrible!'.³⁶ From his account, recorded after Anja's death and Vladek's subsequent destruction of her diaries, Anja emerges as a mentally fragile figure whose survival permanently hinges on her husband's entrepreneurial disposition. According to Sara Horowitz, like *Maus*, many other male-authored narratives portray women as 'peripheral, helpless, and fragile; as morally deficient; or as erotic in their victimization'.³⁷

In this context, by thematising the importance of female co-operation and friendship in the camps, of the challenges of motherhood during and after the Holocaust, and of female inmates' preoccupation with physical appearance and sexuality-related vulnerability, *Le Non de Klara* contributes to the unsilencing of women's Holocaust experiences. Its ambition dovetails with its diary form which, while being a key genre in Holocaust representation, has played a crucial role in feminist recovery of women's voices.³⁸ It is noteworthy that Aaron's choice of the diary form fits in not only with her narrative's feminist goals, but also with her novel's postmodern texture. This is because, firstly, the interaction of the 'fictional code' with the code of the real in a diary ties in with typically postmodern double coding and self-contradictoriness,³⁹ and the fact that the production of the narrative becomes part of the plot reflects the characteristic self-reflexivity of postmodern fiction.⁴⁰ Secondly, emulating the parodic relationship of postmodern texts with established discursive modes, *Le Non de Klara* undermines the diary form in a number of ways, including by making its focus a person other than the narrator.

Le Non de Klara: If This Is a Woman

Klara's post-Holocaust position of negation first becomes apparent through her transgendered appearance. Having entered the lobby of the Lutetia, a hotel that, as signalled in the previous chapter, served as a reception centre for returning deportees, Angélika notices 'un drôle petit homme, au large dans une veste trop boutonnée, un pantalon noir assez fripé tombe sur des chaussures de montagne' [a small, odd-looking fellow wearing a jacket too big for him but buttoned up tight, together with rather crumpled black trousers over a pair of climbing boots].⁴¹ The 'boy' with blond hair, hollow cheeks, and huge eyes, whose androgynous looks are accentuated by the presence of two women flanking 'him', eventually turns out to be Angélika's own sister-in-law. The dislocation of Klara's feminine traits is owed to the men's clothes she is wearing, to her close-cropped hair, and to her emaciated body, which means little flesh around breasts and hips, two areas associated with femininity.⁴² The trope of misrecognition and misleading appearances persists through Angélika's mistaking of a black coat mangled at Klara's feet for a curled-up dog, and through her memory of a woman unable to recognise her own husband returning from captivity. Yet, even witnessing such awkward encounters in her capacity as a volunteer at the Lutetia could not have prepared Angélika for Klara's metamorphosis. The latter is manifest not only in Klara's appearance but also in her rasping voice and her rough manner. That the transformation is in fact intentional transpires from Klara's habit of trimming her hair, from her refusal to wear women's clothes, and from her preference for men's cologne. Accordingly, she rejects her position as a wife by changing her name from 'Schwarz-Roth' to 'Adler' and, showing herself insensitive to Angélika's grief over her brother's death, by proclaiming that had Rainer survived, she would now divorce him (*NK*, 26; *R*, 23). What Klara resents in her late husband are his heroic aspirations which contrasted with her own passive victimisation, a reproach that echoes Simone de Beauvoir's exposure of the contrast between socially-constructed female passivity and men's traditional role as active, controlling subjects.[43] In the light of Jill Conway's study of how gender inflects autobiography, Rainer's response becomes an example of men's expectation that their life should be made up of heroic tales of action, while Klara's trajectory corresponds to women's acceptance of their passivity and of an existence that acquires meaning through love and family.[44] Klara's position could additionally be framed with the valorisation of armed struggle against the Germans by the official narrative on the Occupation, which neglected the victimhood of Jewish deportees.[45] Rebecca Clifford writes:

> Where deportation played a symbolic role in resistance narratives, the focus was entirely on deported resistance fighters; Jewish deportees, having been deported principally because of who they were, rather than because of what they had done, had only a marginal place in such narratives.[46]

Klara's ambiguous gender identity haunts Angélika's diary, as illustrated by the narrator's italicisation of the personal pronoun *elle* [she] or by her direct comment on her sister-in-law's androgynous appearance and behaviour:

> Ce pourrait être un gamin de seize ans, une femme de quarante et on ne sait quoi encore, quelqu'un dont on ne saisirait pas le temporel, en sorte qu'on pourrait dire qu'elle possède toute l'étendue des temporels et tous les modes aussi, jusqu'au neutre de l'objet. (*NK*, 16)
>
> [It might have been a boy of sixteen, a woman of forty, anything — someone whose relation to time was not clear, so you might say she spanned all ages and all fashions, and became neutral, belonging to none.] (*R*, 10)

As well as registering Klara's metamorphosis, Angélika's written record of her sister-in-law's return from deportation hopes to counteract it by narrowing the gap between Klara's pre-war and present selves, and by stabilising the relationship between the two women: 'Depuis trois jours, je ne suis certaine de rien. Klara est revenue. Ce cahier [...] est providentiel... sinon tout va couler, je vais couler' [For three days I haven't been certain of anything. Klara's back. It's lucky I've got this notebook handy [...]. But for it, everything would sink without a trace. *I would sink without a trace*] (*NK*, 9; *R*, 1, translation modified). To corroborate Angélika's faith in the performative power of language, to which I return later, it suffices to quote her diary's opening entry where she utters Klara's name as many as fifteen times and where the name stands either alone or alongside Angélika's and Alban's names. This exercise underscores not only the irreparable ontological damage suffered by Holocaust survivors, but also the destabilising and fragmenting effect of the survivors' trauma on those who come into contact with them.

Before considering Klara's defeminisation in the light of postmodernism's rejection of clearly delineated, essentialist, and totalising identities, and of post-feminism's contestation of the universal and singular conception of 'woman', I will examine Aaron's contribution to the gendering of the Holocaust, including through her sensitivity to the challenge of being a Jewish mother in wartime and post-war Europe. Klara's memories of deportation abound in the tropes that feature in women's Holocaust testimonies and literature, and that relate to women's sexuality and their consequent biological roles as child-bearers and socially constructed roles as main child-carers. One of these tropes is the shaving of heads. Although the same for both sexes, the removal of all hair as part of the initiation to the camp was experienced differently by women for whom 'it symbolise[d] the loss in a concrete way of [their] socially defined identity'.[47] Whereas for men being deprived of their clothes and hair, or having their bodily cavities searched for valuables signified a loss of dignity, autonomy, and external signs of professional and social status, for women, who had been socialised by religious teachings and communal values to behave modestly, the same process amounted to a sexual assault and was highly traumatic.[48] Even non-Jewish female prisoners remember the forcible and violent removal of hair as the most shocking experience,[49] not to mention observant Jewish women who, once married, would wear headscarves or wigs, and who perceived it as 'an act of mutilation and humiliation'.[50] Irrespective of Klara's non-engagement with Judaism, having her head shorn in Auschwitz leaves her with a deep psychological wound: 'Je ne supporte plus les cheveux, c'est ce qui m'a le plus révulsée, ces femmes avec leurs masses de cheveux, les cheveux des femmes ici, elles portent des couronnes, de gros cheveux' [I can't stand hair any more. That's what repelled me the most here — the women with their masses of hair, they wear braids wound round their heads, enormous affairs] (*NK*, 28–29; *R*, 26). And so hair, which has traditionally been a potent coder for femininity, drives a wedge into the female community of the camp, splitting it along the lines of ethnicity and nationality and, consequently, as postfeminist theorists have it, showing 'woman' to be an elusive and fragmented construct.[51] As Klara stresses, only Jewish women had their heads shorn regularly; in contrast, political prisoners were allowed to have short hair and *Kapos* and especially German guards boasted elaborate hairstyles. Indeed, if a woman's complicity with the Nazis grew in proportion to the sumptuousness of her hair, the only detail about a particularly sadistic *Kapo* that Klara deems worth mentioning is her splendid hairdo. Interestingly, Aaron establishes a continuity between the shearing of women's heads in Nazi concentration camps and *la tonte* which, as discussed in the previous chapter, affected thousands of French women accused of intimate relations with the Germans. The episode in which a Frenchman taunts Klara on account of her cropped hair puts on a par the Nazis' shaving of women's heads in the camps and the punishment of *la collaboration horizontale* at the Liberation, thus interconnecting sexist and racist violence.

Klara's defeminisation, indicated by her very short hair, is accentuated by her emaciation that persists as a result of her poor appetite. Intriguingly, Klara's ambiguous relationship with her wasted body, which provokes a combination of self-hatred and self-commiseration, mirrors her conflicted feelings about her native Berlin, a city whose ruins she simultaneously loathes and pities. Klara's complex emotions regarding her physique and national identity may be behind her refusal to remove her trousers during a medical examination even though the doctor is female. It is also possible that, as well as all the horrors she recounts, Aaron's protagonist suffered sexual abuse during deportation, a speculation invited by her metaphorising of her privileged status in Auschwitz as prostitution. As if she had been selling her flesh, as some detainees did when forced to work in brothels or to barter sexual favours for food, Klara feels ashamed of having spoken German in exchange for a more advantageous position.[52] It is therefore not only because of its association with Nazi violence, but also because of her own enforced collusion with her oppressors that Klara resolves not to speak her beloved native tongue:

> J'ai utilisé ma langue comme si elle était mon corps, un corps bafoué, [...] comme un corps méprisé, ma langue, je l'ai faite *putain* [...]. [J]e la poussais devant moi, à lui faire tortiller du cul [...], je lui disais, viens salope, viens aguicher le SS [...], elle peut servir à tout cette *pute*. (NK, 100–01, my emphasis)
>
> [I [...] used my mother tongue as if it was my body, a humiliated body; [...] like a despised body, [...] used my mother tongue like *a whore* [...], I pushed it in front of me, making it wiggle its behind [...], I'd tell her, come on, slut, give the SS the glad eye [...], she can be useful in all sorts of ways, this *trollop*.] (R 109)

An alternative explanation of Klara's refusal to undergo a full medical examination is her aesthetic anxiety about a body that, once very attractive, has been ruined by the two years spent in Birkenau: 'Je suis partie avec un corps acceptable, un visage également, des cheveux blonds et des yeux gris. Je reviens avec un visage ravagé, des cheveux gris, un corps que je n'ose pas regarder et qui n'est pas regardable' [I went there with a decent body, a decent face, fair hair and grey eyes. I come back with a ravaged face, grey hair, a body which I can't bear to look at and which isn't fit to be looked at] (NK, 71; R, 76). Such a reading is invited by the historically grounded scene in which female inmates are shocked by their reflection in a scrap of mirror they have found.[53]

The defeminising impact of deportation on Aaron's protagonist is also signalled by her amenorrhea. Survivor testimonies link the lack of menstruation to malnutrition in ghettos and concentration camps, and establish it as a source of women's procreational anxieties.[54] Waxman points out that in patriarchal Jewish communities the threat of childlessness was not merely emotional but existential.[55] In contrast, women who continued to menstruate suffered discomfort through having no access to sanitary protection, a fact that Klara mentions in relation to the abjection to which prisoners were subjected.[56] According to Terrence Des Pres, depriving inmates of soap and water was part of the Nazis' 'exremental assault' on their victims, that is of their deliberate policy of destroying the victims' dignity, of dehumanising them, and, consequently, of making them easier to brutalise and kill. The Nazis thus also thwarted the prisoners' acts of solidarity or collaboration, for 'one [cannot] respond to the needs of another if both stink, if both are caked with mud and faeces'.[57]

Even if, as Klara's recollections poignantly illustrate, the Nazi system destroyed human (including female) solidarity, the protagonist has fond memories of the three women she knew in Auschwitz. These friendships provided Klara with moral sustenance and, on occasion, saved her life. By recalling that women 'se surveillaient, les amies aidaient amies' [watched over one another, friends helped friends] (*NK*, 90; *R*, 98), Klara echoes both Holocaust testimonies and fiction written by women, which stress the importance of 'camp sisterhood' for survival. In her study of women's Holocaust literature, Lillian Kremer argues that female inmates were more likely than men to nurse each other through typhus and dysentery than their male counterparts, and that they tended to each other's wounds, sustained weaker prisoners through rollcalls, and shared their meagre food rations with those more needy.[58] Yet, as well as lending historical credibility to Aaron's narrative, this rare positive aspect of deportation serves to thematise the devastating effect of the death of Klara's 'camp sisters'. The triple loss disables the young woman's capacity for forming new friendships in Auschwitz and, after her liberation, for reconnecting with her pre-war friends. In the scene of Angélika's and Klara's reunion at the Lutetia, Klara stiffens in response to her sister-in-law's embrace: 'tout son corps dit non' [her whole body [...] saying no] (*NK*, 11; *R*, 3). Similarly, in a later episode, Angélika has the impression that a thick sheet of glass separates her from Klara. As for Agathe, even her key role in saving Victoire's life cannot make the protagonist revoke her refusal to see her former friend. At the same time, Klara cherishes the apparently insignificant yet symbolically charged safety pin she received from Agathe upon her arrest. Once used by mothers and wet-nurses to fasten babies' nappies and hence called in French *épingle de nourrice* [nurse's pin], the safety pin symbolises Klara's bond with her baby daughter, a bond that, however, will also be destroyed.

Suffer Little Mothers

Since the Nazi regime viewed women, as Judith Tydor Baumel notes, 'from a primarily biological standpoint and hence in reproductive terms', Aryan maternity was eulogised and encouraged, whereas Jewish women were perceived as a danger to the purity of the Aryan race.[59] This is reflected in Hitler's pronouncements that 'every child that a woman brings into the world is a battle, a battle waged for the existence of her people', and that 'one gestating Jewish mother posed a greater threat than any fighting man'.[60] Consequently, for Jewish women pregnancy became a capital crime; in many ghettos, Jews were prohibited from marrying and having children, and pregnant women were forced to have an abortion or else were selected for deportation.[61] By the same token, arriving in a concentration camp visibly pregnant or accompanied by small children signified instant death, while women who somehow managed to carry their pregnancies to term, had their infants instantly killed.[62] Otherwise, mother and child would be immediately dispatched to the gas chamber or even tossed alive into the flames of the crematory.[63]

Overshadowed by the Nazi threat from the start, Klara's own motherhood illustrates the above-described reality. Barely a month after giving birth at home and in utmost secrecy, Aaron's protagonist is interned at Drancy. To protect Klara's daughter, Angélika and Alban register her as their own child and change her name from 'Vera' to the French-sounding 'Victoire'. This scenario corresponds to real-life situations where, having been fostered by gentile families, Jewish children would be brought up with new identities and, if they were reunited with their biological parents, would struggle to rediscover their pre-war selves.[64] In Aaron's novel, the change of the child's name has an additional symbolic significance; it indicates the Holocaust's invalidation of the concepts of truth and trust which are the two possible translations of the Russian name 'Vera'. Klara's dissatisfaction with her daughter's new name in turn communicates her scepticism regarding the triumphalist narrative of the end of the war as the Allies' victory over the Nazis. As we will see in Chapter Six, Aaron's protagonist shares the conception of World War II and the Holocaust of Jan Karski (as imagined by Haenel) as an ongoing historical reality which will spill over into post-war decades, continuing through lasting societal and political ramifications, including survivors' and transgenerational trauma.

If Klara's refusal to reconnect with her daughter is easily explained through her traumatisation, the novel additionally anchors it in the images of suffering mothers and children in Birkenau. Since her liberation, Klara has been having nightmares about emaciated Gypsy children with cheeks pierced by protruding bones. These nightmares bring to our attention the still under-represented 'Porajmos', also known as the 'Romani Holocaust', which claimed between twenty-five and fifty per cent of Europe's pre-war Roma and Sinti populations.[65] Klara's ability to mother is also affected by the haunting memory of newborns being murdered, a historically-grounded phenomenon that Aaron renders even more shocking with Klara's use of periphrasis when speaking of a midwife: 'elle aidait pour les enfants à naître' [she helped children to be born] (*NK*, 55; *R*, 58).[66] By specifying that the midwife 'a tué plusieurs enfants' [killed several children] (*NK*, 55; *R*, 58), Klara underscores the absurdities and horrors of *l'univers concentrationnaire* where a woman whose professional duty was to ensure the survival and good health of new mothers and babies, became a murderer of newborns.

What ultimately destroys Klara's maternal instinct is the death of a little boy whom she spontaneously fosters towards the end of her imprisonment and whom she names 'Ulli'. The character of the boy seems to be based on Hurbinek, a disabled three-year-old child whose short and tragic life Levi memorialised in *La tregua* (1963).[67] In the light of Nancy Horowitz's reading of the story of Hurbinek who dies, in Levi's words, 'liberated but not redeemed', as a synecdoche of the survivor's condition, Ulli's role in the novel is to confirm Klara's self-proclaimed spiritual and emotional death in the camp.[68] To such an interpretation point the analogies between Klara and her ward, who are both germanophone, who have both been abandoned in one way or another by their parents, and, finally, who both adopt a stance of refusal. While Klara attributes her survival to the categorical rejection of her pre-war morality and values (*NK*, 68; *R*, 72), Ulli expresses his negating position with persistent silence which he breaks only once to say 'nein' [no]. Guided by the boy's unique utterance, Klara decodes his death as his ultimate rejection of a world that allowed the Holocaust to happen:

> Il a décidé de mourir. Chez un si petit enfant, il y a eu refus. [...] Un doute pour l'éternité... d'ailleurs, ce n'était plus le doute, mais bien l'incroyance totale, incroyance envers un monde qui enlève les mères et fait le malheur énorme. (*NK*, 143)
>
> [He decided to die. In such a young child a refusal. [...] An eternal doubt, or rather no longer a doubt, but total disbelief, disbelief towards a world that steals mothers and creates enormous sorrow.] (*R*, 161)

That Ulli is indeed a projection of Aaron's protagonist is confirmed by Klara's own child-like or rather boyish appearance and behaviour. For example she carries with her a little red briefcase that Angélika compares to the one she used to have for her dolls, but which, ironically, holds Klara's revolver. Also, Klara's stubborn repetition of the phrase 'Che ne feux pas' [I don't vant to] (*NK*, 13; *R*, 7, translation modified) calls to mind the way French children express their disagreement.

Placed in the historical context of female survivors' assumed urge to be reunited with their children or, if they had no children, to start a family, Klara's decision not to rebuild her relationship with Victoire may seem uncharacteristic. Baumel's study suggests that raising a family was the surviving women's paramount concern, even before these women were fully rehabilitated and re-established in their old or new homelands.[69] Having been banned from procreating by their oppressors, women saw bearing healthy offspring as their duty, and, as exemplified by Isabella Leitner's testimony, regarded each new birth as a triumph over the Nazis.[70] More recent research has nuanced this one-dimensional picture of post-Holocaust Jewish motherhood, drawing attention to the estrangement of the former captives from their children. Helga Amesberger remarks that it sometimes took years for the mother to overcome her sense of alienation from the child, and the child's resentment for having been 'abandoned' by its biological parents.[71] Other female survivors chose to remain childless, justifying their decision with their experience of violence. Likewise, the women interviewed by Sara Horowitz spoke of the corrosion of motherhood and wifehood by the Nazi persecution and of their anxiety about passing their trauma on to the next generation.[72] Concurring with this position, Amesberger notes that 'the fate of the children in concentration camps was present in [these women's] minds, and to a certain extent they were afraid that the same fate might also await their children'.[73] Other survivors feared that their maternal instinct may have been eradicated by the conditions prevailing in captivity, while those who did decide to start a family, could not always find happiness in motherhood or even regretted it, an attitude that sometimes resulted in their descendants' serious psychological wounding.[74]

The recorded concerns of surviving women are shared by Aaron's protagonist whose experience of the camp has impaired her maternal potential and who tries to shield her daughter from being shaped by what Marianne Hirsch has called 'traumatic fragments of events that still defy narrative reconstruction and exceed comprehension'.[75]

> Je ne veux pas que [Victoire] renifle cette odeur [de la mort] qu'elle n'a pas encore eu dans le nez. [...] Avec moi, elle n'échappera à Brzezinka. Elle a été épargnée, pourquoi lui infliger les séquelles de ça? [...] Je n'ai rien à lui donner sauf ma douleur et ma folie, ma maladie, c'est bien cela, je suis malade et pas près de guérir. (*NK*, 137–38)
>
> [I don't want [Victoire] to get a whiff of that smell [of death], which she hasn't yet experienced. [...] With me, she wouldn't escape Brzezinka. She's been spared it so far — why inflict its aftermath on her? [...] I have nothing to give her but my pain and my madness, my illness, for that's what it is — I'm ill, and not likely to get better soon.] (*R*, 155)

Klara's refusal to resume the role of wife and mother, and her linked quest for professional independence and creative expression have, however, another purpose in the novel. Notably, they tally with Aaron's critique of women's post-war readiness to reoccupy their traditional positions in society. This is exemplified by Agathe's eagerness to start a new relationship, despite the recent loss of her husband. Likewise, Angélika seems to have no plans for returning to medical studies and instead contents herself with being a doctor's wife. Finally, other female characters of Aaron's novel limit their interests to elegance and glamour.

A Nazi Jew: A Postmodern Identity?

So far, I have concentrated on the external signs of Klara's rejection of her femininity and on her attendant renunciation of motherhood, which I have ascribed to the eroding influence of persecution on the protagonist's maternal instinct and which I have read as Aaron's questioning of the continued validity of traditional gender roles in post-war Europe. I now turn my attention to Klara's efforts to renegotiate other aspects of her identity, which may effectively result in an invalidation of a stable and uniform self in the post-Auschwitz world. Klara's conflicting relationship with both her Jewishness and Germanness, and with her dual status as Holocaust victim and daughter of a Nazi, crystallises and becomes, so to speak, codified in the name 'Sarah Adler' under which she returns from Auschwitz.[76] The full significance of Klara's new name can only be grasped if we view it in the context of the protagonist's family history. From Angélika's reminiscences we learn that in 1933 the professional position of Klara's father became untenable. To remain in the German army, Ulrich Adler divorced his Jewish wife and started an 'Aryan' family. As a sign of her resentment towards her father and her solidarity with her mother, Klara adopted her mother's maiden name 'Schwarz' and then married Angélika's brother who was 'un juif complet' [a complete Jew] (*NK*, 83; *R*, 88). It was also to pay tribute to her law-abiding mother that, once in Paris, Klara adhered to Vichy's anti-Semitic legislation. Unlike Angélika and Rainer, who dissimulated their origins with 'Aryan' identities, Klara registered with the French police as a Jew. In this light, the protagonist's decision to revert to her father's name may seem perplexing, especially given that, as Klara realises when she catches a glimpse of Ulrich Adler in Auschwitz, her father had become part of the Nazis' genocidal machine. Despite its implausibility, Klara's encounter with her father in the camp enables Aaron to intersect patriarchy and anti-Semitism, and to reposition the camp as a site of the conjunction of the two oppressive forces and its female inmates as victims of both racial and gendered violence. Such a re-presentation of *l'univers concentrationnaire* resonates with Claudia Koonz's remark that in the Nazi ideology racism went hand in hand with contempt for women: 'From the earliest beginnings of his Party, Hitler promised to eliminate Jews from "Aryan" society and expel women from public influence'.[77]

The previously outlined circumstances make Klara's adoption of a typically Jewish first name as baffling as her decision to revert to her father's surname. Our bafflement is intensified by the scene in which, having returned to Berlin after her liberation from Auschwitz, Klara murders her mother's former neighbours. Indeed, the protagonist claims that, rather than to punish those she had every reason to suspect of having killed her mother and usurped her mother's property, she pulled the trigger because they had called her 'Sarah'. As Aaron explains in a footnote, Klara's neighbours thus continued to adhere to the 1938 anti-Semitic decree that imposed the names 'Sarah' and 'Israel' on German Jews whose existing names did not disclose their lineage.[78] It needs adding that the couple's linguistic behaviour was only consistent with their overall arrogance: while blaming the war on the Jews, they compared their own wartime hardship — a cousin killed on the Eastern Front and an aunt who perished in the Allied bombings — to Klara's unimaginably horrific ordeal.

In this context, the protagonist's return from captivity as 'Sarah Adler' becomes symptomatic of her affiliation with two mutually conflicting subject positions as part of her post-Auschwitz identity, and can be interpreted, as I will do later, as an interrogation of the victim-victimiser binary. However, the oxymoronic name can equally be regarded in terms of postmodernism's rejection of stable and cohesive subjectivities in favour of ones that are fragmented, dispersed, and constituted by language. According to Victor Burgin, the postmodern subject is 'a precipitate of the very symbolic order of which the humanist subject supposed itself to be the master'.[79] In other words, in contrast to modernists who questioned the humanist subject by attributing its alienation and fragmentation to the multiplicity of available external perspectives, postmodernists do away with the illusion of a subject working towards re-centring in order to achieve a coherent and unique identity.[80] While Lawrence Grossberg explains that the post-humanist subject 'does not exist with a unified identity [but] [...] is constantly remade, reshaped as a mobilely situated set of relations in a fluid context', Zygmunt Bauman regards postmodernity as a propitious ground for the formation of 'liquid' identities which are marked by a chronic lack of stability and deregulation, as they are open to endless transformations through the individual's choices.[81] These remarks can help to understand the unravelling and reshaping of Klara's identity brought about by the Holocaust in which postmodern thinkers recognise the trigger for the changes to subjectivity that they theorise. Yet, considering the positioning of Klara's metamorphosis at the intersection of race and gender, where the two identity markers are construed as reductive, restrictive, and ultimately violent, the reconstruction of the protagonist's post-Auschwitz self could also be deciphered with recourse to postfeminist identity politics. In her influential essay 'The Cyborg Manifesto: Fractured Identities', Donna Haraway cuts herself off from the exclusiveness and essentialism of traditional feminism and instead posits gender, race, and class consciousness as the factors that, brought together, have been 'forced upon us by the terrible historical experience of [...] patriarchy, colonialism and capitalism'. Postulating that identities are 'contradictory, partial and strategic', and that gender, race, and class cannot serve as 'the basis for belief in "essential" unity', Haraway debunks the idea of a unitary female identity as 'a potent political myth'.[82] It is with this vision of 'fractured' identities in mind that I will now endeavour to elucidate the inconsistencies of Klara's negating position. Shifting my attention from the protagonist's rejection of traditional gender roles to her break with Judaism and Germanness, and comparing her stand with the identitary choices of the novel's other characters, I will foreground the interdependence between her fragmented self and the novel's epistolary form, and comment on the tension between the constitutive and oppressive facets of the performative power of discourse structuring Aaron's novel.

The dispersal of Klara's post-Holocaust self is reflected in the equally postmodern fragmentariness of *Le Non de Klara* which follows from the novel's epistolary form. Even though organised by the chronology of the subsequent entries, a diary eschews constraints of narrative thread, logic, and causality.[83] Angélika's narrative strategy, which is conditioned by the limitations of time and memory, by her subjective choices, and by her disposition at the moment of writing, is explained by the following metatextual passage:

> Je saute les préliminaires. Paresse de retrouver le chemin emprunté. Chemin jonché de petits cailloux qu'on écarte ou que l'on repousse, on retient, ne retient pas, selon l'humeur, l'envie, le besoin. Sans savoir pourquoi, on s'arrête, et c'est une place, on reconnaît la place, on s'installe, on ne regarde plus le chemin, on ne repartira plus par là, on ira ailleurs sur d'autres axes qui auront aussi une place au bout. C'est aisé et chaotique à la fois. (NK, 118)

> [I skip the preliminaries. Too lazy to find the place where I should pick up the thread again. The story is a path strewn with pebbles that one sets aside or pushes on further, things that you keep or reject according to your mood or inclination or need. Without knowing why, you suddenly stop. You recognise the place, decide to stay there, you don't care about the path anymore, you won't go that way again, you'll go somewhere else, among other ways that also lead somewhere in the end. The method is easy but chaotic.] (R, 132)

As in the entry introduced by the quoted passage, which relates Klara's disconnected musings on the ramifications of the Holocaust for religion and philosophy, Klara's memories of Auschwitz tend to be presented as non-linear, atemporal, and mostly descriptive fragments punctuated by gaps and silences: 'Ce sont des bribes, elle ne dit pas en continu. [...] L'élocution n'est pas constante [...]. Sa parole advient, on l'entend à un moment, c'est comme l'apparition d'un sous-marin, il était là, invisible, puis on le voit, puis il replonge' [Just scraps from time to time, never anything continuous. There is no continuity in her speech [...]. The words emerge, you hear them for a moment. I'm reminded of a submarine, there all the time but invisible, until suddenly you see it, then it dives again] (*NK*, 31; *R*, 29). If Klara's non-chronological way of remembering her ordeal exemplifies the temporal confusion marking concentrationary experience and its recall, it concurs with the nature of traumatic memory which I discuss at greater length in relation to Haenel's and Littell's novels.[84] Beside Klara's unsolicited, intrusive, and literal reminiscences, her traumata include disturbed sleep patterns, a tendency to associate unrelated situations to the Holocaust, emotional and intellectual distance from non-survivors, and nightmares.[85] The structural unity of Aaron's novel is further undermined through the interlacing of Klara's memories with Angélika's intertextual digressions and direct quotations, and with analeptic passages describing the pre-war life of the novel's main characters and the wartime fortunes of those who escaped deportation. Such a narrative strategy seems particularly apt in a novel that lends itself to a postmodern and postfeminist reading, especially if framed with Rosi Braidotti's assertion that '"fragmentation" has been women's historical condition' and with June's consequent belief that female authors have been embracing 'a disjointed postmodern writing style both to reflect and to resist their historical state of fragmentation'.[86] Importantly, discontinuity has also been identified as a narrative mode capable of rendering Holocaust violence which, with their tendency to arrange events in a linear and logical manner, conventional forms and structures defuse. Instead, they impose on the events of the Holocaust a teleological order and a sense of closure. According to James Young, 'the violent event can exist as such [...] only as long as it appears to stand outside the continuum, where it is apparently unmediated, unframed and unassimilated'.[87] Like Young, Dorota Głowacka isolates the writing of the fragment as an 'effective and ethically viable mode of pursuing the task of "speaking the unspeakable"'. For Głowacka, the fragment's paradoxical power 'lies not only in its centrifugal unframing of the narrative content, but also in its ability to release the power of the untold in the spaces between the scraps of memory'.[88]

Głowacka's thoughts on the suitability of certain literary forms for Holocaust literature follow directly on from Emil Fackenheim's belief that in the post-Holocaust era Jews must endure contradictions and persevere in their fragmented condition.[89] Klara's disseminated identity could therefore be understood as an embodiment of the fragmentariness that, for the German-born theologian, invariably qualifies post-Auschwitz Jewishness. More exactly, Aaron anchors her protagonist's dispersed and self-contradictory self in the Nazis' assault on her status as a fully assimilated middle-class Judeo-German woman. Angélika's flashbacks tell us that, prior to her arrest, Klara was an emancipated, cosmopolitan, erudite, and creative person with clear professional plans. Like Angélika and Rainer, she defined herself by her intellectual and artistic passions, rather than by the religious and cultural practices of her ancestors. None of the three medical students took much interest in their Jewishness, of which Angélika and Rainer learned only as teenagers, and Klara during her parents' divorce. As if anti-Semitism had not concerned them personally, Klara, Angélika, and Rainer laughed at Céline's hysterically Judeophobic outbursts and at Hitler himself. It is therefore without regret that, during the war, Angélika and Rainer shed the last vestiges of their Jewishness, which were their names, and become respectively Solange Blanc and René Leroux. It is noteworthy that their gesture playfully inverts Soazig Aaron's election of a Jewish name as her nom de plume, which, considering the literary resonances of the siblings' new names, alludes to her nascent vocation as a novelist. By calling himself after René Le Roux (1878–1949) who, although from Bordeaux, wrote in the Breton language and under a pen-name with Breton consonance ('Meven Modiern'), Rainer expresses his trust in the ability to reinvent one's cultural and linguistic identity. Even though his name does not ultimately save his life, it enables him to die a heroic fighter's death rather than share his wife's condition of a disempowered and humiliated victim condemned to meaningless suffering. Through her adopted name which, like her brother's, has literary connotations, Angélika, too, identifies with the cultural tradition of her francophone mother. 'Solange Blanc' combines the first name of George Sand's daughter, Solange Clésigner-Sand, with the name of the place where Aurore Dupin (George Sand's real name) had her country retreat. As well as the daughter of a writer, Clésigner-Sand was a novelist in her own right who, like her mother, published under a male pen name ('Dubois de Vavray'). While anticipating her writerly aspirations, manifest in the diary she starts keeping on Klara's return, the name 'Solange Blanc' points to a renewal of Angélika's identity, *blanc* meaning 'white' in English. It needs adding that Angélika is not only cognisant of her French persona's role in her survival, but also finds this persona so comfortable and liberating that once the war is over she decides to have it legalised.

The name changes effectuated by Klara, Rainer, and Angélika, and Angélika's renaming of Klara's daughter as 'Victoire', indicate Aaron's belief in the performative constitution and protean and arbitrary character of identity. The novelist consequently situates her characters within a postmodern logic which, having arisen from the devastation brought about by World War II and the Holocaust, questions the constituting, fixed, secure, uniform, and whole Cartesian ego. In his consequential and unsympathetic analysis of postmodernism, Jameson retraces the move of 'the autonomous bourgeois monad or ego or individual' proper to capitalist society from a position of alienation towards a position of fragmentation, before it is eventually dissolved. Alternatively, Jameson hazards that the bourgeois monad never existed in the first place, but was an 'ideological mirage':[90] 'this construct is merely a philosophical and cultural mystification, which sought to persuade people that they "had" individual subjects and possessed this unique personal identity'.[91] This illusive postmodern subject is, in Jameson's theorisation, additionally unable to imagine its past or present in terms of a coherent experience, which means that its cultural productions cannot result in anything but 'heaps of fragments'.[92]

If the disjointed composition of *Le Non de Klara* sustains Jameson's disparaging view of the postmodern subject's expression, the fluctuating identities of its characters lend support to Waugh's conviction that postmodern identity is 'simply the illusion produced through the manipulation of irreconcilable and contradictory language games'.[93] Exemplified with the adopted identities of the novel's main characters, Aaron's playfulness concerning language is borne out by the correspondence between the identities of these characters and her own self-constitution through her hybrid pen name which holds references to two genders and two cultural traditions. Another language game that Aaron plays with her reader is the use of the letter 'A' at the beginning of her protagonists' names; apart from the already mentioned characters of Angélika, Alban, Agathe, and Adler, the novel includes minor characters called Antoine, Adrien, and Adeline. This unlikely coincidence may be an allusion to Aaron's budding writerly career, 'A' being the first letter of the alphabet, and/or a sign that postmodern authorship entails, according to Bran Nicol, 'the division of the self into other fictional selves'.[94] Aaron may be also suggesting the power of 'Auschwitz' to cast a long shadow over post-war world, while retrospectively besmirching the pre-Holocaust reality.[95] Equally conceivably, Aaron's language games are designed to unsettle a realist reading of her novel and, reinforcing its postmodern character, to remind us of its status as a discursive construct.[96]

The previously described affirmative construction of selfhood through the character's performative agency contrasts with the violent enforcement of an essentialist identity from without dramatised through Klara's persecution as a 'Jew'. By focusing her novel around a woman with Jewish roots but no adherence to Judaism, Aaron foregrounds the Nazis' indiscriminate imposition of a negatively inflected otherness on those whom, for spurious ideological reasons, they had earmarked for annihilation. Rather than de-Judaising the Holocaust, as Cairns has it, Aaron shows how 'Jewishness' was impressed on, to quote Margaret Anne Hutton, 'the religiously observant and the secular, those steeped in Jewish culture and those totally ignorant of it, [and] those who identified as Jews and who did not'.[97] Indeed, in Aaron's novel, 'Jewishness' becomes an exemplar of a totalising and oppressive identity that the author opposes to individuality, differentiation, plurality, hybridity, transience, and undecidability. It could be ventured therefore that Aaron advocates the 'liquid identity' whose advent Bauman connects to the dissolution of all clearly defined and stable contexts provided by class, religion, ideology, and gender, and of the corresponding codes of conduct. But, if the identities of the novel's characters are subject to an ongoing self-definition and self-transformation, they are certainly not, as Bauman would have it, 'privatised' or 'commodified'.

The fact that Aaron's novel considers language as a major force in the formation of identity — be it freely chosen or externally enforced — encourages me to follow Clammer in extending Butler's construction of gender to the category of ethnicity. As in the case of gender or sexual identity which Butler construes as 'performatively constituted by the very "expressions" that are said to be its results', ethnicity creates culturally intelligible subjects, who then perform its discourse at the surface of their bodies through words, gestures, clothes, culinary choices, and so forth.[98] Informed by Clammer's idea of 'performative ethnicity' in circumstances of racial oppression,[99] Klara's adoption of a first name used by the Nazis to stigmatise Jews becomes a cynical form of resistance to the negative labelling through a deliberate heightening of a supposedly unacceptable characteristic, and not, as Cairns claims, a sign of Klara's internalisation of Nazi anti-Semitism.[100] Put differently, it becomes an example of linguistic reclamation exemplified by the resignification of originally derogatory terms such as 'Quaker', 'Protestant', 'Yankee', 'Black', and 'Queer', and widely interpreted as a means of creating group solidarity. For Foucault and Butler, such reappropriations reveal the intrinsic ambivalence of language; while Foucault discusses how homosexuals have enlisted the discourse that pathologised their sexual orientation in defence of their identity, Butler imbues resignifications of pejorative terms with the power to tame, if not to erase completely, their offensive quality.[101]

Before Klara attempts to reclaim and resignify the identity that was brutally imposed on her, the story of her persecution by the Nazis provides an example of Foucault's conceptualisation of discourse as a tool of power regimes and their demagogues. According to the French philosopher, oppressive regimes literally inscribe the subject's body through violent practices such as war, punishment, and branding, and, in so doing, render the body 'docile'.[102] Implicitly endorsing Foucault's belief in the nexus of power and language, and in the corporeality of the enactment of this nexus, Aaron thematises the effect of the Nazi ideology and propaganda on the bodies of her eponymous protagonist and other Jews. The first step in the embodiment of power is the mentioned decree coercing Jews into adopting the names 'Sarah' and 'Israel' as a way of de-individualising, stigmatising, and singling them out for future and more direct persecution. Klara's recognition of the performative force of the Nazi propaganda is visible in her response to Hitler's rabidly anti-Semitic tirades: '"[L]e salaud! on est en train de devenir juif"' ['The swine! Because of him we're turning into Jews'] (*NK*, 41; *R*, 41). After the war, she maintains her confidence in the consolidating impact of Nazi Judeophobia on Jewish identity: 'Hitler donne un coup de main aux Juifs pour qu'ils restent Juifs ou le redeviennent, et c'est faire allégeance à ce caporal minable que de retourner dans le giron du judaïsme' [Hitler is helping Jews to remain Jews, or to become Jews again, and [...] to return to the bosom of Judaism is to pay allegiance to that wretched corporal] (*NK*, 103; *R*, 112). The destructive inscription of the Nazi ideology upon Jewish bodies is then evidenced by Klara's dramatically altered physique which becomes a literal embodiment of the Foucauldian *corps docile*. Among the marks of the concentrationary experience are the protagonist's drastically diminished body weight, grey hair, five missing teeth, and the number tattooed upon her forearm, which in the camp negated her personhood and which, since her liberation, has shocked all those who catch sight of it.

Klara's conviction that her physical and psychological wounds are incurable does not stop her from trying to alleviate the damage she has suffered by renegotiating her ethnic, national, and linguistic identity. She attains this aim by refusing to speak German, a gesture reminiscent of Sylvia Plath's rejection of her father's native tongue. In the writings of the American poet, the German language figures as a 'barb wire snare' from which 'dead men cry', while Otto Plath himself is conflated with a Nazi soldier.[103] Klara's rejection of German, a strategy whose effectiveness Aaron doubts by emphasising her protagonist's strong accent in both French and English, is so systematic that she even replaces 'Auschwitz' and 'Birkenau' with 'Oświęcim' and 'Brzezinka', that is with the Polish names of the villages where the Nazis located the two camps. If Aaron's protagonist temporarily uses French, she plans to limit herself to English which, unlike the languages spoken in the camp, has not been polluted by Nazi violence and by the moral degradation of the victims, including herself. Together with English, Klara hopes to adopt a ubiquitous name such as 'Mary', whose Christian connotations to motherhood make it a curious choice in the light of Klara's renunciation of her own child. She also toys with the idea of replacing her name with a number, which, like her provocative adoption of the name 'Sarah', could be interpreted as an effort to reclaim the negatively charged signifiers that were forcibly attached to her.

'Every Woman Adores a Fascist'

Without refuting my earlier framing of Klara's hybrid and conflicting self with the postmodern doubt regarding the stability and cohesiveness of the subject, I will now recast the protagonist's post-Holocaust identity as a sign of Aaron's contestation of the oppositional construction of the categories of 'victim' and 'perpetrator'. To do this, I return to Klara's choice of the name 'Sarah', which may be read as Aaron's means of criticising those Jews who exploit the Holocaust for political purposes and, more broadly, of condemning the trauma culture that has emerged as a result of the Holocaust. Read more sympathetically, Klara's story could be a vector for foregrounding the enduring traumatisation of Holocaust survivors, the intergenerational transmission of psychological injury, and the risk of a secondary traumatisation. Such a reading is supported by the protagonist's self-proclaimed readiness to return to Auschwitz at any time and by her conscious cultivation of a 'walking corpse' appearance. Six months after her liberation, Klara still has a skeletal body and regularly crops her own hair. Her physical metamorphosis is paralleled by deeper changes; the once polite, gentle, and even bashful young woman has turned into a bad-mannered and aggressive person who will not hesitate to lie, steal, and murder, and who, moreover, boasts about her transgressive behaviour: 'Je sais me cacher, voler, mentir [...]; j'ai les réflexes pour aboutir à peu près à ce que je veux' [I know how to hide, steal, lie [...]; I've acquired the reflexes to be able to do practically anything I want] (*NK*, 105; *R*, 117). As well as by the murder of her neighbours, Klara's newfound propensity for violence is illustrated by her earlier killing of a sadistic *blokova*, in camp parlance a bloc elder. Other examples of the protagonist's transformation include her overreaction to an offhand comment by a Polish woman who had welcomed Klara under her roof in exchange for Russian lessons. Enraged by her hostess's suggestion that her Jewishness explains why she was deported, Aaron's protagonist smashes everything within her reach, throws a cup of tea into the Polish woman's face, and makes off with her overcoat. Similarly, when a Frenchman mistakes her for *une tondue*, Klara punches him so hard that she draws blood.

Since Klara's metamorphosis coincides with her sighting of her father in Auschwitz and her ensuing change of heart regarding him, we are invited to read her behaviour as a result of her contamination by the violence of her oppressors and by the camp's inverted ethical code. As already hinted at, Klara's perplexing attitude towards Ulrich Adler could be productively illuminated by Plath's ambivalence towards her own German father, or could even be construed as a parody of this ambivalence and therefore as another sign of Aaron's typically postmodern self-conscious intertextual reliance on the cultural representations of the Holocaust. Like the American poet, who simultaneously loathes and eroticises Otto Plath and who through her lyrical female persona in her poem 'Daddy' identifies both with the Jews and with the Nazi torturer, Klara espouses Jewish victimhood while engaging in an erotic complicity with fascism.[104] This complicity, which is also likely to be an ironic echo of the eroticisation of the Nazis undertaken by popular culture, is signalled through the protagonist's admiration for Ulrich Adler's good looks, her readoption of his surname, and her use of the diminutive of her father's first name to name the orphaned boy.[105] Another telling detail is Klara's pleasure at handling firearms, a skill that she learned from her father, but which, crucially, horrified her mother. Paradoxically, the protagonist uses a gun to avenge her mother and, also in Berlin, to shoot a rat which she figures as an allegory of the Germans. Turning on its head the Nazis' hateful comparison of Jews to vermin, Klara describes her compatriots as 'des rats, un peuple de rats, mais des rats pleutres' [rats, a nation of rats, but cowardly rats] (NK, 111; R, 123).

The persistent confusion of subject positions, which, as we can see in Chapters Two and Four, can be traced in other French historiographic metafictions about the Holocaust, may exemplify postmodern efforts to displace the dichotomous thinking that undergirds Western philosophy, embodied in strongly valorised opposites such as body/ soul, centre/ margin, self/ Other, man/ woman, and speech/ writing. Relating Derrida's contestation of such binary logic to the Holocaust, LaCapra praises deconstruction for disabling the scapegoat mechanism consisting in 'sharply dividing self and other with the source of anxiety projected onto the nefarious other'.[106] He nevertheless refuses to condone Agamben's elaboration of Levi's notion of the 'Grey Zone', discussed in the previous chapter, as an ethically homogenous 'grey-on-grey world' populated with equally complicit victim-perpetrators.[107] Instead of denying subject positions their distinctiveness, LaCapra recommends an individualised approach where we 'carefully examine the different role in different situations of the grid linking together perpetrator, victim, equivocal perpetrator-victim, collaborator, bystander, rescuer, and so forth'. Ultimately, he proposes that 'the entire grid centred on victimisation' should be overcome by a set of 'more viable and desirable distinctions'.[108]

Le Non de Klara can be seen as an example of the revaluation of subject positions advocated by LaCapra and of the linked rethinking of the relationships connecting them. To begin with, Aaron's novel complicates the victim-perpetrator binary by shining light on the moral corruption of the camp inmates resulting from the devious coercive methods of their captors. Ultimately, however, Klara appears to confuse prisoners with perpetrators, thus ignoring Levi's warning in 'The Grey Zone' against 'this mimesis, this identification or imitation, or exchange of roles between oppressor and victim'.[109] Seemingly following Agamben's over-reading of Levi's essay, Aaron's protagonist reminisces about a happy coexistence of the oppressed with the oppressors: 'Nous avons été là-bas réciproquement avec l'autre, victimes et bourreaux, la joie d'être avec l'autre [...] l'être réciproquement, côte à côte autour de la verité' [Over there, there was a kind of reciprocity between us and them, between victims and victimizers, the pleasure of being with the other [...] of being there in relation to the other, side by side concerned with the truth] (*NK*, 119; *R*, 133, translation modified). Furthermore, *Le Non de Klara* insists on the historically contingent mutability of subject positions, meaning that these positions are changeable rather than fixed, and that, consequently, a victim can become a perpetrator. Accordingly, a modification of circumstances can engender the perpetrator's transformation into a victim. In line with this logic and with the novel's characteristically postmodern anachronism, Klara predicts the formation of the state of Israel and its belligerence:

> Les Juifs vont aboyer en hébreu, [...] ils vont aboyer dans cette langue protégée depuis deux mille ans. La langue des études, des chants et de la prière va aboyer comme n'importe quelle langue. [...] Les Juifs vont tuer aussi. [...] Si les Juifs sont un peuple et qu'ils ont une terre, un pays, alors cette guerre aurait fabriqué un peuple meurtrier de plus. (*NK*, 102)

> [The Jews will bark in Hebrew, [...] they'll bark in a language that has been safe from it for two thousand years. The language of learning, chanting and prayer will start barking like any other language. [...] The Jews will kill too. [...] If the Jews are people and have a land, a country, this war will have created one more murderous nation.] (*R*, 111)

In the quoted passage we can easily discern Aaron's sensitivity to the long-term ramifications of the Holocaust, including for those attacked by Israel. This aspect of the novel has been criticised by Bruno Chaouat who sees in Klara a mouthpiece of current French anti-Israel sentiments. Yet, the ruminations of Aaron's protagonist can be also considered in a broader context, namely as an exposure of the Christian notion of spiritual purification through physical mortification. Should this be Aaron's intention, she is echoing Bauman who states that martyrdom 'is not a warrant for saintliness', or American historian Joseph Amato who criticises those infusing the experience of victimisation with redemptive value: 'nothing guarantees that today's victims won't be tomorrow's victimizers'.[110] Referring specifically to the Holocaust, Gillian Rose states that impotence and suffering 'do not lead to passion for objectivity and justice', but 'to resentment, hatred, inability to trust'. Consequently, the abused 'become the abusers, whether politically as well as physically may depend on contingencies of social and political history'.[111] Like Amato and LaCapra, Anne Rothe believes that it is only when regarded synchronically that victim and perpetrator dwell in distinct subject positions. Conversely, in a diachronic perspective, 'one may occupy these subject positions subsequently in either order and through numerous changes'.[112] To corroborate her comments, Rothe cites Israeli writer Avraham Yehoshua for whom the status of the Jews as victims of the Nazi genocide does not grant them 'a certificate of everlasting righteousness': 'To be moral, you must behave ethically. The test of that is daily and constant'.[113]

By showing Klara failing to rise to Yehoshua's challenge, Aaron destabilises the paradigm of 'the victim innocent and pure, devoid of responsibility', which Erica Bouris calls 'Holocaust theology'.[114] Bouris is thus critical of the narrative of 'unparalleled Jewish suffering' and of 'Jewish innocence', which first crystallised, as both Bouris and Rothe note, in the aftermath of Adolf Eichmann's trial and the publication of Anne Frank's diary, before being instrumentalised by Israel in justifying its military strategy.[115] In contrast, in 1945, which is when Aaron's novel is set, Holocaust survivors were subject to more ambivalent treatment. If some were met with pity and received financial support from fellow Jews from areas unaffected by persecution, others faced suspicion or were demonised as owing their lives to scheming and collaboration.[116] These moods are, however, absent from Aaron's novel whose protagonist is treated with compassion by her family and friends even though, as Angélika eventually admits, Klara's newfound haughtiness and brutality, and the pride she ostensibly takes in her violent behaviour preserve her from sympathy. In fact, the protagonist herself concedes her inability to rise to the received image of a (Holocaust) victim: 'Je ne suis pas une belle figure de victime' [I don't make a very good victim] (*NK*, 29; *R*, 27). Whatever its exact purpose, Aaron's interrogation of the image of Holocaust survivors as sanctified innocents chimes with Levi's observation that survival was often the fruit of prevarications or even achieved at the expense of others, which meant a high percentage of 'privileged' Jews among those who lived through the Holocaust.[117] Aaron's problematisation of victimhood is also consistent with the efforts to nuance the representation of Holocaust participants by the other postmodern novels considered in this book, including *La Cliente*, Littell's *Les Bienveillantes*, and Claudel's *Le Rapport de Brodeck*.

The association of victimhood with the idea of saintliness is only one of the preconceptions related to the Holocaust that is opposed by Aaron's novel. Sharing the position of Haenel's protagonist, whose identification of the Allies' passivity with the Nazis' genocidal violence I discuss in Chapter Six, Klara lashes out at the 'free world' for having done nothing to stop the Holocaust. Together with its survivors who, as she claims, should be put to death along with the perpetrators, Aaron's protagonist ultimately desacralises the Holocaust itself as she divests it of the religious, metaphysical, and ideological meanings with which many inscribe it. In so doing, she may be motivated by the fear of turning apocalyptic events such as the Holocaust and the atomic bombings of Japan into 'founding traumas' which can be then harnessed to dubious political ends and, according to LaCapra, 'pla[y] a tendentious ideological role [...] in terms of the concept of a chosen people or a belief in one's privileged status as a victim'.[118] And so Klara reduces the Holocaust to 'une boucherie, rien de plus' [a sheer butchery, nothing more] (*NK*, 103; *R*, 112), a position she justifies with the fact that the same fate was meted out to the Jews ('le peuple du livre' [people of the Book]) and to the Romanies ('le peuple sans livre' [people without a Book]) (*NK*, 103; *R*, 112).

Conclusions: The Holocaust Victim as a Cyborg

The novel's repeated references to the Porajmos are only one of the signs of Aaron's commitment to postmodern ethics which, as I demonstrate throughout this book, entails being attentive to historically marginalised identities. Among the other symptoms of this commitment are the novelist's efforts to question homogenising and oversimplifying discourses on the Holocaust, and to expose their exploitation for political goals. Also, like the other works considered in this study, *Le Non de Klara* confronts the binaries structuring our understanding of the Jewish tragedy, which some think to be representative of the dichotomous logic that led to the Holocaust and which postmodern thought does its best to deconstruct. While enhancing men's emancipation, the culturally engrained and strongly hierarchised binaries such as nature/culture and mind/body have also, as Christine Everingham asserts, served to constrain women.[119] Consequently, apart from drawing attention to the Romanies and the *Mischlinge* as neglected victims of Nazi violence, Aaron's novel contributes to the belated and still contentious gendering of the Holocaust. *Le Non de Klara* fulfils its feminist goals by staging a woman survivor and addressing uniquely female aspects of persecution. Furthermore, rather than following many male-authored Holocaust novels in casting a helpless and passive female victim, Aaron's narrative stages a protagonist capable of reflecting on her experience and determined to reshape her life and identity regardless of the physical and psychological damage she has suffered. The criticism sparked by Klara's considerations, which are recognisably posterior to the novel's diegetic present and mediated by a secondary witness, can be countered with the novel's postmodern self-awareness of its status as a fictional construct created some eighty years after the Holocaust by a writer separated by generational distance from the events she fictionalises. It is, as Aaron unequivocally shows, with the knowledge of post-war theorisations and cultural representations of the Nazi genocide and with present political concerns in mind that she has written *Le Non de Klara*. Indeed, Aaron seems to be interested precisely in the lasting legacies of the Shoah, which are felt both vertically and horizontally, and in its implications for post-war politics, science, religion, and philosophy. This is evidenced, on the one hand, by Klara's acute awareness of the risk of passing her trauma on to her daughter and by Angélika's observation of the detrimental effects of Klara's testimony on her and her husband's mental wellbeing. On the other hand, the novel registers the collapse of unrestrained trust in religions and ideologies, and bemoans the ramifications of the transformation of the Jews from a diasporic people into a nation state.

Overall, Aaron's evaluation of the post-Auschwitz world is a bleak one, and especially from the female standpoint. The misogynist and racist impulses behind the Holocaust are shown to have undermined a unified female identity as well as female solidarity in the face of patriarchal and racist oppression. Likewise, the matrilineal plot that Aaron creates by attaching the performative agency of Klara, Rainer, and Angélika to the legacy of their mothers is irrevocably destroyed by the forces of patriarchy and anti-Semitism underlying the Nazi ideology as personified by Klara's father. Among the signs of the Holocaust's corrosive effect on feminist values is the renaming of Vera whose original name was a tribute to the Russian heritage of Klara's mother. It is also worth mentioning the disabling of Klara's maternal instinct and capacity for forming female friendships, and the protagonist's erotically-tinged admiration for her own father. Moreover, Aaron's novel pushes the hybridisation of subjectivity, especially that of women, to the point where no reconstruction seems possible. Although Klara's move towards financial autonomy and artistic and professional fulfilment implicit in her emigration to America provides a welcome contrast to the recuperative instinct of European societies in relation to patriarchy, the disintegration of the protagonist's self does not bode well for the future of the (female) subject. *Le Non de Klara* thus seems to advocate 'liquid identity', even if Klara's heterogenous and itinerant self has little to do with the galloping globalisation and consumerism to which Bauman attributes the mobility of our postmodern selves. Rather, it is an outcome of an apocalyptic disaster that has, so it seems, forever invalidated the possibility — or our illusion — of stability and cohesion. In this light, Foucault's 'happy limbo of non-identity' which some feminist critics have identified as the goal of postfeminism, may prove to be a more appropriate concept.[120] Equally helpful could be Haraway's image of the cyborg as a hybrid self 'untied at last from all dependency' and with no aspiration to organic wholeness, a 'creature in a post-gender world' marked by 'transgressed boundaries, potent fusions, and dangerous possibilities'.[121]

The dispersal of female identity thematised by *Le Non de Klara* is, as I have shown in this chapter, matched by the novel's disjointed and palimpsestic texture, and self-contradictory status as a fictional diary. It is also in this sense that Aaron's narrative drifts away from canonical feminist literature which either embraces established narrative structures in the hope of reaching a wider readership with its political message, or espouses discursive forms, such as the diary, thought to be best suited to rendering the female experience.[122] In contrast, Aaron follows in the footsteps of French female writers whose work has been celebrated for its iconoclastic destabilisation of both social and literary conventions.[123] It can be therefore suggested that the eponymous and multivalent 'no' encapsulates the author's own negating position. This position regards, first and foremost, the understanding of the Holocaust as a genocide that targeted only Jews, that affected both genders in the same way, and that can be viewed in terms of the bipolar opposition between saintly victims and vicious perpetrators. In particular, Aaron rejects the polarisation that has run through conceptualisations of the Holocaust along gender lines, with femininity being conflated with nobility, bravery, and goodness, and being set against evil moral ambiguities.[124] The novelist also contests the dominant perception of the Nazi genocide as an event with a happy ending in the form of the liberation of the camps and the return of the deportees to their homes or their resettlement in third countries. Finally, the eponymous refusal appears to be directed at the traditional modalities of writing associated with both Holocaust and feminine literature, which Aaron disrupts by co-opting postmodern narrative strategies, including her parody of both the existing textualisations and theorisations of the Nazi genocide, and of discursive modes that have been associated with Holocaust literature.

Notes to Chapter 3

1. Charlotte Delbo, *Auschwitz, et après I* (Paris: Minuit, 1970), p. 151; *Auschwitz and After*, trans. by Rosette C. Lamont, 2nd edn (New Haven, CT: Yale University Press, 2013), pp. 95–96. Hanna Krall, *The Woman from Hamburg and Other True Stories*, trans. by Madeline G. Levine (New York: Other Press, 2005), p. 16.
2. A biographical blurb presents the author's choice of the name 'Aaron' as a tribute to her great-uncle who had brought her up. Lucille Cairns established, however, that Aaron has no Jewish roots: '"La Mémoire de la Shoah": The Contentious Case of Soazig Aaron's *Le Non de Klara*', *French Studies*, 64.4 (2010), 438–50 (p. 439).
3. *La Sentinelle tranquille sous la lune* (2010) stages a World War I soldier who disappears after having returned from the front.
4. In the year of its publication, the novel won the Prix Emmanuel-Roblès, the Prix du roman de la ville de Carthaix, and the prestigious Bourse Goncourt du premier roman. These were followed by the Prix Amnesty International Belgique, Prix de Limoges, and Prix Inter-Comités awarded in 2003, as well as the Grand Prix des Libraires and Prix de Donne ebree d'Italia awarded in 2004.
5. <http://www.geschwister-scholl-preis.de/preistraeger_2000–2009/2007/eng.php> [accessed 12 May 2017].
6. In 2005 the play was performed at the Théâtre de l'Acacia (Vincennes) and in 2010 at the Théâtre Blocry. Positive reviews of Aaron's novel appeared in *Le Monde* (Patrick Kéchichian, 10 May 2002), *La Croix* (Francine de Martinoir, 17 January 2002), and *Le Canard enchaîné* (Dominique Durand, 16 January 2002).
7. Jorge Semprún, 'Un récit de Soazig Aaron: merci Klara!', *Le Nouvel Observateur*, 1951, 28 March 2002, p. 120.
8. Cairns, '"La Mémoire de la Shoah"; Timo Obergöker, 'Shoah et récit fictionnel, un champ de force délicat: *Le Non de Klara* de Soazig Aaron', in *Témoignages de l'après-Auschwitz dans la littérature juive-française d'aujourd'hui: enfants de survivants et survivants-enfants*, ed. by Annelies Schulte Nordholt (Amsterdam: Rodopi, 2008), pp. 205–18; Danièle Sabbah, '"Il y a eu les retours solitaires [...] au cœur désaffecté de l'âme": *Le Non de Klara* de Soazig Aaron', in *Trauma et texte*, ed. by Peter Kuon (Frankfurt am Mein: Peter Lang, 2008), pp. 311–30; Bruno Chaouat, 'Antisemitism Redux: On Literary and Theoretical Perversions', in *Resurgent Antisemitism: Global Perspectives*, ed. by Alvin H. Rosenfeld (Bloomington: Indiana University Press, 2013), pp. 118–39 (pp. 128–30); Anne-Berenike Binder, 'Soazig Aaron, *Le Non de Klara* — "paroles suffoquées" oder der Desakralisierung der Überlebenden', in *'Mon ombre est restée là-bas': literarische und mediale Formen des Erinnerns in Raum und Zeit* (Tübingen: Max Niemayer, 2008), pp. 117–69.
9. Efraim Sicher, *Breaking Crystal: Writing and Memory after Auschwitz* (Urbana: University of Illinois Press, 1998), p. 301.
10. Marianne Hirsch, *The Generation of Postmemory: Writing and Visual Culture after the Holocaust* (New York: Columbia University Press, 2012). Art Spiegelman, *The Complete Maus* [1986–91] (London: Penguin, 2003).
11. See, for example, Marysia Zalewski, *Feminism after Postmodernism? Theorising through Practice* (London: Routledge, 2003), p. 27.
12. Ann Brooks, *Postfeminisms: Feminism, Cultural Theory and Cultural Forms* (London: Routledge, 1997), p. 4.
13. For theorisations of postfeminism as anti-feminism, see, for example, Stephanie Harzewski, *Chick Lit and Postfeminism* (Charlottesville: University of Virginia Press, 2011); Angela McRobbie, *The Aftermath of Feminism: Gender, Culture and Social Change* (Los Angeles: Sage, 2009); and Heike Mißler, *Cultural Politics of Chick Lit: Popular Fiction, Postfeminism and Representation* (London: Routledge, 2017).
14. Brooks, *Postfeminisms*, p. 4.
15. Hutcheon, *A Poetics of Postmodernism*, p. 18. Brooks, *Postfeminisms*, p. 1.
16. Brooks, *Postfeminisms*, p. 2.

17. Judging postmodernism to be apolitical and ahistorical, some see it as incompatible with feminism's strong political commitment and social function. Another reason for the incompatibility of postmodernism and feminism is, on the aesthetic level, the former's formal experimentations and perceived correlated elitism. In contrast, because of its political engagement, feminist literature wishes to reach as wide a readership as possible and hence relies heavily on the conventions of realism. For a discussion of these misgivings, see Stéphanie Genz and Benjamin A. Brabon, *Postfeminism: Cultural Texts and Theories* (Edinburgh: Edinburgh University Press, 2009), p. 106; and Megali Cornier Michael, *Feminism and the Postmodern Impulse: Post-World War II Fiction* (New York: State University of New York Press, 1996), pp. 1–10.
18. Pamela B. June, *The Fragmented Female Body: The Postmodern, Feminist and Multiethnic Writings of Toni Morison, Theresa Hak Kyung Cha, Phyllis Alexia Perry, Gayl Jones, Emma Pérez, Paula Gunn Allen, and Kathy Acker* (New York: Peter Lang, 2010), p. 4.
19. Patricia Waugh, *Feminine Fictions: Revisiting the Postmodern* [1989] (London: Routledge, 2012), p. 4.
20. Andreas Huyssen, 'Mapping the Postmodern', *New German Critique*, 33 (Autumn 1984), 5–52 (p. 27).
21. Genz and Brabon, *Postfeminism*, p. 110.
22. Cathy S. Gelbin, 'Between Persecution and Complicity: The Life Story of a Former "Jewish Mischling"', *Holocaust Studies*, 11.2 (2005), 74–93 (pp. 74–75).
23. Anna Reading, *The Social Inheritance of the Holocaust: Gender, Culture and Memory* (Basingstoke: Palgrave Macmillan, 2002), p. 15.
24. Myrna Goldenberg, 'Different Horrors, Same Hell: Women Remembering the Holocaust', in *Thinking the Unthinkable: Meanings of the Holocaust*, ed. by Roger S. Gotlieb (Mahwah, NJ: Paulist Press, 1990), pp. 150–66 (p. 163). Yehuda Bauer, *Rethinking the Holocaust* (New Haven, CT: Yale University Press, 2001), p. 167.
25. Joan Ringelheim, 'The Unethical and the Unspeakable: Women and the Holocaust', in *The Holocaust: Theoretical Readings*, ed. by Neil Levi and Michael Rothberg (Edinburgh: Edinburgh University Press, 2010), pp. 169–77 (pp. 169–70). The pioneering works in the field of feminist Holocaust studies are: *Women in the Resistance and in the Holocaust: Voices of Eyewitnesses*, ed. by Vera Laska (Westport, CT: Greenwood, 1983); Judith Tydor Baumel, *Double Jeopardy: Gender and the Holocaust* (London: Vallentine Mitchell, 1998); *Women in the Holocaust*, ed. by Dalia Ofer and Lenore J. Weiztman (New Haven, CT: Yale University Press, 1998); Joan Ringelheim, 'Women in the Holocaust: A Reconsideration of Research', *Signs*, 10.4 (Summer 1985), 741–61; *Different Voices: Women and the Holocaust*, ed. by Carl Ann Rittner and John K. Roth (St Paul, MN: Paragon House, 1993). For a full historiography of gendered approaches to the Holocaust, see Elizabeth R. Baer and Myrna Goldberg, *Experience and Expression: Women, the Nazis, and the Holocaust* (Detroit: Wayne State University Press, 2003), pp. xvii–xxvii.
26. Ringelheim, 'Women in the Holocaust', p. 741.
27. Ringelheim, 'The Split between Gender and the Holocaust, in *Women in the Holocaust*, ed. by Ofer and Weiztman, pp. 340–50 (p. 345). When Ringelheim proposed a conference on women's Holocaust experience, Cynthia Ozick stated that by emphasising the specificity of the women's plight she was complicit in 'eradicating Jews from history' and 'joining up with the likes of [the Revisionists]': ibid., pp. 348–49. Holocaust survivor Helen Fagin expressed the view that feminist agenda can trivialise the Shoah, quoted by Zoë Waxman, *Women in the Holocaust: A Feminist History* (Oxford: Oxford University Press, 2017), pp. 4–5. Lawrence Langer has expressed belief that the two sexes are united by the ultimate sense of loss that is 'beyond gender': 'Gendered Suffering? Women in Holocaust Testimonies', in *Women in the Holocaust*, ed. by Ofer and Weiztman, pp. 351–63 (p. 362). The most virulent of those criticising feminist approach to the Holocaust has been, so it seems, Gabriel Schoenfeld who has called such an approach 'propaganda' and has described feminist writings on the subject as 'execrable' and characterised by 'notes of querulousness and righteous self-regard': 'Auschwitz and the Professors', *Commentary*, 105–06 (June 1998), 42–46.
28. Anna Hardman, *Women and the Holocaust* (London: Holocaust Education Trust, 2000); Waxman, *Women in the Holocaust*.

29. Esther Hertzog, 'Subjugated Motherhood and the Holocaust', *Dapim: Studies on the Holocaust*, 30.1 (2016), 16–34.
30. Sara R. Horowitz, 'Memory and Testimony of Women Survivors of Nazi Genocide', in *Women of the World: Jewish Women, Jewish Writing*, ed. by Judith R. Baskin (Detroit: Wayne State University Press, 1994), pp. 258–82 (p. 256).
31. For an examination of these formerly prohibited aspects of women's experience of persecution, see *Sexual Violence against Jewish Women during the Holocaust*, ed. by Sonja Maria Hedgepeth and Rochelle G. Saidel (Lebanon, NH: Brandeis University Press, 2010).
32. Among the few recent French Holocaust novels by women are Valentine Goby's *Kinderzimmer* (2013) and Colombe Schneck's *La Réparation* (2012).
33. For a full bibliography of women's Holocaust literature, see S. Lillian Kremer, 'Sexual Abuse in Holocaust Literature: Memoir and Fiction', in *Sexual Violence*, ed. by Hedgepeth and Saidel, pp. 177–99 (pp. 196–95).
34. The only full-length studies of Holocaust fiction by women that I am aware of are Kremer, *Women's Holocaust Writing*; Marlene E. Heinemann, *Gender and Destiny: Women Writers and the Holocaust* (New York: Greenwood Press, 1986); Dorothy Bilik, *Immigrant-survivors: Post-Holocaust Consciousness in Recent Jewish American Fiction* (Middletown, CT: Wesleyan University Press, 1981); and Federica K. Clementi, *Holocaust Mothers and Daughters: Family, History and Trauma* (Lebanon, NH: Brandeis University Press, 2013). Of note are also parts of Lucille Cairn's *Postwar Jewish Women's Writing in French* (Oxford: Legenda, 2011); Ellen S. Fine's chapter 'Women and the Holocaust: Strategies for Survival', in *Reflections of the Holocaust in Art and Literature*, ed. by Randolph L. Braham (Boulder, CO: Csengeri Institute for Holocaust Studies, 1990), pp. 79–95; and Sidra DeKoven Ezrahi's chapters on women writers in *By Words Alone: The Holocaust in Literature* (Chicago: University of Chicago Press, 1980).
35. Kremer, *Women's Holocaust Writing*, p. 5. One such exception is David Foenkinos's recent fictionalised account of the life of the German-Jewish painter, Charlotte Solomon, murdered at the age of twenty-six when she was pregnant: *Charlotte* (Paris: Gallimard, 2014).
36. Spiegelman, *The Complete Maus*, p. 160. In his autobiography, Auschwitz commandant Rudolf Höss admitted that 'everything was much more difficult, harsher and more depressing for the women, since general living conditions in the women's camp were incomparably worse', quoted by Sarah Cushman, 'The Auschwitz Women's Camp: An Overview and Reconsiderations', in *The Palgrave Handbook of Holocaust Literature and Culture*, ed. by Victoria Aarons and Phyllis Lassner (Basingstoke: Palgrave Macmillan, 2020), pp. 707–24 (p. 711).
37. Sara R. Horowitz, 'Women in Holocaust Literature: Engendering Trauma Memory', in *Women in the Holocaust*, ed. by Ofer and Weiztman, pp. 364–78 (p. 367). The interviews Spiegelman conducted with those who knew his mother during captivity confirm, however, Vladek's representation of Anja. See Art Spiegelman, *Metamaus: A Look Inside a Modern Classic, Maus* (New York: Pantheon, 2011), pp. 279–88. For an analysis of Anja's representation as a mother, see Helena Duffy, 'The Silence of the Mothers: Representation of Holocaust Motherhood in Art Spiegelman's *Maus* and Philippe Brodeck's *Brodeck*', *Journal of Holocaust Research*, 34.2 (April 2020), 138–54.
38. Amy L. Wink, 'Diaries', in *Encyclopaedia of Feminist Theories*, ed. by Loraine Code (London: Routledge, 2000), pp. 133–35; James Fisher, 'Péter Forgács's *Free Fall* into the Holocaust', in *Visualizing the Holocaust: Documents, Aesthetics, Memory*, ed. by David Bathrick, Brad Prager, and Michael D. Richardson (Rochester, NY: Camden House, 2008), pp. 239–60 (p. 240).
39. Valerie Raoul, *The French Fictional Journal: Fictional Narcissism/ Narcissistic Fiction* (Toronto: University of Toronto Press, 1980), p. vii. Cf. Hutcheon, *A Poetics of Postmodernism*, p. 114.
40. H. Porter Abbott, 'Diary Fiction', *Orbis Litterarum*, 37 (1982), 21–31 (pp. 21–22); and *Diary Fiction: Writing as Action* (Ithaca, NY: Cornell University Press, 1984), p. 9.
41. Soazig Aaron, *Le Non de Klara* [2002] (Paris: Maurice Nadeau pocket, 2004), p. 10 (hereafter referenced as *NK* in the main text); *Refusal*, trans. by Barbara Bray (London: Harvill Secker, 2007), p. 3 (hereafter referenced as *R* in the main text).
42. Monika J. Flaschka, '"Only Pretty Women Were Raped": The Effects of Sexual Violence on Gender Identities in the Concentration Camps', in *Sexual Violence against Jewish Women during*

the Holocaust, ed. by Hedgepeth and Saidel, pp. 77–93 (p. 80). Second-generation poet Lily Brett devotes one of her poems to the breasts of concentration camp inmates. 'It was strange the way the breasts change | first the flesh fell as though dropped from shock | breasts old and young hung | facing the floor | till they disappeared existed no more': *Auschwitz Poems: Gedichte Englisch und Deutsch* (Vienna: Suhrkamp, 2004), p. 164.

43. Simone de Beauvoir, *Le Deuxième sexe. I* (Paris: Gallimard Folio, 1986), p. 265.
44. Jill Ker Conway, *When Memory Speaks: Reflections on Autobiography* (New York: Alfred A. Kopf, 1998), pp. 7, 14.
45. Clifford, *Commemorating the Holocaust*, pp. 31–32.
46. Ibid., p. 35.
47. Heinemann, *Gender and Destiny*, p. 29.
48. Waxman, *Women in the Holocaust*, p. 88; Kremer, 'Sexual Abuse in Holocaust Literature', p. 178. Holocaust survivor Anita Lasker-Wallfish remembered the shaving of the hair as 'the most traumatic experience. It made me feel totally naked, utterly vulnerable and reduced to a complete nobody': *Inherit the Truth* (New York: Thomas Dunn, 2000), p. 72. Dachau and Auschwitz survivor, Livia Britton-Jackson thus commented on the shaving of women's hair in the camps: 'The absence of hair transforms individual women into like bodies. Indistinguishable. Age melts away. Other personal differences melt away. Facial expressions disappear. In their place, a blank, senseless stare emerges on the thousand faces of one naked, unappealing body. We become a monolithic mass. Inconsequential. Shorn heads, nude body, faceless faces': *I Have Lived a Thousand Years* (New York: Simon & Schuster, 1997), p. 77.
49. Kelly Ricciardi Colvin, *Gender and French Identity after the Second World War: Engendering Frenchness* (London: Bloomsbury, 2017), p. 37. A former French political prisoner admits that having her head shorn was 'one of the things that most tormented me during the time I spent in Germany', while another one describes it as 'a violation' and states that 'our femininity was being taken away from us', quoted by Margaret-Anne Hutton, *Testimony from Nazi Camps: French Women's Voices* (London: Routledge, 2005), p. 125.
50. Waxman, *Women in the Holocaust*, p. 88.
51. Donna Haraway, 'The Cyborg Manifesto and Fractured Identities', in *Reading Feminist Theory: Modernity to Postmodernity*, ed. by Susan Archer Mann and Ashly Suzanne Patterson (Oxford: Oxford University Press, 2015), pp. 212–17 (p. 214). Holocaust survivor Judit Magyar Isaacson directly associates the loss of her hair with defeminisation. When remembering her mother after her head had been shaven, Magyar Isaacson states, 'Her pretty face was transformed by the shorn skull: the features stronger, the nose more masculine. Was it a mere hair style that made her feminine?': *Seed of Sarah* (Chicago: University of Illinois Press), p. 67.
52. The rarely tackled subject of prostitution in concentration camps has now been given attention by Hedgepeth and Saidel's edited volume. The editors quote Andrea Dworkin who vociferates against the exclusion of sexual abuse, including forced prostitution, from Holocaust research and commemorations: 'Introduction', in *Sexual Violence against Jewish Women during the Holocaust*, ed. by Hedgepeth and Saidel, pp. 1–10 (pp. 2–3). See also Robert Sommer, 'Sexual Exploitation of Women in Nazi Concentration Camp Brothels', in ibid., pp. 45–60; and Naomi Levenkorn, 'Death and the Maidens: "Prostitution", Rape and Sexual Slavery during World War II', in ibid., pp. 13–28.
53. Erna Rubinstein writes about her sense of defeminisation as a result of the loss of her hair — 'what is a woman without her glory on her head, her hair?' — and Isabella Leitner describes the regrowth of her hair as a return of her identity as a woman. See also Kremer, *Women's Holocaust Writing*, p. 15, and Hutton, *Testimony from Nazi Camps*, p. 112.
54. Flaschka, '"Only Pretty Women Were Raped"', pp. 80–81.
55. Waxman, *Women in the Holocaust*, p. 93.
56. Ibid., p. 94; Kremer, *Women's Holocaust Writing*, p. 181.
57. Terrence Des Pres, *Survivor: An Anatomy of Life in the Death Camps* (Oxford: Oxford University Press, 1976), pp. 51–72 (p. 60).
58. Kremer, *Women's Holocaust Writing*, pp. 16–18, 45. Baumel deems the phenomenon of 'camp sister' as highly important for survival: *Double Jeopardy*, p. 71. Analysing Sara Nomberg-

Przytyk's memoir, Myrna Goldenberg pays attention to the persistent theme of connectedness: 'We are left with the implicit admonition to develop and nurture relationships, to care for one another, and to take responsibility for one another, for in loneliness, there is no protection against violence and despair': 'Memoirs of Auschwitz Survivors: The Burden of Gender', in *Women in the Holocaust*, ed. by Ofer and Weiztman, pp. 327–39 (p. 329).
59. Baumel, *Double Jeopardy*, p. 7. Kremer, *Women's Holocaust Writing*, p. 11.
60. Quoted by Kremer, *Women's Holocaust Writing*, p. 2.
61. David Patterson, 'The Moral Dilemma of Motherhood in the Nazi Death Camps', in *Problems Unique to the Holocaust*, ed. by Cargas, pp. 7–24 (p. 8). Cf. Waxman, *Women in the Holocaust*, pp. 7, 11.
62. Waxman, *Women in the Holocaust*, pp. 335–36.
63. Gisella Perl, *I Was a Doctor in Auschwitz* (New York: International Universities Press, 1948), p. 84.
64. This is exemplified by the personal experience of philosopher and writer, Sarah Kofman, as recorded in her autobiographical narrative *Rue Ordener, rue Labat* (1996), or by Susan Fromberg Schaeffer's novel *Anya* (1974). Helga Amesberger discusses the conflicts with foster mothers who did not want to relinquish their responsibilities, feeling more competent in caring for a child than the returning biological mother: 'Reproduction under the Swastika: The Other Side of the Nazi Glorification of Motherhood', in *Sexual Violence*, ed. by Hedgepeth and Saidel, pp. 139–55 (p. 149). Cf. Waxman, *Women in the Holocaust*, pp. 69, 118–19.
65. Ian Hancock deplores the neglect of the Romani Holocaust or even outright efforts to minimise or deny it, which, as he stresses, sometimes originate with Jewish authors: 'Romanies and the Holocaust: Re-evaluation and Overview', in *The Historiography of the Holocaust*, ed. by Stone, pp. 383–96 (pp. 84–85). On the Romani Holocaust, see also Myriam Novitch, *Le Génocide des Tsiganes sous le régime nazi* (Paris: AMIF and the Ghetto Fighters' House, Israel, 1968), and *The Nazi Genocide of the Roma: Reassessment and Commemoration*, ed. by Anton Weiss-Wendt (New York: Berghahn Books, 2013).
66. Klara's experience finds reflection in the testimonies of Auschwitz survivors who recall newborns being strangled, killed with a lethal injection, beaten to death, or drowned in a bucket of water. This often happened in front of the mother. As an example of the non-morality of *l'univers concentrationnaire*, Langer evokes the murder of a newborn child, recalled by a midwife: 'The Dilemma of Choice in the Deathcamps', pp. 224–25. See also Ruth Elias's examination of Katharina von Kellenbach's 'choiceless choice': 'Reproduction and Resistance during the Holocaust', in *Women and the Holocaust*, ed. by Esther Fuchs (Lanham, MD: University Press of America, 1999), pp. 19–32 (pp. 28–29). Cf. Amesberger, 'Reproduction under the Swastika', p. 144.
67. Primo Levi, *The Reawakening*, trans. by Stuart Woolf (New York: Simon & Schuster, 1965), pp. 25–28. Like Ulli, Hurbinek was about three years old and could not speak. Like Ulli, he said only one intelligible word which the prisoners interpreted as his name. Hurbinek died shortly after the camp's liberation.
68. Nancy Horowitz, *Primo Levi and the Identity of a Survivor* (Toronto: University of Toronto Press, 2016), p. 89.
69. Baumel, *Double Jeopardy*, pp. 236–37.
70. Waxman, *Women in the Holocaust*, p. 114. Isabella Leitner, *Fragments of Isabella: A Memoir of Auschwitz* (New York: Thomas Y. Crowell, 1978), p. 111. Amesberger, 'Reproduction under the Swastika', p. 150.
71. Amesberger, 'Reproduction under the Swastika', p. 149.
72. Horowitz, 'Memory and Testimony of Women Survivors of Nazi Genocide', p. 280
73. Amesberger, 'Reproduction under the Swastika', p. 150.
74. Hutton, *Testimony from Nazi Camps*, pp. 102–03.
75. Hirsch, *The Generation of Postmemory*, p. 5.
76. Considering the homonymy of the French words *non* [no] and *nom* [name], it could be productive to consider the question of Klara's name from a Lacanian perspective. The novel's French title could thus be read as a play on the Lacanian concept of 'le nom du père' as the master signifier,

which would illuminate Klara's ambivalent relationship with her father and, more generally, with patriarchy.

77. Claudia Koonz, *Mothers in the Fatherland: Women, the Family and Nazi Politics* [1987] (New York: Routledge, 2013), p. 3.
78. This footnote is absent from the novel's paperback edition from which I am quoting, but has been preserved in the English translation of the novel (*R*, 176). While the original decree offers the spelling 'Sara', on some documents the name was reproduced as 'Sarah'. For more information regarding the decree, see I. M. Nick, *Personal Names, Hitler and the Holocaust: A Socio-onomastic Study of Genocide and Nazi Germany* (New York: Lexington Books, 2019), p. 57, n. 88.
79. Victor Burgin, *The End of Art Theory: Criticism and Postmodernity* (Basingstoke: MacMillan, 1986), p. 49,
80. Michael, *Feminism and the Postmodern Impulse*, pp. 83–84.
81. Lawrence Grossberg, *Bringing It All Back Home: Essays on Cultural Studies* (Durham, NC: Duke University Press, 1997), p. 189. Bauman first detailed the theory of liquid modernity in 2000, before elaborating it through further works into a complex and comprehensive theoretical system. For an analysis of some of the aspects of Bauman's theory related to the question of identity, see Ann Branaman, 'Gender and Sexuality in Liquid Modernity', in *The Contemporary Bauman*, ed. by Anthony Elliott (London: Routledge, 2007), pp. 117–35; and Anthony Elliott, 'The Theory of Liquid Modernity: A Critique of Bauman's Recent Sociology', in ibid., pp. 46–62.
82. Haraway, 'The Cyborg Manifesto and Fractured Identities', p. 214.
83. Amy Wink notes that, 'rather than view the diary (and women's lives) as fragmented, scholars suggest that the components of a completed diary must be examined to understand the text as a whole'. She quotes Rebecca Hogan's view that 'the seemingly disparate entries can be viewed as a form of parataxis and thus understood [...] as individual writing moments linked together in a diary form': 'Diaries', p. 134. See Rebecca Hogan, 'Engendered Autobiographies: The Diary as a Feminine Form', *Prose Studies*, 14.2 (1991), 95–107.
84. The confusion features in Levi's memoir *If This Is a Man* and is discussed by Henry Krystal in his edited volume *Massive Psychic Trauma* (New York: International University Press, 1968). See also Susanne Hillman, '"Not Living, but Going": Unheroic Survival, Trauma Performance, and Video Testimony', *Holocaust Studies*, 21.4 (2015), 215–35 (p. 215).
85. Kremer, *Women's Holocaust Writing*, p. 24.
86. Rosi Braidotti, *Nomadic Subjects: Embodiment in Contemporary Feminist Theory* (New York: Columbia University Press, 1994), p. 121.
87. Young, *Writing and Rewriting the Holocaust*, pp. 15–16.
88. Dorota Głowacka, 'The Shattered World: Writing of the Fragment and Holocaust Testimony', in *The Holocaust's Ghost: Writings on Art, Politics, Law and Education*, ed. by F. C. DeCoste and Bernard Schwartz (Edmonton: University of Alberta Press, 2000), pp. 37–54 (p. 37).
89. Emil Fakenheim, *Jewish Return into History: Reflections in the Age of Auschwitz and a New Jerusalem* (New York: Schokhen Books, 1978), p. 23.
90. Jameson, *Postmodernism, or the Cultural Logic of Late Capitalism*, p. 15.
91. Fredric Jameson, 'Postmodernism and Consumer Society', in *Postmodern Culture*, ed. by Hal Foster (London: Pluto, 1985), pp. 111–25 (p. 115).
92. Jameson, *Postmodernism, or the Cultural Logic of Late Capitalism*, p. 25.
93. Waugh, *Feminine Fictions*, p. 7.
94. Bran Nicol, *The Cambridge Introduction to Postmodern Fiction* (Cambridge: Cambridge University Press, 2009), p. 78.
95. Reading, *The Social Inheritance of the Holocaust*, p. 11.
96. Hutcheon, *A Poetics of Postmodernism*, p. 53.
97. Cairns, '"La Mémoire de la Shoah"', p. 443. Hutton, *Testimony from Nazi Camps*, p. 134.
98. Judith Butler, *Gender Trouble: Feminism and its Subversion of Identity* [1990] (London: Routledge, 2014), p. 33; John Clammer, 'Performing Ethnicity: Performance, Gender, Body and Belief in the Construction and Signalling of Identity', *Ethnic and Racial Studies*, 38.12 (2015), 2159–66.

99. Clammer, 'Performing Ethnicity', p. 2159.
100. Cf. Cairns, '"La Mémoire de la Shoah"', p. 443.
101. For a discussion of resignifications of derogatory terms, see Gregory Coles, 'Emerging Voices: The Exorcism of Language: Reclaimed Derogatory Terms and Their Limits', *College English*, 76.5 (May 2016), 424–46.
102. Michel Foucault, *Surveiller et punir: naissance de la prison* (Paris: Gallimard, 1975), p. 138; 'Nietzsche, Genealogy, History', in *Language, Countermemory, Practice: Selected Essays and Interviews*, ed. by Donald F. Bouchard (Ithaca, NY: Cornell University Press, 1977), pp. 139–64 (p. 148).
103. For a discussion of Plath's problematic relationship with her father's language, see Laura Frost, '"Every Woman Adores a Fascist": Marguerite Duras, Sylvia Plath, and Feminist Visions of Fascism', in *Sex Drives: Fantasies of Fascism in Literary Modernism* (Ithaca, NY: Cornell University Press, 2001), pp. 120–50 (pp. 142–43).
104. Plath's (ab)use of Holocaust imagery and her ambivalence towards her father has been examined by Jacqueline Rose, *The Haunting of Sylvia Plath* (Cambridge, MA: Harvard University Press, 1992); Al Strangeways, '"The Boot in the Face": The Problem of the Holocaust in the Poetry of Sylvia Plath', *Contemporary Literature*, 37.3 (Autumn 1996), pp. 370–90; Young, *Writing and Rewriting the Holocaust*, pp. 117–33, and Frost, '"Every Woman Adores a Fascist". The controversy surrounding Plath's appropriation of the Holocaust as a metaphor for her personal situation invites me to read Aaron's implicit reference to 'Daddy' as designed to pre-empt the criticism she might face for representing the Jewish tragedy as a non-Jew. In Cairns's view, her adoption of the penname 'Aaron' was intended to 'to induce a lectorial belief that, by virtue of a Jewish lineage, she was morally authorised to "exploit" for fictional purposes a uniquely Jewish experience': '"La Mémoire de la Shoah"', p. 448
105. See Petra Rau, *Our Nazis: Representations of Fascism in Contemporary Literature and Film* (Edinburgh: Edinburgh University Press, 2013).
106. LaCapra, *Writing History, Writing Trauma*, p. 68,
107. Agamben, *Remnants of Auschwitz*, p. 17.
108. LaCapra, *Writing History, Writing Trauma*, pp. xxvi, xxvii.
109. Levi, *The Drowned and the Saved*, p. 32.
110. Zygmunt Bauman, 'The Holocaust's Life as a Ghost', in *Social Theory after the Holocaust*, ed. by Robert Fine and Charles Turner (Liverpool: Liverpool University Press, 2000), pp. 7–18 (p. 12). Joseph A. Amato, *Victims and Values: A History and a Theory of Suffering* (New York: Greenwood Press, 1990), p. 196.
111. Gillian Rose, 'Beginnings of the Day: Fascism and Representation', in *Mourning Becomes the Law: Philosophy and Representation* (Cambridge: Cambridge University Press, 1996), pp. 41–62 (p. 51).
112. Anne Rothe, 'Popular Trauma Culture: The Pain of Others Between Holocaust Tropes and Kitsch-Sentimental Melodrama', in *Interdisciplinary Handbook of Trauma and Culture*, ed. by Yochal Ataria, David Gurevitz, Haviva Pedaya, and Yuval Neria (Basel: Springer, 2016), pp. 51–66 (p. 57).
113. A. B. Yehoshua, *Between Right and Right* (Garden City, NY: Doubleday, 1981), p. 17.
114. Erica Bouris, *Complex Political Victims* (Bloomfield, CT: Kumarian Press, 2007), pp. 52–53.
115. Ibid., p. 59. Rothe, 'Popular Trauma Culture', p. 53. The term 'Jewish innocence' was coined by Mark H. Ellis, *Beyond Innocence and Redemption: Confronting the Holocaust and Israeli Power. Creating a Moral Future for the Jewish People* (Eugene, OR: Wipf & Stock, 1990), p. 2.
116. Peter Novick, *The Holocaust in American Life* [1991] (Boston: Houghton Mifflin, 2000), pp. 68–69.
117. Levi, *The Drowned and the Saved*, pp. 64, 26.
118. LaCapra, *Writing History, Writing Trauma*, p. 81.
119. Christine Everingham, *Motherhood and Modernity: An Investigation into the Rational Dimension of Mothering* (Buckingham, PA: Open University Press, 1994), p. 6..
120. Michel Foucault, *Herculine Barbin*, trans. by Richard McDougall (London: Vintage, 2010), p. xiii.
121. Haraway, 'The Cyborg Manifesto and Fractured Identities', pp. 213–14.
122. Michael, *Feminism and the Postmodern Impulse*, pp. 8–9.

123. Nathalie Edwards, *Voicing Voluntary Childlessness: Narratives of Non-mothering in French* (Bern: Peter Lang, 2015), p. 2.
124. Sara R. Horowitz, 'The Gender of Good and Evil: Women and Holocaust Memory', in *Gray Zones*, ed. by Petropoulos and Roth, p. 168. See also Ingrid Lewis, 'The Jewish Woman as the Epitome of Holocaust Victimhood in the 1960s', in *Women in European Holocaust Films: Perpetrators, Victims and Resisters* (Basingstoke: Palgrave MacMillan, 2018), pp. 147–54.

CHAPTER 4

'Father, don't you see I'm burning?': Jonathan Littell's *Les Bienveillantes* as an Example of Traumatic Metafiction

> Historical trauma is specific, and not everyone is subject to it or entitled to the subject position associated with it.
> — DOMINICK LaCAPRA, *Writing History, Writing Trauma*

> Essayez de regarder. Essayez pour voir.
> [Try to look. Just try and see.]
> — CHARLOTTE DELBO, *Auschwitz, et après I*

> Shallow are the souls that have forgotten how to shudder.
> — LEON KASS, 'The Wisdom of Repugnance'[1]

'This is not how I imagined an eighty-year-old SS veteran speaking or thinking'[2]

Jonathan Littell's *Les Bienveillantes* is frequently cited as representative of the French-language novelists' recent surge of interest in the Jewish tragedy or has even been credited with inaugurating it.[3] Although, as this study demonstrates, this surge had begun a decade earlier with Modiano's *Dora Bruder*, it is undeniable that *Les Bienveillantes* has been the most commented upon recently published French Holocaust novel. Penned by an American with little writing experience but well acquainted with the realities of genocidal conflicts through his work for the NGO Action Against Hunger, *Les Bienveillantes* garnered prestigious French literary prizes, including the Prix Goncourt and the Prix du roman de l'Académie française.[4] It sold some 700,000 copies in its first year on the market and won the praise of eminent figures such as Georges Nivat, Pierre Nora, Pierre Assouline, Julia Kristeva, and Claude Lanzmann.[5] Jorge Semprún even predicted that in the future Littell's novel would exercise greater influence on the collective memory of the Holocaust than historical studies.[6] However, as well as acclaim, *Les Bienveillantes* has aroused condemnation, both in France and beyond.[7] For example, renowned translator Pierre-Émmanuel Dauzat dubbed the novel kitsch, voyeuristic, and pornographic. He accused it of desecrating the victims' memory and corrupting the work of historians, and described Littell's prose as uninspired and clumsy.[8] Some of Dauzat's invectives were repeated by Paul-Éric Blanrue, a journalist connected with negationist circles. While Blanrue classified *Les Bienveillantes* as 'gestaporn', historian Édouard Husson deemed Littell's novel immoral and abject.[9] In a later study co-authored with philosopher Michel Terestchenko, Husson pronounced it dangerous and obscene, before ultimately calling for its boycott.[10]

One of the nodal points of the debates *Les Bienveillantes* ignited has been its protagonist-narrator, a Franco-German lawyer who in 1941 is deployed on the Eastern Front as an officer of the *Sicherheitsdienst*, the intelligence agency of the Nazi Party. Some years later, having settled in northern France under the false identity of a lace factory manager and a model husband and father, Maximilien Aue writes his memoirs. Rather than by remorse, he is motivated by the urge to 'mettre les choses au point pour moi-même' [set the record straight for myself], and 'éclaircir un ou deux points obscurs' [clear up one or two obscure points].[11] Aue's tale begins with Germany's invasion of Russia in June 1941 and ends with the collapse of the Third Reich in May 1945. In between these dates, he assists at executions of Jews by the *Einsatzgruppen* (mobile killing squads), including the Babi Yar massacre where, as well as watching the killings in order to report on them, he delivers 'mercy shots'.[12] Littell's protagonist also partakes in pseudo-scientific discussions about the fate of a Caucasian Judaic tribe, inspects the concentration camps with a view to rationalising labour, and oversees the 1944 deportation of Hungarian Jews. In the meantime, at Stalingrad, Aue suffers a near-fatal head injury and, later, during the fall of Berlin is sentenced to death for biting or, depending on the edition of the book, pinching Hitler's nose. Aue's reminiscences regarding historically documented events are interspersed with his asides regarding his complicated personal life which is conditioned by his deep-seated hatred for his French mother and his frustrated desire for his twin sister, Una. Thus we learn of Aue's puzzlement over the disappearance of his German father after the Great War, of his anger at his mother's remarriage to a Frenchman, and of his mother and stepfather's discovery of Aue's incestuous relationship with Una. Since the forcible separation of the twins, the protagonist's unrequited passion has been channelled into perverted fantasies about his sister, which Aue enacts by engaging in casual acts of passive homosexuality. As expected from a novel that explicitly draws on the story of Orestes's murder of Clytemnestra and Aegisthus to avenge his father Agamemnon, Aue's maternal resentment culminates in his brutal though seemingly unconscious assassination of his mother and stepfather during his leave in 1943.

While prominent commentators, such as philosophers Klaus Theweleit and Daniel Bougnoux, have praised Littell's construction of his protagonist, others have found the author's choice to grant a Nazi 'the privilege of the narrative voice' ethically problematic.[13] Others still have criticised Aue's historical implausibility, and especially his Zelig-like presence in all the important locations of World War II, and his blatant anachronism.[14] While conceding that his protagonist is 'un nazi hors norme, peu réaliste et pas forcément crédible' [an untypical, unrealistic and not necessarily convincing Nazi], in response to such criticism, Littell insisted that a sociologically plausible war criminal would not have made a satisfactory narrator.[15] The novelist's view is reflected in Aue's scornful judgement of the memoirs of Hans

Frank, the head of the general government in German-occupied Poland, as 'confus, geignard, baigné d'une curieuse hypocrisie religieuse' [confused, whining, steeped in a curious kind of religious hypocrisy] (*B*, 12; *KO*, 4–5). Yet more stringent criticism of Aue's character has been voiced by fellow writer Laurent Binet, who has framed his own novelistic account of the 1942 assassination of Reinhard Heydrich as a counterexample of how to depict the Nazi era. Despite its title, rather than on the architect of the 'Final Solution' and brutal governor of the Protectorate of Bohemia and Moravia, *HHhH* focuses on Heydrich's two heroic assassins, Jozef Gabčik and Jan Kubiš.[16] Hence, while setting himself the ethical goal of reinscribing Czechoslovakia's ignored contribution to the war effort into historical consciousness, Binet pledges to avoid fictionalisation and instead to adhere rigorously to the historically documented facts. Correspondingly, the novelist has condemned the lack of historical veracity characterising Littell's protagonist, which he attributes to Aue's postmodern nihilism, as manifest in his detachment, permanent malaise, taste for philosophising, morose sadism, and sexual frustration.[17]

Combined with his own ethically motivated efforts to refocus literary representations of World War II on heroism and victimhood, Binet's identification of Littell's protagonist as 'le miroir de *notre* époque' [the mirror of *our* age] provides a convenient point of departure for my discussion of *Les Bienveillantes*.[18] Continuing my examination of French novelists' deployment of representational strategies found in historiographic metafiction to retrace the events of the Holocaust, in this chapter I consider Maximilien Aue as a quintessentially postmodern protagonist. Yet, rather than likening him, as Binet does, to Michel Houellebecq's depressive and abject antiheroes, I will focus on Aue's war-induced traumatisation, trauma being an essential feature of present-day, that is postmodern, subjectivity.[19] I will therefore reclassify *Les Bienveillantes*, which has so far been categorised as historical literature, 'literature of excess', and traumatic realism,[20] as an example of 'traumatic metafiction', a label proposed by Alan Gibbs to capture the postmodern novel's propensity for representing the effects and processes of trauma, and for providing a metafictional commentary on the expression of psychological injury.[21] As well as from his mental wounding, Aue's postmodern quality proceeds from his 'disconcerting multiplicity', provisionality, and tendency to undermine his own omniscience and reliability, which Hutcheon associates with protagonists of historiographic metafiction.[22] Moreover, as a marginal figure in relation to the programmatically xenophobic and homophobic socio-political system within which he functions, Aue embodies the 'ex-centric' quality of postmodern characters, as Hutcheon designates the marginalisation of these characters by dominant ideologies.[23] Aue owes his marginality to his mixed Franco-German origin, incestuous longing, covert homosexuality, and consequent inability to start a family. While his refusal to comply with the Nazi model of citizenship makes him suspect in Himmler's eyes, and his homosexual trysts get him into trouble with the *Kriminalpolizei*, the double murder of his mother and stepfather that he commits would make him an outcast to any society regardless of its political make-up.[24]

It is not only Aue-the-protagonist but also Aue-the-narrator who is a liminal figure, and this is because of his status as a former perpetrator. Whereas during the post-war years historians relied mostly on German documents and on interrogation records of Nazi criminals, which meant that 'perpetrator history dominated the field', Adolf Eichmann's trial placed public interest squarely on the victims and endowed their testimony with an unparalleled moral authority.[25] During what Annette Wieviorka has famously branded 'l'ère du témoin' [the era of the witness][26] the Nazis have been relegated by historians to the role of the silenced Other.[27] While Susanne Knittel notes that 'engagement with the perpetrator of the Holocaust constitutes a significant blind spot within the discipline of memory studies', Gibbs asserts that the perpetrator's point of view has been 'shunned by cultural trauma theory'.[28] Erin McGlothlin in turn detects a powerful 'taboo, which places the imagination of the consciousness of the perpetrator outside acceptable discourse on the Holocaust'. As a result, 'the *narrative* perspective of the perpetrator, meaning their subjectivity, motivations, thoughts, and desires — have been all but ignored'.[29] Littell himself observes that 'les bourreaux ne parlent jamais' [the perpetrators never speak], a fact that can be ascribed to the implication of guilt and complicity in such a confession.[30] In the novelist's view, our limited interest in perpetrators precludes our full understanding of the whys of extreme violence and, consequently, our ability to prevent future atrocities.[31] Littell's position has been recently echoed by Susanne Knittel and Zachary Goldberg who state that one cannot grasp the root causes of genocide, oppression, and political violence without paying attention to those who carry out or are complicit in such acts.[32] Similarly, James Weller opines that offering a psychological explanation of the perpetrators' behaviour:

> Allows us to understand the conditions under which many of us could be transformed into killing machines. When we understand [...] evil, we will be less surprised by evil, less likely to be unwitting contributors to evil, and perhaps better equipped to forestall evil.[33]

It is perhaps with these concerns in mind that novelists such as Martin Amis, Bernhard Schlink, David Albarahi, and Jodi Picoult have recently produced narratives that mark 'the turn toward the figure of the perpetrator'.[34] In the French domain, the writers' interest in the perpetrator is illustrated by Robert Merle's *La Mort est mon métier* (1952), Michel Tournier's *Le Roi des Aulnes*, Binet's *HHhH*, and Fabrice Humbert's *L'Origine de la Violence* (2010).[35] Accordingly, these novels have elicited ample critical response, including a number of full-length studies.[36]

Since Eichmann's trial, the ethical focus on the survivor's experience has been consecrated by Lanzmann's *Shoah* which, for Debarati Sanyal, only exemplifies the wider move from history to memory, from heroes to victims, from complicity and contamination to innocent suffering, and from agency to trauma. To enter the perpetrator's logic is therefore seen as 'a betrayal of Auschwitz's reign of senseless violence'.[37] In this context, rather than as instituting 'l'ère du bourreau' [the era of the perpetrator], as feared by Charlotte Lacoste, or as testifying to our growing fascination with evil,[38] Littell's espousal of the perpetrator's perspective can be construed as an iconoclastic gesture directed against the survivors' monopoly over Holocaust memory or, in Crownshaw's terms, at stemming 'the universalisation of the victim's identity'.³⁹ Attendant to Littell's challenge to the victim-focused representations of the Jewish tragedy is his refusal to enable what Eric Leake terms 'easy empathy' with the victims, which reassures us that we care about those suffering and which, in Ezra DeKoven Ezrahi's words, is morally safe, albeit mortally dangerous.⁴⁰ In contrast, when listening to a Nazi, we are forced into 'difficult empathy' which 'unsettles us and places easy empathy into question, showing us [...] our shared human capacity to victimize reflected in victimizers'.⁴¹ Put differently, by narrating the Holocaust from the perpetrator's perspective, Littell encourages us to consider our hypothetical response to past atrocities, to their legacies, and to contemporary injustices and human rights abuses.⁴² Unsurprisingly, some have found such a narrative strategy perilous, in that it is potentially capable of manipulating us into sympathising with an evildoer and, as a result, of engendering an uncritical exculpation of a Nazi or even of promoting fascism.⁴³ LaCapra, for instance, has accused Littell of luring us into 'a pseudodialogic relation aimed at generating complicity and even subordination' that smacks of the Nazis' relationship with the *Judenräte*.⁴⁴ Others, in contrast, have noted that Littell not only invites but also hinders readerly engagement, whereby he succeeds at provoking readerly self-examination without fostering identification with the perpetrator protagonist.⁴⁵

My contribution to the already extensive debate surrounding the risks and benefits of emotional engagement with Littell's protagonist lies in my examination of the role of Aue's post-traumatic condition in both enabling and disabling this engagement. Before proceeding, I must, however, clarify my understanding of the reader's relationship with Aue as I imagine Littell intended it. It is undisputable that, to get through the voluminous and frequently harrowing narrative, there must be at least what Rita Felski describes as 'a flash of connection [that] leaps across the gap between text and reader; an affinity or an attunement [that] is brought to light'.⁴⁶ To quote Martha Nussbaum, the narrative must 'place us in a moral position that is favourable for perception and [...] shows us what it would be like to take up that position in life'.⁴⁷ Rather than to identification, implied by Nussbaum, the attunement that Felski has in mind should be tantamount to empathy which LaCapra has conceptualised as 'an affective relation, rapport, or bond with the other recognized and respected as other'. LaCapra distinguishes empathy from identification which is 'an unmediated fusion of self and other where the [...] alterity of the other is not recognized or respected'.⁴⁸ Identification can either lead to the appropriation of the other's pain, as in Henri Raczymow's novel *Un cri sans voix*, or to the denial of trauma by 'recuperating the past in terms of uplifting messages or optimistic, self-serving scenarios', as in Spielberg's blockbuster *Schindler's List*.⁴⁹ LaCapra therefore recommends that our relationship with Holocaust memory be structured by empathy or, more specifically, by 'empathic unsettlement' which means that 'one may imaginatively put oneself in the victim's position while respecting the difference between self and other and recognising that one cannot take the victim's place or speak in the victim's voice'.⁵⁰ Although, for LaCapra, empathic unsettlement predominantly marks the historians' way of approaching victim trauma, he allows for its extension to perpetrators. Our acknowledgment of the mass killers' mental wounding can help these perpetrators, argues LaCapra, to distance themselves from their implication in deadly ideologies and practices, while enabling our recognition of their distinctiveness from the victims and the 'unsettling possibility of their experience and behaviour'.[51]

In the following pages, I will consider the role of Aue's trauma in simultaneously inviting and blocking this ontologically unsettling empathy. More specifically, I will investigate whether Aue's digestive troubles, hallucinations, nightmares, and memory lapses which constitute the symptomatology of his trauma, incite our sympathy or instead disable it. Indeed, by highlighting the protagonist's growing mental instability and tendency to repress inconvenient facts, his trauma symptoms inevitably impair his narratorial reliability and weaken our identification with him. I will focus particularly on Aue's morally discomfiting tendency to narrativise his psychological wounding with anachronistic recourse to images of Jewish suffering, which potentially facilitates readerly distantiation from Littell's protagonist and guards readers from becoming besmirched by sympathy for an unrepentant, self-serving, and deceitful perpetrator. I will also consider such a narrative strategy as a challenge to the traditional association of the trauma paradigm with victimisation where, as Saira Mohamed observes, the concept of trauma 'validates, even extols, the suffering of those whose experiences warrant recognition'.[52] However, rather than condemning Littell for blurring the subject positions of victim and victimiser by focusing on perpetrator trauma, I will propose a more productive interpretation of Aue's recourse to Jewish suffering as a vector for his own mental undoing. To do so, I will draw on Cathy Caruth's reconceptualisation of history as an enmeshment of the victim's and perpetrator's traumas, and of the perpetrator's trauma as an opportunity for the ethical encounter with the Other and the linked articulation of the dead or wounded Other's pain. It is in this theoretical context that I will question both McGlothlin's observation that the perpetrator's account marginalises and deindividualises victims, and LaCapra's more direct accusation that Littell offers scant opportunity for victims to speak.[53] In contrast to these two critics, I will postulate that Aue's psychological damage can open up a creative space for the voicing of Jewish suffering in the face of the oversaturation of media images and cultural figurations of the Holocaust.[54] I will also question whether this controversial representation of Aue's trauma is in fact a way for Littell's novel to manifest its postmodern constructedness through its character's infusion with the author's Jewishness and unreserved sympathy for Holocaust victims.

(Postmodern) History as Trauma and the 'Unwanted Ghost' of the Post-traumatic Perpetrator

Before turning to Aue's psychological injury, I will outline the key tenets of trauma theory and discuss its interconnection with postmodernism and its intersection with the emergent academic field of perpetrator studies. The concept of trauma, which originally meant physical injury, was first used in relation to mental wounding resulting from a sudden emotional shock in the nineteenth century. Sigmund Freud then mobilised it to comprehend the psychological torment suffered by soldiers returning from the Great War.[55] In 1980, the lasting repercussions of combat experienced by Vietnam veterans motivated the official recognition of Post-Traumatic Stress Disorder (PTSD), before the concept gained further currency in the 1990s in connection with the growing acknowledgement of the aftereffects of the Holocaust. This prompted Caruth's deconstructively inspired textual analyses and redefinition of trauma as an overwhelming experience of sudden, catastrophic events that are not fully assimilated as they happen, but haunt the survivor 'exactly and unremittingly, through the unknowing acts [...] and against his or her very will'.[56] Thus redefined, the concept passed from medicine, psychiatry, and psychology into memory studies, acquiring a moral significance. More recently, its use has been broadened to non-Western contexts, and has entered law, sociology, and philosophy.[57] All this has led to the rise of what Anne Rothe calls 'popular trauma culture' which means that trauma has become a prevalent means of how we make sense of and articulate painful experiences, both personal and collective, or even a commodity.[58]

The growing purchase of trauma theory has been linked, on the one hand, to the memory turn of the 1980s, as represented by Pierre Nora's work, and, on the other, to the ethical turn championed by Shoshana Felman and Dori Laub's study of testimony.[59] More pertinently to my discussion of *Les Bienveillantes*, the influence of the concept of trauma has been connected to the advent of postmodernism. James Berger comments on the powerful implication of the concept of trauma for contemporary theory as a 'representational and temporal hermeneutics' that puts 'emphasis on the retrospective reconstruction of the traumatic event' and that is simultaneously constructivist and empiricist in its analysis.[60] The attention that trauma theory pays to the representational means through which mental damage is remembered calls to mind postmodernism's programmatic self-reflectiveness. Moreover, both trauma and postmodern theories subscribe to a conception of history as that which escapes cognitive grasp, but finds articulation — however partial — thanks to narrative structures proper to literature.[61] Correspondingly, both the postmodern and the post-traumatic reject the faith in the notions of objectivity, totalisation, closure, and redemptive meaning attached to traditional historiography, and in the coherence and absolute meaning of language. This position is illustrated by Caruth's reading of Freud's *Moses and Monotheism* (1939), which proposes that the story of the Jews' captivity and return are available today only through the trauma arising from the Israelites' murder of Moses. Caruth thus rejects the experiential and referential model of history, and reframes it as 'a matter of distortion, a filtering of the original event through the fictions of traumatic repression, which makes the event available at best indirectly'.[62] Drawing on Caruth's reading of *Moses and Monotheism*, Paul Crosthwaite posits that the postmodern has reformulated history as trauma, while Naomi Morgenstern identifies trauma as a means of invoking the historical complexity of the subject's experience within the postmodern paradigm.[63] Postmodern and trauma theories are further interconnected through their shared questioning of the boundary between body and mind, which my reading will illustrate with Aue's repeated metaphorisation of his mental torment as psychical disintegration. According to Christa Schönfelder, postmodernism's deconstructive impulse directed at the binaries structuring modernist ontology finds continuation through the blurring by trauma theory of the distinctions between physical injury and mental damage, and between bodily and emotional pain.[64]

The multiple and complex connections between postmodernism and trauma theory are also traceable in literary production. Postmodern fiction, which Amy Elias describes as stamped by a 'post-traumatic imaginary', abounds in shocking episodes, a fact that is hardly surprising considering postmodernism's origins in the apocalyptic events of the 1940s.[65] Furthermore, symbolic processes of signification found in postmodern literature closely resemble those in psychologically wounded individuals, which bear witness to the trauma-induced damage to the symbolic order.[66] This is why postmodern narratives, as my reading of Littell's novel will demonstrate, are punctuated by silences and feature nightmares, memory lapses, and hallucinations.[67] The related breakdown of the unity of the postmodern subject who, as a historically and/or socially marginal figure is often traumatised, indeed matches the disintegration of the traumatised individual. This, in Raz Yosef's view, ties in with trauma becoming co-opted by the discourse of 'identity politics' for oppressed groups such as women, non-whites, and homosexuals.[68] On the formal level, trauma literature, as Anne Whitehead notes, 'overlaps with and borrows from postmodern [...] fiction in its self-conscious deployment of stylistic devices as modes of reflection and critique'.[69] Since trauma narratives simultaneously represent mental wounding and the difficulties attached to its articulation inherent in the traumatic condition, they can be regarded as derivative of historiographic metafiction. In contrast to Rothberg who, notwithstanding his interest in postmodern literature, dismisses the possibility of 'traumatic postmodernism', Morgenstern argues that 'in postmodern fiction, "trauma" (by definition the unnarratable) and narrative have become codependent terms'.[70] Hence, a 'trauma narrative' can be considered a subcategory of historiographic metafiction with which it shares 'resistance to adequate representation'.[71] Following Morgenstern's argument, Gibbs proposes the category of 'traumatic metafiction' to capture the propensity of postmodern literature for representing trauma's effects and processes. Analogically to historiographic metafiction which narrates past events while problematising the very process of their narrativisation, 'traumatic metafiction' dramatises the 'difficulties of representing trauma and the resultant aporias' alongside the traumatic accident and its aftermath.[72]

The label proposed by Gibbs in relation to a corpus of twentieth-century

American novels can be extended to *Les Bienveillantes* whose protagonist is not only a post-traumatic subject but also an inscribed narrator, which, according to Gibbs, is a consistent feature of traumatic metafiction. What additionally speaks for such a categorisation of Littell's novel is the narrator's metafictional reflection on coping with his mental pain by narrativising his traumatogenic experiences. Interestingly, *Les Bienveillantes* also enacts the paradox identified by Gibbs whereby Holocaust analysts resist the idea that Nazis may suffer mental damage despite the fact that the psychological wounding resulting from the act of killing is at the origin of the concept of PTSD, and that the concept of PTSD has been frequently applied to perpetrators.[73] Beside Vietnam veterans, Gibbs lists among PTSD victims the shell-shocked soldiers returning from the Great War and the French policemen torturing prisoners in the Algerian war of independence.[74] Caruth herself has studied the murderous Israelites and Tancred, one of the characters in Torquato Tasso's *Gerusalemme liberata* (1581) whose trauma results from slaying his beloved Clorinda.[75] And yet, due to the recent reassigning of the concept of trauma to victims and survivors, to associate mental damage with perpetrators poses, in Mohamed's view, a risk of rendering the mental pain and crimes of the killers 'more palatable'. She illustrates her concerns with the representation of the veterans of Vietnam, Iraq, and Afghanistan as victims of 'a destructive form of masculinity forced on them by society and military culture'.[76] Indeed, according to Rachel MacNair's pioneering theorisation of perpetrator trauma, research into the mental damage of veterans 'ha[s] explicitly avoided the idea that soldiers have done anything for which they feel guilt'; rather, 'the belief is that PTSD symptoms relate to what the enemy did, not what the soldier did'.[77] MacNair consequently distinguishes between 'post-traumatic stress disorder' and 'perpetration-induced traumatic stress' which, while sharing the symptomatology of PTSD, proceeds specifically from the act of killing. Mohamed, in contrast, suggests that soldiers who kill as part of their military duty should not be classified as perpetrators, and that their psychological damage should be excluded from the category of perpetrator trauma.

As rare examples of the interest in the psychic wounding suffered by perpetrators the quoted studies corroborate MacNair's remark that 'acknowledging [Nazis, slave-catchers, or torturers] as having pain does not occur to many'.[78] Mohamed, too, asserts that 'clinically describable trauma experienced by individuals who are immoral, or whose behaviour should not be empathised with, is neglected in both scholarly and popular accounts of trauma'.[79] Likewise, Raya Morag is aware that her approach may cause 'confusion, opposition, disapproval, or even repulsion', and can be misread as an intention 'to undermine the victim's status in today's culture', 'shake the foundations of trauma ethics', or deny 'our responsibility for healing the victim'.[80] She acknowledges that the perpetrator is 'an unwelcome ghost' 'whose posttraumatic account stands as a profound challenge and hurdle for the society at whose behest s/he was sent'.[81] The vexed nature of perpetrator trauma is best illustrated by the outrage provoked by Caruth's focus on killers, which, relating their criticism to Holocaust representations, Anne Rothe and Ruth Leys have both condemned as leading to the confusion of different subject positions.[82] According to

Leys, if Tancred 'can become the victim of the trauma and the voice of Clorinda's testimony to his wound, then Caruth's logic [...] would turn the executioners of Jews into victims and the "cries" of the Jews into testimony to the trauma suffered by the Nazis'.[83] More generally, Rothe criticises Caruth for claiming trauma to be 'unknowable' and 'unrepresentable', whereby she allegedly denies the survivors the therapeutic potential of testifying, and for mooting the possibility that survivors may traumatise their interlocutors thus becoming themselves perpetrators. Ignoring the Nazis' undisputable awareness of the genocide they carried out, Rothe parsimoniously states that if the Israelites, as Caruth stipulates, were not only traumatized by their murder of Moses, but also committed this murder without experiencing it, 'the Nazis were traumatised by their murder of the European Jews which they likewise did not experience'.[84]

Rothe's scepticism about perpetrator trauma is shared — if on different grounds — by Richard McNally, who underscores the absence of clinical methods pertaining to the detection of PTSD in killers and torturers. He adds that perpetrators respond poorly to treatments developed for victims, since their trauma proceeds from guilt and shame, rather than fear. McNally's linked remark that to address perpetrator trauma may reverse the roles of victim and perpetrator echoes Amit Pinchevski's point that 'perpetrator trauma traffics on a problematic premise: it casts both the aggressor and the victim of aggression under the same category of moral suffering'.[85] LaCapra, too, has warned that the failure to appreciate the moral and political distinction between different kinds of trauma may engender a conflation of the perpetrator (or the collaborator) with the victim.[86] Commenting specifically on Nazi criminals, he argues that perpetrators can go through potentially traumatizing events unscathed: 'Nazi ideology and practice were geared to creating perpetrators able to combine extreme, traumatizing, radically transgressive acts with hardness that, when it succeeded in functioning as psychic armour, foreclosed traumatization of the perpetrator'.[87] And yet, historical record shows that both high-ranking Nazi officials and ordinary soldiers suffered from PTSD;[88] while Christopher Browning's study of the execution battalions confirms the high level of post-traumatic stress among shooters, including cases of suicide and madness,[89] Heinrich Himmler's search for remote killing methods was allegedly motivated by his traumatisation by the mass executions he attended.[90]

The widespread reservations regarding the applicability of the concept of trauma to mass killers have not discouraged scholars from responding to Raul Hilberg's claim that 'without an insight into the actions of the perpetrators one could not grasp history in its full dimension'.[91] Researchers have studied perpetrator trauma in contexts as diverse as the Rwandan genocide, apartheid, and the Israeli-Palestinian conflict.[92] Morag, for example, believes that interest in the post-traumatic perpetrator can forestall facile identification with the victim-position and can lead to an acknowledgement of the perpetrator's status as society's envoy and wider societal responsibility for her or his crimes: 'willingness to acknowledge perpetrators' trauma is required in order to break out of trauma envy, un-speak its language, overcome its entanglement, and build an ethical stand towards the consequence of new war trauma, thus healing the social order'.[93] To this list Mohamed adds the opportunity for the reconciliation of the perpetrators with their victims and their ensuing social reintegration, especially in situations where the two groups continue to live side by side. She hopes that attentiveness to perpetrators' psychological wounding will foster a better understanding of both the killers and the phenomenon of trauma, and, consequently, 'may contribute to preventing crimes in the future'.[94] Finally, research into the killers' mental damage may lead to the recognition of these killers' ordinariness and to the realisation that, if these ordinary men were capable of committing horrific crimes, 'perhaps we all might be able to do the same'.[95]

In the following pages, I will demonstrate that the outlined misgivings regarding perpetrator trauma, and in particular those voiced by Rothe and Leys, could be fuelled by Aue's self-pitying monologue. Indeed, it appears that the narrator uses his traumatisation, whose symptoms repeatedly engage images of Jewish suffering, to destabilise provocatively the divide between himself and his victims. This strategy is anticipated by the metafictional apostrophe to the reader, which details the long-term effects of Aue's mental wounding, traces the origins of this wounding to his exposure to the sight of genocidal horrors, and frames the account that follows as a scripto-therapeutic project. Significantly, Littell's narrator, who on the Eastern Front suffered from diarrhoea, but who is now permanently constipated, analogises this project to the evacuation of excrement, whereby he stresses the enmeshment of bodily and mental ills proper to trauma. In other words, it is in the hope of unblocking the flow of painful and implicitly foul memories, and of healing both his mind and body in the process, that Aue retraces the mass murder of Jews, which he facilitated, witnessed, and on occasion directly perpetrated. Apart from constipation, Littell's protagonist is afflicted by nausea and vomiting, and experiences episodes of strong emotions, intrusive visions, and hypervigilance, in which readers recognise classic symptoms of postcombat pathology:[96]

> Je m'imagine qu'un homme entre avec un fusil de chasse et ouvre le feu; au cinéma ou au théâtre, je me figure une grenade dégoupillée roulant sous les rangées de sièges; sur la place publique, un jour de fête, je vois la déflagration d'un véhicule bourré d'explosifs, la liesse de l'après-midi transformée en carnage, le sang ruisselant entre les pavés, les paquets de chair collés aux murs ou projetés à travers les croisées pour atterrir dans la soupe dominicale. (B, 14)

> [I imagine a man coming in with a shotgun and opening fire; at the cinema or at the theatre, I picture a live grenade rolling under the seats; in a town square on a public holiday I see a car packed with explosives blowing up, the afternoon festivities turned into carnage, blood filling the cracks between paving stones, gobbets of flesh splattered on the walls or smashing through the windows to land in the Sunday soup.] (KO, 6)

The flipside of these symptoms is amnesia, of which Aue provides evidence by denying responsibility for the murder of his mother and stepfather.[97] Yet another characteristic manifestation of the protagonist's trauma are the disturbing images polluting his dreams and the hot flashes whose intensity he likens to that of a crematorium oven. Like the dream which, by showing the protagonist weighed down by a heap of stones, exploits the Judaic tradition of placing pebbles on tombstones, the simile that Aue mobilises to describe an episode of strong emotions foreshadows his tendency to appropriate the experience of the Holocaust's Jewish victims to articulate his own mental pain.[98] However, rather than following Bruno Viard who identified Aue's comparison of his flushed face to a crematorium as 'la plus abominable [...] de toute notre littérature' [the most abominable [...] of all our literature], I will reframe Littell's narrative strategy as illustrative of Caruth's claim that 'one's own trauma is tied up with the trauma of another' and may therefore lead to 'the encounter with another, through the very possibility and surprise of listening to another's wound'. For Tancred's wound, as Caruth postulates in her reading of Tasso's epic, 'is not precisely [his] own but the wound, the trauma, of another', conveying 'the enigma of the otherness of a human voice that cried out from the wound, a voice that witnesses a truth that Tancred himself cannot fully know'.[99] Following Caruth's conceptualisation of trauma, I will argue that Aue's identification with Jewish suffering in representing his own psychological undoing highlights the relationality of traumas in the context of the war and, rather than displace the victim or turn a perpetrator into a victim, inextricably binds Aue's wounding to that of the murdered Jews whose voices are thus defamiliarised and made poignantly audible to the reader.

Don't Look Now

From the textile factory in northern France, whose organisation uncannily recalls a Nazi concentration camp and whose output — lace soiled with graphite and full of holes — seems to be the reification of Aue's memories, we are transported to wartime Ukraine where, as a consequence of his contact with mass death, Littell's protagonist first began to suffer symptoms of trauma. The episodes set in Lutsk and Kharkov provide Littell with an opportunity to ponder the ramifications of one's cognition of horror, which, as we shall see, seems more likely to engender trauma than understanding or moral action. To foreground this point, Littell has cast Aue chiefly as an observer whose function in the novel is emphasised by this surname, Aue calling to mind *das Auge*, 'eye' in German. Furthermore, Aue fancies himself to be permanently equipped with a camera filming everything around him, including himself, and, as a result of his head injury, believes himself to have developed a pineal eye.[100] That such a construction of the protagonist is not intended to limit his culpability transpires from Aue's insistence that bystanders are as guilty as perpetrators. Instead, it strengthens the protagonist's association with trauma, traumatic memory having been described 'in photographic and cinematic terms, as dreams, flashbacks, hallucinations, reality imprints, burnt-in visual impressions, indelible images, events engraved on the mind and etched into the brain, and experiences encoded in iconic rather than linguistic forms'.[101]

Littell's narrator first discusses the dependence of insight on sight in the context of his memories of Lutsk where he is asked to view decomposing and excrement-covered corpses of Poles and Ukrainians, including women and children, murdered by the Soviet People's Commissariat for Internal Affairs (NKVD). In a manner that will become characteristic of his future confrontations with evil, rather than with the victims, Aue is preoccupied with his own adverse reaction to the other's death: 'j'avais beau respirer entre les lèvres, l'odeur m'emplissait les narines, douce, lourde, écœurante. Je déglutis convulsivement pour me retenir de vomir' [I breathed through my mouth, the smell filled my nostrils, sweet, heavy, nauseating. I swallowed convulsively to keep from vomiting] (B, 38; KO, 33). The focus on Aue's discomfort seems to be intended to incite our identification or even sympathy with him, confirming Mohamed's understanding of trauma as 'a moral category that identifies its subject as a person who merits empathy and deserves to be heard'.[102] Referring specifically to *Les Bienveillantes*, Hanna Meretoja indeed remarks that our emotional investment in Aue grows as the text provides evidence of the toll the war takes on his mind and body, even if this investment is inevitably mitigated by the ironic disproportion between the protagonist's minor distress and the death of a thousand innocent victims.[103]

Aue's first encounter with atrocity inspires existential and philosophical asides which reinforce his position as a victim while inscribing the Holocaust into a historical continuum. In Lutsk, for instance, by defining the stench of rotting flesh as 'la signification même de *notre* existence' [the very significance of *our* existence] (B, 39; KO, 33–34, my emphasis), Aue reinterprets suffering and mortality as part of the human condition. For Sanyal, the protagonist's reaction is only consistent with his overall narrative strategy which is meant to lure us into 'contaminating identification' or 'coercive kinship' with an unapologetic Nazi.[104] Having addressed us as his 'frères humains' [human brothers] (B, 11; KO, 3) in his apostrophe to the reader, Aue continues to soften — if not to erode — the lines separating victims and victimisers by insisting on their shared humanity and on the historical contingency of their subject positions. He thus pushes the limits of the 'incrementalist' or 'situationist' view of perpetration, which maintains that perpetration cannot be explained in terms of personality or other inborn dispositions, but, should propitious circumstances arise, is something of which we are all capable.[105] One of the unquestionable aims of Littell's imaginary reconstruction of the Holocaust from the perpetrator perspective is therefore to force us to recognise that we too may be capable of committing atrocities, and to upset our smug conviction that we could never be anything other than a victim or a passive bystander.[106]

To departicularise further the violence he observes, Aue regularly draws on his classical erudition. In Lutsk, he assimilates himself with the young Athenian in Plato's *Republic*, Leontius, who, on seeing bodies of recently executed criminals, 'conçut un désir de les regarder, et en même temps ressentit du dégoût à cette pensée, et voulut se détourner' [felt a desire to look at them, and at the same time loathing the thought he tried to turn away] (B, 97; KO, 98). But, in contrast to Leontius who tries to restrain his intuitive urge to stare at the dead bodies with his rational choice to avert his gaze, Aue forces himself to contemplate the scene against his desire to shut his eyes. Through this reversal of the Platonian dynamic of appetite and reason, Littell raises the question of pornographic attraction to violence, without, however, implicating his protagonist. Significantly, pornographic rhetoric which scholars have used to frame Leontius's reaction, has long been part of the critique of Holocaust representation.[107] According to Carolyn Dean, 'pornographic pleasure' derived from viewing violent images is thought to forestall the 'disinterested indignation' and the 'healthy respect for and outrage at suffering not our own', which are considered appropriate responses to narratives and images of Holocaust pain. It also 'expresses a smug fantasy of being different from others who are otherwise like you, the pleasure of not-having-been a victim'. Put differently, it creates 'an incurable distance' and makes us betray 'those with whom we are trying to identify'.[108] In this light, Littell's intertextual allusion to the *Republic* forces us to interrogate our own gaze at catastrophe and, more pertinently, our engagement with Holocaust imagery and literature. That this is the intention of *Les Bienveillantes* is also suggested by its habit of interspersing descriptions of mass killings with Aue's sexual fantasies and exploits, and by its resultant alignment with the tradition of 'link[ing] pornography and pathological sexuality [...] with pathological (anti-liberal) politics'.[109] Littell's concern with pornographic attraction to Holocaust imagery can also be detected in his imaginary recreations of executions, which systematically eroticise the Nazis' objectification of their victims. As well as by the Kharkov hangings and the Babi Yar massacre which I will discuss shortly, this is exemplified by the historically documented hanging of two Bolshevik Jews in Zhitomir. The German soldiers who have come in throngs to watch Wolf Kieper and Mosche Kogan being hanged jeer and take snapshots which they will then post to their families or use to 'decorate' their quarters. If this manifestation of what Rose would call 'vicarious enjoyment of violence' and what *Les Bienveillantes* itself dubs 'Executionstourismus' [execution tourism] was not enough to convey Littell's condemnation of pornographic attraction to violence, the passage includes the historically unsubstantiated detail of Kieper's involuntary ejaculation at the moment of death.[110] Rather than, as one critic believed, being symptomatic of Littell's 'pornographic voyeurism', the taunting of the victim by the Wehrmacht soldiers in reaction to the ejaculation evidences Littell's denunciation of Holocaust representations thriving on the link between sex and death.[111]

Although centuries-old, the dilemma between looking and averting one's gaze has been, as Angi Buettner contends, crystallised by the Nazi Judeocide, with Holocaust imagery becoming 'functionalised in the development of the aesthetics of a catastrophe'. Correspondingly, the Holocaust has provoked the question of whether exposure to violent events facilitates our understanding of them and ultimately propels us to ethico-political action.[112] Littell's resolve to explore these issues is manifest in the graphic descriptions of violence, to which he subjects the reader, and in his protagonist's indefatigable efforts to understand this violence through his repeated confrontation with mass murder. Aue is convinced that 'le malheur il faut s'y confronter; l'inévitable et la nécessité, il faut toujours être prêt à les regarder en face, et accepter de voir les conséquences qui en découlent; fermer les yeux, ce n'est jamais une réponse' [one has to confront atrocity; one must always be ready to look inevitability and necessity in the face; and accept the consequences that result from them; closing your eyes is never an answer] (B, 82; KO, 81). It is for the same reason that Aue collects 'trophy' photographs taken by soldiers at executions and later enlists a professional photographer to document the Babi Yar massacre. His action is additionally driven by both his horror at the soldiers' scopophilic enjoyment of violence and his desire to expose high-ranking Nazis in Berlin, including Hitler himself, to the sight of the atrocities committed by the German troops on the Eastern Front.

Reflecting Littell's own typically postmodern belief that, rather than clarifying things, enquiry only further obscures them, Aue's endeavour to understand evil through sight proves vain.[113] He admits that 'ces visages, ces yeux effrayés ou effroyablement résignés, ne me disaient rien' [these faces, these terrifyingly resigned eyes told me nothing], and that 'je ne parviendrais jamais à saisir la mort' [I would never manage to grasp death] (B, 161, 162; KO, 168, 170). Instead, as illustrated by the following passage, his presence at executions substantiates the widespread anxiety that sustained contact with violence may lead to vicarious traumatisation and/or numbing.[114] Needless to say, Aue's witnessing the horrors of the Holocaust renders him morally unavailable to counteract them:

> Je retournais régulièrement assister aux exécutions, personne ne l'exigeait, j'y allais de mon propre chef. [...] En m'infligeant ce lamentable spectacle, pressentais-je, je ne visais pas à en user le scandale, le sentiment insurmontable d'une transgression, d'une violation monstrueuse du Bien et du Beau, mais il advenait plutôt que ce sentiment de scandale s'usait de lui-même, et on en prenait en effet l'habitude, on ne sentait, à la longue, plus grand-chose. (B, 170)
>
> [I went back regularly to witness the executions; no one required it, but I went of my own free will. [...] By inflicting this piteous spectacle on myself, I felt, I wasn't trying to exhaust the scandal of it, the insurmountable feeling of a transgression, of a monstrous violation of the Good and the Beautiful, but rather this feeling of scandal came to wear out all by itself, one got used to it, and in the long run stopped feeling much.] (KO, 178)

Aue's Hallucinations

The cognitive and moral ineffectiveness of Aue's presence at mass shootings can be read as an expression of Littell's concern with what Geoffrey Hartman calls the 'desensitizing trend' observed in an age when 'the media make us bystanders of every act of violence and violation'.[115] Aue's recourse to images of Jewish suffering in articulating his own trauma could consequently be considered as a means of re-sensitising his readers to the ordeal of Holocaust victims, that is of combatting empathy fatigue engendered by the oversaturation of media and cultural representations of the Holocaust, and by the Holocaust's metaphorical uses in analysing unrelated atrocities and catastrophes.[116] In my examination of the symptoms of the protagonist's trauma — hallucinations, panic attacks, and nightmares — I will discuss how these symptoms give a new voice to the Holocaust's actual victims while drawing attention to the fictional status of Littell's novel and its protagonist. To achieve this, I will illuminate Aue's belated and reluctant recognition of his implication in the Nazi genocide of Europe's Jews with Caruthian theory wherein trauma becomes the site resonating with the plaintive voice of the dead Other. Tancred's mentioned realisation of his deed on hearing Clorinda's lament rising from the wounded tree is of course one example of the way trauma manifests itself.[117] However, due to the inevitable association between the trope of burning and the Holocaust, including Littell's own extensive reliance on such imagery, even more pertinent is Caruth's deconstruction of the dream of a father haunted by his dead child's accusatory voice. Building on Freud's and Lacan's analyses of the dream, Caruth constitutes trauma as the very identity of the self and of the self's relation to another, as illustrated by the fact that 'the very identity of the father, as subject, is bound up with, or founded in, the death that he survives'.[118] Inspired by this analysis, I will argue that, like the dead child who is asking 'Father, don't you see I'm burning?', the Jews, whose bodies were literarily consumed by fire, remind Aue of his ethical unavailability at the time of their death.

Like most of the symptoms of Aue's mental damage, his hallucinations begin in Ukraine. As he is watching his two fellow officers flirt with local girls, Littell's protagonist is overcome by morbid revulsion, imagining the couples as corpses such as those of 'les Juifs fauchés dans la fleur de l'âge' [Jews mowed down in the prime of life] (B, 89; KO, 89). As well as attaching Aue's trauma to the genocide in which he has become complicit, this unsavoury parallel deflects our empathy from the perpetrator and refocuses it on the victims. Such a reading is particularly encouraged by Felman's reframing of Caruth's discussion of Tancred's trauma with Levinasian philosophy, which leads her to reinterpret trauma as what 'implies a human and ethical dimension in which the Other receives priority over the self.[119] Felman's reformulation of psychological wounding can also throw light on a later episode in which, by figuring Hitler as a rabbi, Aue's troubled mind is once again haunted by the suffering of the Holocaust's Jewish victims. Significantly, the simultaneously grotesque and puzzling apparition immediately follows Aue's meeting with his mentor, Dr Mandelbrod, who, despite his protégé's request for redeployment, pressures him to continue working on the 'Jewish question'. The hallucinatory vision is indeed anticipated by Aue's realisation that 'les Juifs [...] me poursuivaient comme un mauvais rêve au début de la matinée, collé au fond de la tête' [the Jews [...] kept pursuing me like a bad dream early in the morning, stuck in the back of my head] (B, 429; KO, 464). Hence, rather than, as Leys might fear, turning a Nazi into a victim and the cries of the victims into the testimony of their killer's trauma, Aue's mental pain not only disables our empathy for the perpetrator but also makes the victims' voices heard in a new and powerful way.

Even if it is more subtle in this case, Aue's recourse to Holocaust imagery in articulating his mental torment continues through his recollection of the hanging of a young Soviet partisan in Kharkov in the winter of 1941. The scene is based on the real-life execution of Zoya Kosmodemyanskaya who was subsequently propelled by Soviet propaganda to the status of a war heroine and whose posthumous photograph inspired Littell to write *Les Bienveillantes*.[120] Significantly, in an interview Littell calls the photograph of the partisan's martyred body, which shows her neck twisted by the cord and a breast gnawed by wolves, an 'icon'.[121] The term recalls Bessel van der Kolk's qualification of traumatic memories as 'iconic', that is as non-narrative, non-descriptive, and non-declarative.[122] It also brings to mind Caruth's own view that traumatic memory returns in non-symbolic literality, constituting unsolicited, pure, and unmediated intrusion of the traumatic event into the present.[123] Such a construction of traumatic memory helps to understand the implausible reappearance of the partisan's mutilated corpse and its disturbing effect on Littell's protagonist:

> Quel que fût le chemin que je prenais pour me rendre de l'hôtel ou à nos bureaux, je la trouvais toujours couchée sur mon passage, une question têtue, bornée, qui me projetais dans un labyrinthe de vaines spéculations et me faisait perdre pied. (B, 171)
>
> [Whatever path I took to go from the hotel to our offices, I always found her lying in my way, a stubborn, single-minded question that threw me into a labyrinth of vain speculations and made me lose my footing.] (KO, 180)

In line with my earlier reading of the execution of Kieper and Kogan, I argue that one of the aims of the Kharkov episode is to criticise pornographic attraction to violence, which, for Littell, finds embodiment in the aestheticisation or even eroticisation of Kosmodemyanskaya's death by her posthumous photograph. In the scene of the hanging of the partisan, this eroticisation is conveyed through the implausible passage describing German soldiers, including Aue, kissing the condemned woman on the mouth. When it is his turn, Aue suffers mental collapse which he metaphorises as a polymorphous disintegration of his body. And so Aue first burns to cinders, then these cinders form a salt statue which later, too, becomes disjointed and pulverised, before its ashes are scattered by the wind. The imagery used here recalls Aue's comparison of his flushed face to a crematorium, which, as we remember, has met with sharp critique. Similarly, Aue's recourse to the trope of burning in the Kharkov episode has been condemned for appropriating the fate of his future victims and, consequently, has been deemed 'scandalous'.[124] Even if I offer a more productive interpretation of this scene, such a reaction is unsurprising given the established link between incineration and the Jewish tragedy. This link proceeds from the very term 'the Holocaust' which derives from *holokauston*, a Greek word meaning 'a burnt sacrifice offered whole to God', and which was chosen because in concentration camps the bodies of victims were burned whole in crematoria or in open fires.[125] The association between cinders and the Holocaust has been further cemented by Paul Celan's poetry where ember, ash, and smoke are repeatedly cast as what remains of the Nazis' victims.[126]

While the trope of cinders inevitably invokes the Holocaust, the salt statue that Aue turns into makes us think of Lot's wife and, more broadly, of the 'fantasies and fears about the potential for spectatorial damage'.[127] I therefore suggest that, like Aue's earlier intertextual engagement with the *Republic*, his allusion to the 'transhistorical sign' of Lot's wife is intended to broaden the relevance of the protagonist's reaction to the sight of atrocity.[128] What is more, like his reference to Plato's treatise, his citation of the biblical story subjects the source text to a parodic destabilisation. Notably, Aue's use of incineration and petrification as metaphors of his mental disintegration identifies him simultaneously with the woman punished for her curiosity about — or even sympathy for — the victims of God's wrath and with the two cities destroyed by fire and brimstone. Aue's characteristic focus on his own distress and his usurpation of the victim position, to which this double identification points, become even more apparent when recontextualised with a feminist re-appropriation of Lot's wife. Feminist critics have reimagined what the Bible construes as 'a feminine failure of character' as a symbol of patriarchal oppression, that is as a 'woman with no name' who suffers disproportionately to her paltry transgression and who is both entirely defined by her relationship to her husband and framed by her husband's story.[129]

Aue's petrification can be equally made sense of in relation to the myth of Perseus who avoids being turned into stone by deflecting Medusa's murderous gaze with a highly polished shield. The myth is conjured up through Aue's reference to a mirror and description of the partisan's face as framed with 'une crête de méduse' [a Medusa crest] (*B*, 171; *KO*, 180). Let us note that, as he does with the stories of Leontius and Lot's wife, Littell upsets the logic of the Perseus myth as he inverts the victim-perpetrator dynamic by identifying the partisan with the stony-eyed monster and Aue with a victim of her castrating gaze. The protagonist's longing to assume the position of a (Holocaust) victim becomes even more apparent if we recall that Medusa is one of the Gorgons and that Levi, in his essay 'Shame', described those who perished in the camps and who are therefore the Holocaust's only true witnesses as 'those who saw the Gorgon'.[130] Coincidently, Miri Rozmarin establishes a connection between Levi's aporia of witnessing and Lot's wife, whose petrification precludes her from testifying just as death prevented the victims of the Nazi camps from becoming witnesses.[131] And yet, Aue quickly undercuts his own misappropriating gesture of the victim/ witness position by conceding the discrepancy between his cognitive impotence in relation to the mystery of death and the partisan's knowing gaze: 'Lorsque vint mon tour, elle me regarda, un regard clair et lumineux, lavé de tout, et je vis qu'elle comprenait tout, savait tout, et devant ce savoir si pur j'éclatais en flames' [When my turn came, she looked at me, a clear luminous look, washed of everything, and I saw that she understood everything, knew everything, and faced with this pure knowledge I burst into flames] (*B*, 171; *KO*, 180). This suggests that Littell's text does not, after all, recast its perpetrator protagonist as a victim or appropriate and exploit Jewish suffering to voice Aue's trauma. Rather, the motifs of incineration and petrification serve to reinscribe this suffering into the perpetrator's narrative, at the same time subjecting it to defamiliarisation. As I have demonstrated, Littell's narrative strategy is assisted by a combination of intense intertextuality and anachronistic images whose emergence in relation to the Holocaust is posterior to the episode's diegetic present. For, although Aue-the-narrator has full knowledge of the post-war theorisations of the Nazi genocide, in the Kharkov episode the narrative's unmarked descent into the hallucinatory register makes the narrating 'I' merge with the experiencing 'I'. This means that the imagery Aue uses cannot be available to him, which reminds us in turn of his constructedness as narrator and weakens our engagement with him. As we have seen in this section, and as I will continue to contend in relation to the other symptoms of Aue's trauma, this engagement is further mitigated by the protagonist's growing narratorial unreliability and by his unethical attempts to solicit our empathy by focusing our attention on his mental torment with recourse to images of Jewish agony.

Perpetrator Disgust

If in Lutsk and Kharkov Aue still experiences only relatively mild trauma symptoms, his regular participation in the *Aktionen*, as the Nazis euphemistically called mass executions of Jews, Gypsies, and communists, intensifies and diversifies them. Gradually nausea and vomiting are accompanied by diarrhoea, fever, and migraines, not to mention Aue's obsession with the cleanliness of his uniforms. At the same time, the narrator's originally lucid and meticulously documented account of Germany's invasion of the Soviet Union slips into a phantasmagoria, where it is not only the reader but also Aue himself who struggles to ascertain the narrative register of his monologue.

Implied by Aue's previously discussed hallucinatory vision of German officers and their Ukrainian lovers as murdered Jews, the link between the protagonist's trauma and his complicity in the Nazi Judeocide is firmly established by the first *Aktion* that he observes. In preparation for the shooting, the condemned Jews are made to dig their own graves, and as they do so unearth victims of the NKVD. Besides making a mockery of the Nazis' self-proclaimed moral superiority over the Bolsheviks, and supporting Aue's assertion of the sameness of all perpetrators, this fact enables a reframing of the forest as an embodiment of the Caruthian conception of history, where, as Joseph Berger has it, 'each national catastrophe invokes and transforms memories of other catastrophes, so that history becomes a complex entanglement of crimes inflicted and suffered, with each catastrophe understood — that is, misunderstood — in the context of repressed memories of previous ones'.[132] Thus reframed, the forest provides an apt setting for an incident that, if illuminated by Caruth's reading of *Gerusalemme liberata*, can be deciphered as a sign of Aue's trauma and of the entanglement of this trauma with that of the murdered Jews. To begin with, the Ukrainian woods chosen for the *Aktion* can be likened to the magic forest where, seeking building materials necessary for their conquest of Jerusalem, the crusaders staged by Tasso confront their worst anxieties. For instance, on striking a tree with his sword, Tancred fully realises the murder of his beloved Clorinda. In Littell's novel, the forest which is the site of Jewish trauma literally enters Aue's body in the form of the splinters that lodge themselves within his hand.[133] If the fact that Aue seems more concerned with extracting the splinters than with the Jewish victims testifies to his characteristic self-centredness and helps readers to distance themselves from him, the long, thin pieces of wood can be read, as Liran Razinsky and Eric Sandberg have done respectively, as a miniaturisation of the forest and thus as an embodiment of Aue's mental damage.[134] Yet Caruth's theory can not only help us to see the inseparability of Aue's trauma from that of his victims, but also throw light on the protagonist's unlikely composure during the *Aktion*. In tandem with the fact that Aue fails to register the moment of his injury, this composure can be construed as a sign of trauma's unavailability to consciousness at the time of its occurrence. Such a decoding of this episode is supported by the protagonist's consequent inability to enjoy sylvan spaces or even to dwell on his happy childhood memories of the German woods, which have been retroactively tainted by the genocide. Recast in the context of the traditional veneration of the forest by Germans and in particular of the Nazis' integration of the forest into their *Blut und Boden* [blood and soil] ideology, Littell's identification of woodlands as a site of Holocaust trauma becomes even more profoundly ironic.[135]

As well as through the presence of splinters under Aue's skin during the *Aktion*, the protagonist's trauma manifests itself through typical PTSD symptoms, even if the narrator never directly links the genocide he enabled to his poor mental and physical health. His awareness of the link is clear, however, from the causal connection between the *Aktionen* and the abnormal behaviour of other German soldiers, which ranges from sadistic outbursts to suicide. Implicitly endorsing Adorno's claim that indignation over cruelty diminishes in proportion to the dissimilarity of victims and perpetrators, Aue ascribes his fellow Nazis' gratuitous brutality to their recognition of their own and their victims' shared humanity:[136]

> Leurs réactions, leurs violences, leur alcoolisme, les dépressions nerveuses, les suicides, ma propre tristesse, tout cela démontrait que *l'autre* existe [...] en tant qu'humain, et qu'aucune volonté, aucune idéologie, aucune quantité de bêtise et d'alcool ne peut rompre ce lien, ténu mais indestructible. (*B*, 142)

> [Their reactions, their violence, their alcoholism, the nervous depressions, the suicides, my own sadness, all that demonstrated that the *other* exists [...] as a human, and that no will, no ideology, no amount of stupidity or alcohol can break this bond, tenuous but indestructible.] (*KO*, 147)

Likewise, Aue's own sympathy for the victims evidently proceeds from his identification with them. For example, his strong reaction to the Kharkov hanging is provoked by the female partisan's resemblance to Aue's sister, who is Aue's ideal self and love object. The protagonist's regret at the murder of the young pianist Yakov can in turn be traced back to his own unrequited musical ambitions, while his compassion for the Hungarian Jews awaiting deportation is motivated by their apparent similarity to middle-class Germans, that is to a social class that Aue identifies with.

The narrator pushes his interpretation of perpetrator trauma further by analogising suicidal shooters to the Jews who, having been forced to witness the murder of their loved ones, welcome their own death. For instance, he equates executioners with Jewish mothers 'qui devaient regarder tuer leurs enfants sans pouvoir les protéger, qui ne pouvaient que mourir avec eux' [who had to watch their children being killed without being able to protect them, who could only die with them]. Aue further blurs the difference between the two kinds of experience by using similar phraseology to describe them: 'nos hommes souffraient d'un sentiment extrême d'impuissance, eux aussi se sentaient sans défense' [our men suffered from an extreme feeling of powerlessness; they too felt defenceless] (B, 106; KO, 108). Such an explanation of the abhorrence experienced by Aue and other Nazis supports the construction of perpetrator disgust as a 'deep-seated moral impulse [...] that rebels against the act committed or witnessed'.[137] This so-called nativist position has been represented by Hannah Arendt who elucidates the aversion to murder that some Nazis experienced in terms of 'the animal pity by which all normal men are affected in the presence of physical suffering'.[138] Ditte-Marie Munch-Jurisic is sceptical, however, about whether revulsion betrays moral conflict in the perpetrator and whether repugnance is, as Leon Kass puts it, 'the only voice left that speaks up to defend the core of humanity'.[139]

Munch-Jurisic's linked doubts regarding the potential of perpetrator disgust to provoke moral action can help to understand the ethical impotence of Aue's own trauma-related revulsion.[140] Even if Littell's protagonist occasionally recoils from personal involvement in the killing, opposes the methods employed in the genocide, questions the genocide's economic viability, and pities individual victims, his *Weltanschauung* remains essentially unaltered. In fact, Aue's disgust can even be seen as 'morally destructive', as the shock that he initially experienced becomes displaced by indifference, while he himself morphs into a cold-blooded murderer.[141] Having assassinated his mother and stepfather, Aue kills his Romanian lover and, in the novel's closing scene, he murders his best friend and mentor in the *Sicherheitsdienst*, Thomas Hauser. Even if the protagonist's disgust does not turn to sadism, as in the case of some other Nazis, at Babi Yar his pity for a dying woman curdles into murderous rage:

> Je voulais de tout mon cœur me pencher et lui essuyer la terre et la sueur mêlées sur son front, lui caresser la joue et lui dire que ça allait, que tout irait pour le mieux, mais à la place je lui tirai convulsivement une balle dans la tête [...], je continuais à lui tirer dessus et sa tête avait éclaté comme un fruit. (B, 126)

> [I wanted with all my heart to bend over and brush the dirt and the sweat off her forehead, caress her cheek and tell her that it was going to be all right, that everything would be fine, but instead I convulsively shot a bullet into her head [...], I kept shooting at her and her head exploded like a fruit.] (KO, 130)

It therefore appears that Littell has modelled Aue's response to atrocity on that of Himmler who turned the compassion he ought to have felt for the victims towards himself, or of the commandant of Auschwitz, Rudolph Höss, who represented himself as a suffering witness.[142] Instead of saying, as Arendt puts it, 'What horrible things I did to people!', the likes of Himmler and Höss would say, 'What horrible things I had to watch in the pursuance of my duties, how heavily the task weighted upon my shoulders!'[143] For Sanyal, Aue's murder of the Jewish woman at Babi Yar indeed casts him as 'the subject of trauma that is inflicted, paradoxically *by* the victim'. Similarly, she reads the Kharkov hanging as a travesty of the Levinasian face-to-face encounter in that it fails to mobilise the subject's responsibility towards the Other. Consequently, Sanyal fears that Littell's novel 'rationali[ses] sadism as the effect of perpetrators' recognition of their victims' humanity', 'annihilates the victim', and 'perpetuates a "universal grey zone"'.[144]

A more constructive interpretation would suggest that by exposing Aue's efforts to redirect the reader's attention from the agony of the victims to the observing and suffering witness, Littell not only installs a safe affective distance between his reader and his perpetrator protagonist, but, more importantly, reintegrates the suffering of the victims into the perpetrator's self-involved monologue and, through the ironic contrast between the killers' ill health and the genocide they are committing, puts stress on the enormity of Jewish suffering.

The Nazi at the Barber's: Aue's Panic Attacks

Upon his return to Berlin from Stalingrad, where he suffered a near-fatal head wound, Aue additionally experiences anxiety which, like his other symptoms, mobilises Holocaust imagery. Indicated by his constant fear of stepping on a mine or of being hit by shrapnel in the then still tranquil capital, Aue's anxiety manifests itself fully during his visit to a barber shop where it is triggered by the sound of scissors clicking above his head: 'mon cœur battait la chamade, mes entrailles sombraient dans un froid humide, la panique noyait mon corps entier, le bout de mes doigts picotait' [my heart was pounding, my intestines sank into a wet cold, panic drowned my whole body, the tips of my fingers prickled] (*B*, 410; *KO*, 444). The anachronism systematically marking passages describing Aue's trauma makes it possible to conjecture that, notwithstanding the anteriority of this episode to the protagonist's inspection of concentration camps, his panic attack appropriates the experience of their inmates who, as part of their initiation into the camp, had their heads shorn. This anachronism reminds us of the fictionality of Aue's memoir and, together with the unease instilled in the reader by Aue's absorption of the deindividuation and humiliation to which deportees were subjected through the forcible removal of hair, incapacitates the identificatory mechanism. The mimetic illusion is further undermined in this episode through its intense intertextuality, and in particular through its allusions to Edgar Hilsenrath's satirical Holocaust novel *Der Nazi und der Friseur* (1977) and to Claude Lanzmann's interview with the former barber of Treblinka in *Shoah*.[145] With the protagonist of Hilsenrath's novel, Max Schulz, Aue shares not only a first name, but also the status of a Nazi who at least seemingly usurps the victim position. Having assassinated his childhood Jewish friend, Itzik Finkelstein, in the concentration camp of which he was commandant, Schulz steals his victim's identity and moves to Israel where he practices the trade learnt many years earlier in the barber shop owned by Itzik's father. Read in dialogue with *Der Nazi und der Friseur* and Lanzmann's interview with Abraham Bomba who, in Treblinka, cut the hair of women about to be gassed, the scene of Aue's haircut suggests that the protagonist's trauma is bound up with his (over-)identification with Holocaust victims. In fact, while as before reinscribing these victims' voices into the perpetrator's narrative, this episode, especially when considered in relation to Hilsenrath's novel, sounds a warning against trauma envy.

A somewhat different dynamic structures the panic attack Aue has at a party hosted by the commandant of the Lublin concentration camp, Odilo Globočnik.

There, the protagonist's anxiety brings to the surface not only his war trauma, but also what seems to be 'the trauma of birth' in which Otto Rank sought the source of some individuals' sadistic behaviour towards women, especially those pregnant.[146] Aue's panic attack is triggered by the appearance of two emaciated Jewish prisoners of the nearby camp, who are about to be shot by their guards for stealing potato peelings. For Aue, the imminent death of the two Jews spoils the jolly ambiance of the party; floating on his back in an outdoor swimming pool, the protagonist is unable to control his breathing, has the impression that the water around him is growing heavy like a woollen cloak, and is seized by an unreasonable fear that the two corpses will be thrown into the pool transforming its water into blood. Although a liquid environment usually comforts Aue by mentally transporting him back into the intrauterine togetherness with his twin sister, on this occasion even water fails to protect him from the affective impact of the double execution. Indeed, in tandem with the doubling of both the guards and the prisoners, the aquatic context of the scene means that Aue's anxiety can be traced back to his and Una's expulsion from their mother's womb. In Rank's terms, Aue suffers from a trauma that makes itself apparent as:

> The unquenchable hatred of the one who expelled [the traumatised individual]; he really attempts with his fully grown body to go back into the place whence he came as a child, without considering that he thereby tears his sacrifice to pieces.[147]

As well as by Aue's congenital yet unjustified resentment towards his mother and his nostalgia for his antenatal life, such an interpretation is invited by the protagonist's obsession with pregnancy and birth, especially when the delivery is carried out through Caesarean section. Otherwise, Aue's anxiety is clearly rooted in his experience of the Holocaust. As before, however, the protagonist's effort to solicit our sympathy is undercut by the ironic contrast between Aue's own reality and the Jewish suffering that he engages to communicate his distress. In this case, the irony stems from the disparity between the opulence of food and drink at the party and the misery and brutality marking life in the camp, which is encapsulated in the narrator's preposterous comparison of the two gunshots to popping champagne corks.

Tumah and *Taharah*: Bad Dreams and Hot Baths

In line with Freud's identification of the recurring and terrifying nightmares suffered by shell-shocked soldiers as a typical symptom of trauma, Caruth recognises frightening and repetitive dreams as a key manifestation of psychological injury.[148] Consistent with her wider belief in trauma's unmediated nature, she stresses the uncharacteristic literariness of traumatic nightmares. Likewise, other trauma scholars have emphasised these nightmares' freedom from the symbolic transposition, substitutability, condensation, displacement, fantastic elaboration, and secondary revision that characterise ordinary dreams.[149] While through their recurrence, the nocturnal visions tormenting Aue conform with the outlined characterisation of post-traumatic nightmares, their symbolic investment defies the general consensus regarding the literality of what are sometimes considered as 'nighttime flashbacks'.[150] This can be demonstrated with the help of the taxonomy of Aue's dreams proposed by Edith Perry who divides them into 'les rêves de souillure' [dreams of defilement], 'les rêves de métro' [metro dreams], and 'les rêves qui intègrent le contexte historique' [dreams with a historical context].[151] Drawing on Klaus Theweleit's renowned conceptualisation of the fascist's psyche as split into a flowing feminine interiority and an armour-like masculine exterior, Perry observes the shared tendency of Aue's dreams to offset the Nazis' utopian fantasy of a homogenous and orderly society with fluid identities.[152] Consequently, she deciphers Aue's nocturnal visions as betraying his fear of the dissolution of personal boundaries.[153] What interests me, in contrast to Perry, is the cognitive potential of the protagonist's nightmares in relation to his trauma, and their apparent capacity for arousing our empathy with a perpetrator.[154] As we will now see, like the protagonist's hallucinations and panic attacks, Aue's dreams have the power not only to incite but also to foreclose readerly empathy, which they do by assimilating Holocaust imagery.[155] Furthermore, as suggested by Luc Rasson's contention that the novel's oneiric passages subject Nazi discourse to 'persistent delegitimation', these dreams undermine Aue's narratorial reliability and thus weaken our affective engagement with him.[156]

As if reifying the metaphorical remark of a Berlin policeman who, in an episode set in the late 1930s, interrogates Aue on suspicion of homosexuality — '"Vous êtes dans la merde, jeune homme"' ['You're in deep shit, young man'] (B, 70; KO, 69, translation modified) — many of the protagonist's nightmares figure him and his doubles as faecally incontinent. These 'defilement dreams', to use Perry's term, reflect the daytime reality of Aue who, throughout his engagement on the Eastern Front, is afflicted by diarrhoea. But they also appear to carry a symbolic meaning and require decoding. If Aue mostly leaves this job to his reader, he sporadically attempts to expose the repressed content himself. This is exemplified by the nightmare featuring, Voss, a talented linguist whom Aue befriends in the Caucasus:

> Voss, dans une pièce sombre et vide, se tenait à quatre pattes, le derrière dénudé; et de la merde liquide lui coulait de l'anus. Inquiet, je saisissais du papier, des pages des *Izvestia*, et tentais d'éponger ce liquide brun qui devenait de plus en plus foncé et de plus en plus épais. J'essayais de garder les mains propres, mais c'était impossible, la poisse presque noire recouvrait les feuilles et mes doigts, puis ma main entière. Malade de dégoût, je courais me rincer les mains dans une baignoire proche; mais pendant ce temps cela coulait toujours. (B, 285)

> [Voss, in a dark, empty room, was on all fours, his rear end bare, and liquid shit was streaming from his anus. Worried, I seized some paper, some pages from *Izvestia*, and tried to sponge up this brown liquid, which was becoming increasingly darker and thicker. I tried to keep my hands clean, but it was impossible, the almost black pitch covered the pages and my fingers, then my whole hand. Sick with disgust I ran to wash my hands in a bathtub nearby; but during this time it was still streaming.] (KO, 305)

According to Aue's unmistakably Freudian interpretation which follows his description of the dream, Voss has been displaced by Aue while Aue has displaced his own father. The accuracy of such a reading is corroborated by the recurring presence in the protagonist's nightmares of paternal figures who either act as unsympathetic observers of another's physical undoing or as solicitous helpers. What puzzles the narrator is the meaning of the Soviet newspaper whose pages he uses to clean up the excremental mess. The propagandist character of *Izvestia* suggests that it may have displaced the *Völkischer Beobachter*, the mouthpiece of Nazi propaganda, of which Aue happens to be a reader. Seen in this light, the nightmare restages Aue's real-life use of the Nazis' official rhetoric to oppose Voss's scientifically informed dismissal of the notion of race and his ensuing implicit contestation of Nazi ideology. As for the protagonist's vain attempt to keep his hands clean, it no doubt signifies his wish to avoid direct involvement in the genocide.

In a later 'defilement dream', it is the protagonist's sister who is beset by diarrhoea. As Aue passively watches Una's demise, Una's paraplegic and much older husband does the tidying up. The dark and foul-smelling substance escaping from Una's body is offset by the whiteness of her gown, which, apart from purity, signifies the fulfilment of Aue's fantasy to marry his twin.[157] If the stark contrast marking this nightmare mirrors the opposition between the Nazis' ambition to create a racially homogenous society and the genocide they carried out to realise it, the excrement stands for the truth about the 'Final Solution' of which Aue is — as in the dream — a horrified and powerless observer. Evidently dissatisfied with the bystander's role, when interpreting the nightmare, Aue tries to usurp the victim position by comparing his sister, and therefore himself, to those brutalised by the Nazis. He first likens Una to the emaciated Auschwitz prisoners who, during the death marches, defecated as they walked and whose legs, like those of Aue's sister, were caked in excrement. He then seeks an analogy between Una and the Hungarian-Jewish women awaiting deportation, before assimilating his sister with the partisan hanged in Kharkov, whose bowels, as Aue speculates, must have emptied at the moment of death. Aue's identification of Una and thus of himself with Holocaust victims becomes even more apparent if framed with Des Pres's notion of 'excremental assault' to which I referred in Chapter Three. It is noteworthy, however, that the dreams that stage Aue's undoing reverse the logic behind excremental violence as a mechanism designed to destroy the concentration camp inmates' last vestiges of self-worth. Whereas the moral and mental breakdown of the prisoners resulted from the malfunctioning of their bodies, Aue's physical collapse is caused by his psychological wounding.

Considering the designation of Auschwitz as 'the anus of the world', it is only expected that the defilement dreams should intensify during Aue's inspection of the camp.[158] In one nightmare, Littell's protagonist watches himself wandering about the camp in search of the source of the smell that is emanating from the crematoria and whose simultaneously enticing and repelling quality reflects the ambiguity of Aue's earlier responses to mass death. In the dream's second part, the protagonist soils his bed with large quantities of sperm and blood, and then fears an angry reaction from the camp's commandant, Rudolph Höss, who stands for

Aue's prohibitive and authoritarian father. Conversely, in a dream coinciding with a sharp decline in the protagonist's mental health during the 1944 deportation of Hungarian Jews, the father is fleshed out by Himmler. Adopting an affectionate and protective attitude towards Aue who appears here as a *Judelein* [a little Jew], the *Reichsführer* takes the protagonist by the hand as they walk amidst falling bombs and raging fires. That the nightmare conveys the protagonist's identification with the Nazis' youngest victims can be inferred from Aue's memories of an *Aktion* during which he witnessed the murder of Jewish children. While the protracted agony of a Jewish boy reminds Aue of his own masochistic childhood games, a little girl's quest for his protection after her mother has been shot wrenches his heart. The girl takes Aue by the hand and enquires in what he thinks to be Ukrainian '*Gdye mama?*' [Where's mummy?], in response to which Aue leads her up to a shooter and asks him to be gentle with her (B, 106–07; KO, 109).[159] In the light of Caruth's claim about the interconnectedness of victim's and killer's traumas, rather than inciting our empathy for Aue's mental torment, his nightmare brings to the fore the tragedy of the genocide's (youngest) victims.

In the nightmare that concludes the sequence of dreams featuring the paternal figure, we finally come across Herr Aue senior himself. This time, Aue-the-child is surrounded by soldiers wearing World War I uniforms and pointing sharp spears at him as he is emptying his bowels into the snow. Apart from the by now familiar purity-defilement binary, the dream contains two phallic symbols — the faeces and the spear — which, if interpreted through a Freudian lens, reveal Aue's simultaneous erotic desire for his father and fear of him.[160] To be understood more completely, the dream needs to be contextualised with the revelations regarding the crimes committed by Aue's father during the Great War. These revelations make the protagonist interrogate his own political allegiance, since his father is widely considered a pioneer of National Socialism. The much longed-for identification with the father is further impeded by the photograph accompanying the information about the father's wartime misconduct and featuring several horsemen in mismatched uniforms. Due to the photograph's grainy quality, Aue fails to ascertain which of the men is his father. All this unleashes an unprecedented crisis in the protagonist's mental and physical health, a crisis announced precisely by the described nightmare which restages (albeit in a distorted form) the scene in the photograph.

To Perry's category of the 'metro dreams' belong nightmares in which Aue misses train connections, gets lost in underground corridors, and is pursued by inspectors for fare-dodging.[161] To nuance Perry's reading of these visions as a reflection of the chaos overwhelming the Third Reich, I regard them as additionally alluding to the crucial role of transport in the Nazis' extermination project and so as a sign of Aue's war-induced traumatisation. Significantly, the metro dreams are triggered by the introduction of the Saurer gas van whose exhaust was used by the *Einsatzgruppen* for mass killings before gas chambers and crematoria came into use. The metro dreams become more frequent at Stalingrad where, in Aue's exhausted mind, fantasy and reality become increasingly blurred. In a scene with ambiguous narrative status,

Aue's friend and colleague Thomas suffers a seemingly fatal stomach injury. The injury happens at the very moment when Aue himself childishly insists on entering the metro in the hope of reliving his student days in Paris where, at night, he and his friends would roam the metro's empty tunnels. Instead of re-experiencing the joys of camaraderie and transgressive behaviour, be it in the form of trespassing or homosexual sex, Aue faces the gory spectacle of the network of Thomas's steaming intestines sprawled across snow-covered ground. The hallucinatory sequence restages the purity-defilement opposition structuring other manifestations of Aue's mental damage and, as in the case of the forest, transforms a site of youthful and erotically tinged games into a traumatogenic space.

In the third and final category of Aue's nightmares, Perry situates those with historical content. In one of these visions, Aue sees himself as a great Squid God ruling over a beautiful underwater city of white marble, who, one day, acting on a whim, expels all the citizens. The dream that Eaglestone deciphers as communicating the Holocaust's incomprehensibility and that Perry decodes as anticipating Aue's writerly vocation, squid being an ink-producing animal, can equally be interpreted as an ironic comment on the Nazis' tentacular territorial expansion, aspiration to control and perfection, and arbitrary ideas regarding who should belong to their world.[162] Such a reading follows from the nightmares that will torment Aue in Auschwitz and that, ironically, cast the concentration camp as the fulfilment of Nazi Germany's utopian fantasy of a perfectly homogenous and regulated society:

> Je parcourais [...] une cité immense, sans fin visible, d'une topographie monotone et répétitive, divisée en secteurs géométriques, et animée d'une circulation intense. Des milliers d'êtres allaient et venaient, entraient et sortaient des bâtiments identiques, remontaient des longues allées rectilignes, descendaient sous terre par des bouches de métro pour ressortir à un autre endroit, incessamment et sans but apparent. [...] je constatais que ces hommes et ces femmes ne se distinguaient les uns des autres par aucun trait particulier, tous avaient la peau blanche, les cheveux clairs, les yeux bleus, pâles, perdus, les yeux de Höss, les yeux de mon ancienne ordonnance Hanika. (B, 571)

> [I was travelling [...] through an immense city, without any visible end, its topography monotonous and repetitive, divided into geometric sectors, its way animated with an incessant flow. Thousands of beings came and went, entered and exited identical buildings, walked along long, straight avenues, plunged underground through subway entrances to emerge at some other place, constantly and without any apparent aim. [...] I noticed that the men and women weren't distinguished from one another by any special characteristic; they all had white skin, light-coloured hair, blue, pale, lost eyes, Höss's eyes, the eyes of my old orderly Hanika.] (KO, 620)

Hounded by bad dreams at night, during his days at Auschwitz Aue constantly yearns for a bath. The same craving seizes him after he witnesses an *Aktion*, executes an elder of a Caucasian Judaic tribe, or joins a shooting party. Like the protagonist's trips to swimming pools, these baths are indubitably meant to assuage his trauma, which they potentially achieve by helping Aue regress to the intrauterine life he longs for. The combination of the protagonist's systematic assimilation of Jewish suffering in voicing his anguish and the fact that his hallucinations and nightmares are structured by the purity-defilement dichotomy makes it also possible to relate his yearning for aquatic environment to the Judaic *mikvah* ritual. The ritual is indeed designed for achieving spiritual purity (*tumah*) and is performed, for example, after abnormal excretion of bodily fluids, such as semen or menstrual blood (*taharah*). Whether or not Aue (sub)consciously exploits Jewish religious tradition to alleviate the symptoms of his trauma, his submersions are of varied efficacy. For instance, his visit to the Pushkin Baths in Pyatigorsk after the execution of an old *Bergjude* [Mountain Jew] reinvigorates him and restores, even if only temporarily, his mental equilibrium. This positive effect may, however, be attributed to the therapeutic properties of sulphur baths and/or to the Oedipal satisfaction that Aue derives from the murder of a paternal figure. Another possible reason for Aue's sense of relief is the old *Bergjude*'s comforting conception of death as a return to the mother's womb. Conversely, the bath that Aue takes after witnessing the agony of Jewish children proves ineffective. Having made use of the water left boiling on the stove in a *shtetl* freshly emptied of its inhabitants, Aue continues to be tortured by the memory of those whose lives have been so brutally interrupted. His ultimate recognition of the inefficacy of water as an antidote to his trauma can be gleaned from the statement concluding his exposure of the Nazi crimes to a young German war widow: 'aucun bain, aucune piscine ne suffirait à laver de telles paroles' [no bath, no swimming pool would be enough to wash away such words] (B, 750; KO, 822).

Conclusions

Aue's pessimism regarding his ability to overcome his psychological wounding undoubtedly proceeds from the persistence of his symptoms into the post-war years. His last resort is writing, even if, resembling the graphite-stained lace produced by his factory, his text is full of gaps and covered in filth.[163] Nevertheless, voicing trauma can, as Rothe believes, minimise psychological dysfunction or, as LaCapra has it, counteract the tendency to sacralise trauma or convert it into a founding or sublime event.[164] Whether Aue's strategy has scripto-therapeutic and/or wider societal benefits is, however, beside the point.[165] Rather, Littell's imaginary reconstruction of the Holocaust from the perspective of a post-traumatic perpetrator is, as my discussion of *Les Bienveillantes* has demonstrated, intended to unsettle the narrative conventions dominant in the Holocaust's cultural representations which habitually adopt the survivor's point of view and invite 'easy empathy' or identification (in LaCapra's sense) with those persecuted. As an exemplar of historiographic metafiction, or rather of its traumatic strand identified by Gibbs, *Les Bienveillantes* inscribes the paradigmatic testimonial mode, yet simultaneously unsettles it by giving the floor to a perpetrator. The novel thus goes against the efforts, in Karyn Ball's formulation, to 'discipline the Holocaust', which means the exclusion of 'insufficiently rigorous', 'immoral', 'profane', or 'pornographic' representations of the Jewish genocide.[166] These efforts have occasioned the emergence of a highly conventionalised, not to say formulaic 'Holocaust metanarrative' which is victim-focused and which, according to Anna Hunter, leads to unchecked identifications with the victims' suffering and, ultimately, 'acts as a screen between the cultural imagination and the damaging effects of the Holocaust'.[167] To put it in Rose's terms, *Les Bienveillantes* challenges the straightjacket of 'Holocaust piety' or 'fascism of representation' which have served to preclude a full exploration of the 'why' of the murderous rage unleashed in the name of modernity and with the assistance of technological progress.[168] That said, Littell's novel does not share Rose's hope for a better understanding of the killer more generally, a hope that also undergirds studies of perpetrator trauma. Instead, it lays bare the limited cognitive potential of the encounter with violence, its attendant impotence to incite moral action, and, if Aue's case is anything to go by, the danger that exposure to atrocity may produce traumatisation and compassion fatigue.

Littell's other main reason for casting a post-traumatic perpetrator is, as I have argued, to render him less alien to twenty-first-century readers familiar with the reconceptualisation of history as trauma, or at least with a historiography that, under the influence of trauma and memory studies, has begun to accommodate the mental pain silenced by positivist historians. Put differently, by figuring Aue as a post-traumatic and therefore postmodern subject, Littell enables the readerly engagement necessary for his protagonist to become, to borrow Jenni Adams's formulation, 'a catalyst to ethical thought'.[169] More specifically, our 'unsettling empathy' with Littell's narrator is designed to make us reflect on our own positionality in relation to both the legacies of past atrocities and current violations of human rights. To put it in Morag's terms, *Les Bienveillantes* forces us to ponder our implication in the crimes carried out on our behalf, that is on 'the relationship between direct and indirect complicity in perpetration, which on the collective level are dialectic rather than exclusive of each other'.[170] Littell, however, as we have seen, adroitly controls the reader's affective investment in Aue with irony, with dreams and hallucinations that weaken his narrator's reliability, and with his protagonist's routine attempts to cannibalise Jewish suffering for the purpose of expressing his own mental pain. This strategy, as I have contended, has further purposes, including exposing the dangers of overidentification with victims and opening up an original narrative space for articulating the agony of those victims. I suggest therefore that, like in the case of the majority of the writers considered in this study, Littell's use of the narrative strategies characteristic of historiographic metafiction is both productive and ethical. More specifically, the novelist pays attention to a neglected subject perspective in discourses surrounding the Holocaust, encourages his readers to reconsider their own implication in the evil surrounding them, and, finally, strives to counteract 'Holocaust fatigue' with a text that is a cognitively and morally transformative experience.[171]

Notes to Chapter 4

1. Lacapra, *Writing History, Writing Trauma*, p. 78. Delbo, *Auschwitz, et après I*, p. 137. Leon R. Kass, 'The Wisdom of Repugnance', in *The Ethics of Human Cloning*, ed. by Leon R. Kass and James Q. Wilson (Washington, DC: AEI Press, 1998), pp. 3–60 (p. 19).

2. Laurent Binet, 'Exclusive: The Missing Pages of Laurent Binet's *HHhH*', *The Millions*, 16 April 2012 <https://themillions.com/2012/04/exclusive-the-missing-pages-of-laurent-binets-hhhh.html> [accessed 1 July 2018].
3. Grégoire Leménager, 'Génération Littell', *Le Nouvel Observateur*, 5 July 2010 <https://bibliobs.nouvelobs.com/romans/20100705.BIB5425/generation-littell.html> [accessed 5 July 2010].
4. Littell was deployed in war zones in Bosnia, Afghanistan, and Chechnya.
5. Georges Nivat, '*Les Bienveillantes* et les classiques russes', *Le Débat*, 144 (March-April 2007), 56–65; Pierre Nora and Jonathan Littell, 'Conversation sur l'histoire et le roman', *Le Débat*, 144 (March-April 2007), 25–44; Julia Kristeva, 'De l'abjection à la banalité du mal: conférence avec Jonathan Littell, Centre Roland Barthes, 24.04.2007' <http://www.kristeva.fr/abjection.html> [accessed 12 October 2008]; Claude Lanzmann, '*Les Bienveillantes*, vénéneuse fleur du Mal', *Le Journal du Dimanche*, 3114, 17 September 2006, p. 14; and 'Une documentation impeccable mais... Lanzmann juge *Les Bienveillantes*', *Le Nouvel Observateur*, 2185, 21–26 September 2006, p. 14. It needs noting that before applauding the novel, Lanzmann first expressed his scepticism.
6. Jorge Semprún, 'Ohne die Literatur Stirb die Erinnerung', *Frankfurter Allgemeine Zeitung*, 8 February 2008, p. 35.
7. For the German reception of the novel, see Wolfgang Asholt, 'A German Reading of the German Reception of *The Kindly Ones*', in *Writing the Holocaust Today: Critical Perspectives on Jonathan Littell's 'The Kindly Ones'*, ed. by Aurélie Barjonet and Liran Razinsky (Amsterdam: Rodopi, 2012), pp. 221–38; and Klaus Theweleit, 'On the German Reaction to Jonathan Littell's *Les Bienveillantes*', *New German Critique*, 36.1 (Winter 2009), 21–34; for the Polish reception, see Helena Duffy, 'La Bienveillance de la critique polonaise: An Analysis of the Polish Reception of *The Kindly Ones*', in *Writing the Holocaust Today*, ed. by Barjonet and Razinsky, pp. 239–56; for the French and American reception, see Richard J. Golsan, 'The American Reception of Max Aue', *SubStance*, 39.1 (2010), 174–83; and '*Les Bienveillantes* et sa réception critique: littérature, morale, histoire', in *L'Exception et la France contemporaine: histoire, imaginaire et littérature*, ed. by Marc Dambre and Richard J. Golsan (Paris: Presses Sorbonne Nouvelle, 2010), pp. 45–56.
8. Pierre-Émmanuel Dauzat, *Holocauste ordinaire: histoires d'usurpation. Extermination, littérature, théologie* (Paris: Bayard Centurion, 2007), pp. 57, 70, 29, 72, 59.
9. Paul-Éric Blanrue, *Les Malveillantes: enquête sur le cas Jonathan Littell* (Paris: Scali, 2006), p. 109. Édouard Husson, 'La Vraie Histoire des *Bienveillantes*', *L'Histoire*, 320 (May 2007), 6–19 (p. 18).
10. Édouard Husson and Michel Terestchenko, *Les Complaisantes: Jonathan Littell et l'écriture du mal* (Paris: De Guibert, 2007), p. 50.
11. Jonathan Littell, *Les Bienveillantes* (Paris: Gallimard, 2006), pp. 11, 13 (hereafter referenced as *B* in the main text); *The Kindly Ones*, trans. by Charlotte Mendel (London: Vintage, 2010), pp. 3, 5 (hereafter referenced as *KO* in the main text).
12. Between 29 and 30 September 1941, the Nazis murdered over thirty thousand people, mainly Jews, at Babi Yar.
13. Daniel Bougnoux, 'Max Aue, personage de roman', *Le Débat*, 144 (March-April 2007), 66–69; Theweleit, 'On the German Reaction of Jonathan Littell's *Les Bienveillantes*'. Susan Rubin Suleiman, 'When the Perpetrator Becomes a Reliable Witness: On Jonathan Littell's *Les Bienveillantes*', *New German Critique*, 106 (Winter 2009), 1–19 (p. 2).
14. Samuel Moyn compared Aue to Zelig and Forrest Gump: 'A Nazi Zelig: Jonathan Littell's *The Kindly Ones*', *Nation*, 3 December 2009 <https://www.thenation.com/article/nazi-zelig-jonathan-littells-kindly-ones/> [accessed 12 January 2010]. Cf. Eaglestone, *The Broken Voice*, p. 55. See also Jeremy Popkin, 'A Historian's View of *The Kindly Ones*', in *Writing the Holocaust Today*, ed. by Barjonet and Razinsky, pp. 187–200 (p. 198), and Dominick LaCapra, 'Historical and Literary Approaches to the "Final Solution": Saul Friedländer and Jonathan Littell', in *History Literature and Critical Theory* (Ithaca, NY: Cornell University Press, 2013), pp. 95–119 (pp. 100–01).
15. Jonathan Littell and Samuel Blumenfeld, 'Il faudra du temps pour expliquer ce succès', *Le Monde*, 17 November 2006 <https://www.lemonde.fr/livres/article/2006/11/16/jonathan-littell-il-faudra-du-temps-pour-expliquer-ce-succes_835008_3260.html> [accessed 25 April 2009]. The English translation of the interview can be found at <https://thekindlyones.wordpress.com/littell-interview-with-samuel-blumenfeld/> [accessed 25 April 2009].

16. The title is the initialism for 'Himmlers Hirn heißt Heydrich' [Hitler's Brain is Called Heydrich].
17. Binet, *HHhH*, p. 326; *HHhH*, Chapter 204. Aue's postmodern character has also been noted by Sanyal who calls him 'a discomfiting blend of postmodern picaresque and Bataillean abjection': *Memory and Complicity*, p. 189.
18. Binet, *HHhH*, p. 326; *HHhH*, Chapter 204. In the pages removed from the novel's final version, Binet thus describes Littell's protagonist, 'The SS veteran Aue is an intellectual who sleeps with his sister, kills his parents, actively participates in genocide, sucks off Robert Brasillach, survives a bullet in the head, is never separated from his Flaubert, and enjoys rolling in his shit from time to time. For a guy who is just like you and me, that is quite a list!': 'Exclusive'.
19. Nicole A. Sütterlin, 'History of Trauma Theory', in *The Routledge Companion to Literature and Trauma*, ed. by Colin Davis and Hanna Meretoja (New York: Routledge, 2020), pp. 11–22 (p. 11). This view is shared by Nancy K. Miller and Jason Tougaw, 'Introduction', in *Extremities: Trauma, Testimony and Community*, ed. by Nancy K. Miller and Jason Tougaw (Urbana: Illinois University Press, 2002), pp. 1–24 (p. 1); and J. Roger Kurtz, 'Introduction', in *Trauma and Literature*, ed. by J. Roger Kurtz (Cambridge: Cambridge University Press, 2018), pp. 1–17 (p. 1).
20. The novel has been categorised as 'literature of excess' by Liran Razinsky, 'History, Excess and Testimony in Jonathan Littell's *Les Bienveillantes*', *French Forum*, 33.3 (Fall 2008), 69–87; as historical fiction by Ned Curthoys, 'Evaluating Risk in Perpetrator Narratives: Resituating Jonathan Littell's *The Kindly Ones* as Historical Fiction', *Textual Practice*, 31.3 (2017), 457–75, and Popkin, 'A Historian's View of *The Kindly Ones*'; and as traumatic realism by Hanna Meretoja, 'Narrative Dynamics, Perspective Taking, and Engagement: Jonathan Littell's *Les Bienveillantes*', in *The Ethics of Storytelling: Narrative Hermeneutics, History and the Possible* (Oxford: Oxford University Press, 2018), pp. 217–54, and LaCapra 'Historical and Literary Approaches to the "Final Solution"', p. 95.
21. Alan Gibbs, *Contemporary American Trauma Narratives* (Edinburgh: Edinburgh University Press, 2014), p. 88.
22. Hutcheon, *A Poetics of Postmodernism*, pp. 11–12.
23. Ibid., p. 35.
24. For a discussion of Aue's marginality, see Anda Rădulescu, 'Max Aue de Jonathan Littell: un marginal des plus controversés', *Analele Universității din Craiova*, 1 (2012), 263–70, and Peter Tame, 'Lieux réels et lieux imaginaires dans *Les Bienveillantes*', in *'Les Bienveillantes' de Jonathan Littell*, ed. by Murielle Lucie Clément (Cambridge: OpenBook, 2010), pp. 213–30 (p. 218).
25. Christopher R. Browning, 'German Memory, Judicial Interrogation, Historical Reconstruction: Writing Perpetrator History from Postwar Testimony', in *Probing the Limits of Representation*, ed. by Friedländer, pp. 22–36 (p. 26).
26. Annette Wieviorka, *L'Ère du témoin* [1998] (Paris: Pluriel, 2013). Jürgen Matthäus, 'Historiography and the Perpetrators of the Holocaust', in *The Historiography of the Holocaust*, ed. by Stone, pp. 197–215. Holocaust historiography has been marked by the dearth of interest in perpetrators apart from a few studies dedicated to individual perpetrators, such as Hannah Arendt, *Eichmann in Jerusalem: A Report on the Banality of Evil* (New York: Penguin, 2006), Gita Sereny's biography of the Treblinka commandant Frantz Strangl, *Into the Darkness: An Examination of Conscience* (New York: Vintage, 1974), and some rare studies of groups of perpetrators, for example: Christopher R. Browning, *Ordinary Men: Reserve Police Battalion 101 and the Final Solution in Poland* (New York: HarperCollins, 1992); Ian Rich, *Holocaust Perpetrators of the German Police Battalions: The Mass Murder of Jewish Civilians, 1940–1942* (London: Bloomsbury, 2018); Wendy Lower, *Hitler's Furies: German Women in the Nazi Killing Fields* (New York: Vintage, 2014); Guenter Lewy, *Perpetrators: The World of Holocaust Killers* (Oxford: Oxford University Press, 2017).
27. Richard Crownshaw, 'Perpetrator Fictions and Transcultural Memory', *Parallax*, 17.4 (2011), 75–89 (p. 77). Cf. Erin McGlothlin, 'Theorizing the Perpetrator in Bernard Schlink's *The Reader* and Martin Amis's *Time's Arrow*', in *After Representation: Holocaust, Literature, and Culture*, ed. by R. Clifton Spargo and Robert M. Ehrenreich (New Brunswick, NJ: Rutgers University Press, 2008), pp. 210–21 (p. 213).

28. Suzanne Knittel, *The Historical Uncanny: Disability, Ethnicity, and the Politics of Holocaust Memory* (New York: Fordham University Press, 2014), p. 132. Cf. Browning, 'German Memory, Judicial Interrogation, Historical Reconstruction', p. 27. Gibbs, *Contemporary American Trauma Narratives*, p. 19. This blind spot has been remedied by the recently published *The Routledge International Handbook of Perpetrator Studies*, ed. by Susanne C. Knittel and Zachary J. Goldberg (New York: Routledge, 2020).
29. McGlothlin, 'Theorizing the Perpetrator', p. 213.
30. Littell and Blumenfeld, 'Il faudra du temps pour expliquer ce succès'. Hilary Earl, 'Nazi Perpetrators and the Law: Postwar Trials, Courtroom Testimony, and Debates about the Motives of Nazi War Criminals', in *The Routledge International Handbook*, ed. by Knittel and Goldberg, pp. 109–19 (p. 109).
31. Jonathan Littell and Assaf Uni, 'The Executioner's Song', *Haaretz*, 29 May 2008 <https://www.haaretz.com/1.4985953> [accessed 25 April 2009].
32. Susanne C. Knittel and Zachary J. Goldberg, 'Introduction', in *The Routledge International Handbook*, ed. by Knittel and Goldberg, pp. 1–4 (p. 1).
33. James Weller, *Becoming Evil: How Ordinary People Commit Genocide and Mass Killing* (Oxford: Oxford University Press, 2007), p. xvii.
34. Martin Amis, *Time's Arrow* (1991); Bernhard Schlink, *Der Vorleser* (1995); David Albarahi, *Götz and Meyer* (1998); Jodi Picoult, *The Storyteller* (2013); and Edgar Hilsenrath, *Der Nazi und der Friseur* (1977). For a more exhaustive survey of perpetrator literature, see Pettitt, *Perpetrators in Holocaust Narratives*, pp. 1–2.
35. Among germanophone perpetrator novels is Hans Kelson's *Der Tod der Widersachers* (1959).
36. Crownshaw, 'Perpetrator Fictions and Transcultural Memory', p. 75. Full-length studies of perpetrator fiction include Erin McGlothlin, *Second-generation Holocaust Literature: Legacies of Survival and Perpetration* (Rochester, NY: Camden House, 2006), pp. 143–227; Pettitt, *Perpetrators in Holocaust Narratives*; Rau, *Our Nazis*; and *Representing Perpetrators in Holocaust Literature and Film*, ed. by Jenni Adams and Sue Vice (London: Vallentine Mitchel, 2013).
37. Sanyal, *Memory and Complicity*, pp. 182–83.
38. Charlotte Lacoste, 'L'Ère du bourreau', *Esprit*, 347.8–9 (August-September 2008), 254–57; and 'La Fascination du mal: une nouvelle mode littéraire', *Cité*, 45 (2011), 168–74. Denis Peschanski, 'Les Bienveillantes, roman à controverse', *Libération*, 7 November 2006 <https://www.liberation.fr/evenement/2006/11/07/les-bienveillantes-roman-a-controverse_56610> [accessed 5 June 2008].
39. Crownshaw, 'Perpetrator Fictions and Transcultural Memory', p. 75.
40. Eric Leake, 'Humanizing the Inhumane: The Value of Difficult Empathy', in *Rethinking Empathy through Literature*, ed. by Meghan Marie Hammond and Sue J. Kim (New York: Routledge, 2014), pp. 175–85 (p. 175). Ezra DeKoven Ezrahi, 'Acts of Impersonation: Barbaric Spaces as Theatre', in *Mirroring Evil: Nazi Images/ Recent Art*, ed. by Norman L. Kleeblatt (New York: The Jewish Museum, 2001), pp. 17–38 (p. 19).
41. Leake, 'Humanizing the Inhumane', p. 175.
42. LaCapra, 'Historical and Literary Approaches to the "Final Solution"', p. 96; Meretoja, 'Narrative Dynamics, Perspective Taking, and Engagement', p. 245.
43. According to James E. Young, the perpetrator's perspective arouses the fear that it may 'reperpetrate' his crimes: 'Holocaust Documentary Fiction: The Novelist as Eyewitness', in *Writing and the Holocaust*, ed. by Berel Lang (New York: Holmes & Meier, 1988), pp. 200–15 (p. 209).
44. LaCapra, 'Historical and Literary Approaches to the "Final Solution"', p. 96.
45. See, for example, Erin McGlothlin, 'Narrative Perspective and the Holocaust Perpetrator: Edgar Hilsenrath's *The Nazi and the Barber* and Jonathan Littell's *The Kindly Ones*', in *The Bloomsbury Companion to Holocaust Literature*, ed. by Adams, pp. 159–77 (p. 162). For discussions surrounding empathy/ identification with Aue, see: LaCapra, 'Historical and Literary Approaches to the "Final Solution"', pp. 96–100; Curthoys, 'Evaluating Risk in Perpetrator Narratives'; Charlotte Lacoste, *Séductions du bourreau* (Paris: Presses universitaires de France, 2010); Suleiman, 'When the Perpetrator Becomes a Reliable Witness'; Susan Rubin Suleiman, 'Performing Perpetrator as Witness: Jonathan Littell's *Les Bienveillantes*', in *After Testimony: The Ethics and Aesthetics of*

Holocaust Narrative for the Future, ed. by Jakob Lothe, Susan Rubin Suleiman, and James Phelan (Columbus: Ohio State University Press, 2012), pp. 99–119; Steven Ungar, 'Out of the Past: The Perpetrator Portrait as Literary and Historical Exercise', *Yale French Studies*, 121 (2012), 185–203; Meretoja, 'Narrative Dynamics, Perspective Taking, and Engagement'; and Stephanie Bird, 'Perpetrator and Perpetration in Literature', in *The Routledge International Handbook of Perpetrator Studies*, ed. by Knittel and Goldberg, pp. 301–10.
46. Rita Felski, *Uses of Literature* (Oxford: Blackwell, 2008), p. 23.
47. Martha C. Nussbaum, *Love's Knowledge: Essays on Philosophy and Literature* (Oxford: Oxford University Press, 1990), p. 162.
48. LaCapra, *Writing History, Writing Trauma*, pp. 213, 27, n. 31.
49. Ibid., p. 78.
50. LaCapra, *Writing History, Writing Trauma*, p. 78; *History in Transit*, p. 125.
51. LaCapra, *Writing History, Writing Trauma*, pp. 41, 79.
52. Saira Mohamed, 'The Contours and Controversies of Perpetrator Trauma', in *The Routledge International Handbook of Perpetrator Studies*, ed. by Knittel and Goldberg, pp. 265–75 (p. 269). Cf. Sütterlin, 'History of Trauma Theory', p. 17, and Rothe, 'Popular Trauma Culture', p. 52.
53. McGlothlin, 'Narrative Perspective', p. 161. LaCapra, 'Historical and Literary Approaches to the "Final Solution"', p. 97.
54. LaCapra, *History in Transit*, p. 134. Cf. Carolyn J. Dean, *The Fragility of Empathy after the Holocaust* (Ithaca, NY: Cornell University Press, 2004). Dean quotes the position that our overexposure to atrocity, especially as mediated through visual images, desensitises us to the suffering of others (p. 7). She cites Barbie Zelizer's argument that new visual media generate 'moral habituation', which means that the more one sees the less one feels. Barbie Zelizer, *Remembering to Forget: Holocaust Memory through the Camera's Eye* (Chicago: Chicago University Press, 1999), p. 214.
55. Sigmund Freud defined 'traumatic neurosis' as 'a consequence of an extensive breach being made in the protective [psychic] shield against stimuli': 'Beyond the Pleasure Principle', in *The Standard Edition of the Complete Psychological Works of Sigmund Freud*, trans. and ed. by James Strachey and others, 24 vols (London: Hogarth Press, 1954–74), XVIII, 7–64 (p. 31).
56. Cathy Caruth, 'Introduction to Part I: Trauma and Experience', in *Trauma: Explorations in Memory*, ed. by Cathy Caruth (Baltimore, MD: Johns Hopkins University Press, 1995), pp. 3–12 (pp. 4–5); *Unclaimed Experience, Trauma, Narrative and History* (Baltimore, MD: Johns Hopkins University Press, 1996), p. 2.
57. See, for example, Chapter 3 'The Future of Trauma' in Lucy Bond and Stef Craps, *Trauma* (New York: Routledge, 2020), pp. 103–31; and Stef Craps, 'Beyond Eurocentrism: Trauma Theory in the Global Age', in *The Future of Trauma Theory: Contemporary Literary and Cultural Criticism*, ed. by Sam Durrant and Robert Eaglestone (New York: Routledge, 2013), pp. 45–62.
58. Anne Rothe, *Popular Trauma Culture: Selling the Pain of Others in the Mass Media* (New Brunswick, NJ: Rutgers University Press, 2011. For an overview of the development of the trauma concept, see, for example, Davis and Meretoja, 'Introduction', in *The Routledge Companion*, ed. by Davis and Meretoja, pp. 1–8; and Sütterlin, 'History of Trauma Theory'. See also Miller and Tougaw, 'Introduction', p. 2.
59. Nora, *Les Lieux de mémoire*. Shoshana Felman and Dori Laub, *Testimony: Crises of Witnessing in Literature, Psychoanalysis and History* (New York: Routledge, 1992).
60. James Berger, 'Review: Trauma and Literary Theory', *Contemporary Literature*, 38.3 (Autumn 1997), 569–82 (p. 572).
61. Caruth, 'Introduction to Part I', pp. 6–7.
62. Caruth, *Unclaimed Experience*, pp. 13, 16.
63. Crosthwaite, *Trauma, Postmodernism and the Aftermath of World War II*, p. 1. Naomi Morgenstern, 'The Primal Scene in the Public Domain: E. L. Doctorow's *The Book of Daniel*', *Studies in the Novel*, 35.1 (Spring 2003), 68–88 (p. 70).
64. Christa Schönfelder, *Wounds and Words: Childhood and Family Trauma in Romantic and Postmodern Fiction* (Bielefeld: Transcript, 2013), p. 66.
65. Amy J. Elias, *Sublime Desire: History and Post-1960s Fiction* (Baltimore, MD: Johns Hopkins University Press, 2001), p. 50.

66. Valentina Adami, *Trauma Studies and Literature: Martin Amis's 'Time's Arrow' as Trauma Fiction* (Frankfurt am Main: Peter Lang, 2008), p. 7.
67. David Gurevitz, 'Literature as Trauma: The Postmodern Option — Franz Kafka and Cormac McCarthy', in *Interdisciplinary Handbook of Trauma and Culture*, ed. by Ataria and others, pp. 3–26 (p. 3).
68. Raz Yosef, *The Politics of Loss and Trauma in Israeli Cinema* (New York: Routledge, 2011), p. 10.
69. Anne Whitehead, *Trauma Fiction* (Edinburgh: Edinburgh University Press, 2004), p. 3. Similarly, Roger Luckhurst attributes the limited critical attention to trauma fiction to the dominance of postmodernism as critical paradigm: *The Trauma Question* (New York: Routledge, 2008), p. 87.
70. Rothberg, *Traumatic Realism*, p. 186. One of the postmodern narratives Rothberg examines is Spiegelman's *Maus*. Rothberg's term 'traumatic realism' responds to the combination of ordinary and extreme elements that characterise the Nazi genocide, and thus reconciles the two opposing positions — the realist and the antirealist — dominating the discourses surrounding the Holocaust. By 'realist' approach Rothberg understands the positions of 'historians and others who assert the necessity of considering the Holocaust according to the "scientific" procedures and inscribing the events within continuous historical narratives'. Conversely, according to the 'antirealist' position, 'the Holocaust is not knowable or would be knowable only under radically new regimes of knowledge' (p. 4). Rothberg rejects the label 'traumatic postmodernism' on the grounds that, while obsessed with trauma, postmodernity shows it to have lost its disruptive edge. Also, while 'postmodernism is precisely what remains of the wounding of the referential and metahistorical claims', it aims to 'salvage an Americanized modernity over against the ruins of Europe' (p. 186).
71. Morgenstern, 'The Primal Scene in the Public Domain', p. 71.
72. Gibbs, *Contemporary American Trauma Narratives*, pp. 88, 89.
73. Ibid., pp. 89, 18. This paradox has also been observed by Luckhurst: *The Trauma Question*, p. 5. Cf. Bernhard Giesen, 'The Trauma of Perpetrators: The Holocaust as the Traumatic Reference of German National Identity', in *Cultural Trauma and Collective Identity*, ed. by Jeffrey C. Alexander and othes (Berkley: University of California Press, 2004), pp. 112–54 (p. 114).
74. Franz Fanon examines the case of a police inspector who consulted him to complain of classic symptoms of trauma resulting from torturing prisoners in Algeria. These symptoms included loss of appetite, nightmares, insomnia, and intolerance to noise. The man also chain-smoked and displayed uncharacteristically violent behaviour towards his wife and children, including a baby. He blamed his condition on 'the troubles', and thus on the Algerians themselves, and saw no reason for stopping his 'work': *Les Damnés de la terre* (Paris: François Maspero, 1961), pp. 202–04.
75. These two cases are addressed by Caruth in *Unclaimed Experience*: 'Introduction: The Wound and the Voice' (1–10), and by 'Unclaimed Experience: Trauma and the Possibility of History (Freud, *Moses and Monotheism*)' (pp. 11–25).
76. Mohamed, 'The Contours and Controversies of Perpetrator Trauma', p. 268.
77. Rachel M. MacNair, 'Psychological Reverberations for the Killers: Preliminary Historical Evidence for Perpetration-induced Traumatic Stress', *Journal of Genocide Research*, 3.2 (2001), 273–78; and *Perpetration-induced Traumatic Stress: The Psychological Consequences of Killing* (New York: Praeger, 2002), p. 206. MacNair notes that researchers of perpetrator trauma focus 'primarily on the experience and aftermath of severe deprivation, victimisation and personal life-threat' rather than on 'the moral conflict, shame, and guilt produced by taking life in combat'. Cf. Shira Maguen and others, 'The Impact of Killing in War on Mental Health Symptoms and Related Functioning', *Journal of Traumatic Stress*, 22.5 (2009), 435–43 (p. 435).
78. Rachel M. MacNair, 'Perpetration-induced Stress in Combat Veterans', *Peace and Conflict: Journal of Peace Psychology*, 8.1 (2002), 63–72 (p. 63).
79. Saira Mohamed, 'On Monsters and Men: Perpetrator Trauma and Mass Atrocity', *Columbia Law Review*, 115 (2015), 1157–1216 (p. 1167).
80. Raya Morag, 'Perpetrator Trauma and Current Israeli Documentary Cinema', *Camera Obscura*, 27.2 (2012), 93–132 (p. 93); and *Waltzing with Bashir: Perpetrator Trauma in the Cinema* (London: I. B. Tauris, 2013), p. 4.

81. Morag, *Waltzing with Bashir*, p. 4.
82. For an overview of this criticism, see Rothberg, *Multidirectional Memory*, pp. 88–90. The most vocal critics of Caruth's theory have been: Ruth Leys, *Trauma: A Genealogy* (Chicago: University of Chicago Press, 2000), pp. 292–97; Amy Novak, 'Who Speaks? Who Listens? The Problem of Address in Two Nigerian Trauma Novels', *Studies in the Novel*, 40.1–2 (2008), 31–51; and Sigrid Weigel, 'The Symptomatology of the Universalized Concept of Trauma: On the Failing of Freud's Reading of Tasso in the Trauma of History', trans. by Georgina Paul, *New German Critique*, 90 (Autumn 2003), 85–94.
83. Leys, *Trauma*, p. 297.
84. Anne Rothe, 'Irresponsible Nonsense: An Epistemological and Ethical Critique of Postmodern Trauma Theory', in *Interdisciplinary Handbook of Trauma and Culture*, ed. by Ataria and others, pp. 181–94 (pp. 191–92). To defend Caruth's strategy, David Quint points out that Caruth's intertwining of different traumas ties in with the 'overlapping and contradictory identities' in Tasso's poem: *Epic and Empire: Politics and Generic Form from Virgil to Milton* (Princeton, NJ: Princeton University Press, 1993), p. 244. This in turn indicates the multidirectionality of trauma which Rothberg detects in Fanon's identification of the same psychopathologies in victims and perpetrators of racism: *Multidirectional Memory*, p. 95.
85. Richard J. McNally, *Remembering Trauma* (Cambridge, MA: Harvard University Press, 2003), pp. 85–86. Amit Pinchevski, *Transmitted Wounds: Media and the Mediation of Trauma* (Oxford: Oxford University Press, 2019), p. 84.
86. Dominick LaCapra, *History and Memory after Auschwitz* (Ithaca, NY: Cornell University Press, 1998), pp. 41–20.
87. LaCapra, *History in Transit*, p. 113.
88. High-ranking Nazi official Erich von dem Bach-Zelewski is reputed to have said to Himmler, 'Look at the eyes of the men in this *Kommando*, how deeply shaken they are! These men are finished for the rest of their lives. What kind of followers are we training up here? Either neurotics or savages'. Robert Jay Lifton, *The Nazi Doctors: Medical Killings and the Psychology of Genocide* (New York: Basic Books, 1986), p. 159.
89. Browning, *Ordinary Men*, pp. 55–70. Raul Hilberg mentions frequent nervous breakdowns and systematic abuse of alcohol among members of the killing squads: *The Destruction of European Jews* (Chicago: Quadrangle Books, 1961), p. 218. Cf. Rudolph Hoess, *Commandant of Auschwitz: The Autobiography of Rudolph Hoess*, trans. by Constantine Fitzgibbon (London: Weidenfeld & Nicolson, 1959), p. 163. Jean-François Steiner discusses the psychological repercussions suffered by members of the killing squads: *Treblinka*, trans. by Helena Weaver (New York: Simon & Schuster, 1967), p. 73.
90. MacNair, 'Psychological Reverberations', p. 276. Historian Peter Padfield suspects that the account of Himmler's adverse reaction to a mass execution of Jews in Minsk in 1942, reported by his sub-commander Karl Wolff, may be fabrication: *Himmler: Reiseführer-SS* (London: Cassell, 2001), pp. 342–43.
91. Raul Hilberg, *The Politics of Memory: The Path of a Holocaust Historian* (Chicago: Ivan R. Dee, 1996), p. 61.
92. Mohamed, 'On Monsters and Men'; Susanne Schaal and others, 'Mental Health 15 Years after the Killings in Rwanda: Imprisoned Perpetrators of the Genocide Against the Tutsi versus a Community Sample of Survivors', *Journal of Traumatic Stress*, 26.4 (2012), 446–53; Morag, *Waltzing with Bashir*, and 'Perpetrator Trauma'; Michelle E. Anderson, 'Perpetrator Trauma, Empathic Unsettlement, and the Uncanny: Conceptualisations of Perpetrators in South Africa's Truth Commission Special Report', *Journal of Perpetrator Research*, 2.1 (2018), 95–118.
93. Morag, *Waltzing with Bashir*, pp. 6, 7–8.
94. Mohamed, 'The Contours and Controversies of Perpetrator Trauma', p. 271.
95. Mohamed, 'On Monsters and Men', p. 1165.
96. McNally, *Remembering Trauma*, pp. 106–07.
97. Bessel A. van der Kolk and Jose Saporta, 'Biological Response to Psychic Trauma', in *International Handbook of Traumatic Stress Syndromes*, ed. by John P. Wilson and Beverley Raphael (New York: Springer, 1993), pp. 28–48 (p. 41). McNally states that perpetrator amnesia is restricted to the most violent aspects of their crime: *Remembering Trauma*, p. 211.

98. Bruno Viard, 'Les Silences des *Bienveillantes*', in *'Les Bienveillantes' de Jonathan Littell*, ed. by Clément, pp. 73–86 (p. 82).
99. Caruth, *Unclaimed Experience*, pp. 8, 3.
100. Razinsky, 'History, Excess and Testimony in Jonathan Littell's *Les Bienveillantes*', p. 71. Elsewhere, Liran Razinsky states that Aue 'functions as an eye turned towards everything around him': 'Not the Witness We Wished for: Testimony in Jonathan Littell's *Kindly Ones*', *Modern Language Quarterly*, 71.2 (June 2020), 175–96 (p. 185, n. 20).
101. Gary Weissman, *Fantasies of Witnessing: Postwar Efforts to Experience the Holocaust* (Ithaca, NY: Cornell University Press, 2004), p. 133.
102. Mohamed, 'On Monsters and Men', p. 1173.
103. Meretoja, 'Narrative Dynamics, Perspective Taking, and Engagement', p. 221.
104. Sanyal, *Memory and Complicity*, pp. 189, 191. For a discussion of the confusion of victims and perpetrators, and of all kinds of perpetrators in Littell's novel, see Liran Razinsky, 'We Are All the Same: Max Aue, Interpreter of Evil', *Yale French Studies*, 121 (2012), 140–54, and 'The Similarity of Perpetrators', in *Writing the Holocaust Today*, ed. by Barjonet and Razinsky, pp. 47–60. For a critique of Littell's narrative strategy, see LaCapra, 'Historical and Literary Approaches to the "Final Solution"'.
105. These views have been championed, on the one hand, by Arendt's report on Eichmann's trial and, on the other, by Stanley Milgram's and Philip Zimbardo's Yale University and Stanford Prison experiments. The situationist approach has recently been challenged by, for example, Zachary J. Goldberg, who mobilises Kantian theory to stress the subject's free choice between adherence to morality and satisfaction of her 'sensuous desires': 'What's Moral Character Got to Do with It? Perpetrators and the Nature of Moral Evil', in *The Routledge International Handbook of Perpetrator Studies*, ed. by Knittel and Goldberg, pp. 74–83.
106. Cf. Earl, 'Nazi Perpetrators and the Law', p. 115.
107. Hendrik Lorenz speculates that Leontius is a necrophile and derives sexual pleasure from gaping at the corpses: 'The Analysis of the Soul in Plato's *Republic*', in *The Blackwell Guide to Plato's 'Republic'*, ed. by Gerasimos Santas (Oxford: Blackwell, 2006), pp. 146–55 (p. 152). Dean, *The Fragility of Empathy*, p. 4.
108. Dean, *The Fragility of Empathy*, pp. 20, 19, 21.
109. Ibid., p. 20.
110. Rose, *Mourning Becomes the Law*, p. 50. Dean, *The Fragility of Empathy*, p. 152, n. 51.
111. See Peter Kuon, 'From "Kitsch" to "Splatter": The Aesthetics of Violence in *The Kindly Ones*', in *Writing the Holocaust Today*, ed. by Barjonet and Razinsky, pp. 33–45 (pp. 33–34).
112. Angi Buettner, *Holocaust Images and Picturing Catastrophe: The Cultural Politics of Seeing* (Farnham: Ashgate, 2011), pp. 12, 4–5. Buettner cites American journalist Philip Gourevitch who, when writing about the Rwandan genocide, compares himself and his reader to Leontius. Gourevitch states that the reader already knows about the genocide and so it is not self-knowledge or moral lesson that she or he seeks in his book: 'Among the Dead', in *Disturbing Remains: Memory, History, and Crisis in the Twentieth Century*, ed. by Michael S. Roth and Charles G. Salas (Los Angeles: Getty Research Institute, 2001), pp. 63–76 (p. 65).
113. In an interview, Littell stated: 'Un écrivain pose des questions en essayant d'avancer dans le noir. Non pas vers la lumière, mais en allant encore plus loin dans le noir, pour arriver dans un noir encore plus noir que le noir de départ' [A writer asks questions as he tries to make his way through the darkness. Not towards the light, but further into the darkness, to arrive at a darkness even darker than his starting place]. Littell and Blumenfeld, 'Il faudra du temps pour expliquer ce succès'.
114. Felman and Laub (*Testimony*, p. 2), Dean (*The Fragility of Empathy*, p. 23), and LaCapra (*Writing History, Writing Trauma*, p. 102) all allow for the possibility of transmission of trauma.
115. Geoffrey Hartman, 'Public Memory and its Discontents', *Raritan: A Quarterly Review*, 13.4 (Spring 1994), 24–40 (p. 25).
116. As early as 1980, an article in *The New York Times Magazine* quoted Wiesel wondering whether a saturation point had been reached and whether mentioning the Holocaust produced apathy. A year later, Deborah Lipstadt made a similar comment, and in 1989 the education editor of *The*

New York Times, Joseph Berger, wrote of 'a general jadedness, even a fatigue of the Holocaust. The subject has lost its ability to shock, to stir wonder, to wring tears'. Paula E. Hyman, 'New Debate on the Holocaust', *The New York Times Magazine*, 14 September 1980 <https://www.nytimes.com/1980/09/14/archives/new-debate-on-the-holocaust-has-the-popularization-of-this-tragedy.html> [accessed 1 April 2020]; Deborah E. Lipstadt, 'Invoking the Holocaust', *Judaism*, 30.3 (Summer 1981), 335–43 (p. 342); Joseph Berger, 'The Peril of Vulgarisation', *Dimensions: A Journal of Holocaust Studies*, 5.1 (1989), 3–6 (p. 4). For a more recent discussion of 'Holocaust fatigue', see Samantha Mitschke, 'The Sacred, the Profane, and the Space in Between: Site-specific Performance at Auschwitz', *Holocaust Studies*, 22.2–3 (2016), 228–43. For a discussion of compassion fatigue, see Dean, *The Fragility of Empathy*; for the use of the Holocaust as a metaphor for other catastrophes and atrocities, see Buettner, *Holocaust Images and Picturing Catastrophe*.
117. Caruth, *Unclaimed Experience*, p. 3.
118. Ibid., p. 95.
119. Shoshana Felman, *The Juridical Unconscious: Trials and Traumas in the Twentieth Century* (Cambridge, MA: Harvard University Press, 2002), pp. 173–74.
120. For a discussion of the creation of Soviet War Heroes, including that of Zoya Kosmodemyanskaya, see Helena Duffy, *World War II in Andreï Makine's Historiographic Metafiction: No One is Forgotten, Nothing is Forgotten* (Amsterdam: Brill, 2018), pp. 102–04. Post-Soviet sources indicate that Kosmodemyanskaya may have been killed by Soviet peasants rather than the Germans for having torched a stable full of horses. Elena L. Seniavskaia, 'Heroic Symbols: Reality and Mythology of the War', *Russian Studies in History*, 37.1 (Summer 1988), 61–87 (pp. 76–78).
121. Littell and Blumenfeld, 'Il faudra du temps pour expliquer ce succès'.
122. For a discussion of the 'iconic' character of traumatic memories, see Leys, *Trauma*, pp. 245–54.
123. Caruth, 'Introduction to Part I', p. 5
124. Sanyal, *Memory and Complicity*, p. 195.
125. Michael Barenbaum, 'Holocaust: European History', *Encyclopaedia Britannica* <https://www.britannica.com/event/Holocaust> [accessed 6 July 2017].
126. See Derrida's reading of Celan's poetry in 'Poetics and Politics of Witnessing'.
127. Martin Harries, *Forgetting Lot's Wife: On Destructive Spectatorship* (New York: Fordham University Press, 2007), p. 8.
128. Ibid., p. 7.
129. Miri Rozmarin, 'Staying Alive: Matricide and the Ethical-political Aspects of Mother-daughter Relations', *Studies in Gender and Sexuality*, 17.4 (2016), 242–53 (pp. 248–49). Janice Haaken, *Pillar of Salt: Gender, Memory, and the Perils of Looking Back* (New Brunswick, NJ: Rutgers University Press, 1998), p. 1; and Alison Stone, 'Stealing Lot's Wife and Daughters from the Bible: A Response to Rozmarin's "Staying Alive"', *Studies in Gender and Sexuality*, 17.4 (2016), 254–61(p. 257).
130. Levi, *The Drowned and the Saved*, p. 64.
131. Rozmarin, 'Staying Alive', p. 249.
132. Berger, 'Review', p. 570.
133. I pursue this argument in my essay 'Space of Trauma/ Space of Freedom'.
134. Razinsky, 'The Similarity of Perpetrators', p. 53; Eric Sandberg, '"This Incomprehensible Thing": Jonathan Littell's *The Kindly Ones* and the Aesthetics of Excess', *The Cambridge Quarterly*, 43.3 (2014), 231–55 (p. 243).
135. Michael Imort, 'Wilhelmine Forestry and the Forest as a Symbol of Germandom', in *Germany's Nature: Cultural Landscapes and Environmental History*, ed. by Thomas Lekan and Thomas Zeller (New Brunswick, NJ: Rutgers University Press, 2005), pp. 55–80 (pp. 57–59). Cf. Boria Sax, *Animals in the Third Reich: Pets, Scapegoats, and the Holocaust* (New York: Continuum, 2000), p. 15.
136. Theodor Adorno, *Minima Moralia: Reflections from Damaged Life*, trans. by E. F. N. Jephcott [1951] (London: Verso, 2005), p. 105.
137. Ditte-Marie Munch-Jurisic, 'Perpetrator Disgust: A Morally Destructive Emotion', in *Emotions and Mass Atrocity: Philosophical and Theoretical Explorations*, ed. by Thomas Brudholm and Johannes Lang (Cambridge: Cambridge University Press, 2018), pp. 142–61 (p. 146).

138. Arendt, *Eichmann in Jerusalem*, p. 106.
139. Kass, 'The Wisdom of Repugnance'.
140. Munch-Jurisic, 'Perpetrator Disgust', p. 154.
141. Ibid.
142. Eric J. Sundquist, 'Mr. Styron's Planet', in *Shades of the Planet: American Literature as World Literature*, ed. by Wai Chee Dimock and Lawrence Buell (Princeton, NJ: Princeton University Press, 2007), pp. 103–40 (p. 116).
143. Arendt, *Eichmann in Jerusalem*, p. 106.
144. Sanyal, *Memory and Complicity*, pp. 195, 197, 187.
145. *Der Nazi und der Friseur* was originally written in German, but, having failed to find a German publisher, was first published in English as *The Nazi Who Lived as a Jew* (1977), later republished as *The Nazi and the Barber* (2013).
146. Otto Rank, *The Trauma of Birth* [1924] (London: Routledge, 1999), pp. 35–36. Since symptoms of anxiety bear traces of asphyxiation, confinement, and constriction, Rank identified the experience of birth as the primary trauma.
147. Ibid., p. 36.
148. The dreams of the Great War veterans challenged Freud's theory that humans are driven by the 'pleasure principle' (the subject's search for the elimination of tension). They led him to advance the existence of another force which is the self-destructive death drive aiming to return the organism to its earlier, non-organic form: 'Beyond the Pleasure Principle', pp. 13–14. Caruth, 'Introduction to Part I', pp. 7–11.
149. Bessel A. van der Kolk and Onno Van der Hart, 'The Intrusive Past: The Flexibility of Memory and the Engraving of Trauma', in *Trauma: Explorations in Memory*, ed. by Caruth, pp. 158–82 (p. 172); McNally, *Remembering Trauma*, p. 108–11.
150. For a discussion of conflicting positions regarding posttraumatic nightmares, see Leys, *Trauma*, pp. 231–45.
151. Edith Perry, 'Rêves et fantasmes dans *Les Bienveillantes*', in *'Les Bienveillantes' de Jonathan Littell*, ed. by Clément, pp. 125–39 (p. 128).
152. Klaus Theweleit, *Male Fantasies. I: Women, Floods, Bodies, History*, trans. by Stephen Conway (Cambridge: Polity Press, 1987).
153. Perry, 'Rêves et fantasmes dans *Les Bienveillantes*', p. 133. This hypothesis explicitly underpins Littell's study of the Belgian fascist, Léon Degrelle. Jonathan Littell, *Le Sec et l'humide* (Paris: Gallimard, 2008).
154. Jenni Adams, 'Reading (as) Violence in Jonathan Littell's *The Kindly Ones*', in *Representing Perpetrators*, ed. by Adams and Vice, pp. 25–46 (p. 28).
155. Ibid., p. 29. Luc Rasson, 'How Nazis Undermine Their Own Point of View', in *Writing the Holocaust Today*, ed. by Barjonet and Razinsky, pp. 97–110.
156. Rasson, 'How Nazis Undermine Their Own Point of View', p. 107.
157. Aue expresses the desire to marry Una when the siblings meet in Zurich. He does so by citing a description of a Jewish wedding in Proust's *Jean Santeuil*. He also breaks a wine glass, which can be regarded as part of the Jewish wedding ritual. His reunion with Una results in the conception of the twins, Tristan and Orlando. Aue's wish is confirmed by the long hallucinatory vision that follows his head injury.
158. Wiesław Kielar, *Anus Mundi: Five Years in Auschwitz*, trans. by Susanne Flatauer (London: Penguin, 1982).
159. As Cyril Aslanov points out, Aue is speaking Russian, not Ukrainian: 'Visibility and Iconicity of the German Language in *The Kindly Ones*', in *Writing the Holocaust Today*, ed. by Barjonet and Razinsky, pp. 61–74 (p. 68).
160. In his analysis of the Wolf-Man's case, Freud identified the child's faecal column with the father's penis, and the child's defecation as a sign of his excitation. Sigmund Freud, 'From the History of Infantile Neurosis', *Standard Edition of the Complete Psychological Works of Sigmund Freud*, trans. and ed. by Strachey, XVII, pp. 7–122 (p. 80).
161. Perry, 'Rêves et fantasmes dans *Les Bienveillantes*', p. 133.
162. Eaglestone, *The Broken Voice*, p. 57; Perry, 'Rêves et fantasmes dans *Les Bienveillantes*', p. 139.

163. For a discussion of the two opposing positions on the possibilities and benefits of voicing trauma, see Leigh Gilmore, *The Limits of Autobiography: Trauma and Testimony* (Ithaca, NY: Cornell University Press, 2001), pp. 6–7.
164. Rothe, 'Irresponsible Nonsense', p. 185. LaCapra, *History in Transit*, p. 123.
165. Suzette A. Henke, *Shattered Subjects: Trauma and Testimony in Women's Life-writing* (Basingstoke: Palgrave Macmillan, 1998), p. xxii. The term 'scripto-therapeutic' designates the recovery and reconstruction of traumatic events so as to make sense of them.
166. Karyn Ball, *Disciplining the Holocaust* (New York: State University of New York Press, 2008), p. 8.
167. Anna Clare Hunter, '"To Tell the Story": Cultural Trauma and Holocaust Metanarrative', *Holocaust Studies*, 25.1–2 (2019), 12–27 (p. 13).
168. Rose, *Mourning Becomes the Law*, p. 41.
169. Adams, 'Reading (as) Violence in Jonathan Littell's *The Kindly Ones*', p. 28.
170. Morag, *Waltzing with Bashir*, p. 7.
171. Mitschke, 'The Sacred, the Profane, and the Space in Between', p. 231.

CHAPTER 5

'The Dog and the Wolf':
Philippe Claudel's *Le Rapport de Brodeck* as a Postmodern Beast Fable

We Germans, who are the only people in the world who have a decent attitude towards animals, will also assume a decent attitude towards these human animals. But it is a crime against our own blood to worry about them.
— HEINRICH HIMMLER, speech given to the
SS-Ausbildungslager, Sennheim, 5 June 1943

Ce que l'animal est privé de la possibilité de témoigner selon les règles humaines d'établissement du dommage, et qu'en conséquence tout dommage est comme un tort et fait de lui une victime *ipso facto*.

[This is because the animal is deprived of the possibility of bearing witness according to the human rules for establishing damages, and as a consequence, every damage is like a wrong and turns it into a victim *ipso facto*.]
— JEAN-FRANÇOIS LYOTARD, *Le Différend*[1]

Introduction

The beast fable that has inspired the title of this chapter tells the story of a dog that offers regular food to a starving wolf in exchange for his loyalty to a human master. Seeing the mark that a collar has left on the dog's neck, the wolf decides that it is better to go hungry and to be free than to be a fat slave. Aesop's fable 'The Dog and the Wolf' constitutes one of the intertexts of Philippe Claudel's *Le Rapport de Brodeck* (henceforth *Le Rapport*) whose characteristically postmodern parodic engagement with the genres of the fairy tale and the fable is the focus of this chapter. More specifically, in the following pages I will examine the epistemological, ethical, and political implications of *Le Rapport*'s playful and subversive dialogue with the genres that, while being associated with children's literature, programmatically shun realism and aspire to assert ahistorical and universal meanings. What interests me in particular is the import of Claudel's use of the allegorical method for our understanding of the philosophical sources of the Holocaust, of its lasting legacies, and of the man-animal divide as an ontological structure legitimating our exploration and ill-treatment of both other humans and non-human animals.

Published in 2007 to great critical acclaim, *Le Rapport* is the ninth novel of a prolific writer and filmmaker who, without being Jewish, believes that all post-war literature must address the Holocaust in one way or another.² Claudel's dramatisation of the Nazi genocide of the Jews in *Le Rapport* is also symptomatic of his conception of war as a condition that is both ongoing and revelatory,³ and of his sustained interest in the two world wars which have punctuated the landscape of his native Lorraine with military cemeteries and monuments.⁴ More broadly, *Le Rapport* signals Claudel's long-standing commitment to representations of socially marginalised and persecuted alterity, manifest through his attention to the stigmatisation of ex-convicts, to the plight of immigrants, and to the suffering of patients with physical or mental illness.⁵

As anticipated by the novel's close intertextual relationship with 'The Dog and the Wolf', *Le Rapport* is set in a realm of fable, which means that its figuration of the Nazi genocide is located outside history. Among the few temporal markers is a recently ended armed conflict which bears many hallmarks of World War II, and an earlier war whose description brings to mind World War I. As vague as the novel's temporal setting is its location: the action takes place in a nameless village nestling in a mountainous and sylvan landscape and bordering a powerful germanophone country. The novel opens with the assassination of an enigmatic and benevolent newcomer to the village, nicknamed in the local dialect 'de Anderer', whose troubling alterity has undermined the efforts of the local men to forget their persecution of ethnic difference in the context of their wartime collaboration with the occupying forces. To explain the murder to the authorities, the villagers ask Brodeck, the best educated man in the village, who possesses a typewriter and normally reports to the local administration on the changes in the fauna and flora, to produce an exonerating account of the *Anderer*'s stay in the village. Significantly, the killing of the stranger replicates the persecution that during the war Brodeck himself suffered, and Brodeck's collusion with the stranger's killers repeats his own enforced collaboration with his oppressors. This becomes evident from the analeptic passages that tell us of Brodeck's arrival in the village as a child refugee in the company of an old woman, Fédorine, of his studies in the capital of the neighbouring country, of his meeting with his future wife, Émelia, and of the rise of racial violence that put an end to Brodeck's stay abroad. The brutal attack on the 'Fremdër' community, as the novel calls those with uncharacteristically dark hair and swarthy complexion, which the protagonist witnessed and whose characterisation is modelled on *Kristallnacht*, is followed by the invasion of Brodeck's country by the 'Fratergekeime', so-named on account of their linguistic and cultural affinity with the protagonist's compatriots.⁶ As a *Fremdër*, Brodeck is denounced by his neighbours and deported to a camp whose wrought-iron gate and daily selections and executions inevitably suggest Auschwitz. And so, while the *Fremdër* clearly stand for the Jews, the *Fratergekeime* are thinly disguised Nazis. Led by Captain Adolf Buller, whose name shows phonological kinship with that of Adolf Hitler, they march under banners reminiscent of the red-and-white flags marked with a swastika, and use coercive methods that invoke those of the actual Nazis.

To examine Claudel's simultaneous use and contestation of the allegorical method, I will read *Le Rapport* through two connected theoretical lenses. The first of these is constituted by the works of French postmetaphysical philosophers who have questioned the hierarchies structuring our relationship with the animal world and have often done so with reference to conventional narrative genres, including the fable. Derrida, for example, has exposed the fable as complicit in our centuries-long abuse of animals, and Lyotard, as evident from one of this chapter's epigraphs, has posited the animal as the ultimate victim of the 'differend'.[7] Levinas has in turn endeavoured to wrest the dog from its enslavement by the categories of human intelligibility, and Deleuze and Guattari have conceptualised man's accommodation of minoritarian identities as 'becoming-animal'. My other theoretical perspective is Hutcheon's theory of parody as a quintessentially postmodern narrative mode which, by 'signal[ling] ironic difference at the heart of similarity', tallies with her conception of postmodernism as a self-contradictory enterprise that participates in conventional values and discursive models only to undermine them.[8] It is important to stress that Hutcheon dissociates eighteenth-century parody from its postmodern avatar whose range of intent is broader, embracing irony, scorn, and playfulness.[9] Contemporary parody therefore repeats with a critical distance, marking difference rather than similarity,[10] and does so with a view to enabling a disruptive confrontation with a discursive world of socially defined meaning systems, both past and present.[11] More generally, Hutcheon inscribes the postmodern revival of parody into the rejection of the Romantic emphasis on the originality of art and of the consequent efforts of Romantic artists to mask any sources of their work through 'cunning cannibalisation'.[12] In contrast, postmodern art openly admits its incorporation and recontextualisation of past narratives, which it often undertakes in a meta-discursive environment.[13] Significantly, Hutcheon aligns the disdain of postmodernism for the Romantic veneration of originality with the 'current crisis of the entire notion of the subject as a coherent and continuous source of signification'.[14] It is this connection between postmodernism's taste for parody and its interrogation of 'the empiricist, rationalist, humanist assumptions of our cultural systems, including those of science', that is key to my reading of *Le Rapport*'s critical relationship with genres that have been a conduit for humanist ideology.[15] Having known their heyday in the eighteenth and nineteenth centuries, the fable and the fairy tale have championed human exceptionalism and social hierarchies. Presented as natural constructs, these have sanctioned the othering not only of non-humans, but also of ethnic, religious, sexual, and gender subcategories of humanity.

The Holocaust Fairy Tale

Le Rapport's parodic approach to established narrative conventions is recognisable, firstly, in its critical engagement with the testimonial mode.[16] However, while testimony seems a more likely choice of a narrative model for Holocaust fiction, a novel about the Nazis' attempted annihilation of European Jewry that deploys fabular structural devices and themes may appear ethically questionable. This is because such a novel unites two incompatible narrative modes — history and fairy tale — where the former demands strict adherence to truth and accurate interpretation of facts, while the latter can be seen, as Kevin Paul Smith puts it, as a 'simple stor[y] that functions in the vernacular as a synonym for lies'.[17] Furthermore, the programmatic rejection of realism, which fairy tales and fables achieve through their inherent universality and timelessness, and rhetorical devices such as zoomorphism, may seem at odds with the events of the Nazi genocide. As discussed in Chapter Four, these events are often thought to be firmly rooted in a specific spatio-temporal setting and therefore best suited to realist representations. In other words, the emplotment of the Holocaust as a fairy tale may be seen as compromising the specificity of a historical reality that some believe to be unique or at least exceptional.[18] For instance, Elizabeth Schreiber regards fiction about the Nazi Judeocide as anchored in time and place more strongly than any other literature, and Sidra DeKoven Ezrahi believes that Holocaust writers see themselves chiefly as 'witnesses or transmitters of historical events that are fixed in time and space'.[19]

These anxieties can be countered with a number of arguments. Firstly, animalisation of humans can be an apt rhetorical device in narrativisations of a genocide anticipated by the expulsion of certain ethnic and social groups from under the protective umbrella of humanity. Kári Driscoll observes that Holocaust memory has been haunted by the language of animality, with perpetrators being dubbed 'beasts' and 'butchers', and victims being compared to 'lambs going to the slaughter' and to 'cattle'.[20] Secondly, the spatio-temporal obliqueness characterising fairy tales and fables can be enlisted in the reinsertion of the Nazi genocide into the continuum of man's oppression of otherness, be it human or non-human. Thirdly and finally, stories whose popularity coincided with the glorification of man's intellectual and moral superiority over both animals and some fellow men can offer a suitable framework for an interrogation of the philosophical origins of the Holocaust in the rationalism of the Enlightenment. Put differently, fables and fairy tales can enable a questioning of the legitimacy of the ontological divide between man and animal, and a meditation on the responsibility of this divide for man's ill treatment of non-humans and of humans who fail to conform to the normative standard provided by man.

Revisionist retellings of fairy tales are not uncommon, especially among postmodern writers; however, these most frequently pertain to gender and sexuality.[21] Less often postmodern fairy tales, which have also been called 'antitales', serve to address concerns such as war, social injustice, ideological conflicts, and trauma.[22] As for the Holocaust, its events have been retold with recourse to fabular themes and devices by writers such as Jerzy Kosinski, whose *Painted Bird* (1965) teems with demons, witches, and giants; Spiegelman, whose *Maus* resorts to zoomorphic recasting of humans as animal species; Yaffa Eliach, whose *Hasidic Tales of the Holocaust* (1988) abound in fanciful miracles; and Jonathan Safran Foer, whose magical realist aesthetics in *Everything Is Illuminated* (2002) serve to question the recoverability of the past.[23] Among narratives with a more direct relationship to fairy tales are Jane Yolen's *Briar Rose* (1992) which retells the slaughter of Jews at the Chełmno camp with references to *Little Red Riding Hood*, *Bluebeard's Castle*, *Hansel and Gretel*, *Pied Piper of Hamelin*, and, naturally, *Sleeping Beauty*. Further examples are provided by Chava Rosenfarb's short story 'Royt Feigele' (2004), Judy Budnitz's *If I Told You Once* (1999), and Louise Murphy's *The True Tale of Hansel and Gretel* (2003).[24] In the German context, where conjoining fairy-tale motifs with the subject of the Holocaust became acceptable in the 1970s,[25] we find Edgar Hilsenrath's *Der Nazi und der Friseur*, Günter Grass's *Die Rättin* (1986) and *Die Blechtrommel*, and Ruth Klüger's *weiter leben: eine Jugend* (1992).[26] In 1997, Roberto Benigni extended the use of fairy-tale narrative strategies to Holocaust cinema with *La vita è bella* which introduces itself as 'a simple story but not an easy one to tell. Like a fable, there is sorrow, and, like a fable, it is full of wonder and happiness.'[27]

The existing studies of a Holocaust literature that seeks inspiration in fabular stories agree that fairy tales can provide an antidote to the reported unspeakability of the Nazi genocide.[28] Jenni Adams considers a departure from realism as a possible answer to 'the opaqueness of the events and the opaqueness of language as such', and Judith Kerman welcomes it in the light of the incredulity with which the Jews themselves received the rumours of persecution.[29] Kerman illustrates her point with Yolen's *The Devil's Arithmetic* (1988) where the news of the unfolding mass killings is qualified as 'fairy tales'.[30] The widely postulated unavailability of the horrors of the Holocaust to language invites its reframing as a traumatogenic event which, in Adams's formulation, 'cannot be known in any existential or experiential sense, as it is incompatible with linguistic or narrative knowledge'.[31] For both Adams and Elizabeth Baer, the inherently traumatic character of Holocaust memory constitutes an argument for using fabular imagery and structures; Baer, for example, posits the capacity of anti-realist narratives, and especially of fairy tales, to foreground both the survivor's trauma and the resistance of traumatic memories to discourse.[32] María Jesús Martínez-Alfaro goes further by postulating the therapeutic potential of fairy tales which 'symbolically reflect our unconscious fears and desires'.[33] She cites the use by psychoanalysts of metaphoric expressions borrowed from myth and folk tales, and quotes Jack Zipes's observation that fairy tales rely on metaphors to conquer the terror emanating from specific historical struggles against bestial and barbaric forces.[34]

As well as verbalising and possibly countering trauma, fairy tales may enable a better understanding of the Holocaust since in these tales overpowering evil finds embodiments in villains, while fairy-tale heroes are faced by an uncanny and incomprehensible world. In Margarete Landwehr's terms, fairy tales provide 'powerful and evocative metaphors that portray unspeakable horrors, a role that everyday language cannot fulfil as successfully'.[35] Similarly, Peter Arnds notes that, due to their key attributes — violence and unreality — fairy tales lend themselves 'to the representation of [...] extreme political violence and the victim's loss of reality'.[36] Landwehr identifies fairy tales as potential templates for Holocaust narratives also due to their focus on ordinary people with fears and weaknesses; for her, 'the insignificant, the neglected, the helpless' are a mirror of the oppressed Jews with 'their marginalized and diasporic identity'. At the same time, the anxiety of confronting overwhelming and destructive natural forces staged by fairy tales conveys some of the terror felt by Jewish victims.[37]

In the same vein, Baer observes that Holocaust narratives imitate fairy tales where 'the oppressed [...] usually win in the end over the wealthy, royalty, and the evil presences in the world'.[38] The formulaicity shared by fairy tales and Holocaust narratives highlighted by the critic's comment has encouraged Anna Hunter to state that, notwithstanding the apparent incongruity of the Jewish catastrophe and the fabular world, the fairy tale and the 'Holocaust story' are both conventionalised canons with certain similarities.[39] In contrast, Martínez-Alfaro believes in the ability of fairy-tale motifs to undermine the 'sanctioned Holocaust metanarrative'.[40] As opposed to the formula that relies on the unproblematic good/ evil binary and, correspondingly, ushers readers into an easy empathy with the morally irreproachable victim, Holocaust stories inspired by fairy tales unsettle this pattern by undermining clear-cut dichotomies, such as that of victim/ victimiser, and by forestalling our identification with the protagonist through the effects of silence and secrets.[41]

Yet another possible advantage of using fabular motifs in Holocaust fiction is their potential for bridging the epistemological gap that, according to Philippe Codde, separates third-generation Holocaust writers from the events they narrativise.[42] Hunter adds that, by resorting to fairy-tale motifs, these authors can overcome their perceived lack of authority and, by framing the Nazi genocide with the familiar, can facilitate the engagement of their readers with a past that lies outside their experience and appears unknowable. At the same time, fabular structures can provide a welcome screen separating the depicted horrors from readers whose textual engagement depends on their ability to decipher the signs encoded within fabulous narrative devices and motifs.[43]

Magical Numbers, Archetypal Characters, and Typical Chronotopes in *Le Rapport*

Smith's structuralist taxonomy of the intertextual uses of fairy tales in contemporary literature provides a useful framework for a discussion of Claudel's complex engagement with the genre. In *Le Rapport*, we find, among other types of references, 'allusions', which Smith defines as implicit references to a fairy tale in the text, and which take the form of numbers thought to be magical, such as three, six, and seven. For instance, when describing events reminiscent of *Kristallnacht*, Claudel pictures *three* men who beat to death an elderly *Fremdër*. In the concentration camp where Brodeck is held, *three* crows assist at the daily hanging and in the sties belonging to the village mayor pigs are separated into *three* distinct categories. As in fairy tales where episodes tend to repeat themselves, the *Anderer*'s accusatory lamentations can be heard on *three* consecutive nights following the slaughter of his horse and donkey by the villagers.[44] As for the other two numbers, seven men decide Brodeck's handover to the *Fratergekeime*, and Brodeck's journey to the concentration camp lasts six days.

As well as with allusions, *Le Rapport* teems with 're-visions' ('putting a new spin on an old tale'), 'fabulations' ('crafting an original fairy tale'), 'architectural/ chronotopic' references ('fairytale setting/ environment'), and 'metafictional comments'.⁴⁵ Furthermore, Claudel's novel refers to fairy tales directly by describing Brodeck as 'le voyageur de la fable' [the traveller in the fable] and characterising the *Anderer* as someone who has come out of 'une vieille fable pleine de poussière et de mots perdus' [a dusty old fable full of obsolete words].⁴⁶ Similarly, when describing the racially motivated attacks modelled on *Kristallnacht*, Claudel's narrator attributes to the streets lined with shattered glass 'une dimension scintillante, merveilleuse et féerique' [a sparkling, marvelous, magical dimension, like the setting of a fairy tale] (*RB*, 224; *B*, 183).

More visibly than with other fairy-tale traditions, *Le Rapport* engages with the Grimm Brothers' *Children's and Household Tales* (1812), a choice that befits the novel's Germanic aura. Claudel's particular interest in the Grimms' tales may also be linked to their entanglement in the rise and fall of Nazism.⁴⁷ According to Arnds, the Nazis misappropriated the tales by turning them into 'the prime vehicle in supporting their Aryan policies', which in 1945 resulted in their ban by the Allied forces who condemned their 'nasty "Teutonic" nature'.⁴⁸ That said, Florian Weber's novel *Grimms Erben* (2012) demonstrates that the tales can be equally invested with subversive potential in relation to Nazi ideology. Zacharias Buchmann, the novel's protagonist, plans to publish the tales by his brother, Ignaz, in resistance to the Nazis and, after Ignaz is murdered in Treblinka, entrusts the task to his grandson.

Unlike Weber, rather than to the forces of light, Claudel connects the Grimms' tales to the forces of darkness. This is suggested by the fact that the date of the collection's original publication — 1812 — is engraved upon the door leading to a secret room that plays the role of the fabular 'forbidden chamber'. As for the 'Café Schloss', inside which the secret room is located, it fulfils the function of another ominous fairy-tale locale, the castle, and shares the castle's association with doom, malevolence, and violence. It is noteworthy that the typically negative connotations of the castle, established by *Jack and the Beanstalk* or *Beauty and the Beast*, have been exploited by Yolen's reworking of *Sleeping Beauty* in *Briar Rose*.⁴⁹ Inspired by Abraham Bomba's testimony in Lanzmann's *Shoah*, Yolen's novel is set in the castle-cum-concentration camp of Chełmno where 145,000 Jews and 5,000 Gypsies were murdered. In *Le Rapport*, equipped with a secret room, the Café Schloss reminds us specifically of the castle in *Bluebeard* whose eponymous protagonist uses the forbidden chamber to store the bodies of his dead wives.⁵⁰ In Claudel's novel, the private room hosts the meetings of 'De Erweckens'Bruderschaft' [Brotherhood of Awakening], a mysterious and self-appointed council of seven powerful men who take weighty decisions such as those concerning the denunciation of Brodeck and Simon Frippman to the *Fratergekeime*, and, later, the assassination of the *Anderer*. The part of the murderous ogre is played by Orschwir, the village mayor who may not have a blue beard, but whose eyes are intensely blue and face purple, and whose stove is decorated with blue and green tiles. Apart from the 'forbidden chamber', *Le Rapport* reproduces the two other key details of *Bluebeard* that have been isolated by Antti Aarne and Stith Thompson's structuralist typology of fairy-tale elements. While the 'person allowed to enter all chambers except one' finds embodiment in Brodeck, 'Taboo: eating human flesh' is enacted through the consumption of the *Anderer*'s remains by the mayor's pigs.[51] However, like other authors for whom *Bluebeard* has been 'a fruitful field of criticism', Claudel ends up subverting the tale by doing away with its happy ending (at least for the latest wife).[52] Instead, Claudel ends his novel with the triumph of the ogre-like mayor and his accomplices who, having coerced Brodeck into compromising collusion with the *Anderer*'s killers, force him into exile.

Apart from the castle, Claudel's novel engages another major fairy-tale chronotope which is the forest. Once again, this strategy is consistent with *Le Rapport*'s indebtedness to the Grimms' tales which, according to Zipes, identified the forest as the holder of 'essential truths about German customs, laws and culture' at the time when the *Volk* needed reuniting.[53] More broadly, the forest is 'a common fairy tale locale', especially if its geographical position remains unspecified.[54] Studies dedicated to fairy tales demonstrate that the role of the forest is ambiguous. That it can be either deadly or unconventional, free, and alluring is illustrated by *Hansel and Gretel* where the children first get lost in the woods before emerging from them richer and wiser.[55] Similarly, while in *Snow White* the forest has an enchanting potential, in *Little Red Riding Hood* it is a stage for dangerous temptations and the dwelling-place of predatory males. Claudel's novel has clearly co-opted iconographies of the fairy tale by preserving the forest's fabular duality. More specifically, in *Le Rapport*, the forest provides a contrast to the Bruegelesque village and the perilous capital, and is a source of both aesthetic pleasure for the *Anderer* and of livelihood for many villagers, including Brodeck himself.[56] At the same time, the forest is cast as an all-engulfing and menacing force which, in the traumatised mind of the novel's protagonist, becomes metonymically connected to the *Fratergekeime*. Such an association is unsurprising considering that in German iconography, the national love of forests has been at times linked to militarism, including to that of the Nazis.[57] Echoing Elias Canetti's comparison of the Germans to a 'marching forest', Brodeck fears that the hut which has been sheltering his writing from the ill-founded curiosity of his neighbours, will be razed by trees on the march.[58] Claudel confirms this negative investment of the forest with the episode in which Brodeck, Émelia, and Émelia's daughter, Poupchette, venture into the woods. The protagonist first notices that a pond has tripled in size, which is an ominous sign in itself. In addition, the trough standing in the pond's midst and once capable of stirring pleasant associations with a floating vessel, now resembles a tomb. Alarmed by this morbid vision, Brodeck hurries back to Émelia and Poupchette, but, as if in a nightmare, slips on the marshy ground and sinks into holes and quagmires which emit 'des bruits qui ressemblaient à des plaintes mourantes' [sounds like the groans of the dying] (*RB*, 202; *B*, 164). The negative representation of the forest is ultimately crystallised by its failure to protect three fugitive *Fremdër* girls from the sexual violence and murderous rage of the occupying soldiers and their local accomplices.

The forest's ambivalence is further borne out by the symbolic investment of its flora. This is exemplified by Ernst-Peter Limmat's gift to Brodeck of black-coloured and funnel-shaped fungi called 'trompettes de la mort'. The evil symbolism of the mushrooms which were once believed to be trumpets played by the dead is strengthened when Limmat joins the jury of Brodeck's report. Yet, the woods are also home to the valley periwinkle which is mentioned by Brodeck's fellow deportee, Moshe Kelmar, as a countermeasure to the horrors of their interminable train journey. Indeed, it is in tribute to Kelmar who let himself be beaten to death by the guards on the way to the camp, that the protagonist vainly searches for the mythical plant. His speculation that nature has suppressed it to punish human wickedness both endows the natural environment with agency and suggests the novel's critique of man's domination, exploitation, and oppression of human and non-human otherness. The fact that, rather than in the wild, Brodeck eventually locates the flower in the *Anderer*'s almanac is in turn a sign of *Le Rapport*'s typically postmodern awareness that the reality it is describing is experienced textually rather than empirically. That said, the *Anderer*'s warning against the unreliability of the written word articulates the novel's limited trust in the textual sources which serve as the basis for cultural representations of historical events such as *Le Rapport* itself.

To return to the intertextual relationship of Claudel's novel with well-known fairy tales, its 'incorporation', as Smith calls an explicit reference in the text, of *Pied Piper of Hamelin* and *Snow White* is as destabilising as that of *Bluebeard*. Elements of the two tales structure Brodeck's childhood memory of an earlier war, exile, and parental loss, which in themselves constitute a typical fairy-tale opening.[59] To lure the four-year-old orphan away from his burnt-down village, Fédorine offers him a gleaming red apple and the child follows her 'comme si elle avait été un joueur de flûte' [as if she were a piper] (*RB*, 28; *B*, 16). Claudel's novel thus playfully turns the apple from a tool of persecution (which is its role in *Snow White*) into a token of generosity, and transforms the pied piper from a figure of vengeance into one of (grand)motherly compassion. Another interesting detail of this episode is the rabbit travelling on Fédorine's cart. The animal comforts the traumatised orphan and lends him its species' fabular connotations of timidity, fearfulness, and vulnerability. The rabbit's remedial properties are restated later in the novel when, during his return journey from captivity, Brodeck is treated by an uncharacteristically welcoming stranger to a hearty meal consisting of rabbit and carrots. As well as Brodeck's physical strength, the dish restores his faith in men and his own sense of humanity. However, Claudel's reduction of the rabbit to a mere source of man's physical and emotional sustenance, and his exploration of the animal's traditional symbolic investment seem at odds with *Le Rapport*'s pro-animal agenda. Claudel's use of the rabbit clashes in particular with his novel's efforts to free animals from their stereotypical role as, to put it in Steve Baker's terms, 'the objectified other, fixed and distanced by the controlling look of the empowered human'.[60]

As with its representation of different animal species, to which I will return later, *Le Rapport*'s treatment of female stereotypes found in fairy tales consists in a simultaneous inscription and challenge of them. This is illustrated by the character of Fédorine who, although portrayed as 'une sorcière cabossée' [a battered old witch] (*RB*, 28; *B*, 16) and further associated with witchcraft through her cat, undermines the fairy-tale image of a cannibalistic witch and evil stepmother. Conversely, Brodeck's wife easily falls into the category of the persecuted beauty in the style of

Rapunzel, Snow White, and Cinderella. Émelia's alignment with passive femininity is reflected in her occupation as embroiderer, not to mention her characteristic silence and docility.[61] Her vulnerability only increases as a consequence of her brutalisation by the *Fratergekeime* and their local collaborators, which plunges her into aphasia and strips her of all agency. This plot development nevertheless creates a rare opportunity for Claudel's novel to gender wartime violence and to dramatise the protracted after-effects of the sexual abuse and exploitation that many Jewish women suffered during the Holocaust.[62]

Suggested by the characterisation of Émelia, the view of beauty as synonymous with moral virtue is undermined by the peripheral character of the wife of the concentration camp commandant. Moreover, 'Zeilenessiniss' [The Eater of Souls], as the inmates nickname the commandant's wife due to her keen participation in the daily executions, serves to interrogate the fairy-tale stereotype of the all-good mother. More generally, since the beautiful young blonde nurses her baby as she watches men being hanged, her character serves Claudel to undermine the association of motherhood with innocence, moralism, purity, and selflessness.[63] Her character thus demonstrates that carnophallogocentrism — a term that adds carnivorism to aggressive manhood and rationality construed by Derrida as fundamental preconditions of Western metaphysics — is not uniquely bound up with masculinity.[64] In the narrower context of Holocaust representations, the commandant's wife is a parody of the way Nazi women have been portrayed in popular culture, and especially in Nazisploitation cinema.[65] If such stereotypes are meant to convey Nazi sadism, female violence being more culturally aberrant than male brutality, Claudel heightens this effect by figuring the Nazi female as a Madonna.[66] Incidentally, like the statuesque blond staged by the horror film *Ilsa: She-wolf of the S.S.* (1974), *Zeilenesseniss* is lynched by the prisoners on the camp's liberation.[67] The character of the commandant's wife may additionally be intended to foreground the complicity of ordinary German women in Nazi atrocities and their biological role in promulgating the Aryan race.[68]

Claudel's novel not only critically revisits age-old fairy tales and the stereotypes they propagate, but also engages in what Smith calls 'fabulation' ('crafting an original fairy-tale'). That these tales nevertheless rely on well-known and recurrent fairy-tale motifs is evidenced by the following description of the stories made up by Fédorine:

> Je me souviens de tous les contes que Fédorine a dans sa mémoire, où des objets parlent, [...] des châteaux en une nuit traversent des plaines et des montagnes, [...] des reines dorment durant mille ans, [...] des arbres se muent en seigneurs, [...] leurs racines se dressent, enlacent des gorges et les étouffent et [...] certaines sources peuvent guérir les blessures et les immenses chagrins. (*RB*, 85)

> [I thought of all the tales that Fédorine knows by heart, stories in which objects speak, chateaux cross mountains and plains in a single night, queens sleep for a thousand years, trees change into noble lords, roots spring from the earth and strangle people, and springs have the power to heal festering wounds and soothe overwhelming grief.] (*B*, 64)

Reflecting the dark aura of Brodeck's own story, Fédorine's tales have a sinister quality. This is anticipated by the phonological kinship between 'Tibipoï', the name of the land in which they are set, and 'Pitchipoï' which is the Yiddish word that the Jews held in Drancy used to refer to the unknown place they believed they were heading for.[69] The ill-boding resonance of Fédorine's tales is soon enacted by the story of the poor tailor Bilissi which, while bookending Brodeck's own narrative, constitutes its *mise en abîme*. The story goes as follows: one day, Bilissi opens the door to three masked and armed knights who commission a garment for the king. On two subsequent days, the knights return to ask the tailor to carry out further work for which he is remunerated with the loss of his mother and wife. Fearing for the life of his daughter, Bilissi declines payment for the third garment. The knights reply that the child the tailor thinks to have is a mirage and that his refusal of payment means that he has lost his only chance of becoming a father. The enigmatic and portentous sentence closing the first part of Bilissi's story — 'C'est ainsi bien souvent quand il est bien trop tard' [Things are often thus, when it is far too late] — sets the tone for its second and final part, as well as for Brodeck's own dark tale which, like many 'anti-tales', is stamped by disenchantment rather than enchantment (*RB*, 19; *B*, 7). This means that the story of Bilissi, who shares Brodeck's vulnerability and veiled Jewishness, and whose family is, like that of Brodeck, composed of three women, foreshadows the protagonist's victimisation by the rich and mighty, and his decision to protect his family by going into exile.[70]

Brodeck and the Animal Fable: Animals Behaving Badly

As well as from fairy tales, Claudel's novel borrows from fables, which are defined as stories where animals attain human traits to dispense moral wisdom.[71] The fable was popularised by Aesop, Jean de La Fontaine, and Ivan Krilov, before being famously revisited by George Orwell's 1945 political satire. In contrast to *Animal Farm* which, despite its author's documented concern with animal welfare, emulates fabular anthropocentrism and exploitation of the characteristics that men have ascribed to different species, contemporary reworkings of the genre depart from the notion that men and animals are separated from each other by an unbreakable divide.[72] These fables also try to restore ontological independence to animals and, rather than casting them as allegories of human vice and folly, make them characters in their own right.[73]

When it comes to the use of the fable as the narrative model in Holocaust literature, it has no doubt been encouraged by the proliferation of animal metaphors in discourses on the Nazi era. The best-known examples of works drawing on animal imagery are those by Spiegelman and Kosinski, even though the approaches of the two authors differ significantly.[74] Claudel's narrative technique is closer to Kosinski's in that, rather than casting men as beasts as does Spiegelman, he endows his human characters with animal features. For instance, Brodeck compares the camp guards to crows scavenging on prisoners' corpses, a collaborator to rat droppings, broken shop windows to jaws of dead animals, and the village folk to a herd of animals. What *Le Rapport* also shares with *The Painted Bird* is its protagonist's equivocal identity, its lack of precise historical and geographical markers, and its aspiration to fabular universality and timelessness, suggested by the allusion of the title of Kosinski's novel to Aesop's 'The Bird in Borrowed Feathers'.[75]

Furthermore, like *The Painted Bird*, *Le Rapport* is studded with mini-fables. However, rather than casting anthropomorphised animals whose exemplary behaviour educates readers, these parables invite men to imitate the immoral conduct of animals and, consequently, suggest Claudel's disparaging view of the fable as the voice and tool of carnophallogocentric power. Chronologically, the first of the mini-fables is narrated by Adolf Buller whose story about the butterfly species, *Rex flammae*, serves to manipulate the peasants into denouncing the *Fremdër*. As well as of Hitler himself, Buller is thus cast as a parody of those Nazis who keenly used animal behaviour to make larger arguments about humans. In the Third Reich metaphors drawn from the natural world were abused and the roles of animals and humans blurred. For example, the opposition between the victor and the vanquished, which underpinned Nazi ideology, was modelled on the distinction between predator and prey.[76] Claudel ridicules such biological determinism with a parable in which the butterflies welcome other species in favourable conditions, but, as soon as food becomes scarce, expel the outsiders from their midst. The tale satirises the Nazis' fetishised concept of the *Volksgemeinschaft* which designated 'a racially homogenous, socially conformist, performance oriented and hierarchically structured society' realised by 'educating the "well suited" and "eradicating" the supposedly "unsuitable"'.[77] To strengthen the ridiculing effect of his parody, Claudel focuses his tale around insects rather than large predatorial mammals, such as wolves and lions with which real-life Nazis liked to identify.[78]

Later in the novel, Buller's recourse to animal allegories with the intention of coercing his victims into collaboration is replicated by Orschwir in relation to Brodeck. To dispel the protagonist's qualms about colluding with the *Anderer*'s killers, the mayor encourages him to imitate the oldest and, in his view, the wisest of his pigs. Orschwir's tale clearly parodies *Three Little Pigs* which, according to Bruno Bettelheim, narrates our renunciation of the pleasure principle for the reality principle. The three pigs which Bettelheim sees as one and the same character, mark our progression from immaturity to maturity as we shed earlier forms of existence and move on to higher ones.[79] In line with this psychoanalytical model, Orschwir's pigs represent three different phases in human life: innocence, gratuitous violence, and what the mayor calls wisdom, but what in fact is viciousness and moral corruption. Furthermore, the oldest pigs lack the capacity for thinking, empathy, and memory, that is the faculties that are widely identified as uniquely human and that supposedly distinguish man from animal: 'Ils ne connaissent pas le remords. Ils vivent' [They know nothing of remorse. They live] (*RB*, 51; *B*, 35).[80] In this light, Orschwir urges Brodeck to part with the hallmarks of, to put it in Agamben's terms, meaningful human life and to embrace 'bare life', or what Derrida calls a 'life without qualities, without qualification'.[81]

Claudel further subverts *Three Little Pigs* by shifting our attention from allegorical pigs to actual animals. He thereby echoes the endeavour of postmetaphysical philosophers, such as Derrida and Levinas, to liberate animals from their centuries-old symbolic appropriation.[82] Unlike in the children's story, here all the pigs, whatever their age, are equally vulnerable to exploitation. That the animals have no chance of outsmarting their predator is obvious from the scene where trucks cart away carcasses to shops and panic-stricken pigs to abattoirs, and which thus displaces the happy ending of the original story. In rewriting the closure of the original fairy tale, Claudel also discards the zoomorphism of evil and, by unmasking its human face, rescues the wolf from his negative fabular connotations. Finally, the novel erodes the distinction between devouring and eating established by *Three Little Pigs* and embodied respectively in the wolf's carnophallogocentric appetite and in the third pig's vegetarian diet of apples and turnips. By ingesting the *Anderer*'s body, the pigs not only adopt the carnivorous habits of their human victimiser, but also become complicit in a murder that follows from the very drive for control and domination of otherness that is behind our abuse of animals.

At the end of the novel, the mayor reiterates his message with the parable of the shepherd and the flock. Figuring himself as the shepherd, Orschwir believes it to be his duty to ensure the safety of his people who, figured as sheep, 'ne s'intéressent qu'à ce qu'elles voient sous leurs pattes et juste devant leurs têtes' [are interested only in what they see under their feet and right in front of their eyes] (*RB*, 367; *B*, 307). Popularised by Plato, who was already alert to the danger that the statesman-as-shepherd may exploit his flock under the pretext of protectiveness and care, the paradigm of 'pouvoir pastoral' [pastoral power] has been replaced by Foucault with the model of the statesman-as-weaver. Rather than nourishing and caring for his people, the weaver's task is to 'associer des temperaments contraires (fougeux et modérés) [...] rassembler les vivants "en une communauté qui repose sur la concorde et l'amitié" et [...] tisser ainsi "le plus magnifique de tous les tissus"' [bind together different contrasting temperaments (spirited and moderate) [...] bring together these lives 'in a community that rests on concord and friendship' and [...] weave 'the most magnificent of fabrics'].[83] By putting the pastoral metaphor into Orschwir's mouth Claudel lends support to Plato's misgivings. At the same time, he endorses the Foucauldian alternative to the model of the sovereign-as-shepherd with his protagonist, whose name derives from the French verb *broder* [to embroider].

The final mini-fable embedded in Brodeck's story is presented by the protagonist himself as a conclusion to his investigation of the mass death of foxes. In contrast to the other animal parables, here beasts imitate men when they die a self-inflicted death. Brodeck is led to such an interpretation of the demise of the foxes by the fact that, like men, foxes are thought to be capable of killing for sheer pleasure. In this way, the novel destabilises the idea of man's exceptionality based on, among other things, the belief that suicide is an exclusively human response to psychological pain.[84] Propagated by thinkers across history, this belief has also been advanced in the context of the Holocaust.[85] Before committing suicide himself, Levi, in his essay 'Shame', opposed the animal state of the camp inmates to the survivors' regained humanity, manifest in their capacity for experiencing guilt regarding their own good fortune and for ending their own lives.[86] In this light, the mass death of the foxes allegorises the inability of Holocaust survivors to live with the memory of those who perished and whose death sometimes facilitated their own survival. Such a reading is invited by the stories of Moshe Kelmar and Diodème, whose suicides are attributed to their wartime conduct. Kelmar's death, for example, results from his refusal to live with the memory of the theft of water that he and Brodeck committed on the train, and that may have precipitated the unavoidable death of a young mother and her baby. Coincidentally, Kelmar's story recalls Levi's confession of his and his fellow inmate's decision not to share with other prisoners the few drops of water they found stagnating in a pipe.[87] As for Diodème, who is a would-be-writer and the protagonist's alter-ego, his death follows his passivity in the face of Brodeck's deportation, of the rape and murder of the *Fremdër* girls, of the rape and attempted murder of Émelia, and, finally, of the assassination of the *Anderer*. Such a reading is invited by Diodème's choice to die by the river, at the very spot where the peasants buried the *Fremdër* girls and where they later drowned the *Anderer*'s horse and donkey with the intention of ousting him from the village.

'Jews and Dogs Not Welcome'

By providing a reflection of the human suicides narrated by *Le Rapport*, the tale of the collective death of foxes feeds into the novel's structural opposition between a humiliating but potentially life-saving demoralisation and a rewarding, albeit costly, moral integrity. The notions of servitude and dignity are embodied in *Le Rapport* respectively by the dog and by the fox and the dog's other wild cousin, the wolf who, according to a minor character of the novel, shares the fox's capacity for suicide. Claudel's choice of the dog as the main allegory is unquestionably grounded in the long history of domestication or — to abandon the misleading euphemism — of subjugation of this animal. In an autobiographical essay 'Nom d'un chien ou le droit naturel', Levinas notes that in the popular imagination the dog is 'la bête ayant perdu l'ultime fierté de nature sauvage' [the beast that has lost the last noble vestiges of its wild nature]. It is the image of the dog as '[un] chien couchant, [...] un méprisable chien servile' [crouching, servile [and] contemptible] that is no doubt responsible for the presence of canine similes in anti-Semitic rhetoric from early Christianity to the Third Reich.[88] Although the degrading comparisons of Jews to rats or lice dominated the Nazi parlance, the epithet 'dog' also served as an expression of contempt.[89] Survivors of concentration camps recall that, when setting their German shepherds on inmates, guards would call the former 'men' and the latter 'dogs'.[90] The derogatory analogy has also found its way into literature, as exemplified by Heinrich Heine's ironic poem 'Prinzessin Sabbat' (1851) which casts a Jew as a filthy scavenging dog who regains his human form only once a week, on Fridays. More recently, in André Schwarz-Bart's Holocaust novel *Le Dernier des Justes* (1959), Ernie Levy transforms into a dog as a result of internalising the Nazis' anti-Semitic rhetoric.[91]

In *Le Rapport*, the dog occupies a complex position, beginning with the dogs guarding prisoners in the concentration camp. In keeping with the novel's fairy-tale aura, Claudel figures the guard dogs as fabular creatures reminiscent of the three enormous and terrifying dogs found in Hans Christian Andersen's tale *The Tinderbox* (1835). He describes them as 'des dogues au pelage miel, aux gueules retroussées dont les yeux bavaient des larmes un peu rouges' [mastiffs with coats the colour of honey and curled up lips and eyes that drooled reddish tears] (*RB*, 30; *B*, 17). Rather than serving to thematise the 'biopolitical paradox' consisting in the simultaneous enlistment of animals in the service of biopolitics and their enslavement by it, the guard dogs are simply part of Claudel's characterisation of *l'univers concentrationnaire*.[92] Their other role is to prepare the scene for Brodeck's demoralisation and dehumanisation in the camp, which takes the form of him becoming the canine servant of the guards. As 'Chien Brodeck' [Brodeck-the-Dog] (*RB*, 30; *B*, 18), the protagonist walks on all fours, eats food using only his mouth, wears a collar and lead, licks the boots of the guards, and barks or dangles his tongue on command (*RB*, 30; *B*, 17).[93] By thus reifying Brodeck's loss of dignity, Claudel inscribes the fabular figuration of the dog as man's slave in return for his keep and endorses the moral of Aesop's 'The Dog and the Wolf' that, as Judith Still puts it, 'agreeing to be a servant, or slave, only moderates the violence that will be meted out'.[94]

At the same time, in a characteristically postmodern fashion, *Le Rapport* challenges the stereotypical treatment of the dog by casting an actual animal that resolutely rejects man's egregious imposition of his will. The posture of the stray mongrel who lives in Brodeck's village is encapsulated by his name, 'Ohnmeist', which combines the German words *ohne* [without] and *Meister* [master]. The dog's crossbreed status defies in turn the pseudo-scientific notion of pedigree and, consequently, denounces the violence that we have imposed on animals through unnatural selection in pursuit of satisfying our own aesthetic or practical needs.[95] According to Hilda Kean and Philip Howell, animal eugenics has been linked to interhuman racism, as suggested by the concern that the idea of pedigree can 'bleed over into the concepts of "race" and rank ("good stock"), culture and civility ("good breeding"), that are still used to separate the human sheep from the human goats'.[96] Similarly, LaCapra asserts that 'the notion of purity of breed has racist overtones, including the quasi-ritual horror of mixing breeds' and recognises kennel clubs as 'the last bastions of unexamined racism, reproducing, vis-à-vis other animals, barriers and attitudes that have been challenged with respect to humans'.[97] Pushing the comparative approach further, Boria Sax links animal eugenics to the Nazis' obsession with the concept of pure race, which the Nazis applied to humans and animals alike. This is evidenced by the fact that, just as they praised pedigree dogs and despised mongrels, the Nazis deemed Jews as a racially impure ethnic group that, as Sax sardonically concludes, therefore had to be euthanised.[98]

The quoted comments enable us to see *Ohnmeist* as a vector for Claudel's criticism of pure breeding, hierarchy of races, and the dog's customary role as man's faithful companion, guide, or servant. However, one could argue that by naming the dog, the novel subjugates him through an imposition of an externally constructed identity. For Derrida, this process is illustrated with Adam's assertion of his authority over the animals in Genesis or even through the use of the word 'animal' which, when deployed in its totalising singular form, is 'une appellation que des hommes ont instituée, un nom qu'ils se sont donné le droit et l'autorité de donner à l'autre vivant' [an appellation that men have instituted, a name they have given themselves the right and the authority to give to another living creature].[99] Andrew Benjamin additionally observes that the excluding mechanism behind the singular noun has also been applied to Jews whose identity has been, like that of animals (and especially of dogs), invariably constructed from without and consists of a denial of both universality and particularity.[100] To expose such a derogatory perception of the dog and at the same time to offset Brodeck's demoralisation and disempowerment in the camp, Claudel endows *Ohnmeist* with dignity and agency. This agency, to draw on Howell's taxonomy, takes the 'agonistic' form, meaning 'actions that push back against the pressures and presumptions of the human-dominated world'.[101] Having refused to belong to anyone for years, at the end of the novel *Ohnmeist* returns to the wild. The dog's agency is also of the 'assembled' type, manifesting itself in his relations with humans.[102] More specifically, appreciating the *Anderer*'s non-discriminatory attitude, *Ohnmeist* lets himself be caressed by the stranger's hand and, after his assassination, howls and lowers his head and tail. He then transfers his fondness to Brodeck in whom he must recognise the *Anderer*'s avatar as well as a creature relegated, like himself, to the other side of the human-animal divide and, consequently, discriminated against.

The interaction between *Ohnmeist* and Brodeck can be productively framed with Levinas's rare attempt to extend his ethics beyond the human in the context of his captivity during World War II.[103] The essay 'Nom d'un chien ou le droit naturel' credits a wandering dog with the power to re-graft on to the Franco-Jewish POWs 'la peau humaine' [the human skin] of which the Nazis had stripped them.[104] In reward for his cheerful barking, the prisoners bring the dog into the fold of humanised animality by giving him a human name — 'Bobby' — even though, by choosing an English name, they maintain a safe ontological distance between themselves and the dog. Read more positively, the dog's name situates him as a beacon of the longed-for liberation by the Anglo-American Allies,[105] a reading that tallies with Levinas's cross-referencing of his imprisonment with the exodus of the Jews from Egyptian slavery and with Ulysses's homecoming.[106] Brodeck's relationship with *Ohnmeist* simultaneously echoes and alters Levinas's encounter with Bobby. As opposed to the philosopher who is interested in the stray dog only insofar as he can throw light on the human condition, which means that Bobby is merely an agent of the prisoners' rehumanisation and a promise of their future freedom, Claudel is concerned with *Ohnmeist*'s own quest for independence from man and from his derogatory conception of the dog as a species. Furthermore, despite overtly rejecting allegories and even briefly elevating Bobby to the position of 'le dernier kantien de l'Allemagne nazie' [the last Kantian in Nazi Germany], Levinas denies the dog both ethics and *logos*, thus keeping him within the narrow confines of compliance and silence to which Bobby's ancestors have been relegated by the Bible.[107] In contrast, Claudel exposes the offensive stereotype of canine servility and endeavours to free the dog from what Derrida terms 'la réappropriation anthropo-théomorphique' and sees as synonymous with the denial of animal agency and the condemnation of animals to 'aphasic inability'.[108] The novelist achieves such a re-presentation of animality with the final pages of *Le Rapport*, which narrate Brodeck and *Ohnmeist*'s departure from the village and the dog's return to the wild. In the light of the mass death of foxes, *Ohnmeist*'s metamorphosis into a beautiful and mature fox confirms his agency and suggests his inscrutability to the human mind. If the foxes were to be read as stand-ins for moral men such as Kelmar, the ending of *Ohnmeist*'s story would point in turn to a post-Holocaust regeneration of humanity. Such a positive interpretation of Claudel's otherwise bleak tale is further encouraged by the analogy between Brodeck and Aeneas who, after the fall of Troy, set out to found a new civilisation in Rome.

Hope, however, is dissipated through Brodeck's ultimate self-distanciation from normative humanity. His position is indicated by his donning of the *Anderer*'s fur cap, gloves, and slippers, and by his last-minute decision to leave behind his typewriter, a gesture that can be deciphered as his rejection of language. That Claudel simultaneously shares and queries the dominant conception of speech as a defining attribute of humanity can be inferred from the fact that Brodeck's dehumanisation in the camp culminates in aphasia and that his rehabilitation is signalled by his renewed ability to speak. At the same time, the novel shows language to be a tool of oppression, as illustrated by its coercive use in the camp, by the exploitation of fabular rhetoric by Buller and Orschwir, and, finally, by the villagers' enlistment of Brodeck's writing skills to justify their murder of the *Anderer*. Moreover, *Le Rapport* criticises language for its inability to safeguard humanity from descent into savagery. Disappointed by poetry which, as Brodeck puts it, 'ne connaît pas les chiens' [knows nothing of dogs] (*RB*, 46; *B*, 30), the protagonist burns all his books on return from captivity. He thus denounces a culture that has failed to prevent horrific interhuman violence, to accommodate the loss of dignity experienced by its victims, and, being narrowly anthropocentric, to account for the suffering of non-human animals. If illuminated with Deleuze and Guattari's philosophy, the shared exile of Brodeck and *Ohnmeist* can be construed as a deterritorialisation or, as the philosophers alternately call it, as 'devenir-animal' [becoming-animal].[109] Becoming-animal is neither resemblance nor imitation nor identification; it is neither progress nor descent, and does not result in man's metamorphosis into an animal. Rather, it concerns an opening to alterity which in Claudel's novel takes the form of oppressed animality, be it human or non-human. In this context, *Le Rapport*'s closure tells us that, to transcend Western metaphysics and the animal-human divide that is at its core, today's writer must 'become animal'. In Deleuze and Guattari's terms, this means that, instead of prolonging the enslavement of animals through anthropomorphic allegories and their construction as man's ultimate Other, the purveyor of new fables must enter a symbiotic relationship with them and oppose their disempowerment.

The Animal Holocaust

While it is clear that in *Le Rapport* Claudel advances a pro-animal agenda, it needs to be established what discursive means he employs to achieve this in a novel that, despite its allegorical aura, is undoubtedly about the Holocaust. Of specific interest is how *Le Rapport* interconnects interhuman violence, as emblematised by the Nazi genocide, to the abuse that animals have suffered at our hands. In other words, how does Claudel's novel negotiate the vexed analogy between the Holocaust and our centuries-old mistreatment of non-humans? Although the term 'animal holocaust' which is used to refer to this mistreatment has been operational only since the 1990s, the comparison between racism and speciesism is significantly older. Already in the 1940s, Adorno stated that the possibility of pogroms is decided

> in the moment when the gaze of a fatally-wounded animal falls on a human being. The defiance with which he repels this gaze — 'after all, it's only an animal' — reappears irresistibly in cruelties done to human beings, the perpetrators having again and again to reassure themselves that it is 'only an animal', because they could never fully believe this even of animals.[110]

Inverting Adorno's argument, more recently, David Sztybel, Charles Patterson, Peter Singer, and Karen Davis have all mobilised Holocaust rhetoric to draw attention to our cruel treatment of non-humans. As Timothy Costelloe points out, these scholars demonstrate similarities in 'the mind-numbing scale' of the two sets of horrors, in the methods (e.g. production-like techniques) and euphemistic language used both by the Nazis and the meat industry, and in the secrecy surrounding the concentration camps and the slaughterhouses and laboratories.[111] Moreover, they argue that, just as women or slaves have been brought into the same cultural universe as white men, one day it may no longer be permissible to treat animals as we do.[112] Some of these thinkers additionally postulate that for as long as we continue abusing animals, we will ill-treat other humans.[113] Others in turn opine that, rather than becoming ossified in its sacrosanct uniqueness, the Holocaust should be a moral lesson of relevance to the way we live today.[114] This position has been championed by Matt Prescott, the director of PETA, who, in defence of his organisation's 2003 campaign 'Holocaust on Your Plate', argued that the victims of Nazi violence should be honoured through our recognition of the will to live in those suffering today.[115] Yet, as evidenced by the controversy surrounding the campaign, the comparison between the Jewish tragedy and industrial farming continues to raise strong objections. Its detractors accuse it of offending the memory of Holocaust victims, of trivialising the genocide,[116] and, despite the evidence of the economic agenda of the 'Final Solution', of eroding the difference in the motivations for the two forms of violence.[117]

Among those advocating animal rights with recourse to Holocaust imagery are major writers such as Nobel Prize laureates Isaac Bashevis Singer and J. M. Coetzee, Margarete Yourcenar, and Hélène Cixous, as well as prominent philosophers including Derrida, LaCapra, and Élisabeth de Fontenay.[118] It is noteworthy that some of these writers and thinkers are Jewish or even have a familial connection to the Holocaust.[119] For instance, Singer, who lost most of his family in Nazi-occupied

Poland, has created protagonists who proclaim that to animals every man is a Nazi and that, consequently, animals live 'an eternal Treblinka'.[120] Even more vocal is the eponymous protagonist of Coetzee's novel *Elizabeth Costello* (2003), who, drawing on the stock tropes of the beast fable, states that 'we are surrounded by an enterprise of degradation, cruelty and killing which rivals anything that the Third Reich was capable of, indeed dwarfs it, in that ours is an enterprise without end'.[121]

In contrast to Coetzee or Cixous, Claudel avoids the direct comparison between concentration camps and abattoirs. Instead, he uses a range of narrative strategies that potentially sensitise his readers to the parallels between the two kinds of violence. For example, in *Le Rapport* men are put to death in ways reminiscent of animal slaughter; while in the village the *Fratergekeime* use an axe to decapitate insubordinate peasants, in the camp they resort to a butcher's hook to hang prisoners. The hook which, however outlandish it may seem, finds reflection in the historical reality of the Nazi era, is part of the systematic dehumanisation of the victims. This dehumanisation is also communicated by the label the condemned men are made to wear around their necks and reading 'ICH BIN NICHTS' ['I am nothing'] (*RB*, 79; *B*, 59), or by the main protagonist's transformation into 'Chien Brodeck'.[122] The assimilation of future human victims with animals is also illustrated by the scene in which, to warn the protagonist against non-compliance, Brodeck's neighbour, Göbbler, gratuitously squashes a small and gracious snail. Göbbler's ruthless gesture repeats the peasants' drowning of the *Anderer*'s horse and donkey in an act of warning, which in turn echoes the real-life Nazis' confiscation or destruction of pets belonging to Jews in preparation for their murder of the Jews themselves.[123] *Le Rapport* thus lends support to Driscoll's apt observation that it is the animalisation of beings that makes their death of no concern, and that, in order to be killed with impunity, animals themselves have to be animalised.[124]

Analogically to likening victims to animals, Claudel casts the two key persecutors of human otherness as livestock breeders. Orschwir and Göbbler are instrumental in Brodeck's deportation, in the rape and murder of the *Fremdër* women, and in the rape and attempted murder of Brodeck's wife. If the two men are also deeply implicated in collaboration with the *Fratergekeime,* Göbbler is additionally assimilated with real-life Nazis through a name that conflates those of Goebbels and Himmler. To dispel any doubt as to Claudel's intentions, suffice it to say that Göbbler shares the original occupation of Himmler who 'after his commercial failure as a chicken breeder, elected to become a breeder of human beings'.[125] As befits a novel charged with a fabular aura, the immorality of Orschwir and Göbbler is externalised through their physical repulsiveness. The negative characterisation of the mayor, who is described as 'aussi laid comme un régiment barbare' [as ugly as an entire barbarian regimen] (*RB*, 36; *B*, 23) and whose smiles come across as grimaces, is enhanced through the association of his remotely located house with the labyrinth, the *château*, and the forest. Consequently, Orschwir is metonymically aligned with the Minotaur and Bluebeard, yet, significantly, *Le Rapport* replaces the human victims of these cannibalistic monsters with pigs from whose suffering and death Orschwir profits. Equally loathsome and terrifying is Göbbler who never smiles, who reminds Brodeck of gnomes and monsters, and who exudes 'l'odeur des crottes de poules et de leurs plumes, [...] [une odeur] écœurante, corrompue comme celle des tiges pourries' [the smell of chicken feathers and chicken droppings, [...] a sickening, corrupt odour like that of rotting flower stems] (*RB*, 317; *B*, 262). While his grey and pointy teeth conjure up a predatorial mammal, Brodeck fears that Göbbler's similarly inhuman gaze will gouge out his own eyes.

To interlink further the different strands of oppression it thematises, Claudel's novel shows the persecution of the *Fremdër*, the assassination of the *Anderer*, and the breeding of pigs for slaughter to be all hidden from public view. Sztybel notes a resemblance between the policy of concealment surrounding the Nazis' genocidal programme and the 'exclusion of public scrutiny concerning slaughterhouses and animal laboratories where arguably some of society's most systematic and heinous injustices against animals occur'.[126] Similarly, comparing the two types of oppression, Derrida observes in relation to industrial farming and slaughter of animals that 'les hommes font tout ce qu'ils peuvent pour dissimuler ou pour se dissimuler cette cruauté, pour organiser à l'échelle mondiale l'oubli ou la méconnaissance de cette violence que certains pourraient comparer aux pires génocides' [men do all they can in order to dissimulate this cruelty or to hide it from themselves, in order to organize on a global scale the forgetting or misunderstanding of this violence that some would compare to the worst cases of genocide].[127] In *Le Rapport*, this dissimulation is enacted through the remoteness of both the concentration camp and Orschwir's farm, through the secrecy surrounding the assassination of the *Anderer*, and through the methodical destruction of both the stranger's remains and Brodeck's report. All these processes uncannily replicate not only the Nazis' efforts to conceal the 'Final Solution' from the public and to erase all its traces, but also the 'concern for the disposal of animal remains' accompanying factory farming.[128]

The systematic exploitation by the villagers of farm and wild animals is underscored by the *Anderer*'s contrasting respect and kindness towards all creatures. That, in return, animals trust him is evidenced by *Ohnmeist*'s mentioned fondness of the stranger and by the *Anderer*'s relationship with his own horse and donkey. The two animals, respectively named Mademoiselle Julie and Monsieur Socrate, reply to their master's words with meaningful looks and 'des mots d'animaux' [animal words], challenging the notion that animals only *react* but do not *respond* which runs through Aristotelian, Cartesian, Kantian, Heideggerian, and Levinasian philosophy (*RB*, 64; *B*, 46).[129] The phrase 'des mots d'animaux' itself invokes Derrida's neologism 'l'animot' which, containing the French noun *mot* [word], aims to grant to animals language and the ability to name. Intended to sound similar to the plural *animaux*, the term additionally frees animals from the totalising singular *l'animal* which, suppressing the difference between individual creatures, is, in Derrida's words, 'un premier crime contre les animaux, contre des animaux' [a crime of the first order against the animals, against animals].[130] Mademoiselle Julie is further humanised through her opposition to mules and donkeys whom the narrator describes as '[d]es bêtes très bêtes, avec rien d'humain en elles et aucun souvenir sur le dos' [real, beastly beasts, with nothing human about them and nothing to remind us of the past] (*RB*, 62; *B*, 45). While apparently derisive, such a figuration of draft animals in fact highlights the unfairness of conflating stupidity (*la bêtise*) with animality by dint of the nominalisation of the adjective *bête*. Interestingly, in trying to render this wordplay, the novel's English translator, John Cullen, has reached for a similarly unjust connection between animals and bestiality. According to Derrida, bestiality, like stupidity, is a characteristic proper to man alone, a fact that Claudel foregrounds by naming the *Anderer*'s donkey after the father of Western philosophy, Socrates, and thus rescuing him from his fabular connection to stupidity, stubbornness, and ill-will.[131]

'I'm right because yes, I'm called Lion'

Claudel's characterisation of Orschwir and Göbbler as carnophallogocentric creatures who persecute alterity and who sanction their murderous behaviour with animal parables, supports Derrida's conception of the fable as the site of both authoritarian speech and devouring.[132] The philosopher's position can be seen as exemplary of the 'restraint and scepticism' with which animal studies and ecocriticism have regarded the fable.[133] Scholars have criticised in particular the genre's inherent anthropocentrism and reliance on naïve, narcissistic, and trivial anthropomorphism.[134] Fables have also been suspect because animals feature in them only as part of their moralistic function and, having 'no physical or psychological existence in their own right', are 'merely vehicles for the human'.[135] Critics have also claimed that in fables 'humans project their own thoughts and feelings onto other species because they egotistically believe themselves to be the centre of the universe'.[136] Others, however, posit that the fable allows for the problematisation of the man-animal relationship, and consider it as central to postcolonial ecocriticism.[137] For example, Sebastian Schönbeck is convinced that, through its capacity for 'theoriz[ing] and problematiz[ing] the relation of texts, animals, and environments', the fable can be pertinent to animal studies and to ecocriticism whose texts 'include the fables both as a method and an object of research'.[138]

An example of such a text is Derrida's essay 'L'Animal que donc je suis' (1999) which, while depending on fabular imagery, criticises the genre. Derrida distances himself from the fable by blaming it for 'apprivoisement anthropomorphique, un assujettissement moralisateur, une domestication. Toujours un discours *de* l'homme; sur l'homme; voire sur l'animalité de l'homme, mais pour l'homme, et en l'homme' [anthropomorphic taming, a moralising subjection, a domestication. Always a discourse *of* man, on man, indeed on the animality of man, but for and as a man].[139] Accordingly, Derrida calls for novel approaches to the fable so that animals may be rescued from its zoopoetics and restored to their true selves.[140] In *La Bête et le souverain* (2001–03), the philosopher in turn identifies the fable as the voice of authority that legitimates and perpetuates social inequality and injustice. He instantiates this claim with La Fontaine's 'The Wolf and the Lamb' which announces its discursive strength with its opening moral: 'La raison du plus fort est toujours la meilleure' [The reason of the strongest is always the best]. In other words, the fable identifies with the Wolf and the reader with the Lamb.[141] In the same text, Derrida zoomorphises the fable as the Lion whose authority proceeds not so much from the rule of law as from his enunciatory power and physical prowess: 'Eh bien, j'ai raison parce que oui, j'ai raison parce que oui, je m'appelle le lion et que vous allez m'écouter, je vous parle, prenez peur, je suis le plus vaillant' [Well, I am right because yes, I'm right because yes, I'm called Lion and, you'll listen to me, I'm talking to you, be afraid, I'm the most valiant].[142]

If for Derrida the fable is the voice of the sovereign whose reign is inexorably tainted with dictatorship, Claudel exposes the genre's complicity in perpetuating the unjustifiable dominion of man over both other men and animals, or, to put it succinctly, in asserting that 'might makes right'.[143] Le Rapport's intention is evident not only in Brodeck's reference to La Fontaine's 'The Wolf and the Lamb' through his comment that, since the war, wolves have outnumbered lambs, but also in the mini-fables embedded in its plot (RB, 59; B, 42). Imitating La Fontaine's tale, Bilissi's story opens with a foreboding moral that simultaneously predicts and legitimates the undeserved violence the tailor suffers from the all-mighty yet invisible king. To put it in the terms of Louis Marin, whose work inspired Derrida's thoughts on the fable, the mini-fables included in Le Rapport teach us about a social order where 'violence will always lie at the origin of law; power will always be the basis of morality; and law and morality will never be anything but a justification of power'.[144] Yet, crucially Claudel does not allegorise the fable as a predatory mammal but, even if Orschwir and Göbbler bear zoomorphic features, gives it human form. In addition, like Derrida's reading of 'The Heifer, the Goat and the Ewe in Society with the Lion',[145] by gendering violence Le Rapport corroborates Still's view that while being a wolf to man, man is in particular a wolf to women.[146]

Conclusions

Le Rapport's criticism of the fable as a discourse that programmatically condones social injustice and disguises power as law and morality cannot be separated from its inscription of the genre and of some of the stereotypes it has promulgated, such as those concerning women and certain animal species. As well as critically engaging with a genre that, summed up in the image of the Cartesian animal-machines,[147] has been accused of legitimating the abominations of colonialism, slavery, genocidal violence, and 'unjustifiable uses and abuses of other animals', the novel amply draws on fairy tales which in turn have been suspected of embroilment in Nazism.[148] The intensely self-conscious and subversive nature of Claudel's reliance on the two narrative modes reflects Hutcheon's claim regarding the inability of postmodern novels to escape implication in 'the historical, social, ideological contexts in which they have existed and continued to exist'. More specifically, by simultaneously espousing and contesting the two discursive models through parody, Claudel's novel supports Hutcheon's reconceptualisation of imitation as a 'perfect postmodern form'.[149] Distancing herself both from Avraham Shlonsky's view of parody as a means of desacralising and dethroning literary norms, and from Kristeva's understanding of it as consolidating the law, Hutcheon regards parody as 'a custodian of artistic legacy' whose agenda can nevertheless be revolutionary.[150] As I have demonstrated in this chapter, such a redefinition of parody suits Claudel's novel. This is because, while liberally borrowing from a range of fairy tales and fables, *Le Rapport* unmistakably sides with postmetaphysical philosophy's querying of a logic that structures and is promoted by the two genres, ensconcing man's exceptionalism and consequent right to dominate non-humans and some subcategories of humanity. To be more precise, Claudel mobilises fabular tropes and narrative devices to draw attention to the entanglement of human and animal worlds, and to the resultant porosity of the human/ animal divide. He also questions the allegorical connotations of animal species and the ethics of animal allegory itself, and, correspondingly, attempts to liberate animals from the reductive singularity, dumbness, and muteness to which we have confined them. As a postmodern novel, *Le Rapport* therefore buttresses de Fontenay's recognition of postmodernism and postmetaphysical philosophy as the two forces that jointly 'ruinent, dans ces implicites et bien-pensants fondements, la foi humaniste et toujours encore secrètement créationniste que nous avons dans le caractère unique de l'histoire humaine' [ruin the humanist and always still secretly creationist faith we have in the unique character of human history and its implicit self-righteous foundations].[151]

Apart from calling attention to the embroilment of fairy tales and fables in the stigmatisation and oppression of otherness, Claudel's narrative strategy assists, as we have seen, his defamiliarisation of ubiquitous Holocaust tropes, such as the dehumanisation of the victims. The paradigmatic timelessness and universality of fairy tales and fables permit Claudel in turn to wrest the Holocaust from its perceived and unproductive uniqueness, redirecting our focus to its philosophical origins in modernity and to its continuing import on present reality. In so doing, Claudel follows, among other thinkers, Zygmunt Bauman who argues that it is only by regarding it as part of modernity, that is of the cult of homogeneity, normality, and efficacy, that the Nazi genocide can become a lesson for the society in which we live.[152] *Le Rapport*'s parody therefore enacts one of the aims of imitation, which is to ridicule contemporary customs or politics through the recasting of works of the past or, to put it in Hutcheon's terms, to re-examine the past in the light of present concerns.[153] More specifically, Claudel's use of parody emulates Derrida's deconstruction of sovereignty, which, far from being simply a historical exercise, 'bears significantly on the contemporary situation'.[154] Without negating the specificity of the Holocaust, Derrida draws on the structures of the fabular genre to connect it to phenomena such as factory farming and the war on terror. Similarly, Claudel foregrounds the ramifications of the Holocaust and links it to other forms of oppression, at the same time emphatically contrasting wartime and post-war intolerance towards alterity with pre-war hospitality. Once prevalent, this hospitality is shown to have been irredeemably destroyed by the *Fratergekeime* who morally corrupted not only their own kind and their collaborators, but also their victims.

In short, Claudel's postmodern reworking of the fabular genre invites us to extend our preoccupation with interhuman violence to the animals who have for centuries served our multifarious, including discursive, needs. *Le Rapport*'s message therefore echoes not only the writings of Derrida, Deleuze and Guattari, and de Fontenay, but also of LaCapra who has recently called for the humanities to abandon their narrow focus on the human and to bring the animal out of its position as 'the more or less covert "other" or even scapegoat of an idea of the human'.[155] However, despite Claudel's pro-animal politics, one cannot resist the impression that, like many studies of the non-human, his novel is first and foremost a study of humanity.[156] The function of the animals in his novel is to provide analogical or contrasting illustrations of human behaviour, as illustrated by Claudel's use of the rabbit's traditional connotation of timidity or by his use of *Ohnmeist* to offset Brodeck's loss of moral rectitude and, later, to accentuate his rejection of corrupt and brutal humanity. Consequently, in *Le Rapport* animals are often maintained in their traditionally subservient roles, including being exploited through allegoric phantasies. This is further exemplified by Orschwir's pigs or by the snail squashed by Göbbler, who continue to be trapped in their roles as didactic devices, rather than being allowed to assume the rank of cognisant and moral creatures. Closely linked to his novelistic treatment of animals is Claudel's evident perception of humanity as a valid ontological notion. This is even though its two traditional hallmarks — language and dignity — have been exposed by postmetaphysical philosophy as discursive constructs. They have also been posited as part of a history that is but an anthropocentric autobiography, and have been shown, including by Claudel's novel itself, to be as easily connected to animals as they are detached from man.[157]

Notes to Chapter 5

1. Himmler quoted by Terence O'Reilly, *Hitler's Irishmen* (Cork: Mercier Press, 2008), p. 165. Jean-François Lyotard, *Le Différend* (Paris: Minuit, 1983), p. 50; *The Differend: Phrases in Dispute*, trans. by Georges Van Den Abbeele (Manchester: Manchester University Press, 1988), p. 28.
2. *Le Rapport de Brodeck* won the Prix Goncourt des Lycéens, the Prix des Libraires du Québec (2008), the Prix des Lecteurs — Le Livre de Poche (2009), and the Independent Foreign Fiction Prize (UK, 2010). The novel has also become a set text in schools across France and beyond, and has been adapted by the highly regarded cartoonist Manu Larcenet as a *bande dessinée*: *Le Rapport de Brodeck*, 2 vols (Paris: Dargaud, 2015–16).
3. Mélanie Carpentier, 'Le Conteur humaniste: interview de Philippe Claudel', *Le Figaro*, 10 March 2006, <http://www.evene.fr/livres/actualite/interview-philippe-claudel-petite-fille-monsieur-linh-295.php> [accessed 1 February 2016]; Lucie Geffroy, 'Philippe Claudel: la guerre pour obsession', *L'Orient Littéraire*, 166 (April 2020), <http://www.lorientlitteraire.com/article_details.php?cid=33&nid=5808> [accessed 10 October 2020].
4. Emily Greenhouse, 'Interview: Philippe Claudel', trans. by Emily Greenhouse, *Granta*, 111 (30 June 2010) <https://granta.com/interview-philippe-claudel/> [accessed 10 September 2016].
5. Ibid. Claudel has addressed stigmatisation of ex-convicts in *Le Bruit des trousseaux*, 2002, and *Il y a longtemps que je t'aime*, 2008); the plight of immigrants in *La Petite Fille de Monsieur Linh*, 2005; and illness in *L'Arbre du pays Toraja*, 2016, and *Avant l'hiver*, 2013.
6. The term *Fremdër* seems to be alluding to the concept of *Fremdkörper* [foreign body] which the Nazis used in opposition to *Volkskörper* [the German people's body] and which designated all elements, including Jews, alien to it. On 9 and 10 November 1938 (*Kristallnacht*), the Nazis vandalised and looted Jewish homes, businesses, and institutions, and killed and injured many Jews themselves.

7. Lyotard, *Le Différend*, p. 12; *The Differend*, p. 28.
8. Hutcheon, *A Poetics of Postmodernism*, p. x.
9. Linda Hutcheon, *A Theory of Parody: The Teachings of Twentieth-Century Art Forms* (London: Routledge, 1985), p. 6.
10. Ibid.
11. Hutcheon, *A Poetics of Postmodernism*, p. 6.
12. Hutcheon, *A Theory of Parody*, p. 8.
13. Ibid., p. 7.
14. Ibid., pp. 4–5.
15. Hutcheon, *A Poetics of Postmodernism*, p. 6.
16. As part of his contestation of the testimonial mode, Claudel both complicates the survivor's moral integrity and undermines his narratorial reliability. Furthermore, rather than focusing the reader's attention on the past, he sets the action of his novel in the post-war present. He thus emphasises the lasting ramifications of wartime violence for both individuals and communities. Finally, by offering no scope for reconciliation and redemption, his novel adopts an uncharacteristically pessimistic tone.
17. Adrienne Kertzer, '"Don't You Know Anything?": Childhood and the Holocaust', in *The Bloomsbury Companion to Holocaust Literature*, ed. by Adams, pp. 121–38 (p. 125); and Anna Clare Hunter, 'Tales from Over There: The Uses and Meanings of Fairy-tales in Contemporary Holocaust Narrative', *Modernism*, 20.1 (2013), 59–57 (p. 60). Kevin Paul Smith, *The Postmodern Fairy Tale: Folkloric Intertexts in Contemporary Fiction* (Basingstoke: Palgrave Macmillan, 2007), p. 1.
18. I have addressed this in my 'Philippe Claudel's *Brodeck* as a Parody of the Fable or the Holocaust Universalized', *Holocaust Studies*, 24.4 (2018), 503–26.
19. Elizabeth Schreiber, '*Car cela devient une histoire*: Representation of the Holocaust in the Imaginative and Collective Memoirs of Charlotte Delbo', in *Re-examining the Holocaust*, ed. by Kluge and Williams, pp. 2–38 (p. 4). Ezrahi, *By Words Alone*, p. 150.
20. Kári Driscoll, 'Perpetrators, Animals, and Animality', in *The Routledge International Handbook of Perpetrator Studies*, ed. by Knittel and Goldberg, pp. 192–205 (p. 196).
21. María Jesús Martínez-Alfaro, 'Rewriting the Fairy Tale in Louis Murphy's and Lisa Goldstein's Holocaust Narratives', *European Journal of English Studies*, 20.1 (2016), 64–82 (p. 64). See, for example, Christina Bacchilega, *Postmodern Fairy Tales: Gender and Narrative Strategies* (Philadelphia: Pennsylvania University Press, 1997).
22. *Anti-tales: The Uses of Disenchantment*, ed. by Catriona McAra and David Calvin (Newcastle upon Tyne: Cambridge Scholars Publishing, 2011). The essays gathered in this volume testify to the broad spectrum of concerns raised by contemporary rewritings of fairy tales.
23. Jenni Adams, *Magic Realism in Holocaust Literature: Troping the Traumatic Real* (Basingstoke: Palgrave Macmillan, 2011), p. 34.
24. Other Holocaust narratives that engage with Hansel and Gretel are Peter Rushforth's *Kindergarten* (2006) and Eliza Granville's *Gretel and the Dark* (2014).
25. Peter Arnds, 'On the Awful German Fairy Tale: Breaking Taboos in Representations of Nazi Euthanasia and the Holocaust in Günter Grass's *Die Blechtrommel*, Edgar Hilsenrath's *Der Nazi & der Friseur*, and Anselm Kiefer's Visual Art', *German Quarterly*, 75.4 (Autumn 2002), 422–39 (p. 423).
26. Fairy-tale narrative strategies are related to magic realism and the fantastic. See Adams, *Magic Realism in Holocaust Literature*; *The Fantastic in Holocaust Literature and Film: Critical Perspectives*, ed. by Judith Kerman and John Edgar Borning (Jefferson, NC: McFarland, 2015); and Michael Yogev, 'The Fantastic in Holocaust Literature: Writing and Unwriting the Unbearable', *Journal of the Fantastic in the Arts*, 5.2 (1993), 32–49.
27. Quoted by Casey Haskins 'Art, Morality, and the Holocaust: The Aesthetic Riddle of Benigni's *Life Is Beautiful*', *Journal of Aesthetics and Art Criticism*, 59.4 (Autumn 2001), 373–84 (p. 374).
28. Leon Yudkin, 'Is Aharon Appelfeld a Holocaust Writer?', in *The Holocaust and the Text: Speaking the Unspeakable*, ed. by Andrew N. Leak and George Paizis (Basingstoke: Palgrave Macmillan, 2000), pp. 142–58 (p. 146).
29. Adams, *Magic Realism in Holocaust Literature*, p. 26.

30. Jane Yolen, *The Devil's Arithmetic* (New York: Viking Kestrel, 1988), p. 67.
31. Adams, *Magic Realism in Holocaust Literature*, p. 26.
32. Elizabeth R. Baer, 'A Postmodern Fairy Tale of the Holocaust: Jane Yolen's *Briar Rose*', *Studies in American Jewish Literature*, 24 (2005), 145–52 (p. 149).
33. Martínez-Alfaro, 'Rewriting the Fairy Tale in Louis Murphy's and Lisa Goldstein's Holocaust Narratives', p. 66.
34. Jakob A. Arlow, 'Metaphor and the Psychanalytic Situation', *Psychanalytic Quarterly*, 43 (1979), 363–85; Jack Zipes, *Spells of Enchantment: Wondrous Fairy Tales of Western Culture* (New York: Penguin, 1991), p. 9.
35. Margarete J. Landwehr, 'The Fairy Tale as Allegory for the Holocaust: Representing the Unrepresentable in Yolen's *Briar Rose* and Murphy's *Hansel and Gretel*', in *Fairy Tales Reimagined: Essays on New Retellings*, ed. by Susan Reddington Bobby (Jefferson, NC: McFarland, 2009), pp. 153–67 (pp. 155, 157).
36. Arnds, 'On the Awful German Fairy Tale', p. 423.
37. Landwehr, 'The Fairy Tale as Allegory for the Holocaust', pp. 156, 157.
38. Baer, 'A Postmodern Fairy Tale of the Holocaust', p. 150.
39. Hunter, 'Tales from Over There', p. 60.
40. Hunter, '"To Tell the Story"'.
41. María Jesús Martínez-Alfaro, 'The Estrangement Effect in Three Holocaust Narratives: Defamiliarising Victims, Perpetrators and the Fairy-tale Genre', *Journal of the Spanish Association of Anglo-American Studies*, 42.1 (June 2020), 37–56 (p. 42).
42. Philippe Codde, 'Transmitted Holocaust Trauma: A Matter of Myth and Fairy Tales?', *European Judaism: A Journal for the New Europe*, 42.1 (Spring 2009), 62–75 (p. 64).
43. Hunter, 'Tales from Over There', p. 60.
44. D. L. Ashliman, *Folk and Fairy Tales: A Handbook* (Westport, CT: Greenwood Folklore Handbooks, 2004), p. 7.
45. Smith, *The Postmodern Fairy Tale*, p. 10. The remaining categories are: 'authorized' (explicit reference to a fairy tale in the title), 'writerly' (implicit reference in the title), and 'incorporation' (explicit reference in the text).
46. Philippe Claudel, *Le Rapport de Brodeck* (Paris: Stock, 2007), pp. 371, 194 (hereafter referenced as *RB* in the main text); *Brodeck*, trans. by John Cullen (New York: Anchor Books, 2010), pp. 310, 157 (hereafter referenced as *B* in the main text).
47. Jack Zipes, *Grimm Legacies: The Magic Spell of the Grimm Folk and Fairy Tales* (Princeton, NJ: Princeton University Press, 2014), p. 118.
48. Arnds, 'On the Awful German Fairy Tale', pp. 422–23. Jack Zipes, 'The Contamination of the Fairy Tale, or the Changing Nature of the Grimms' Fairy Tales', *Journal of the Fantastic in the Arts*, 11.1 (2000), 77–93 (p. 71).
49. Smith, *The Postmodern Fairy Tale*, p. 49.
50. Having its origins in the story of Gilles de Rais, *Bluebeard* is more frequently attributed to French author Charles Perrault than to the Grimms. Although originally included in the Grimms' tales, *Bluebeard* was removed because of its French origins. Smith, *The Postmodern Fairy Tale*, p. 11. Maria Tatar, however, identifies the pre-Perrault versions of the story as bearing similarity to the tales narrated by the Grimms' 'Fitcher's Bird' and 'The Robber Bridegroom': 'Bluebeard', in *The Oxford Companion to Fairy Tales*, ed. by Jack Zipes (Oxford: Oxford University Press, 2000), p. 56.
51. Smith, *The Postmodern Fairy Tale*, p. 27.
52. Ibid., p. 10. See, for example, Casie Hermansson, *Reading Feminist Intertextuality through Bluebeard Stories* (New York: Edwin Mellen, 2001), and works of fiction such as Margaret Atwood, *Bluebeard's Egg* (1983), Kurt Vonnegut, *Bluebeard* (1988), Max Frisch, *Blaubart* (1982), and Angela Carter, *The Bloody Chamber* (1979).
53. Jack Zipes, *The Brothers Grimm: From Enchanted Forests to the Modern World* (Basingstoke: Palgrave Macmillan, 2002), p. 68. A year after *Children's and Household Tales*, the Grimms published a journal entitled *Old German Forests* as part of their ambition to reactivate German people's interest in the customs, norms, and laws that bound them together.
54. Landwehr, 'The Fairy Tale as Allegory for the Holocaust', p. 158.

55. Zipes, *The Brothers Grimm*, p. 65.
56. France Grenaudier-Klijn, 'Landscapes Do Not Lie: War, Abjection and Memory in Philippe Claudel's *Le Rapport de Brodeck*', *Essays in French Literature and Culture*, 47 (November 2010), 87–107 (p. 97).
57. Jeffrey K. Wilson, *The German Forest: Nature, Identity, and the Contestation of National Symbols, 1871–1914* (Toronto: University of Toronto Press, 2012), pp. 178–79.
58. Elias Canetti, *Crowds and Power*, trans. by Carol Stewart (New York: Seabury, 1978), p. 173.
59. Bruno Bettelheim, *The Uses of Enchantment: The Meaning and Importance of Fairy Tales* (London: Penguin, 1976), p. 8.
60. Steve Baker, *Picturing the Beast: Animals, Identity and Representation* (Urbana: University of Illinois Press, 2001), p. 158.
61. I have addressed Claudel's representation of women (and of mothers in particular) in Duffy, 'The Silence of the Mothers'.
62. These questions have long been marginalised by Holocaust studies. See, for example, Monika J. Flaschka, 'Sexual Violence: Recovering a Suppressed History', in *A Companion to the Holocaust*, ed. by Simone Gigliotti and Hilary Earl (Hoboken, NJ: John Wiley, 2020), pp. 469–86; and '"Only Pretty Women Were Raped"'.
63. Bettelheim, *The Uses of Enchantment*, p. 67. Jodi Vandenberg-Daves, *Modern Motherhood: An American History* (New Brunswick, NJ: Rutgers University Press, 2014), p. 22.
64. Daniel Birnbaum and Anders Olsson, 'An Interview with Jacques Derrida on the Limits of Digestion', *e-flux Journal*, 2 (January 2009) <https://www.e-flux.com/journal/02/68495/an-interview-with-jacques-derrida-on-the-limits-of-digestion/> [accessed 6 July 2022].
65. The stereotype is loosely based on real-life figures of Ilse Koch, the sadistic and reputedly sex-crazed wife of the commandant of Buchenwald, and of Irma Grese, a particularly cruel guard at Ravensbrück, Auschwitz-Birkenau, and Bergen-Belsen. See Lewis, *Women in European Holocaust Films*, pp. 83–99.
66. Frost, *Sex Drives*, p. 154.
67. Ibid.
68. Koonz, *Mothers in the Fatherland*, pp. 53–90.
69. In the biography of the German-Jewish painter Charlotte Salomon, Mary Lowenthal Felstiner writes that 'For some, Pitchipoï was the nonsense name of a legendary village, "one of the Yiddish names used by Polish Jews". For some, "the word resonated like an eternal curse, the place of a pogrom or ghetto"': *To Paint Her Life: Charlotte Salomon in the Nazi Era* (New York: Harper Perennial, 1994), p. 198. The expression can also be found in André Schwarz-Bart, *Le Dernier des Justes* (Paris: Seuil, 1959), p. 402; *The Last of the Just*, trans. by Stephen Baker (New York: Atheneum, 1961), p. 351.
70. Anne Kershen explains the proliferation of Jewish tailors with the biblical prohibition against wearing garments combining linen and wool. To ensure garments conformed to this law, Jews only used co-religionist tailors. Shoemaking and tailoring businesses were also easy and cheap to establish. 'For a people accustomed to dispersal, occupations which were adaptable to any society at any time would always survive': *Uniting the Tailors: Trade Unionism among the Tailors of London and Leeds, 1870–1939* (London: Routledge, 1995), p. 8. Sébastien Hogue observes similarities between Bilissi's tale and Claudel's earlier novel, *La Petite Fille de Monsieur Linh* whose eponymous protagonist deludes himself about having a baby granddaughter. Hogue suggests that Fédorine, Emélia, and Poupchette are but a product of Brodeck's imagination, which undermines the protagonist's narratorial reliability: 'Oublier ou se souvenir? Culpabilité et mémoire dans *Le Rapport de Brodeck* de Philippe Claudel' (unpublished Masters dissertation, Université de Laval, 2015), pp. 92–93.
71. Georges Van den Abbeele, 'Fable', *Historical Materialism*, 16.4 (2008), 233–38.
72. Daphne Patai, 'Political Fiction and Patriarchal Fantasy', in *George Orwell's 'Animal Farm'*, ed. by Harold Bloom (New York: Infobase, 2009), pp. 3–22 (p. 3). Valerie Meyers, 'Animal Farm: An Allegory of Revolution', in ibid., pp. 23–34 (p. 27).
73. Márcia Seabra Neves, 'La Néo-fable animalière: devenir-animal et métamorphose', in *Le Néo: sources, héritages et réécritures dans les cultures européennes*, ed. by Karine Martin-Cardini and Jocelyne Aubé-Bourligueux (Rennes: Presses universitaires de Rennes), pp. 279–93, paragraph

17.
74. For a discussion of Spiegelman's use of animal imagery, see Stanislav Kolář, *Seven Responses to the Holocaust in American Fiction* (Ostrava: Universum, 2004), pp. 152–56.
75. Ezrahi, *By Words Alone*, p. 152.
76. Sax, *Animals in the Third Reich*, pp. 19–22, 23. Hitler likened himself to a wolf and the future generations of Germans to predators (p. 34).
77. Detlev Peukert, *Volksgenossen und Gemeinschaftsfremde: Anpassung, Ausmerze und Aufbegehren unter dem Nationalsozialismus* (Cologne: Bund-Verlag, 1982), p. 295.
78. Sax, *Animals in the Third Reich*, p. 34.
79. Bettelheim, *The Uses of Enchantment*, p. 43.
80. Dominick LaCapra, *History and its Limits: Human, Animal, Violence* (Ithaca, NY: Cornell University Press, 2009), p. 151.
81. Giorgio Agamben, *Homo Sacer: Sovereign Power and Bare Life*, trans. by Daniel Heller-Roazen (Stanford, CA: Stanford University Press, 1989). Jacques Derrida, *The Beast and the Sovereign. Volume 1*, trans. by Geoffrey Bennington (Chicago: University of Chicago Press, 2009), p. 326.
82. Jacques Derrida, 'L'Animal que donc je suis (à suivre)', in *L'Animal autobiographique*, ed. by Marie-Louise Mallet (Paris: Galilée, 1999), pp. 251–301 (p. 287); 'The Animal that Therefore I Am', trans. by David Wills, *Critical Inquiry*, 28.2 (Winter 2002), 369–418 (p. 405).
83. Michel Foucault, 'Omnes et singulatim: vers une critique de la raison politique', *Le Débat*, 4.41 (1986), 5–36 (p. 6).
84. Andrew Bennett discusses this myth from a historical perspective: *Suicide Century: Literature and Suicide from James Joyce to David Foster Wallace* (Cambridge: Cambridge University Press, 2017), pp. 26–28.
85. Among these thinkers have been Roman scholar Josephus, Rousseau, Goethe, Levinas, Cioran, Camus, and Derrida.
86. This is exemplified by the self-inflicted death of Jean Améry, Jerzy Kosinski, Tadeusz Borowski, Paul Celan, Piotr Ranviera, and Primo Levi himself. Levi, *The Drowned and the Saved*, pp. 56–57.
87. Ibid., pp. 60–61.
88. Emmanuel Levinas, 'Nom d'un chien ou le droit naturel', in *Difficile liberté: essais sur le judaïsme* (Paris: Albin Michel, 1976), pp. 199–202 (p. 200); 'The Name of a Dog or Natural Rights', in *Difficult Freedom: Essays on Judaism*, trans. by Seán Hand (Baltimore, MD: Johns Hopkins University Press, 1990), pp. 151–53 (pp. 151–52).
89. Referring to the Nazis and the Jews, Hitler compared them to cats and mice respectively. Sax, *Animals in the Third Reich*, p. 34. The comparison is further exemplified by the propaganda film *Der Ewige Jude*, which opens with the image of swarming rats and the narrator's explanation: 'Just as the rat is the lowest of animals, the Jew is the lowest of human beings', quoted by Charles Patterson, *Eternal Treblinka: Our Treatment of the Animals and the Holocaust* (New York: Lantern Books, 2001), p. 48. Cf. Amon Goeth's tirade in *Schindler's List*, where the sadistic Nazi compares Helen Hirsch to a rat. See Dan MacMillan, 'Dehumanisation and the Achievement of *Schindler's List*', in *The Holocaust: Memories and History*, ed. by Victoria Khiterer (Newcastle: Cambridge Scholars Publishing, 2014), pp. 311–34 (pp. 325–26). Kenneth Stow, *Jewish Dogs: An Image and its Interpreters: Continuity in the Catholic-Jewish Encounter* (Stanford, CA: Stanford University Press, 2006). Cf. Sax, *Animals in the Third Reich*, p. 81.
90. Charles Patterson mentions Kurt Franz's dog Barry in Treblinka, or the Jaworzno camp where similar commands were issued: *Eternal Treblinka*, pp. 123–24. In Schwarz-Bart's novel, an SS sets his dog on a deportee, shouting '"*Homme, déchire ce chien!*"' ['Man, destroy that dog!']: *Le Dernier des Justes*, p. 417; *The Last of the Just*, p. 368.
91. More recently, Asher Kravitz has narrated the Holocaust from the canine perspective. His 2007 novel attempts to reinscribe pets into the history of the persecution, where they can occupy the position of either victim or (unwilling) perpetrator, or, as in the case of the novel's protagonist, Caleb, of both: *The Jewish Dog*, trans. by Michal Kessler (New York: Penlight Publications, 2015).
92. Driscoll, 'Perpetrators, Animals, and Animality', p. 200. It is noteworthy that some survivors identified guard dogs as fully-fledged perpetrators with quasi-human motivations and genuine

eagerness to serve their masters. Yves Béon writes that 'the killer dogs seem to know all about Dora and the terror that must be sustained. They are cogs in the New Order that grips Europe implacably. They are confident in it; it will never fail them': *Planet Dora: A Memoir of the Holocaust and the Birth of the Space Age* (Boulder, CO: Westview Press, 1997), p. 43.

93. Brodeck's animalisation mirrors Levi's discussion of 'useless violence' which he exemplifies with the lack of spoons in Auschwitz. Without spoons 'the daily soup could not be consumed in any other way than by lapping it up as dogs do'. Levi, 'Useless Violence', in *The Drowned and the Saved*, pp. 83–101 (p. 91). A similar scenario can be found in Judith Kerr's YA novel *When Hitler Stole Pink Rabbit* (1971), which describes a famous professor who, once imprisoned in a Nazi camp, 'had to sleep in a dog kennel [...] and [had] to bark' (London: HarperCollins, 2008 [1971], p. 115).
94. Still, *Derrida and Other Animals*, p. 74.
95. Sax, *Animals in the Third Reich*, p. 83.
96. Hilda Kean and Philip Howell, 'Writing in Animals in History', in *The Routledge Companion to Animal-human History*, ed. by Hilda Kean and Philip Howell (London: Routledge, 2019), pp. 3–28 (p. 17).
97. LaCapra, *History and its Limits*, p. 155.
98. Sax, *Animals in the Third Reich*, pp. 83, 84.
99. Derrida, 'L'Animal que donc je suis', p. 247; 'The Animal that Therefore I Am', p. 386.
100. Andrew Benjamin, *Of Jews and Animals* (Edinburgh: Edinburgh University Press, 2010), pp. 186, 4.
101. Philip Howell, 'Animals, Agency and History', in *The Routledge Companion to Animal-human History*, ed. by Kean and Howell, pp. 197–221 (p. 204).
102. Ibid., p. 207. The third type of agency is 'ascribed agency'. Howell exemplifies it with medieval trials of animals or with circus animals whose 'human' behaviour is the effect of 'the brutal affair of ropes, pullies and hooks'. This sort of agency is construed through the lens of human power and privilege, 'rehears[es] and rehash[es] anthropocentric attitudes', and ultimately engenders the effacement of animals' true agency (p. 197).
103. David L. Clark, 'On Being "The Last Kantian in Nazi Germany": Dwelling with Animals after Levinas', in *Configuring the Human in Western History*, ed. by Jennifer Ham and Matthew Senior (New York: Routledge, 1997), pp. 165–98 (p. 166).
104. Levinas, 'Nom d'un chien ou le droit naturel', p. 201; 'The Name of a Dog or Natural Rights', p. 153.
105. Marie Daney de Marcillac, 'Fables philosophiques d'Emmanuel Levinas et de Michel Serres: Ulysse et les bêtes', *Littérature*, 4.168 (2012), 71–84 (p. 75).
106. Levinas, 'Nom d'un chien ou le droit naturel', p. 200; 'The Name of a Dog or Natural Rights', p. 152. Some might disagree with such a reading of Levinas's essay. Peter Atterton, for example, wonders whether, going against the humanism stamping his philosophical enterprise, Levinas grants the dog the position of a full moral agent: 'Dog and Philosophy: Does Bobby Have What It Takes to Be Moral?', in *Face to Face with Animals: Levinas and the Animal Question*, ed. by Peter Atterton and Tamra Wright (New York: State University of New York Press, 2019), pp. 63–92.
107. Levinas, 'Nom d'un chien ou le droit naturel', p. 202; 'The Name of a Dog or Natural Rights', p. 153. This is surprising given that, as Richard Nash points out, Levinas systematically ignores animals or even polices the species border: *Animal Nomenclature: Facing Other Animals* (New York: Routledge, 2006), p. 101.
108. Derrida, 'L'Animal que donc je suis', p. 269; 'The Animal that Therefore I Am', p. 387.
109. Gilles Deleuze and Félix Guattari, *Mille plateaux* (Paris: Minuit, 1980), p. 291.
110. Adorno, *Minima Moralia*, p. 105. Published in 1951, the text had been written between 1945 and 1949.
111. Timothy M. Costelloe, 'The Invisibility of Evil: Moral Progress and the "Animal Holocaust"', *Philosophical Papers*, 32.2 (2003), 109–13 (p. 115). Costelloe quotes Hilberg who likens the operations of the death camps to the 'complex mass production methods of a modern plant'. Hilberg, *The Destruction of European Jews*, p. 863. Charles Patterson observes similarities between the tunnel that was used in Bełżec, Sobibór, and Treblinka to feed Jews into gas chambers and

that used in slaughterhouses. He notes that, like the guards at Sobibór and Treblinka who called the tunnel *Himmelfahrtstrasse* [Road to Heaven], an American food scientist calls the conveyor she designed to funnel animals to their deaths the 'Stairway to Heaven': *Eternal Treblinka*, pp. 112–13.

112. Costelloe, 'The Invisibility of Evil', pp. 125–26, 128.
113. Steven Wise, *Rattling the Cage: Towards Legal Rights for Animals* (Cambridge, MA: Perseus Books, 2000), p. 252. This argument was already put forward by Edgar Kupfer-Koberwitz in the writings he produced during his imprisonment in Dachau, *Die Tierbrüder: Eine Betrachtung zum Ethischen Leben* (Hamburg: Höcker Verlag, 2010); *Animal Brothers: Reflections on an Ethical Way of Life*, trans. by Ruth Mossner, in *Compassionate Spirit* <https://compassionatespirit.com/wpblog/books/animal-brothers/> [accessed 6 June 2022].
114. Buettner, *Holocaust Images and Picturing Catastrophe*, p. 111.
115. Matt Prescott, 'Letter to the Jewish Community', quoted by David B. MacDonald, 'Pushing the Limits of Humanity? Reinterpreting Animal Rights and "Personhood" through the Prism of the Holocaust', *Journal of Human Rights*, 5.4 (2006), 417–37 (p. 429).
116. For an overview of the campaign and its detractors, see Buettner, *Holocaust Images and Picturing Catastrophe*, p. 106; and MacDonald, 'Pushing the Limits of Humanity?', pp. 427–29. In scholarship, Emily Miller Budick calls the use of the Holocaust in defence of animal rights 'a poorly chosen comparison at best' and at worst 'downright absurd and offensive'. She goes on to state that whereas 'enslavement and murder of humans is wrong', 'it is not obvious, especially given the history of human development (hunting and farming), why the slaughter of animals is wrong'. Her argument is therefore based on the fact that Blacks and Jews belong to the same species as white people, whereas animals do not, and that they can therefore be subject to any abuse. To buttress her argument, she states without any evidence that 'slave owners have always known that their slaves were humans like themselves': *The Subject of Holocaust Fiction* (Bloomington: Indiana University Press, 2012), pp. 230–31. In literature, this position is embodied by the fictional character Stern who, in J. M. Coetzee's *Elizabeth Costello* (2003), accuses the Australian novelist of blasphemy.
117. The eponymous protagonist of J. M. Coetzee's *Elizabeth Costello* rebuffs this argument by pointing out that it is of little interest to the victims whether their bodies are utilised or not after their death. Costello also stresses the utilitarian aspect of the Holocaust. She conjures up a scenario where she compliments the hostess on her lamp that, as it turns out, has been made out of 'the skins of young Polish-Jewish virgins': *Elizabeth Costello* (New York: Viking, 2003), p. 66. Likewise, Derrida dismisses the difference in ideological underpinning of the compared phenomena by asking us to imagine that, instead of burning the Jews, the Nazis 'avaient décidé d'organiser par insémination artificielle la surproduction et la surgénération de Juifs, de Tziganes et d'homosexuels qui, toujours plus nombreux et plus nourris, auraient été destinés [...] au même enfer, celui de l'expérimentation génétique imposée, de l'extermination par le gaz ou par le feu. Dans les mêmes abattoirs' [had decided to organize an overproduction and overgeneration of Jews, gypsies, and homosexuals by means of artificial insemination, so that, being more numerous and better fed, they could be destined [...] for the same hell, that of the imposition of genetic experimentation or extermination by gas or by fire. In the same abattoirs]. Derrida, 'L'Animal que donc je suis', p. 47; 'The Animal that Therefore I Am', p. 395.
118. J. M. Coetzee, *The Lives of Animals* (1999); Hélène Cixous, *Le Jour où je n'étais pas là* (2000); Marguerite Yourcenar, *Les Yeux ouverts: entretiens avec Mattieu Galey* (1980). Derrida, 'L'Animal que donc je suis'; Élisabeth de Fontenay, *Sans offenser le genre humain: réflexion sur la cause animale* (Paris: Albin Michel, 2008), and *Le Silence des bêtes: la philosophie à l'épreuve de l'humanité* (Paris: Fayard, 1998); LaCapra, *History and its Limits*, pp. 149–89.
119. Cf. MacDonald, 'Pushing the Limits of Humanity?', p. 418. Holocaust survivors include Alex Hershaft, who founded the Farm Animals Rights Movement (FARM). PETA's director Matt Prescott is not only Jewish, but lost relatives in the Holocaust. When hitting back at the campaign's opponents, he stressed that many of PETA's supporters were Jewish and that the campaign itself had been funded by a Jewish philanthropist: 'Pushing the Limits of Humanity?', pp. 429–30. Mark Gold relates the case of Edgar Kupfer-Koberwitz, a survivor of Dachau,

who refused to eat meat because, as he put it, 'I cannot nourish myself by the suffering and by the death of other creatures': *Animal Rights: Extending the Circle of Compassion* (Oxford: Jon Carpenter, 1995), p. 25. Other works that make the comparison between the holocausts of animals and the Jews include: Peter Singer, *Animal Liberation* (New York: Avon Books, 1990); Sax, *Animals in the Third Reich*; Karen Davis, *The Holocaust and the Henmaid's Tale: A Case for Comparing Atrocities* (New York: Lantern Books, 2005); Tom Regan, *The Case for Animal Rights* (Los Angeles: University of California Press, 1983); Roberta Kalechofsky, *Animal Suffering and the Holocaust: The Problem with Comparisons* (Marblehead, MA: Micah Publications, 2003); and Wise, *Rattling the Cage*.
120. Isaac Bashevis Singer, 'The Letter Writer', in *The Séance and Other Stories* (New York: Farrar, Straus & Giroux, 1968), p. 270. Although the protagonist, Herman Gombiner, did not experience Nazi violence first-hand, his New York life is structured according to a pattern reminiscent of Holocaust experience: having lost his job when the Hebrew publishing house he works for closes, Gombiner confines himself to his room (a sort of ghetto). When his boiler explodes and leaves him without heating, Gombiner contracts pneumonia and nearly dies. As he is too ill to feed his mouse, Huldah, who allegorises European Jewry, also nearly dies, yet in the end they both survive, promising a rebirth of the Jewish people. The same idea is put in the mouth of another of Singer's protagonists, Joseph Shapiro, who states, 'when it comes to animals, every man is a Nazi': *The Penitent* (New York: Farrar, Straus & Giroux, 1968), p. 39.
121. Coetzee, *Elizabeth Costello*, p. 65.
122. On Hitler's order, the executions of the participants of the Stauffenberg plot were carried out by hanging the victims from meat hooks. Carl Müller Frøland, *Understanding Nazi Ideology: The Genesis and Impact of Political Faith*, trans. by John Irons (Jefferson, NC: McFarland, 2020), p. 262.
123. In the spring of 1942, German Jews were requested to give up their pets. In the Kovno Ghetto, the murder of the Jews was preceded by the destruction of their pets inside a synagogue. Avraham Tory, *Surviving the Holocaust: The Kovno Ghetto Diary*, ed. by Martin Gilbert, trans. by Jerzy Michałowicz (Cambridge, MA: Harvard University Press, 1990), p. 67; and Saul Friedländer, 'Introduction', in *Probing the Limits*, ed. by Friedländer, pp. 1–21 (p. 21). In cinema, violence against Jewish-owned pets has been portrayed by Bob Fosse's *Cabaret* (1972) where the Brown Shirts slit the throat of Nathalia Landauer's beloved dog. In literature, this situation finds reflection in Prager, *Eve's Tattoo*.
124. Driscoll, 'Perpetrators, Animals, and Animality', p. 195.
125. Jochen von Lang, *The Secretary: Martin Bromann, the Man Who Manipulated Hitler*, trans. by Christa Armstrong and Peter White (New York: Random House, 1979), p. 84. Charles Patterson lists other high-ranking Nazis with farming backgrounds: Rudolph Höss (the commandant of Auschwitz), Victor Hack and Hans Hefelmann (key personnel in the euthanasia programme), and Kurt Franz (the last commandant of Treblinka): *Eternal Treblinka*, pp. 101–02 (p. 107).
126. David Sztybel, 'Can Treatment of Animals be Compared to the Holocaust?', *Ethics & the Environment*, 11.1 (2006), 97–132 (p. 112).
127. Derrida, 'L'Animal que donc je suis', p. 276; 'The Animal that Therefore I Am', p. 394.
128. According to Gérard Wajcman, forgetting was planned, rationalised, and factored into the genocidal project: *L'Object du siècle* (Paris: Verdier, 1998), p. 270. Sztybel notes that the flesh of killed mink is fed to the mink who are still alive: 'Can Treatment of Animals be Compared to the Holocaust?', p. 112.
129. Derrida, 'L'Animal que donc je suis', p. 283; 'The Animal that Therefore I Am', p. 400.
130. Ibid., p. 289; p. 416.
131. Derrida, *The Beast and the Sovereign*, pp. 68, 447.
132. For a discussion of the connection between speech and devouring in the context of Derrida's philosophy, see Chris Danta, '"Might Sovereignty be Devouring?": Derrida and the Fable', *SubStance*, 43.2 (2014), 37–49.
133. Sebastian Schönbeck, 'Return to the Fable: Rethinking a Genre Neglected in Animal Studies and Ecocriticism', in *Texts, Animals, Environments: Zoopoetics and Ecopoetics*, ed. by Frederike Middelhoff and others (Freiburg: Rombach, 2019), pp. 111–26 (p. 111). Schönbeck quotes Harriet Ritvo, *The Animal Estate: The English and Other Creatures in the Victorian Age* (Cambridge, MA: Harvard University Press, 1987); Erica Fudge, *Animal* (London: Reaktion Books, 2002);

and John Simons, *Animal Rights and the Politics of Literary Representation* (Basingstoke: Palgrave Macmillan, 2002).

134. Joshua Schuster argues that fables are counterproductive to the pursuit of real knowledge about animal minds and to the articulation of animal rights: 'Fables: On the Morals of Marianne Moore's Animal Monologues', in *The Ecology of Modernism: American Environments and Avant-garde Poetics* (Tuscaloosa: University of Alabama Press, 2015), pp. 22–46.
135. Simons, *Animal Rights and the Politics of Literary Representation*, p. 119.
136. Lorraine Daston and Gregg Mitman, 'Introduction', in *Thinking with Animals: New Perspectives on Anthropomorphism*, ed. by Lorraine Daston and Gregg Mitman (New York: Columbia University Press, 2005), pp. 1–14 (p. 4).
137. Daney de Marcillac, 'Fables philosophiques d'Emmanuel Levinas et de Michel Serres', p. 72. Graham Huggan, '"Greening" Postcolonialism: Ecocritical Perspectives', *Modern Fiction Studies*, 50.3 (Autumn, 2004), 701–33. Karen Dawn and Peter Singer demonstrate that Coetzee shares his character's view on animal rights: 'Converging Convictions: Coetzee and His Characters on Animals', in *J. M. Coetzee and Ethics*, ed. by Anton Leist and Peter Singer (New York: Columbia University Press, 2010), pp. 109–18.
138. Schönbeck, 'Return to the Fable', p. 112.
139. Derrida, 'L'Animal que donc je suis', p. 287; 'The Animal that Therefore I Am', p. 405.
140. Ibid., p. 255; p. 374.
141. Danta, '"Might Sovereignty Be Devouring?"', pp. 41–42.
142. Derrida, *The Beast and the Sovereign*, pp. 291–92.
143. Still, *Derrida and Other Animals*, p. 5.
144. Louis Marin, *Food for Thought*, trans. by Mette Hjort (Baltimore, MD: Johns Hopkins University Press, 1989), p. 82.
145. Derrida, *The Beast and the Sovereign*, p. 287. Still pays further attention to the grammatical gender of the animals in Derrida's bestiary, including those of *la bête* and *le souverain*: *Derrida and Other Animals*, p. 13.
146. Still, *Derrida and Other Animals*, pp. 6, 304–57.
147. Derrida, 'L'Animal que donc je suis', p. 272; 'The Animal that Therefore I Am', p. 391.
148. Dominick LaCapra, *Understanding Others: Peoples, Animals, Pasts* (Ithaca, NY: Cornell University Press, 2018), p. 64.
149. Hutcheon, *A Poetics of Postmodernism*, pp. 25, 11.
150. Hutcheon, *A Theory of Parody*, p. 75.
151. Fontenay, *Sans offenser*, pp. 44–45; *Without Offending Humans: A Critique of Animal Rights*, trans. by William Bishop (Minneapolis: University of Minnesota Press, 2012), pp. 20–21.
152. Bauman, *Modernity and the Holocaust*.
153. Henryk Markiewicz, 'On the Definitions of Literary Parody', in *To Honour Roman Jakobson: Essays on the Occasion of His 70th Birthday, 11 October 1966*, 3 vols (The Hague: Mouton, 1967), II, 1264–72 (p. 1265); Hutcheon, *A Poetics of Postmodernism*, p. 19.
154. Matthew Chrulew and Chris Danta, 'Fabled Thought: On Jacques Derrida's *The Beast & the Sovereign*', *SubStance*, 43.2 (2014), 3–9 (p. 8).
155. LaCapra, *Understanding Others*, p. 62.
156. Timothy Clark, *The Cambridge Introduction to Literature and the Environment* (Cambridge: Cambridge University Press, 2011), p. 187.
157. Derrida, 'L'Animal que donc je suis', p. 280; 'The Animal that Therefore I Am', p. 398.

CHAPTER 6

A Poor Pole Enters the Ghetto: Yannick Haenel's *Jan Karski* as a Witness to the Differend

> What will I tell him, I, a Jew of the New Testament,
> Waiting two thousand years for the second coming of Jesus?
> My broken body will deliver me to his sight
> And he will count me among the helpers of death:
> The uncircumcised.
>
> — Czesław Miłosz, 'A Poor Christian Looks at the Ghetto'

Introduction

The final verse of the poem by Czesław Miłosz quoted in the epigraph provides a convenient point of departure for my reading of *Jan Karski*, a novel that, using postmodern themes and representational strategies, confronts the growingly contentious subject of Polish-Jewish wartime relations.[1] It does so by retracing the life of a Polish diplomat and resistance fighter who has been described as the key to understanding these relations.[2] During World War II, Jan Romuald Kozielewski (1914–2000), better known under his *nom de guerre* 'Jan Karski', acted as one of the couriers between the resistance movement in occupied Poland and the Polish government-in-exile residing in Paris and, after Germany's invasion of France, in London. As part of his diplomatic missions, which in 1942 took him to England and in 1943 to Washington, the Polish emissary alerted the world to the genocide of the Jews that the Nazis were carrying out on Polish soil. Having failed to obtain a response from politicians, leaders of various churches, writers, or other persons of influence, in 1944 Karski published his memoirs, *Story of the Secret State*, and then, as part of the promotion of the book, gave some two hundred lectures all around the United States. In the terms of Hilberg's taxonomy of the participants of the Holocaust, Karski, who was a Catholic, was one of the messengers who brought 'the dire news of annihilation to the outside world'.[3] To borrow Bauman's formulation, he was one of those who was convinced that 'evil is not all-powerful' and that 'it can be resisted', and therefore '*chose moral duty over the rationality of self-preservation*'.[4] As we know today, Karski's endeavours failed to move the world to action, since for the Allies assisting the Jews was, as Hilberg puts it, 'at best a subordinated interest':

'The currency of the war was the bullet, shell, bomb; those who did not have these means were the war's forgotten poor'.[5]

Through their subject and form, the two poems that Miłosz created in reaction to the 1943 uprising in the Warsaw Ghetto and the Nazis' consequent destruction of the Ghetto raise questions that are also central to Haenel's novel. Broadly, these questions pertain to Polish responses to the Holocaust, which, since the fall of the Berlin Wall and the resulting discussion of ideas previously censored by the communist regime, have become subject to heated debates both in Poland and beyond. More specifically, if read paratextually and intratextually, Miłosz's poetry addresses literature's ethical responsibility to oppose social injustice by detecting and exposing indifference to evil. I am referring here in particular to the poet's own misgivings about his two poems; despite having been recognised by Yad Vashem as a Righteous Among the Nations and credited by fellow writers with saving 'the honour of Polish poetry', the Nobel Prize laureate judged his poems 'immoral' as they thematised 'the act of dying from the standpoint of an observer'.[6] While 'A Poor Christian Looks at the Ghetto' interrogates the passive onlooker's moral responsibility towards witnessed atrocity and her or his ensuing sense of guilt, 'Campo di Fiori' additionally bemoans the indifference of bystanders by juxtaposing the image of the burning Ghetto with that of non-Jewish Poles riding on a merry-go-round outside its walls. To universalise the Gentile Poles' shocking inertia, 'Campo di Fiori' frames the destruction of the Ghetto with similarly contrasting images from the past: the carefree ambiance of a food market and the public burning of the Italian free-thinker Giordano Bruno in punishment for holding opinions contrary to the Catholic doctrine.

As opposed to Miłosz's scathing portrait of Polish responses to the slaughter of the Jews, Haenel's narrative centres its attention on a man who repeatedly risked his life so that he might see the mass annihilation of Europe's Jewry with his own eyes and thus become a more credible witness. He then indefatigably rallied the British and American administrations to stop the extermination process. With his literary representation of Karski, Haenel, as I will argue in the first part of the chapter, intervenes in the ongoing discussions concerning Polish-Jewish co-existence, and in particular the Polish people's wartime inaction in the face of — or even their active participation in — the destruction of the Jews who had for generations lived in their midst. Although Polish wartime anti-Semitism had featured prominently in survivor narratives, for example Spiegelman's *Maus*, the public debate on the topic was ignited only by Lanzmann's *Shoah* in which many in Poland saw a tendentious portrayal of non-Jewish Poles.[7] Such a defensive reception must be contextualised within Polish post-war historiography of World War II. Controlled by the regime and subject to strict censorship, post-war historical studies narrowly focused on Polish resistance and suffering, neglecting the tragedy of Polish Jews who in fact constituted the majority of the victims of the Nazis' murderous occupation of Poland.[8] The year following the release of *Shoah* saw the screening of Andrzej Wajda's adaptation of Jerzy Andrzejewski's novella, *Wielki Tydzień* (1945) [Holy Week], another contemporaneous literary portrayal of the destruction of the

Warsaw Ghetto.[9] In contrast to Wajda's film which, screened only briefly before being shelved, passed literally unnoticed, Jan Błoński's essay 'The Poor Poles Look at the Ghetto' (1987) aroused heated discussions about Polish people's wartime responses to the Holocaust.[10] In the essay, published in the progressive Roman Catholic journal, *Tygodnik Powrzechny*, Błoński flatly rejected the notion of Poland's complicity in the genocide, at the same time deploring his fellow countrymen's dismissal of the questions regarding Polish-Jewish relations. He also urged the Poles to come to terms with their wartime past, for their soil 'ha[d] been tainted [with Jewish blood] for all time'.[11] However emotional and polarised, the reactions to Błoński's attempt at undermining the dominant narrative of Poland's wartime history and the linked silencing of the memory of a genocide that took place on Polish soil, pale in comparison with the outcry caused by Jan Gross's *Neighbours: The Destruction of the Jewish Community in Jedwabne, Poland* (2001).[12] Mobilising, to borrow Ball's expression, 'visceral poetics' through gut-wrenching descriptions of brutality, Gross's study brought to light the murder of some 1,600 Jews by the non-Jewish inhabitants of a small Polish town.[13] The account of what happened in Jedwabne in July 1941 opened up a path for further revelations.[14] These dealt a blow to Poland's self-image as a nation-martyr which, as a result of the war, lost not only nearly two million of its non-Jewish inhabitants, but also a large chunk of its territory and political sovereignty.[15] *Neighbours* also undermined the external perception of two separate histories as far as wartime Poland is concerned: one of the Polish population which, like other occupied nations, suffered under the German yoke, and the other one of the Jews whose ordeal has been seen as part of the transnational narrative of the Holocaust. That the matter has not been laid to rest is evidenced by the sustained efforts of Poland's government, since 2015 led by the national-conservative party, Prawo i Sprawiedliwość [Law and Justice], to criminalise any discussion of Polish involvement in the Holocaust.[16]

Thus contextualised, Haenel's representation of the Nazi genocide from the perspective of a non-Jewish witness and rescuer sets out to score several political goals. Apart from providing a counternarrative to the increasingly dominant conception of Polish people as complicitous in the Nazi programme of the 'Final Solution', *Jan Karski*'s ambition is to bring into the spotlight the Polish resister's heroic actions which, at least in the French-speaking world, have been neglected. At the time Haenel was writing his novel, the French translation of Karski's memoirs had been out of print for many years and even his interview in *Shoah* had been largely forgotten. Indeed, Haenel's other major aim is, as I will demonstrate in this chapter, to straighten the record set by Lanzmann's film which included the Pole's forty-minute testimony without, however, mentioning his rescue mission. Furthermore, like Gross's *Neighbours* — albeit with a radically different emphasis — Haenel's narrative aims to counter the prevailing view of the separateness of Polish and Jewish wartime histories. *Jan Karski* achieves this not only by concentrating on a man who displayed extraordinary dedication to the Jewish cause, but also by foregrounding the activities of the Polish government-in-exile and of the resistance movement at home aimed at assisting Poland's Jewish population. Finally, as part of its crusade to restore Poland's good name, *Jan Karski* revives a historical narrative that, having emerged in the mid-1960s, indicted the apathy of the Allies in the face of the Nazi genocide. Picking up on the allegations made by historians, *Jan Karski* charges wartime Britain and America with the crime of non-assistance. Correspondingly, it construes Western accusations of Polish anti-Semitism as a means of deflecting attention from the Western nations' own deeply entrenched anti-Jewish prejudice. Finally, *Jan Karski* rejects the widely accepted redemptive and conclusive significance of the Nuremberg trials. Rather, it posits them as a means of installing a complicity of silence over the Allies' shared responsibility for the Holocaust and other crimes committed during World War II, such as the Soviets' 1940 massacre of some twenty-two thousand Polish officers and members of social elites in the Katyń forest.

Haenel's narrative thus fulfils two of the functions of eyewitness accounts, which are to attest to the suffering of the exploited and wounded, and to provide a 'counter-discourse' to the existing philosophical and historiographic representations of past events.[17] It also, as I will contend in the second part of the chapter, challenges literary realism and biography, which many consider the most appropriate rhetorical modes in which to represent the Holocaust. Instead, *Jan Karski* co-opts a characteristically postmodern approach, as manifest in, among other narrative strategies, its meta-fictionality, interdiscursivity, and generic heterogeneity. Put differently, by incongruously fusing biography, testimony, and literary invention, Haenel's narrative complies with Hutcheon's definition of historiographic metafiction as a narrative mode that rejects 'the impulse to sameness [...] and homogeneity, unity and certainty', in order to be 'a complex institutional and discursive network of élite, official, mass, popular cultures that postmodernism operates in'.[18] Moreover, through its self-reflexive and critical espousal of the testimonial mode, Haenel's narrative aligns itself with the programmatically self-contradictory ethos of postmodern historical literature, as theorised by Hutcheon, which undercuts the very narrative conventions it inscribes. Notably, while demonstrating the rare potential of testimony to articulate subjective and traumatic narratives, *Jan Karski* draws attention to its narrativity, constructedness, and consequent affinity with fiction. Finally, in line with postmodern fiction's attentiveness to the voices of marginalised groups and individuals, Haenel's ethically-charged novel revisits a life story that has been liminalised and distorted, and, accordingly, challenges dominant historical narratives, as exemplified by its questioning of America's moral superiority over Nazi Germany.

Elsewhere I have identified Haenel's narrative as an act of metawitnessing, a term that Derrida has coined in response to Paul Celan's poetry and that, analogous to metafiction, designates a secondary testimony accompanied by a metatextual meditation on the aporias attached to the act of bearing witness.[19] Pursuing this interpretation, I will contend that what *Jan Karski* testifies to is not so much the events of the Holocaust, which are well known by now, but to the fact that the Jews' pleas for help, which Karski mediated on their behalf, were repeatedly ignored. It also bears witness to the post-war silencing of Karski's efforts to alert the world to the Jewish tragedy, and to the world's indifference to the terrible news of which he was bearer. In other words, Haenel's narrative draws attention to the wrongs that both the Jews and Karski suffered when the Pole's desperate appeals went unheeded and, later, when Lanzmann manipulated his testimony and, in so doing, misrepresented his wartime diplomatic missions. I will thus posit the scenario staged by *Jan Karski* as an example of the differend (*différend*), a term with which Jean-François Lyotard has designated the incompatibility between the discursive codes of the plaintiff and of the judicial, political, or social framework within which the plaintiff presents her or his damage (*dommage*). It is this incompatibility that, by making the damage incommunicable, turns it into a wrong (*tort*).[20] I will conclude the chapter by postulating that, rather than appropriating Karski's voice, as some of Haenel's critics have intimated, the non-Jewish third-generation novelist raises a range of vital questions regarding the nature and historical usefulness of testimony, and its future in the face of the impending absence of direct witnesses to the Holocaust. By testifying to the differend(s) rather than to the events of the Nazi genocide themselves, Haenel answers Lyotard's call to postmodern writers to create original affective and narrative responses to the victims' wrongs. He thus bears witness to the metareality of these wrongs, that is to the impossibility of their articulation for lack of witnesses and/or suitable discursive means.

'A False Testimony' and 'a False Novel'

The two most virulent critics of Haenel's novel have been the Holocaust historian Annette Wieviorka and Lanzmann himself, who dubbed *Jan Karski* respectively 'a false testimony' and 'a false novel'.[21] Borne out by the two derogatory labels, the generic instability of Haenel's narrative is apparent already from its cover; whereas the book's title suggests that we are about to read a biography and therefore a work adhering to the principle of veracity, the category *roman* [novel] places Haenel's narrative under the rubric of literary invention.[22] To dispel this confusion, the author's note scrupulously distinguishes between the documentary character of Parts I and II, and the 'fiction intuitive' [intuitive fiction] of Part III.[23] What this means in practice is that Haenel's narrative opens with an ekphratic description of Karski's appearance in *Shoah*, which is followed, in Part II, by a recapitulation of his memoirs, *Story of the Secret State*. Positioning himself as a candid viewer, the narrator of Part I records his impressions of the Pole's testimony in front of Lanzmann's camera, a testimony marked with 'thick affect', as Ball terms an identification with past violences as if they were still actively present.[24] During the interview, Karski relates his encounter with two Jewish leaders in September 1941 in Warsaw, and his clandestine and perilous infiltration of the Warsaw Ghetto where he witnessed Dantesque scenes of human misery.[25] Part II then summarises the main points of the Pole's memoirs: Karski's participation in the short-lived defence of his homeland in September 1939, his internment by the Soviets and escape from their captivity later the same year, and his work for the Polish Resistance where, thanks to his multilingualism, photographic memory, and diplomatic training and experience, he was entrusted with the role of a courier. Before Karski's journey to England, the Resistance arranged his meeting with the leaders of the Bund and the Zionists, who urged him to inform the government-in-exile and its allies of the mass murder of Jews taking place in occupied Poland. The two men also requested that the German people be made aware of the atrocities committed on their behalf and that German cities be bombed in retaliation. To make Karski more trustworthy, the men took him into the Ghetto and later arranged his visit to the transit camp of Izbica Lubelska (which at the time Karski mistook for Bełżec).[26] The following description of the Pole's diplomatic missions contains harrowing details of his capture, arrest, and torture by the Gestapo, of his attempt to take his own life, and of his successful escape from the hospital where he was recovering from the attempted suicide. From Part II, we also learn about the Polish emissary's London interview with the Judeo-Polish socialist politician Szmul Zygielbojm, of his meetings with various Polish and British officials and, finally, of his journey to America where he was to speak with Jewish and Christian leaders, congressmen, writers, and journalists, and where, on 28 July 1943, he met President Roosevelt himself.

The third and final part of the novel, whose fictionality Haenel has justified with the paucity of information about Karski's post-war life, presents itself as the Pole's posthumous testimony to his fruitless efforts to save his homeland from Soviet control and the Jews from Hitler. Significantly longer than Parts I or II and strikingly different in tone to both, Part III is narrated by an imaginary Karski who reminisces about his unrelenting endeavours to stop the annihilation of Europe's Jewry. A long passage is dedicated to the Pole's interview with Roosevelt, which the imaginary Karski recalls in farcical terms, depicting the president as a simultaneously apathetic and lustful conformist. Ventriloquising Karski's thoughts, Haenel makes the reader privy to the Pole's enduring sense of failure resulting from his unsuccessful attempts to stop Poland's handover to Stalin and to mobilise the Allies' support for the dying Jews. The fictional Karski then vociferates against those who, by portraying the Poles as virulent anti-Semites, whitewash themselves of Judeophobia. Furthermore, while expressing his admiration for *Shoah*, he settles the score with Lanzmann who had misled him into believing that his project was to be about rescue efforts before including his testimony in a film that offers a one-sided view of Polish bystanders to the Holocaust. Haenel's Karski ultimately condemns the British and American passivity regarding the Jewish catastrophe and posits humanity as a concept discredited by the crimes committed during World War II and by their subsequent politically motivated distortion and obfuscation.

It is largely, though not exclusively, Haenel's invention of Karski's testimony that became the target of the vehement criticism exemplified by the tirades of Lanzmann and Wieviorka. Having first met with quasi-unanimous critical acclaim, some three months later the book gave rise to a polemic whose ferocity matched that of the debates provoked by Littell's *Les Bienveillantes*, even if the two novels were contested for different reasons.[27] Despite centring his novel on an indisputably positive character and doing nothing to offend the memory of the Jews whose cause Karski so tirelessly championed, Haenel was blasted with vitriolic and often absurd accusations. Since this controversy has already been addressed in some detail, I will restrict myself to a restatement of those points which are immediately pertinent to my discussion of, on the one hand, Haenel's re-presentation of Polish-Jewish relations and the Allies' passivity, and, on the other, his self-conscious and self-questioning approach to the genre of testimony.[28] The attack on Haenel was first launched in December 2009 by Wieviorka who implicitly equated *Jan Karski* with Wilkomirski's hoax testimony of his childhood survival of the Holocaust. The historian also accused the novel of anachronistic anti-Americanism and, invoking the 1946 Kielce pogrom, of offering a sentimentalised view of Polish-Jewish relations.[29] Finally, she denounced Haenel's inadmissible disregard for historical *truth* which, in her view, the novelist had replaced with a number of his own *truths*.[30] Echoing Wieviorka's outburst, Lanzmann charged the novelist with falsifying history by, for instance, misrepresenting Karski as a whimpering and cantankerous character, and misconstrued Haenel's analysis of *Shoah* as an act of plagiarism.[31] Many of these invectives were then repeated by other critics,[32] including in Karski's homeland, before the debate moved from the press to scholarly journals where Haenel found more supporters than detractors.[33]

'A Catholic Jew'

To return to Miłosz's wartime poems, their representativeness of the Polish people's wartime response to the Holocaust is unquestionably limited; while 'A Poor Christian Looks at the Ghetto' stages the impotent pity of the Poles for the Jews being murdered, 'Campo di Fiori' thematises their callous indifference towards the genocide. In reality, some non-Jewish Poles quietly welcomed the Germans' programme of extermination or even profiteered from Jewish deaths. Others, pejoratively called *szmalcownicy* [extortioners], tracked down Jews hiding in order to blackmail them or, encouraged by financial rewards from the German authorities, betrayed them and those sheltering them.[34] Worse still, some, as in Jedwabne and other places, took advantage of the vulnerability of the Jews and murdered them themselves. However, as evidenced by the prominence of Polish names among those Yad Vashem has honoured as Righteous Among Nations, many also defied the draconian measures the Germans took against anyone helping Jews and assisted their Jewish neighbours — whether their aid was selfless or financially motivated.[35] It is worth adding that Poland was the only German-occupied country with an organisation dedicated to helping Jews, which was established and supported by the government. Operating under the threat of death from the Nazis, members of the Council for Aid to Jews (Żegota) saved thousands of lives.[36]

With his retelling of the life of a Catholic Pole who took enormous risks to become an eyewitness to the reality of the ghettos and the camps, and who then promoted the Jewish cause right until the end of the war, Haenel singles out a rare — though not isolated — response to the Holocaust by a non-Jewish member of Poland's population. Karski's empathetic attitude has often been ascribed, including by himself, to his origins in the multicultural city of Łódź where on the eve of

World War II a third of the population was Jewish.[37] In fact, Karski's links with the Jewish people and commitment to the memory of the Holocaust continued well into the post-war period. In 1964 he married the Polish-Jewish dancer and choreographer, Pola Nireńska (née Perla Nirensztajn), who had lost seventy-four members of her family in Nazi-occupied Poland and who, haunted by her loss, eventually committed suicide. As well as being recognised by Yad Vashem as a Righteous Among the Nations, Karski was awarded honorary citizenship of Israel. After his death, Kaddish was said at his funeral, which, according to his long-time friend, was 'something [Karski] would have liked'.[38] In Haenel's narrative, the Pole's hybrid identity is reflected in his statement to Elie Wiesel: 'Je suis un catholique juif' [I am a Catholic Jew], which the novelist has based on Karski's pronouncement at the 1981 Liberation of the Concentration Camps Conference.[39]

Notwithstanding Karski's unquestionable sympathy for the Jews and the general perception of his wartime heroics promulgated by, among others, Karski himself, it is obvious that his wartime diplomatic missions were chiefly to do with the Polish war effort and Poland's position in the postwar world.[40] The resistance movement at home and the government-in-exile were more alarmed by the threat of Poland's transferal to the Soviet zone of influence after the re-establishment of peace than by the massacre of Poland's Jews. This is corroborated by Karski's own contemporaneous reports which reveal that Jewish matters occupied, as David Engel puts it, 'a relatively small portion of his attention, both in Britain and in the United States'.[41] In contrast to these facts, Haenel's portrayal of Karski reflects the popular image of him as 'the man who tried to stop the Holocaust', as he became known thanks to the testimonies he made following the release of *Shoah* and to his 1994 biography.[42] To be more exact, Haenel's narrative creates an impression that the Pole's endeavours were dedicated in equal measure to ensuring Poland's post-war political independence and to rescuing Jews. Such a representation of Karski's mission may have been motivated by the novelist's intention to reconnect Polish and Jewish wartime histories which had been separated in Karski's homeland.[43] In post-war Poland, Jewish memories were subsumed within the ideologically-driven metanarrative of Poland's heroic struggle against the Nazis, and the Jews themselves were effectively excluded from 'the mnemonic community'.[44] According to Daniel Levy and Natan Sznaider, the end of communism only entrenched this separation, with the Holocaust having emerged as a transnational phenomenon that was to provide a new point of reference for future-oriented Europe in the Second Modernity.[45] Conversely, Haenel's novel systematically interweaves the abandonment of the Jews by the Western powers and Poland's betrayal by the Allies and its resulting post-war loss of sovereignty. Furthermore, inspired by Karski's use of direct discourse when he recalls the pleas of the two Jewish leaders in front of Lanzmann's camera, Haenel's narrative melds Karski with the murdered Jews. The conduit for this melding is the prophetic figure of Moses, credited with leading the Jews out of their Egyptian slavery into the Promised Land. Like baby Moses, whose bulrush basket was carried by the waters of the Nile, the fictional Karski is transported by the flow of his story, his vessel being a pillow-lined bathtub standing in the middle of his Washington hotel room. At the end of the narrative, which revisits Karski's physical and psychological collapse following his infiltration of Izbica Lubelska, the Pole is no longer figured as a potential saviour, but as a crucified Christ who, seized by doubt and the realisation of his impotence as rescuer, considers dying together with those he has failed to save to be the only ethical course of action.

If Haenel's focus on Karski could be deciphered in terms of his intention to enmesh the wartime plight of non-Jewish Poles with that of their Jewish neighbours, I see it mainly as an effort to counter the perception of Poles as fervent anti-Semites who at best passively watched the Jewish tragedy and at worst played an active role in it. Although, contrary to Wieviorka's indictment of Haenel's novel, the fictional Karski acknowledges the existence of Polish anti-Jewish prejudice, he refuses to see his homeland reduced to this phenomenon, as if other nations, including the French, were immune to it. To stress the unfairness of the progressively dominant representation of Poland, Haenel's Karski justifies his decision not to return to his homeland after the war with his anxiety of being seen, as a Pole, as complicitous in the genocide. Having been elected by the Germans to be the vast killing field, a fact that some historians have attributed to the Polish people's supposedly endemic anti-Jewish sentiment,[46] Poland, Karski asserts, will become synonymous with the mass murder of Europe's Jews: 'Et même si les Polonais ont été victimes des nazis, et victimes des staliniens, même s'ils ont résisté à cette double oppression, le monde verra toujours dans les Polonais les bourreaux, et dans la Pologne le lieu du crime' [And even if the Poles were victims of the Nazis, the victims of the Stalinists, even if they resisted against this twofold oppression, the world would always see the Poles as executioners and Poland as the scene of the crime] (*JK*, 153; *M*, 140). Ironically, it was in 2012 at a ceremony during which Karski's wartime heroics were posthumously acknowledged with the Presidential Medal of Freedom, that, by invoking 'Polish death camps', Barack Obama provided an example of the misrepresentation of Poland lamented by Haenel's narrative.[47] To oppose this, in his view, unfair image of Karski's homeland, Haenel romanticises Poland by, for example, describing it as a scapegoated country that has been 'mal-aimé, mal-traité' [unloved, ill-treated] and by equating it with 'l'éternelle douceur [eternal gentleness] (*JK*, 120, 162; *M*, 110, 148). In so doing, Haenel glosses over the ambiguity marking Polish society's wartime reactions to the Holocaust, instantiated by the fact that Pola Nirenska's beloved sister, Franka, did not find help among her non-Jewish friends when she managed to escape from the Ghetto.[48] His novel conveniently draws a veil over the resentment that Karski's wife consequently harboured against Poland and that she externalised by refusing to speak her native language, including with her Polish husband. Even more problematically, by engaging in an unchecked equation of Polishness with resistance, the novelist extends Karski's courage and moral integrity to all Poles.[49] This means that, even if this is to counter a one-sided and necessarily biased portrayal of wartime Poland, Haenel himself is guilty of simplifying a complex historical reality.

Un di Velt hot geshvign[50]

Haenel's refutation of the charge of anti-Semitism levelled at the Polish nation is concomitant with his lashing out at Western liberal democracies which, to deflect attention from their own wartime failure to save the Jews, have foregrounded Polish anti-Jewish sentiment: 'Ils s'acharnent à couvrir la Pologne d'infamie [...] parce qu'il leur donne l'illusion de les blanchir, eux qui d'une manière ou une autre ont collaboré avec les nazis' [They continue to heap Poland with infamy [...] because it gives them the illusion of cleansing themselves, even though they all collaborated one way or another with the Nazis] (*JK*, 120; *M*, 110). The fictional Karski substantiates this argument by reminding us of the Western Allies' sustained unwillingness to listen to reports on the ongoing genocide and to calls for action. He invokes the vote of the American Congress against saving Jews, Roosevelt's refusal to receive the rabbis seeking help for their European brethren, and the Allies' decision to ignore various opportunities to save Jews, such as the bombing of Auschwitz and the rescue of seventy thousand Jewish-Romanian refugees. Rather than to simple bureaucratic inertia, the fictional Karski ascribes the Allies' wartime attitude to a complex combination of political cowardice, legal technicalities, and entrenched anti-Semitic sentiment. He also mentions the American administration's fear of having to accommodate large numbers of immigrants in the context of the approaching elections. He even insinuates that the reduction in the Jewish population was something the Allies secretly welcomed: 'le consensus anglo-américain masquait un intérêt commun contre les Juifs' [the Anglo-American consensus masked a shared interest *against* the Jews] (*JK*, 129; *M*, 118). To the British and American passivity, Haenel's Karski opposes the well-documented efforts of the Polish underground movement and government-in-exile to expose Nazi atrocities on Polish soil and to assist the Jews.[51]

In indicting the apathy of the Allies, Haenel's protagonist reiterates the arguments that have been put forward as of the late 1960s when, inspired by the silence of Pope Pius XII, journalist Arthur Morse broke the ground in the field.[52] Morse was then followed by historians Henry Feingold, David Wyman, Monty Penkower, and Deborah Lipstadt, who continued to uncover the American administration's knowledge of the progressing genocide. They also condemned its inadequate response to the plight of the Jews escaping Nazi Germany in the 1930s and, later, to the mass slaughter of the Jews who had remained in Nazi-occupied Europe. And, even if the tone of recent scholarship has been more measured and some of the arguments more nuanced, a consensus remains that 'British and American officials worked assiduously to block emigration to their countries, backed by an unsympathetic public and politicians unwilling to consider the humanitarian aspects of the situation'.[53]

With its attack on the Allies, *Jan Karski* questions Hilberg's taxonomy of Holocaust actors, where, according to Kristina Morina and Krijn Thijs, the bystander category is not only the 'broadest and the vaguest', but also carries 'assumptions about the personal responsibility and culpability of "the other"'.[54] Tony Kushner concurs with this position by noting that the bystander category is 'as unquestioned today

[...] as it was absent from consideration in 1945', at the same time observing that the bystander's role has caused much 'soul-searching and anger in recent years'.[55] Through his contribution to these debates, Haenel does not limit himself to foregrounding the passivity of the Allies in the face of the genocide, but puts it on a par with Nazi violence: 'en se détournant du mal, et en refusant d'entendre qu'il existe, on se met à en faire partie. Ceux qui refusent d'entendre le mal deviennent les complices du mal' [by turning away from evil, by refusing to hear that it exists, people become part of it. Those who refuse to hear about evil become its accomplices] (*JK*, 129; *M*, 118). Haenel's resolute implication of the Allies in the Holocaust resonates less with Hilberg's definition of bystanders as those who were present during the genocide than with an act of complicity which, while being normally understood as being 'a knowing accomplice or accessory to a crime', is redefined by Mary Fulbrook as 'know[ing] about a crime, possibly even witness[ing] it personally, but fail[ing] to act by seeking to prevent it'.[56] To illustrate the equation of inaction with perpetration, Haenel has the fictional Karski identify with the Nazis when, disguised as a Ukrainian guard, he enters a concentration camp but is unable to alleviate the suffering he witnesses. Karski's powerlessness renders him, in his own view, as culpable as the perpetrators, and the only way to move away from the position of guilt would be to commune with the victims in death. Haenel reinforces his point through his protagonist's assimilation of the White House, where the actual Karski met Roosevelt, with the Soviet camp for Polish POWs where he was held in 1939, and with the headquarters of the Gestapo where he was brutally interrogated in 1941. Imputing the Nazis' anti-Semitism to the Allies, the imaginary Karski states that 'chaque fois qu'un collaborateur de Roosevelt ou de Churchill se demandait quoi faire des Juifs, il se posait la même question qu'Hitler' [whenever a member of Churchill's or Roosevelt's administration wondered what to do about the Jews, he was asking the same question as Hitler was asking] (*JK*, 131; *M*, 120).

Such a re-presentation of the Allies, in which Wieviorka recognises Haenel's retroactive projection of contemporary anti-American sentiments, dovetails with the novelist's questioning of the conception of the end of the war as a victory: 'Il n'y a pas eu de vainqueurs en 1945, il n'y a eu que des complices et menteurs' [There were no victors in 1945, there were just accomplices and liars] (*JK*, 115; *M*, 105). The very fact that six million Jews were allowed to perish undermines the possibility of seeing 8 May 1945 as a day of triumph and glory. The subsequent bombings of Hiroshima and Nagasaki, the Soviets' use of the freshly emptied Nazi concentration camps to intern their perceived opponents, and the Western powers' new betrayal of the central European states in February 1945 at Yalta, which repeated the 1938 Munich conference, undermine the linear narrative of twentieth-century history. Instead, these facts promote a circular vision of the past, where the war is an ongoing condition rather than a completed historical event. And so, for Haenel's Karski, instead of providing a sense of closure and redemption, the Nuremberg trials are a cover up for the Allies' shared responsibility for the Holocaust. What the trials also revealed was the bankruptcy of the concept of 'humanity', since the

Holocaust, in the fictional Karski's redefinition, was not a crime *against* but *by* humanity. Consequently, Haenel's protagonist identifies 1945 not as the year of the re-establishment of peace but as 'la pire année dans l'histoire du XXe siècle' [the worst year in the history of the twentieth century] (*JK*, 167; *M*, 153). This is because 1945 saw the falsification of responsibility for the Holocaust, for the Katyń massacre, and for other wartime crimes.

As for Karski himself, Haenel portrays him as a minoritarian figure whose lonely crusade continues beyond the end of the war. The Pole's position, as imagined by the French novelist, is indicated by his decision to retain his *nom de guerre* and to keep wearing the great coat he received upon first landing on American soil. As well as to Franz Kafka's Joseph K., who becomes fatally lost in the labyrinthine structures of heartless, arbitrary yet all-powerful bureaucracy, Haenel's Karski likens himself to the solitary and defiant figure in Rembrandt's painting *The Polish Rider* (1637). Contextualised by Haenel's romanticised portrait of Poland as a victim of the treachery of powerful nations, Karski's affinity with the nobleman revives the vision of Polish history as one of heroic resistance and lost causes. Unable to return to active service in occupied Poland, Karski resists by bearing witness, including during his sleepless nights. Seated on the very sofa from which he spoke into the lens of Lanzmann's camera, Haenel's Karski incantates the messages given to him by the Jews of Warsaw and the names of his fellow officers murdered on Stalin's orders in Katyń. Haenel thus reposits testimony as a strategy for opposing evil and for confronting those who choose to ignore it. His conception of testimony as an ethical imperative and an act of resistance is embodied by Karski's anxiety that his writing of his memoirs in his Washington hotel room may be interrupted at any moment by the intrusion of an SS officer.

As well as being intended, more generally, as a rejoinder to the allegations of Polish wartime passivity towards — or even complicity in — the Jewish tragedy, the fictional Karski's monologue specifically targets Lanzmann's misrepresentation of the Polish emissary in *Shoah*. Haenel's narrative, firstly, opposes the reduction of the Pole's wartime activities to his infiltration of the Warsaw Ghetto, whereby *Shoah* glosses over his commitment to galvanising the Western Allies into action. Secondly, Haenel's Karski objects, however parenthetically, to Lanzmann's manipulative use of Polish peasants whom the film director gathered in front of a Catholic church and whose indifference and slighting comments he used to underscore the perennial character of Christian anti-Semitism.[57] Finally, the Pole, as imagined by Haenel, complains about having been misled by Lanzmann's assurances of his sympathy for the Polish people and promise to cover rescue efforts. Having been interviewed by Lanzmann in 1978, the real-life Karski was contractually prevented from bearing witness until the release of the documentary in 1985. That said, the novel's positive overall evaluation of *Shoah* reflects Haenel's admiration for the French director's work. Despite the differences between Lanzmann and Haenel, *Jan Karski* imitates what LaCapra has described as *Shoah*'s 'postmodern and poststructuralist tendencies in reading and interpretation'.[58] As we will see in the second part of this chapter, Haenel's subscription to the representational ethos championed by Lanzmann manifests itself in his novel's privileging of testimony over traditional historiography, or perhaps in calling for historiography to accommodate traumatic testimony with its non-linear temporality. As well as valorising trauma and rejecting chronology and the cause-and-effect logic in favour of a circular and reiterative structure,[59] *Jan Karski*, like *Shoah*, emphasises the inseparability of our understanding of the past from the reality in which this past is retrieved and pieced together, and insists on the shared constructedness of fiction and testimony. Finally, the film and the novel are united in their generic ambiguity, with *Shoah* having been identified by LaCapra as 'a disturbingly mixed generic performance' and by its director himself as neither a documentary, nor a historical film, nor even a film about the Holocaust.[60]

Testimony and History

By according the paramount importance to eyewitness narratives, *Shoah*, according to Shoshana Felman, institutionalised 'the age of testimony'.[61] Echoed some years later by Wieviorka's 'l'ère du témoin' [the era of the witness], Felman's term points to an important shift in the perception of survivor testimony occasioned by Eichmann's highly mediatised trial. Prior to the trial, notwithstanding the proliferation of eyewitness accounts both contemporaneous and posterior to the Holocaust, witnesses had been marginalised by mainstream cultural memory and historiography alike.[62] For Stone, who follows here Agamben, this situation was paradoxical, considering that the term 'history' derives from *hístor* which is 'in origin the eyewitness, the one who has seen'.[63] And yet, early Holocaust historians such as Léon Poliakov and Hilberg preferred written documents to testimonies, and especially those produced by the Nazis.[64] By the same token, if they drew on eyewitness accounts at all, they reached for the interrogation records of perpetrators rather than for statements by survivors.[65] This may seem less surprising if we remember that Holocaust historiography had been born of the efforts to prosecute the crimes of National Socialism and that history remains in thrall to the politics of powerful men and, as Tom Lawson puts it, claims 'to be able to see the past more wholly, more objectively, than any one witness constrained by their personal experiences'.[66]

Irrespective of the launch in the 1980s and 1990s of major initiatives aiming to record the memories of remaining Holocaust survivors, incorporation of the victims' voices other than as a tokenistic illustration of the Nazis' crimes has been, according to Tony Kushner, 'an unresolved dilemma in historical writing on the Holocaust'.[67] As a result, the discipline is now divided into historians invested in hard epistemologies and those who, under the influence of Lyotard's philosophy, White's model of narrative history, and Caruth's trauma theory, lend a sympathetic ear to affect, emotions, and imagination, and recognise that the past is inevitably shaped by present questions and concerns.[68] To the former camp belongs, for example, Lucy Dawidowicz who has complained of the witnesses' factual errors regarding names and dates, and of their poor understanding of the events to which they testify. As opposed to eyewitness accounts which she has described as 'more hazard than help', Dawidowicz has praised the 'sublime' and demanding work of historians who, thanks to their necessary distance, are capable of 'discerning truth from falsehood and certainty from doubt'.[69] Hilberg in turn considers all testimonies to be alike, and Pierre Vidal-Naquet regards 'facts' as superior to 'interpretations', and written documents as more helpful than subjective recollections.[70] Even Wieviorka has expressed concern about the difficulty of creating a rigorous historical analysis from affectively-charged testimonies which risk fragmenting and defocusing the historical occurrence in its totality.[71] Finally, Arendt has dismissed traumatic testimony as politically dangerous, for it entails 'dwelling on horrors' which cannot be truly communicated and which may foster fascination with bestiality.[72]

Commenting on this widespread scepticism towards eyewitness accounts, LaCapra regrets that 'historians have not yet worked out altogether acceptable ways of "using" testimonies' which, laden with affect, continue to pose 'an important challenge to history'.[73] Similarly, Dean observes that testimony has been embedded 'within a set of contested rhetorical and often implicitly negative claims about victims'.[74] Young, too, notes that many historians find testimonies incompatible with traditional notions of objectivity and reliability, and that 'the more dispassionate a text seems, the more rhetorically veracious and authentic it becomes'.[75] Since, as Dean puts it, 'credibility of testimony is associated with distant reserve', historians impose their own rigour and composure on the victims who, to be credible, must show that they have mastered the symptoms of their suffering and moved on from their losses.[76] This is why conventional or, to borrow Dean's qualifier, 'minimalist' historiography and survivors' accounts continue to be regarded as mutually incompatible representational modes.[77] For LaCapra, this 'minimalist' historiography is, however, unsuitable when it comes to limit events such as the Holocaust, since it is stamped by 'unqualified objectification, formal analysis, or harmonizing, indeed redemptive narrative'. Conversely, testimony offers 'something other than purely documentary knowledge by trying to understand experience and its aftermath, including the role of memory and its lapses, in coming to terms with — or denying and repressing the past'.[78] Maintaining this distinction, Stone criticises positivist historiography (which he disparagingly calls 'historism') for making Holocaust stories conform to the principles of chronology, logic, and closure, for expunging or at least domesticating trauma, and for insisting on the essential 'pastness' of the past. This sense of finality is achieved by imposing on Holocaust memory 'the classical device of soteriology: catastrophe and redemption, whether this comes in the shape of the liberation of the camps, the founding of the state of Israel, or resettlement in America'.[79]

Discussions regarding the helpfulness of testimony regularly cite a specific eyewitness account of the 1944 *Sonderkommando* uprising in Auschwitz. Interviewed by Holocaust survivor and psychologist, Dori Laub, the witness recalled seeing four chimneys in flames, whereas in reality only one crematorium had been blown up. What for historians further undermined the witness's credibility was her failure to recall the name of her work squad or her lack of concern for how the clothing she smuggled out of her workplace for her fellow inmates had been sourced. The gaps in the woman's knowledge made her account 'hopelessly misleading in its incompleteness' and called into question its validity. For Laub, conversely, what the woman testified to was 'historical truth'. Namely, the woman bore witness to the unprecedentedness and sheer incredibility of an uprising in Auschwitz 'where Jewish armed revolts just did not happen, and had no place'.[80] In line with Laub's observation, Saul Friedländer insists on the importance of victims' voices which reveal 'the clarity of insight and the total blindness of the human beings confronted with an entirely new and utterly horrifying reality', and which 'put the Nazis' actions into full perspective'.[81] Likewise, Young regards the factual errors made by witnesses as valuable evidence of what people saw, as opposed to what actually happened, and therefore 'historically authentic' since 'embodying the victim's grasp of events at the time'.[82] For LaCapra, the testimony to the *Sonderkommando* uprising additionally captures the dissonance between the agendas of history and testimony, which — and this pertains to my discussion of *Jan Karski* — he identifies as an example of the differend.[83]

Among the questions related to the place of testimony in the reconstruction of the past that are put forward by Haenel's novel is that concerning the accuracy of eyewitness accounts. This question is raised when the imaginary Karski recalls mistaking Izbica Lubelska for Bełżec, and the resulting doubts of historians regarding his credibility as a witness. In response to these doubts, the fictional Karski reminds us that wartime conditions did not lend themselves to topographical precision and that certain details could not be reliably established or had to be altered for security or diplomatic reasons. This explains why the identity of the two Jewish leaders Karski met in Warsaw could not be ascertained until after the war, with some ambiguity still surrounding the Zionist.[84] Likewise, written in 1944, Karski's memoirs had to conceal the exact particulars of resistance activities in wartime Poland for fear of exposing those fighting the Germans. It is for political reasons in turn that the memoirs identify the Ukrainian guards at Izbica Lubelska as Estonians, western Ukraine having been an integral part of pre-war Poland. Haenel's Karski also explains why he concealed his disappointment with the American response to the plight of Poland as a nation-state and of its Jewish citizens. In 1944, when the memoirs were written and published, the Polish government-in-exile which, it must be stressed, facilitated and financed the production of *Story of the Secret State*, was still counting on the support of the Western Allies. Political concerns aside, Karski's written testimony was also inflected by editorial pressures, as exemplified by its publisher's insistence on the inclusion of a romantic subplot.

These details confirm Young's conviction that testimony is shaped by a wide range of factors, such as the circumstances of its making, its intended purpose, the language in which it is made, not to mention the witness's gender, level of education, and political convictions. Young notes, for instance, that wartime testimonies were meant to generate an immediate response and, for safety reasons, often withheld important information. This means that witnesses had to be careful about disclosing plans for resistance and used misleading names and details. In contrast, in post-war accounts earlier experiences are contextualised in terms of the later ones, and the vision of the survivor's experience is teleologically unified in the full knowledge of the outcome. Young also observes that, whereas ghetto diaries written in Hebrew 'locate events in the sanctified linguistic sphere of scripture', those composed in Yiddish 'br[ing] into sharper relief the details of daily life and its hardships'.[85] Additionally, the process of writing itself necessarily entails a modification of memory by the context within which it takes place; rather than being a static record of the past, testimony evolves with time, bringing together elements of past and present, and responding to the listeners' expectations.[86] Finally, testimony is inevitably shaped by the surrounding discourses and by the efforts of its author to make her or his accounts comply with existing narrative models.[87] This means that, as Young states, testimony largely depends 'on the myths, figures, and ideologies comprising the survivor's world and language'. But, while the 'constructed and interpretative' quality of written testimony is widely acknowledged, oral accounts are often viewed as unadorned and therefore more credible.[88] Langer, for example, has expressed his belief that because 'the raw material of oral Holocaust narratives [...] resists the organizing impulse of moral theory and art', '[a] kind of unshielded truth emerges from them'.[89] Conversely, Hartman asserts that, through the choices regarding filming, production, and interviewer's questions, 'video texts are still texts and not unmediated experience'.[90]

Hartman's view of video testimony as far from being unmediated or unvarnished finds corroboration in Haenel's metafictional commentary on Karski's interview in *Shoah*. The commentary draws attention to the fact that the Pole's testimony was carefully staged and choreographed, before the filmed material itself was scrupulously edited. Such a handling of the witness and the recorded material serves, as it has been claimed, *Shoah*'s overarching aim which, according to the editor of the documentary, Ziva Postec, was to demonstrate that the Holocaust took place and, contrary to the dominant view of the Jews as passive victims, that the Jews resisted.[91] Lanzmann himself admits that the film was driven by his obsessive fear of savage and cold Eastern Europe (as opposed to the civilised west which, he claims, could have never become the stage for the Holocaust), and by his intention to situate the 'Final Solution' as the pinnacle of centuries-old Christian anti-Semitism.[92] Neal Ascherson further speculates that Lanzmann wished to establish a causal link between Polish anti-Jewish prejudice and the Nazis' decision to situate their killing centres in Poland and the success of the extermination programme.[93] This would explain Lanzmann's choice to interview Polish peasants in front of a church and the 'obtrusive' presence of the church steeple in the film's opening sequence.[94] As Sue Vice deduces from the testimonies of rescuers excluded from *Shoah*'s final version, and as Lanzmann himself makes clear with his cinematic answer to Haenel's novel, *Le Rapport Karski* (2010), *Shoah* was also intended to articulate its director's belief that the Jews could not have been saved.[95] All this has led LaCapra to conclude that, despite Lanzmann's protestations of his film's status as 'fiction du réel' [fiction of the real],[96] *Shoah* can be judged as a historical documentary and can therefore be accused of 'represent[ing] the past in a misleading and ideologically tendentious manner'.[97]

In *Jan Karski*, the constructedness of the Pole's interview in *Shoah* and its openness to multiple interpretations is borne out by the narrator's comments on the interplay between the interviewee's narrative and the images unfolding in the background. When the camera focuses on the Statue of Liberty, the narrator wonders whether this is meant to disembody Karski's message so that it reaches the viewer with greater force, or to create an ironic contrast between America's status as a symbol of freedom and prosperity and the confinement and deprivation suffered by the Jews. Pursuing the latter interpretation, in Part III the fictional Karski assimilates the Statue of Liberty with Roosevelt and, consequently, reimagines it as a hateful figure that has morphed from an emblem of justice into one of hypocrisy. Haenel's narrator detects a similarly ironic comment on the disconnectedness of America's self-perception and its wartime failure to come to the rescue of the Jews in the presence on screen of the American flag, the White House, and the surroundings of the Capitol. As these images appear, the narrator reads them as a visual summary of the 'impassibilité monumentale de la démocratie américaine' [monumental composure of American democracy] (*JK*, 22; *M*, 12). In the superimposition of the two Jewish leaders' apocalyptic vision of the total annihilation of their people, relayed by Karski, over the images of the victims' belongings piled up in the Auschwitz-Birkenau Museum, Haenel's narrator again senses Lanzmann's intention to connect the predicted scale of the extermination to America's recalcitrant response to the Jews' desperate pleas for help. He is similarly alert to Lanzmann's camerawork, to the interviewer's and interviewee's imperfect use of English and the resultant ambiguities of their statements, to the conformity of Karski's testimony to the narrative modes of a spy novel and a biblical tale, and to the Pole's trauma. These elements confirm the inherent metatextuality of video testimony which, for Young, is a prime example of postmodern history. In other words, the value of video testimonies lies not 'in their supposed neutrality as source material, but in their record of "telling history"', as they 'retain the process of construction, the activity of witness'.[98] This is why Felman regards *Shoah* as a documentary that, more than about the Holocaust, is about 'the limits of the witness and of witnessing'.[99]

Testimony and Trauma: Acting Out, Not Working Through

The potential for testimony to articulate the trauma produced by the Holocaust and other limit events has been widely recognised, including by Lyotard, LaCapra, Felman, and Laub. In contrast to these thinkers, Eaglestone questions the helpfulness of trauma theory in understanding survivor testimonies since it strips agency from the witnesses and revictimises them. Moreover, trauma theory is premised on the possibility of working through, of redemptive healing, and, ultimately, of the recovery and forgetting that Holocaust experience precludes.[100] Such an assertion may surprise considering that it is conventional historiography that, while being blamed for trying to smooth over, control, and obliterate trauma,[101] has been associated with the very quest for redemption, closure, and forgetting that Eaglestone ascribes to trauma theory.[102] Eaglestone's suspicion regarding the ethics of the use of the concept of trauma when it comes to eyewitness accounts is tested by *Jan Karski* which, in line with Laub's position, shows trauma as a prerequisite of Holocaust testimony. At the same time, Haenel's novel supports LaCapra's view of the severely traumatised subjects as forced to act out or relive their trauma, yet unable to overcome it.[103] Put differently, while positing the trauma that resulted from the Polish emissary's enduring sense of failure and culpability as the key to understanding the wrongs that the Jews and their messenger suffered at the hands of the indifferent free world, *Jan Karski* disconnects trauma from the possibility of closure and redemptive working through. Instead, the novel simultaneously shows its effect to be limited to acting out and underscores the inability of conventional language to voice traumatogenic experiences. *Jan Karski* achieves such a figuration of mental pain, on the one hand, through its reiterative and open-ended structure which emulates the unusual temporality of traumatic memory, and, on the other, by locating the impetus for testimony in the witness's sense of moral duty to the dead rather than in her or his hope for transcending trauma.

When questioned about making *Shoah*, Lanzmann admits that he was not interested in memories, but wanted his interviewees to re-enact the past, as if they were actors. This is illustrated by the cut-throat gesture that the French director encouraged Polish bystanders to perform in repetition of the sadistic, as Lanzmann interprets it, sign they made when seeing trains heading for Treblinka.[104] A more relevant example is the director's much criticised retraumatisation of his witnesses by forcing them to relive the tragic events, a strategy that has made LaCapra suggest that Lanzmann's criterion for selecting interviewees was indeed their capacity for reliving their trauma.[105] Taking up a similar position, Ascherson attributes Lanzmann's exclusion of Władysław Bartoszewski's testimony to the Polish resister's calm composure.[106] As opposed to Bartoszewski who, as Lanzmann recalls it, recited information but failed to relive the past, and whom Laub would describe as 'a fully lucid, unaffected witness', Karski is visibly disturbed by his memories.[107] The Pole therefore embodies Freud's concept of 'acting out', defined by LaCapra as one's 'tendency to relive the past, to be haunted by ghosts or even to exist in the present as if one were still fully in the past, with no distance from it'.[108] Karski's profound psychological injury is manifest from the start of the interview when he leaves the frame sobbing. Rather than editing out this false start, Lanzmann films the empty space, just as he later films Karski's silences as the Pole struggles to contain his emotion or to find adequate words.

It is, among other things, the discrepancy between the witness's traumatogenic experience and the available discursive means that prompted Laub's redefinition of the Holocaust as 'the event-without-a-witness'.[109] Laub's term finds its starkest illustration in the physical collapse of survivor and writer Yehiel Dinur at Eichmann's trial, which, for Dean, 'transforms his testimony into a form of symbolic speechlessness'. Haenel's recapitulation of Karski's interview in *Shoah* clearly supports the view that, due to the attendant trauma, Holocaust experience is inimical to conventional language and that witnessing is, as Dean puts it, 'a dissonant, discontinuous and fragmented narrative'.[110] Indeed, for Haenel, the difficulty Karski experiences in expressing what he saw in the Ghetto, the difficulty that manifests itself through the fragmentariness and discontinuity of the Pole's narrative, is an eloquent sign of his trauma:

> Ses phrases sont courtes, directes, entourées de silence. [...] Chacune de ses paroles garde trace de cet empêchement qu'il a eu au début, lorsqu'il est sorti du champ. On dirait même qu'elles sont fidèles à l'impossibilité de parler. Jan Karski ne peut pas occuper cette place de témoin [...], et pourtant il l'occupe, qu'il le veuille ou non. (*JK*, 14)

> [His sentences are short, direct, encircled by silence. [...] Each of his words bears a trace of the difficulties he experienced at the beginning, when he moved out of frame. It is as if his words reflect the impossibility of speaking. Jan Karski cannot play the role of witness [...], and yet it is his, whether he likes it or not.] (*M*, 4)

The narrator's assertion that what Karski is trying to say 'ne peut se dire qu'à *travers une parole brisée*' [can in fact only be said in broken language] (*JK*, 14; *M*, 4) encapsulates the aporia attached to both trauma and the Holocaust, which must be voiced, but which struggle to find their way into the available language. According to Laub, 'there are never enough words or the right words to articulate the story that cannot be fully captured in *thought, memory* and *speech*'.[111] In Haenel's novel, Laub's remark finds embodiment in Karski's unease regarding the word 'hell' whose rhetorical strength proves insufficient to communicate the atrocious scenes he observed, but which he uses for lack of a more adequate term. Otherwise, as Haenel's narrator conjectures, Karski would have been trapped in silence or would have suffocated. In the end, the Pole's language grows sparse and broken, conveying the wretchedness of the described scenes:

> Les phrases de Karski n'ont pas de souffle. Elles sont minuscules, un mot, deux mots, pas plus. [...] Maintenant, le langage n'a plus de vie, il ne cherche plus à convaincre ni à expliquer, il ne pourra secourir personne. De pauvres visions s'accrochent à de pauvres mots: oignons, biscuits, yeux, seins. Ces mots-là ne sauvent pas. (*JK*, 29)

> [Karski's sentences are now breathless. They are short, one word, two words, no more. [...] Now his language is lifeless, he is no longer trying to convince or explain, he will not be able to help anyone. Impoverished visions attach themselves to impoverished words: onions, biscuits, eyes, breasts. Such words save no one.] (*M*, 18)

Haenel's narrator moots the possibility that trauma is what defines the witness, as it enables the translation of a horrific experience into inadequate language: 'Est-ce la souffrance qui fait le témoin?' [Is it suffering that makes a witness?] (*JK*, 31; *M*, 21) Such a redefinition of the witness reflects its Greek translation (*martis* [martyr]) which interlocks testimony and suffering. While for Agamben, the idea of martyrdom is misplaced in the context of the Holocaust, as it would 'justif[y] the scandal of meaningless death', he concedes that 'witnessing' and 'martyrdom' can become linked. Indeed, the Greek term derives from the verb 'to remember': 'The survivor's vocation,' concludes Agamben, 'is to remember; he cannot *not* remember'.[112]

The disjointedness of the Pole's testimony is mirrored by the hybridity and fragmentariness of *Jan Karski*. Commenting on the construction of his novel, Haenel states that:

> Il faudrait en passer par des registres à priori différents, et sans doute opposés. [...] Je ne voulais pas écrire un récit linéaire; c'était impossible pour rendre compte des brisures de la vie de cet homme. Alors, [...] j'ai écrit des chapitres avec des modes narratifs différents.[113]
>
> [It was necessary to adopt essentially different and undoubtedly mutually exclusive registers. [...] I didn't want a linear narrative; it would have been impossible to thus render the discontinuities in the life of this man. And so [...] I wrote chapters with different narrative modalities.]

Haenel's narrative approach tallies with Young's claim that, to articulate the violence of the Holocaust, writers must abandon the harmonising conventions of realism. This is because realism resolves violence by inserting the narrated events into the historical continuum and stripping them of their particularity, and by failing to 'preserve in narrative the very *dis*continuity that lends events their violent character'.[114] *Jan Karski*'s much criticised generic instability can thus be ascribed to Haenel's intention to convey both the violence marking the Polish resister's story and his lasting psychological injury which, as illustrated by Holocaust literature, invites distortion, disrupts genres, and threatens to collapse distinctions.[115]

According to Stone, narratives such as Ruth Klüger's *weiter leben*, Georges Perec's *W ou le souvenir d'enfance* (1975), and Saul Friedländer's *When Memory Comes* (1978) indeed challenge 'historist temporality' and reflect the survivor's memory which is neither linear nor does it dutifully rest in the past, instead incessantly engulfing the present with affect.[116] LaCapra, too, sees the traumatised witness as incapable of dichotomising the past and the present, a position illustrated by *Shoah* which, for Lanzmann, is marked by 'l'abolition de toute distance entre le passé et le présent' [the erasure of all distance between the past and the present].[117] To erode this distance, *Shoah* refuses to rely on archival footage, instead presenting us with the Holocaust's lasting traces. Among these are traumatised Jewish survivors, sympathetic, indifferent, or anti-Semitic Polish bystanders, conceited perpetrators, Jewish homes resettled by Catholic Poles, and the troubling persistence of the road sign 'Treblinka'. To stress the endurance of the Holocaust's legacies, Lanzmann closes *Shoah* with the image of a rolling train, which echoes that of the Saurer van travelling down a German motorway in the film's opening sequences.[118]

To reach an analogous effect, Haenel's circular narrative systematically (con)fuses temporal levels through, for example, the use of the present tense in Parts I and II.[119] For Haenel, Karski's quasi-physical entrapment in the traumatogenic past is additionally revealed by his repeated use of the adverb 'now' which, however, rather than a sign that the traumatic event 'continues to the present and is current in every respect', may just be a simple discourse marker announcing a new thought.[120] Where Haenel is definitely correct is in his assessment of Karski's use of the present tense as a way of reliving his passage through the Ghetto: 'il parle au présent, il n'y a plus de distance avec ce qu'il décrit' [He is now using the present tense, he has no distance from what he is describing] (*JK*, 28; *M*, 18).¹²¹ The Pole's return to the past is also palpable in his use of direct speech when relaying the message of the Jewish leaders and in his attendant identification with them. Like the two men, distraught at their helplessness in relation to the massacre of their people, thirty-five years later Karski himself fails to maintain his composure.

Haenel's description of Karski's words as condemned to 'une répétition désespérée' [hopeless repetition] (*JK*, 20; *M*, 10) confirms Laub's characterisation of the traumatic subject as someone who lives in the grip of a past reality and who, while being unable to assimilate this past, engages in 'its ceaseless repetitions and reenactments'.¹²² In the concluding part of his novel, Haenel imagines how wartime trauma affected the former messenger's post-war life in America. Having failed to mobilise a response from the world, Karski withdraws from public life to dedicate himself to university teaching. The novel depicts him suffering from insomnia, depression, and digestive problems which contrast with Roosevelt's peaceful ingestion of food in the scene of his interview with the Polish courier. Whereas the President regurgitates the news of the Jewish tragedy along with his copious dinner, Karski, on leaving the White House, is overcome by nausea. This detail makes his failure to communicate his message in Washington tantamount to his experience of abject impotence in Izbica Lubelska which, too, he leaves seized by uncontrollable retchings.

Karski's Story as a Differend

Haenel's fictionalised representation of the Polish diplomat's meeting with Roosevelt may be regarded as the novel's focal scene as it sums up the injustice that *Jan Karski* sets out to address and possibly redress. To use Lyotard's terms, this injustice proceeds from the asymmetry between the idioms used by Karski and the president, and between their moral and political agendas. Put simply, the interview scene foregrounds Roosevelt's unwillingness to listen to the Polish emissary's message so that he would not to be obliged to act upon it. Having been so far contextualised with the oppositional relationship between testimony, which is subjective and capable of articulating trauma, and history, which serves the interests of the victors and thus occludes past injustices, Haenel's retelling of Karski's story can be equally productively framed with Lyotard's concept of the differend and with his call for a rethinking of representational modes in the post-Auschwitz world. Driven by moral aims, these representational modes or discursive genres, as Lyotard names the rubrics providing rules for linking phrases with specific goals in mind, must accommodate testimony.¹²³ At the same time, they must articulate the impossibility of testimony provoked by the murder of first-hand witnesses during the Holocaust and/or by the inability of survivors to voice their experiences in the available idioms. Correspondingly, the new narrative modes should adjudicate the wrongs arising from the discursive impotence of the witnesses. This means that, as I will now argue, rather than usurping Karski's voice or falsifying history, as Haenel's critics have claimed, with his 'thickly affective' retelling of the Polish resister's story,

Haenel answers Lyotard's summons to postmodern writers to elaborate morally-inflected ways of linking phrases so that past injustices and their lasting legacies can finally be heard.[124] In other words, Haenel embraces the ethical challenge with which Lyotard presents the postmodern writer and which consists in listening attentively and sympathetically to the wrongs, both past and present, before seeking novel narrative means to put these wrongs into words and to do justice to them.

Lyotard's conceptualisation of the differend must be seen as a continuation of his contestation of modernity's universalising metanarratives (*grands récits*) of progress, socialism, abundance, and knowledge, which he first offered in *La Condition postmoderne* (1979).[125] In this context, rather than a place-marker that anchors memories or even 'a negative concept for the anonymous, bureaucratic, and instrumental erasure of proper names that took place in the camps', 'Auschwitz' becomes the negation of history as the Enlightenment's metanarrative of progress through reason.[126] Yet, paradoxically, 'Auschwitz' also enacted the Enlightenment's perniciously 'rational' ends as the carefully planned, orchestrated, and industrialised mass murder of Europe's Jews.[127] These ideas are more fully developed in *Le Différend* which, apart from prolonging Lyotard's questioning of modernity's *grands récits*, responds to the rise of *négationnisme* in France.[128] More specifically, in 1978, Robert Faurisson denied the existence of gas chambers on the grounds of the absence of direct witnesses to the murderous installations.[129] As well as the endpoint of modernity with its historical process and rational reason, 'Auschwitz' thus becomes for Lyotard the ultimate embodiment of the differend, that is of a situation where, for lack of discursive means, the victims' *damage* turns into an inexpressible *wrong*. Without explicitly urging historians to abandon their empiricist rigour, Lyotard, inspired by Faurisson's exploitation of positivist historiography based on the creed that seeing is believing, identifies 'Auschwitz' as a turning point in historiography. He therefore invites scholars to take into account not only testimony, but also both its metareality which is the destruction of testimony, and the feeling of injustice and wrong: 'Non le témoignage, mais ce qui reste du témoignage quand il est détruit [...], le sentiment' [Not only the testimony, but also what is left of the testimony when it is destroyed [...], namely, the feeling]. Rather than in professional historians who in the absence of documents will claim to hear nothing but silence, Lyotard puts his faith in lay persons [*les communs*]. They will *sense* in this silence a sign which is not a validatable referent, but an indication that something that cannot be articulated in the existing idioms must nevertheless be put into phrases: 'C'est l'enjeu d'une littérature, d'une philosophie [...] de témoigner des différends en leur trouvant des idiomes' [What is at stake in a literature, in a philosophy [...] is to bear witness to the differends by finding idioms for them].[130]

In Haenel's novel, the differend suffered by the Jews and their messenger finds its starkest expression in the Polish emissary's interview with Roosevelt. This episode has been strongly criticised for violating the historical record by, among other things, ignoring the actual Karski's reportedly favourable impression of the president.[131] It is plain, however, that Haenel does not aspire to a faithful representation of what passed between Karski and Roosevelt, which in any case is impossible to establish with any accuracy.¹³² Instead, his historically inexact, metafictional, intertextual, and anachronistic reconstruction of the meeting exposes the incompatibility of the Pole's morally-guided arguments with Roosevelt's political protocol, and, correspondingly, the dissonance of the discursive genres used by the two men. This dissonance is exemplified by the contrast between Karski's impassioned account of the situation in Poland and Roosevelt's clichéd and vacuous promises of the triumph of good over evil, and of post-war peace and prosperity. To the Polish emissary's report, Roosevelt also reacts with the occasional 'I understand' which, rather than as a sign of the president's empathy, the fictional Karski reads as one of Roosevelt's reluctance to acknowledge the message he is hearing. Karski's interpretation is confirmed by the president's stifled yawns which, as the Pole imagines, are intended to infect him with his interlocutor's apathy.

Haenel further underlines the asymmetry of the two men's political agendas and idioms through oppositions such as that between the overcrowded camps and ghettos where Jews are indiscriminately murdered or die from hunger and disease, and the bourgeois comfort of Roosevelt's office which is filled with plush sofas, porcelain tureens, and elegant women. As the Jews are being denied their most basic rights, the president, comfortably seated in an armchair, is digesting a sumptuous meal while building up his appetite for additional pleasures, suggested by his interest in his secretary's legs. Haenel frames the undeliverability of Karski's message with the Pole's status as a marginal figure vainly trying to challenge the accepted rhetoric of power. As Meg Jensen notes with reference to narratives by slaves or, more recently, female victims of sexual abuse, if a testimony contests the dominant social, cultural, or political narratives, it may fail to attain the status of plausibility. Jensen's view that the credibility of testimony depends on 'the position of subject/narrator within complex social, historical and cultural spaces' finds reflection in the fictional Karski's choice to introduce himself to the president as 'Nobody' (*JK*, 124; *M*, 114).¹³³ The Pole's awareness of the inconsequentiality of his visit to the White House can also be detected in his superposition of Roosevelt's photograph at the Yalta conference, where Poland's post-war fate was sealed, over his direct memory of his meeting with the president. Haenel's Karski then recontextualises the failure of his mission with the Americans' suspicion of Catholics and of Poles whom they regard as rabid anti-Semites. Having vainly testified in front of Roosevelt and other members of the American administration and, earlier, in front of the British war cabinet, the Supreme Court judge Felix Frankfurter, the Apostolic Delegate in Washington, leaders of Jewish and Christian organisations, and, later, through his memoirs, public lectures, and press articles, Haenel's Karski grasps the incommunicability of his message: 'il y avait quelque chose d'intransmissible dans ce message, quelque chose qu'on ne pouvait entendre, et qui peut-être ne sera jamais entendu' [there was something untransmittable in that message, something that could not be heard, and perhaps will never be heard] (*JK*, 119; *M*, 109).¹³⁴

The wrongs that the Jews and their messenger have endured find further expression in the tropes of deafness, wax-filled ears, and the silence that eventually takes hold of the Pole himself. The despondency to which Haenel's Karski succumbs because of his unsuccessful mission lends support to Laub's view that an unsympathetic response to testimony can retraumatise the witness. Laub cites Haim Gouri's documentary *The 81ˢᵗ Blow* (1974) which, by narrating the story of a man whose narrative of suffering is not being believed, shows that 'the absence of an empathetic listener or [...] of an addressable other, an other who can hear the anguish of one's memories and thus recognize their realness, annihilates the story'.[135] It is such disbelief that, according to Lyotard, creates the differend. This is especially so if, as in Faurisson's case, it perfidiously takes advantage of the victims' silence and of traditional historiographical methodology. To do justice to the victim's wrong, one therefore needs to institute not only new significations and referents, but also new addressees.[136] As if responding to this suggestion, Haenel assumes the position of the receiver of the Pole's testimony, who, in Laub's terms, listens to it 'truly'.[137] Seen in this light, Haenel's metatextual account of Karski's interview in *Shoah* enables him to take up the position of those who heard the Pole's message with incredulity or who believed it, but failed to act upon it. Haenel also displaces Lanzmann himself whose insistent and insensitive questioning led to his interviewee's visible retraumatisation, and who subsequently manipulated the filmed material so that it would suit the ideology of *Shoah* and, later, of *Le Rapport Karski*.[138]

Haenel does not, however, limit himself to a compassionate reception of Karski's account. He also demonstrates that traumatic testimony unsettles the boundary between the witness and the listener, endowing the latter with a participative role in the testimonial process or even making her or him, as Laub would put it, a 'co-owner of the traumatic event'.[139] Wiesel has extended the chain of witnessing even further, namely to readers of Holocaust memoirs and viewers of video testimonies.[140] Similarly, an exploration of the cognitive potential of the former concentration camps has inspired Janet Jacobs to contend that these 'memorialscapes' can turn their visitors into 'witnesses of the atrocities of the past'.[141] Yet, such 'cloning of witnesses', as Rothe judgmentally calls the extension of the witness function beyond survivors, has also attracted criticism.[142] Despite allowing the possibility of secondary traumatisation, LaCapra, for example, fears that the identification of the vicarious witness with a victim may lead to scenarios such as Wilkomirski's identity theft or Lanzmann's desire to compensate for having escaped persecution through exploitative and selfish identification with his traumatised interviewees.[143] Objecting to such misgivings, Dean believes that they masquerade as efforts 'to return to an empirical history of injury' and 'advocate a mode of testimony commensurable with the mastery of symptoms'.[144] Ball in turn argues that the identification of secondary witnesses with survivors is inevitable, however determinately they guard themselves against the 'identitarian neutralisation of difference, [...] a thematization of the other as a projection of the same'.[145]

In *Jan Karski*, Haenel brings to the fore the inescapability of the listener's identification with the victim by drawing our attention to Karski's fusion with the Jewish leaders on whose behalf he is witnessing thirty-five years after the events. It is not only through the use of direct discourse, but also through his tone of voice, facial expressions, and violent gestures that Karski morphs into those who tasked him with informing the world of the massacre of their people: 'Jan Karski ne recourt plus seulement au discours indirect, il se met à transmettre directement les paroles des deux hommes, *comme si c'étaient eux qui parlaient par sa bouche*' [Jan Karski now stops using only indirect speech, and starts relaying the two men's words directly, *as if they are speaking through him*] (*JK*, 17; *M*, 7, my emphasis). Imitating this approach in Part III, which could be read as Haenel's transferential implication in the Polish messenger's story, the novelist himself becomes a disembodied carrier of Karski's voice or, to put it in Laub's terms, a vicarious witness whose exposure to the survivor's pain has imbued him with the authority to testify. Such a reading of *Jan Karski* reveals an important difference between Haenel and those who, as Weissman has it, engage in 'fantasies of witnessing' by confusing direct experience with historical knowledge.[146] Instead, it is possible to categorise Haenel's self-conscious narrative as an example of 'proxy-witnessing', a term Susan Gubar uses to designate scenarios where those affected by the pain of the direct witness feel compelled to testify to it through artistic means.[147] *Jan Karski* equally corresponds to the paradigm of 'post-witnessing', as Diana Popescu dubs the investigative or imaginary efforts of writers to understand the meaning of the Holocaust for them and for the times they live in, irrespective of their connection of the genocide.[148] Indeed, apart from retelling Karski's story, Haenel's text explores the identity of the witness and, in so doing, interrogates its author's own situatedness as someone separated from the Holocaust by generational distance and lacking deep personal connection to the described events. *Jan Karski* thus not only probes the future of testimony in the post-witness era but also suggests that fiction should assume the moral responsibility for addressing and redressing past injustices and their legacies.

Haenel's recapitulation of Karski's interview in *Shoah* is punctuated by questions regarding the ontological status of the witness. The camera's focus on the Pole's tear-filled and bulging eyes invites the narrator to identify the witness as someone who occupies a privileged cognitive and topographical position in relation to the events she or he relays, or, in plain terms, that the witness is someone *who has seen*. This definition concurs with 'the western law of evidence', which, as Felman speculates, must have inspired the two Jewish leaders to take Karski into the epicentre of the Jewish carnage.[149] Haenel, however, moots the possibility that it is trauma which, by transforming words from signifiers into embodied signs, qualifies one as a witness. He ultimately decides that it is 'plutôt la parole, l'usage de la parole' [speech, the use of speech] (*JK*, 31; *M*, 21) that turns one into a witness. In this way, he opens the witness category to those defined as secondary witnesses, second-degree witnesses, proxy witnesses, witnesses by adoption, prosthetic witnesses, witnesses of witnesses, or witnesses of testimony.[150] Significantly, such a redefinition enables the author himself to embrace the witness position and to present his novel as a text that, in contrast to historiographies written from the perspective of victors, is committed to the cause of those exploited and wronged. What this means in practice is that *Jan Karski* denounces the Anglo-American indifference to the plight of the Jews and exposes the post-war obfuscation of this indifference through the narrative of the Allies' moral superiority over the Nazis, their self-image as the liberators of the Jews, and the convenient view that the details about the genocide became available only after the liberation of the camps.[151] Finally, Haenel capitalises on his witness position to deplore the Allies' wartime betrayal of Poland and the politically motivated and, in his view, grossly unfair lumbering of Karski's homeland with the charge of anti-Semitism.

Conclusions: Postmodern Literature as a Witness

A story about the failure of language to communicate the Jewish tragedy to the world, *Jan Karski* paradoxically attests to Haenel's conviction about the potential (and moral obligation) of literature to testify to the differends resulting from the world's indifference to the Pole's rescue efforts and from Lanzmann's subsequent silencing of them. The novel's typically postmodern self-contradictoriness is also apparent in Haenel's critical espousal of the genre of testimony, which is both the subject and the form of *Jan Karski*, but which the novel shows to be akin to fiction. This is due to testimony's constructedness, historical, political, and cultural contingency, openness to a plurality of interpretations, and vulnerability to manipulation. Haenel's paradoxical treatment of testimony as part of his rejection of established modes of expression makes him, in Lyotard's sense, a model postmodern writer who develops new idioms in order to unsilence the wrongs created by the inadequacy of conventional narrative means.[152] As Lyotard and others have postulated, 'Auschwitz' has rendered suspect traditional discursive genres, be they historical or literary, by revealing their complicity in the thinking that had led to the Holocaust and their impotence in relation to articulating the aftershocks of the genocide.[153] As illustrated by Faurisson's abuse of the very empirical methodology on which historians rely to safeguard the Holocaust from its deniers, these cognitive modes have additionally proven open to exploitation by negationists.

It is in this context that we must reconsider *Jan Karski*'s much criticised generic instability, as well as its fragmentariness and circularity, which all support its rejection of the resolution, logic, catharsis, and redemption marking conventional Holocaust narratives.[154] As we have seen, the structure of Haenel's novel also helps to thematise Karski's traumatisation as part of its wider ambition to listen patiently and compassionately to the wrongs, traumas, and silences that 'Auschwitz' has created. Troubled by Karski's 'thickly affective' interview in *Shoah* and by the anonymity of the Pole's post-war life, Haenel imagines this life to have been stamped by guilt, by a sense of failure, and by resulting depression. And, as Haenel shows us, such a life cannot be inserted into the linear and teleologically oriented metanarrative of twentieth-century history, which draws a neat line under the Holocaust with the Nuremberg trials and the survivors' return to their homelands or resettlement in other countries. Instead, his novel points to the lasting impact of the Holocaust on post-war realities, including current global politics.

In Ball's terms, Haenel's narrative stands in opposition to the 'thinly affective' style of historiography, which is suggestive of affective mastery and intellectual rigour. Such a style is incompatible with traumatogenic events, including the

Holocaust, as it embodies the 'unsettling capacity for dissociating from cruelty as it takes place, even and perhaps especially when we are complicit in it'.[155] As well as to avoid a 'thinly affective' rhetoric which, as Ball warns, 'might marginalise and therefore exacerbate another's precarity', and to generate affective and moral responses from his readers, Haenel has mobilised the testimonial genre because of its inherent metatextual potential to convey the impossibility of testimony.[156] As I have demonstrated, while drawing attention to testimony's cognitive gaps, contradictions, and inaccuracies, *Jan Karski* lays bare the aporia of witnessing, which consists in the simultaneous need for shocking experiences to be articulated and the difficulties of doing so in the available language. Furthermore, the novel's self-conscious engagement with testimony, as well as its polyphonic composition and intense interdiscursivity mirror the structure and texture of the Pole's account in *Shoah*, which styles itself on existing narrative conventions and incorporates other voices. While thus underscoring testimony's inevitable absorption of other texts and conformity with established discursive models, through its overt anachronism *Jan Karski* draws attention to the tendency of witnesses to recast past events in the light of present concerns and to use testimony to create new insights into current realities.

By having Karski speak from beyond the grave, Haenel finally points to the encroaching absence of direct witnesses and the consequent need for literature to relay testimony by assuming its informative, ethical, and performative function. Haenel's suggestion does not square, however, with the widespread view of testimony and literature in oppositional terms, or with the perception of Holocaust fiction as testimony's poor cousin or even as an ethically irresponsible form spreading falsehoods about the genocide.[157] And yet, as *Jan Karski* confirms, testimony has undeniable literary origins, literary features, and the capacity to convey 'testimonial truths'.[158] At the same time, much of Holocaust fiction depends on the concept of testimony as a rhetorical trope.[159] According to Alan Rosen, even a Holocaust novel that invents characters and scenes is a testimony, since the testimonial value of literature lies in its ability to communicate the moral, religious, and psychological experiences of the genocide, rather than the sheer facts. This means that 'literature may be able to bear witness, not in spite but because of invention and imagination'.[160] Pondering the same question, Felman argues that by involving literature in action, World War II and the Holocaust have softened generic distinctions.[161] The case of Camus whom Felman emphatically describes as a '*non-Jewish* European writer' and whose works, without directly addressing the Nazi genocide, have made their way into the canon of Holocaust literature, can be instructive in the analysis of *Jan Karski* which is marked by a similar ethics, engagement, and paradoxical admixture of pessimism and optimism. Indeed, in the fictional Karski's faith in the written word, notwithstanding the failure of his message, one recognises Haenel's own confidence in the transformative power of his writing: 'le livre [peut] déplacer des montagnes: s'il dit la verité, un livre transforme le monde' [a book [can] move mountains: if it tells the truth, then a book can change the world] (*JK*, 135; *M*, 124).

Notes to Chapter 6

1. Czesław Miłosz, 'A Poor Christian Looks at the Ghetto', in *Selected Poems* (New York: Seabury Press, 1973), p. 49.
2. Robert Kostro, 'Tradycja i otwartość' [Tradition and Openness], *Tygodnik Powrzechny*, 17, (21 April 2014) <https://www.tygodnikpowszechny.pl/tradycja-i-otwartosc-22632> [accessed 12 January 2019].
3. Raul Hilberg, *Perpetrators, Victims, Bystanders: Jewish Catastrophe 1933–1945* (New York: Harper-Collins, 1992), p. 217.
4. Bauman, *Modernity and the Holocaust*, p. 207.
5. Hilberg, *Perpetrators, Victims, Bystanders*, p. 249.
6. Cited by Jan Błoński, 'The Poor Poles Look at the Ghetto', in *Jews and the Emerging Polish State*, ed. and trans. by Antony Polonsky (= special issue of *Polin: Studies in Polish Jewry*, 2 (2008), 321–36 (p. 323). Together with his brother, Andrzej, Czesław Miłosz provided hiding for Sławomir Tross and his wife. He also helped Felicja Wołkomińska, her sister and sister-in-law, who had crossed over to the 'Aryan' side on the eve of the Ghetto Uprising. The Trosses died in the Warsaw Uprising. Wołkomińska survived the war and in 1957 emigrated to Israel. 'Czesław Miłosz (1911–2004)', Ośrodek 'Brama Grodzka — Teatr NN' <http://teatrnn.pl/leksykon/artykuly/czeslaw-milosz-19112004/> [accessed 12 December 2019].
7. For a discussion of the debates surrounding *Shoah*'s portrayal of Poland, see Sue Vice, 'Poland: The Ethics of Filming', in *Shoah* (Basingstoke: Palgrave Macmillan, 2011), pp. 73–79. Writing in 1986 in *Der Spiegel*, Micha Brumlik argued that *Shoah* cannot be seen as anti-Polish as the only hero of the film (apart from the victimised Jews) is a Pole: 'Der zähe Schaum der Verdrängung', *Der Spiegel*, 8 (1986) <https://www.spiegel.de/spiegel/print/d-13518094.html> [accessed 12 February 2021].
8. Dieter Pohl, 'War, Occupation and the Holocaust in Poland', in *The Historiography of the Holocaust*, ed. by Stone, pp. 89–119.
9. Rachel F. Brenner, 'Holocaust *Memories* and Polish Catholic Identity: Cultural Transmutations of Warsaw Ghetto Uprising', in *The Palgrave Handbook of Holocaust Literature and Culture*, ed. by Victoria Aarons and Phyllis Lassner (Basingstoke: Palgrave Macmillan, 2020), pp. 233–50 (p. 233).
10. Błoński's essay was first published as 'Biedni Polacy patrzą na getto', *Tygodnik Powrzechny*, 2 (1987), 1, 4.
11. Błoński, 'The Poor Poles Look at the Ghetto', pp. 328, 329, 321.
12. Jan T. Gross, *Neighbours: The Destruction of the Jewish Community in Jedwabne, Poland* (Princeton, NJ: Princeton University Press, 2001). The book was first published in 2000 in Polish as *Sąsiedzi: Historia zagłady żydowskiego miasteczka*.
13. For a detailed analysis of Gross's narrative strategy, see Karyn Ball, 'Tales of Affect, "Thick" and "Thin": On Distantiation in Holocaust Historiography', *Holocaust Studies*, 20.1–2 (2014), 179–217 (pp. 192–96).
14. Apart from Jedwabne, other small Polish towns became the scene of wartime anti-Semitic violence. These include Radziłów, Wąsosz, Szczuczyn, Goniądz, Bzury, and Rajgród. See Anna Bikont, *The Crime and the Silence: Confronting the Massacre of Jews in Wartime Jedwabne*, trans. by Alissa Valles (New York: Farrar, Straus & Giroux, 2004).
15. This figure has been disputed. See, for example, Joshua D. Zimmerman, 'Changing Perception in the Historiography of Polish-Jewish Relations during the Second World War', in *Contested Memories: Poles and Jews during the Holocaust and its Aftermath*, ed. by Joshua D. Zimmerman (New Brunswick, NJ: Rutgers University Press, 2002), pp. 1–16 (p. 2). As recently as 1 March 2021, the chief rabbi of Poland, Michael Joseph Schudrich, mentioned the figure of three million non-Jewish victims of the Nazi regime: 'Rabin Schudrich: Jeśli nawet komuś się to nie podoba, w Polsce jestem u siebie (Wywiad)' [Rabbi Schudrich: Even if Some May Not Like It, Poland is My Home (Interview)], *Wirtualna Polska*, 1 March 2021 <https://wiadomosci.wp.pl/rabin-schudrich-nawet-jesli-komus-sie-to-nie-podoba-w-polsce-jestem-u-siebie-wywiad-6613058256014304a> [accessed 2 March 2021]. External sources usually give a figure of between

1.8 and 1.9 million. See, for example, the Holocaust Encyclopedia, United States Holocaust Memorial Museum, 'Polish Victims' <https://encyclopedia.ushmm.org/content/en/article/polish-victims> [accessed 2 March 2021].

16. On the eve of Holocaust Remembrance Day in 2018, Poland passed a law criminalising the false attribution of Nazi crimes to the Polish nation or state. The law was vehemently opposed by the US and Israeli administrations, which led to its mitigation in June 2018. Criminal offence has been replaced with civil offence, which, in practical terms, meant that contravening the law could result in a fine, rather than a prison sentence. The efforts to suppress discussion of Polish complicity are exemplified by the 2021 trial of two prominent Holocaust scholars whose recent book quotes a testimony identifying a Polish man as responsible for Jewish deaths: *Dalej jest noc: losy Żydów w wybranych powiatach okupowanej Polski* [Night Without End: The Fate of Jews in Selected Counties of Occupied Poland], ed. by Barbara Engelking and Jan Grabowski, 2 vols (Warsaw: Centrum Badań nad Zagładą Żydów, 2018).

17. Carolyn J. Dean, 'Witnessing', in *The Routledge Companion to Literature and Trauma*, ed. by Davis and Meretoja, pp. 109–20 (p. 110). Fransiska Louwagie, *Témoignages et littérature d'après Auschwitz* (Amsterdam: Brill, 2020), p. 18.

18. Hutcheon, *A Poetics of Postmodernism*, pp. 42, 21.

19. Helena Duffy, 'The Ethics of Metawitnessing in Yannick Haenel's *Jan Karski*', *Dapim*, 32.1 (2018), 1–21.

20. Lyotard, *Le Différend*, p. 24; *The Differend*, p. 5.

21. Annette Wieviorka, 'Faux témoignage', *L'Histoire*, 349 (January 2010) <http://www.lhistoire.fr/faux-témoignage> [accessed 12 September 2016]. Wieviorka first voiced her negative opinion of *Jan Karski* when she was Alain Finkielkraut's guest on the radio programme *Répliques* (31 October 2009) and Emmanuel Laurentin's guest on *Fabrique de l'histoire* (9 December 2009). Claude Lanzmann, 'Jan Karski de Yannick Haenel: un faux roman', *Les Temps modernes*, 657 (January-March 2010) <https://www.cairn.info/revue-les-temps-modernes-2010-1-page-1.htm> [accessed 12 September 2016].

22. Ann Jefferson, *Biography and the Question of Literature in France* (Oxford: Oxford University Press, 2007), pp. 21–22. Jefferson adds that the 'supposedly unadorned nature of the truth offered by biography has regularly been contrasted with the embroidered truths of poetry' (p. 22).

23. Later, Haenel also redefined Parts I and II as fictional. Marc Dambre, 'Entretien avec Yannick Haenel: précisions sur *Jan Karski*', in *Mémoires occupées: fictions françaises et Seconde Guerre mondiale*, ed. by Marc Dambre (Paris: Presses Sorbonne Nouvelle, 2013), pp. 233–42 (p. 237).

24. Ball, 'Tales of Affect, "Thick" and "Thin"', p. 179.

25. The meeting resulted from the co-operation between Armia Krajowa (Home Army) and Żydowski Związek Wojskowy (Jewish Military Union).

26. Set up after the extermination of Izbica Lubelska's Jewish population, the camp accommodated deportees from many European countries, including Poland itself. From there, Jews were sent to die in Bełżec and Sobibór. The camp was liquidated in the spring of 1943.

27. *Jan Karski* won the Prix Interallié and the Prix du roman FNAC, while Haenel himself, who up until then had been relatively unknown, was made Chevalier de l'Ordre des Arts et des Lettres and received the Order of Merit of the Republic of Poland.

28. Duffy, 'The Ethics of Metawitnessing', pp. 3–5. For further details on the exchanges between Haenel and his critics, see Manuel Bragança, 'Faire parler les morts: sur *Jan Karski* et la controverse Lanzmann-Haenel', *Modern and Contemporary France*, 23 (2015), 35–46; and Richard J. Golsan, 'L'"Affaire Jan Karski": réflexions sur un scandale littéraire et historique', in *Mémoires occupées*, ed. by Dambre, pp. 183–90.

29. The pogrom, in which both Polish police and civilians took part, claimed the lives of forty-two Jews, leaving another forty injured.

30. Wieviorka, 'Faux témoignage'.

31. Lanzmann, 'Jan Karski de Yannick Haenel'.

32. See, for example, Jean-Louis Panné, *Jan Karski, le 'roman' et l'histoire* (Saint-Malo: Pascal Galodé, 2014), pp. 31–33.

33. Among the academic responses to Haenel's novel are: Richard J. Golsan, 'The Poetics and Perils

of Faction: Contemporary French Fiction and the Memory of World War II', *Romanic Review*, 105 (2014), 53–68; Carrard, 'Historiographic Metafiction, French Style'; Bragança, 'Faire parler les morts'; Pawel Hladki, '"Qui témoigne pour le témoin?" Question de la liberté littéraire à l'exemple de *Jan Karski* de Yannick Haenel', *Études romanes de Brno*, 33 (2012), 57–67; Evelyne Ledoux-Beaugrand, 'Les Restes d'Auschwitz: intertextualité et postmémoire dans *Jan Karski* de Yannick Haenel et *C'est maintenant du passé* de Marianne Rubinstein', *Études françaises*, 49 (2013), 145–62; and 'Emprunt et bricolage: traces mémorielles de la Shoah dans *Drancy Avenir* et *Jan Karski*', *French Forum*, 39 (Winter 2014), 143–57; and Henry Ravenhall, 'The Untimely Subject: Reporting Discourse and Bearing Witness in Villehardouin's *La Conquête de Constantinople* and Yannick Haenel's *Jan Karski*', *Interfaces*, 7 (2020), 1–28.

34. The term *szmalcownicy* is derived from the German noun *Schmalz* [lard] and refers to the blackmailers' pecuniary gain.
35. Zimmerman notes that, 'Unlike in Western Europe where the punishment for harbouring Jews was not severe, Poles were subjected to the death penalty for the same act'. In a footnote, he mentions the figure of between two to three hundred Poles murdered for harbouring Jews: 'Changing Perception in the Historiography of Polish-Jewish Relations during the Second World War', pp. 8–9, n. 36. Gary E. Rubin, 'The Film *Shoah*: Understanding Polish and Jewish Responses', *Shofar*, 4.2 (Winter 1986), 33–35 (p. 34).
36. <https://www.yadvashem.org/odot_pdf/Microsoft%20Word%20-%206392.pdf> [accessed 2 May 2018]. See also Tadeusz Piotrowski, 'Assistance to the Jews', in *Poland's Holocaust: Ethnic Strife, Collaboration with Occupying Forces and Genocide in the Second Republic 1918–1947* (Jefferson, NC: McFarland, 1998), pp. 112–28.
37. John Besemeres, 'Jan Karski's Valiant Failures', in *A Difficult Neighbourhood: Essays on Russia and East-central Europe Since World War II* (Canberra: Australian National University Press, 2016), pp. 49–62 (p. 50). Holocaust Encyclopaedia, United States Holocaust Memorial Museum, 'Lodz' <https://encyclopedia.ushmm.org/content/en/article/lodz> [accessed 18 April 2018].
38. Michael Szoper, 'Jan Karski: Personal Reflections on the Life of a Saint', *Polish Review*, 59.4 (2014), 73–80 (p. 74).
39. Yannick Haenel, *Jan Karski* (Paris: Gallimard, 2009), p. 176 (hereafter referenced as *JK* in the main text); *The Messenger*, trans. by Ian Monk (Melbourne: Text Publishing, 2011), p. 161 (hereafter referenced as *M* in the main text). In the address at the Liberation of the Nazi Concentration Camps Conference, Karski states 'I am a Christian Jew': 'Jan Karski', in *The Liberation of the Nazi Concentration Camps 1945: Eyewitness Accounts of the Liberators*, ed. by Brewster S. Chamberlin and Marcia Feldman, (Washington, DC: United States Holocaust Memorial Council, 1987), pp. 176–81 (p. 181).
40. Jan Karski, *The Great Powers and Poland, 1919–1945: From Versailles to Yalta* (Washington, DC: University Press of America, 1985), p. 461.
41. David Engel, 'Jan Karski's Mission to the West, 1942–1944', *Holocaust and Genocide Studies*, 5.4 (1990), 363–80 (p. 364). The reports, according to Engel, additionally show that the efforts Karski made on behalf of the Jews were on his own initiative and that the government-in-exile 'does not appear to have been interested in employing its courier as the striker of a tocsin for the fate of its mortally threatened citizens' (p. 364). Karski confirmed during the interview with Lanzmann, 'You realise that throughout my entire mission, for me the Jewish problem was not the only problem. For me the key problem was Poland, the Curzon Line, Soviet demands, Communists in the underground movement, fear for the Polish nation. [...] This was the emphasis'. Lanzmann, *Shoah*, original typescript, United States Holocaust Memorial Museum, pp. 55–56 <https://collections.ushmm.org/film_findingaids/RG-60.5006_01_trs_en.pdf> [accessed 1 April 2019]. In fact, during the war the Nazi crimes against Jews were hardly a prominent concern for the Allies. According to Kim Christian Priemel, it was only at a conference in Moscow in October 1943 that the mass murder of the Jews was discussed as part of the Nazis' genocidal policies: 'War Crimes Trials, the Holocaust, and Historiography, 1943–2011, in *A Companion to the Holocaust*, ed. by Gigliotti and Earl, pp. 173–89 (p. 175).
42. This is how Karski was referred to by his biographers, E. Thomas Wood and Stanisław M. Jankowski: *Karski: How One Man Tried to Stop the Holocaust* (New York: John Wiley, 1994).

43. For example, Ezrahi remarks that 'the prevailing concern of [Polish] literature is with the implication of the Holocaust for the Pole or for Poland, rather than for the victim, who often appears more as a mystical echo of the past than as a real, suffering Jew': *By Words Alone*, p. 233, n. 28. This position has been shared by Monika Adamczyk-Garbowska, 'Polish Literature on the Holocaust', in *Literature of the Holocaust*, ed. by Alan Rosen (Cambridge: Cambridge University Press, 2013), pp. 150–63 (p. 151), but opposed by Madeline Levine, 'The Ambiguity of Moral Outrage in Jerzy Andrzejewski's "Wielki Tydzień"', *Polish Review*, 32.4 (1987), 385–99 (p. 386).
44. Larry Ray and Sławomir Kapralski, 'Introduction to the Special Issue: Disputed Holocaust Memory in Poland', in *Disputed Holocaust Memory in Poland*, ed. by Larry Ray and Sławomir Kapralski (= special issue of *Holocaust Studies*, 25.3 (2019)), 209–19 (p. 213). See also Jean-Charles Szurek, 'Shoah: de la question juive à la question polonaise', in *Au sujet de 'Shoah'*, ed. by Deguy, pp. 357–82.
45. For an analysis of these processes, see Ray and Kapralski, 'Introduction to the Special Issue'. Daniel Levy and Natan Sznaider, *The Holocaust and Memory in the Global Age*, trans. by Assenka Oksiloff (Philadelphia: Temple University Press, 2006), p. 4.
46. See, for example, Helen Fein, *Accounting for Genocide: National Responses and Jewish Victimisation during the Holocaust* (New York: Free Press, 1979). Zimmerman cites other scholars sharing this opinion, including Wiesel's thesis that 'only where the indigenous populations were themselves eager to become "Judenrein" did the cattle trains with their suffocating human cargo roll swiftly into the night': 'Changing Perception in the Historiography of Polish-Jewish Relations during the Second World War', p. 3; Elie Wiesel, 'Eichmann's Victims and the Unheard Testimony', *Commentary*, 32 (December 1961), 510–16 (p. 511).
47. 'Obama Angers Poles with Death Camps', BBC, 30 May 2012 <https://www.bbc.com/news/world-europe-18264036> [accessed 18 April 2018].
48. Weronika Kostyrko, *Tancerka i Zagłada. Historia Poli Nireńskiej* [A Dancer and the Holocaust: A History of Pola Nireńska] (Warsaw: Czerwone i Czarne, 2019).
49. This is how Karski is remembered in the testimonies of those who knew him personally. See, for example, Besemeres, 'Jan Karski's Valiant Failures'. Sławomir Grünberg's documentary *Karski or the Lords of Humanity* (2015) contains a series of interviews that confirm this position.
50. This is the title of Elie Wiesel's novel, originally written in Yiddish and subsequently published in French as *La Nuit*. The text was first published in Brazil in 1954. The title translates as 'And the World Was Silent'.
51. The Polish government in exile repeatedly publicised information about the Nazi crimes and issued numerous and urgent calls for intervention. Dariusz Stola, 'The Polish Government-in-exile: National Unity and Weakness', *Holocaust Studies*, 18.2–3 (Autumn/Winter 2012), 95–118; and 'The Polish Government-in-exile and the Final Solution: What Conditioned its Actions and Inactions?', in *Contested Memories*, ed. by Zimmerman, pp. 85–119.
52. Tom Lawson, '"The Deputy": Bystanders to the Holocaust', in *Debates on the Holocaust* (Manchester: Manchester University Press 2010), pp. 86–124 (p. 103). Arthur Morse, *While Six Million Died: A Chronicle of American Apathy* (New York: Random House, 1968).
53. Paul A. Levine, 'On-lookers', in *The Oxford Handbook of Holocaust Studies*, ed. by Peter Hayes and John K. Roth (Oxford: Oxford University Press, 2002), pp. 156–69 (p. 159). Among the studies quoted by Levine is David Wyman, *The Abandonment of the Jews: America and the Holocaust 1941–1945* (New York: Pantheon, 1984); Monty N. Penkower, *The Jews Were Expendable: Free World Diplomacy and the Holocaust* (Chicago: University of Illinois, 1983); and Deborah Lipstadt, *Beyond Belief: The American Press and the Coming of the Holocaust 1933–1945* (New York: Free Press, 1986).
54. The other two categories in Hilberg's taxonomy are 'victims' and 'perpetrators'. Kristina Morina and Krijn Thijs, 'Introduction: Probing the Limits of Categorisation', in *Probing the Limits of Categorisation: The Bystander in Holocaust History*, ed. by Kristina Morina and Krijn Thijs (New York: Berghahn Books, 2019), pp. 1–14 (pp. 1, 2).
55. Tony Kushner, 'Britain, the United States and the Holocaust: In Search of a Historiography', in *The Historiography of the Holocaust*, ed. by Stone, pp. 253–75 (p. 256).
56. Mary Fulbrook, 'The Making and Un-making of Perpetrators: Patterns of Involvement in Nazi

Persecution', in *The Routledge International Handbook of Perpetrator Studies*, ed. by Knittel and Goldberg, pp. 25–36 (p. 30).
57. Vice rejects these accusations by arguing that the film is not concerned with the Poles but, unable to film those murdered, tries to glean from the testimonies of non-Jewish Poles the final moments of the lives of the killed Jews: 'Poland', pp. 76–78.
58. LaCapra, *History and Memory after Auschwitz*, p. 97.
59. Lanzmann speaks of his rejection of a linear narrative in 'Le Lieu et la parole', pp. 421, 423.
60. Ibid., pp. 414, 423. LaCapra, *History and Memory after Auschwitz*, pp. 96–98.
61. Felman, 'The Return of the Voice', p. 206. For a discussion of *Shoah's* complex generic status, see Sue Vice, 'Documentary or "Fiction of the Real"', in *Shoah*, pp. 22–37.
62. Wieviorka, *L'Ère du témoin*; and 'The Witness in History', trans. by Jared Stark, *Poetics Today*, 27.2 (Summer 2006), 395–96 (p. 389). Cf. Donald Bloxham, *Genocide on Trial: War Crimes Trials and the Formation of Holocaust History and Memory* (Oxford: Oxford University Press, 2001).
63. Giorgio Agamben, *Infancy and History: Essays on the Destruction of Experience*, trans. by Liz Heron (London: Verso, 1993), p. 94.
64. LaCapra, *Writing History, Writing Trauma*, p. 100.
65. Tony Kushner, 'Holocaust Testimony, Ethics, and the Problem of Representation', *Poetics Today*, 27 (Summer 2006), 283–84 (p. 277).
66. Tom Lawson, '"Holocaust Testimonies": The Ruins of Memory and Holocaust Historiography', in *Debates on the Holocaust*, pp. 270–304 (pp. 272–73).
67. Kushner, 'Britain, the United States and the Holocaust', p. 256. Holocaust testimonies have been recorded by the Fortunoff Video Archive at Yale University and by the USC Shoah Foundation founded by Steven Spielberg. See Jeffrey Shandler, *Holocaust Memory in the Digital Age: Survivors' Stories and New Media Practices* (Stanford, CA: Stanford University Press, 2017).
68. Ball, 'Tales of Affect, "Thick" and "Thin"', pp. 180–81. Ball ascribes the reluctance of some scholars to embrace anything but scientific detachment and commitment to empirically recovered facts to their professional survival as respected academics (p. 182). If I understand Ball's argument correctly, she equates such an attitude with the dissociation of bystanders from the cruelty perpetrated in their midst.
69. Lucy S. Dawidowicz, *The Holocaust and the Historians* (Cambridge, MA: Harvard University Press, 1981), pp. 177, 129.
70. Raul Hilberg, 'I Was Not There', in *Writing and the Holocaust*, ed. by Berel Lang (New York: Holmes & Meier, 1988), pp. 17–25 (p. 19). Pierre Vidal-Naquet, 'L'Épreuve de l'historien: réflexions d'un généraliste', in *Au sujet de 'Shoah'*, ed. by Deguy, pp. 270–88 (p. 274). Cf. Pierre Vidal-Naquet, 'Memory and History', trans. by David Ames Curtis, *Common Knowledge*, 5.2 (1966), 14–20 (p. 14).
71. Wieviorka, *L'Ère du témoin*, pp. 123, 180.
72. Hannah Arendt, *The Origins of Totalitarianism* (San Diego: Harcourt Brace, 1979), p. 144.
73. LaCapra, *Writing History, Writing Trauma*, pp. 113, 110.
74. Carolyn Dean, *Aversion and Erasure: The Fate of the Victim after the Holocaust* (Ithaca, NY: Cornell University Press, 2017), p. 143.
75. Young, *Writing and Rewriting the Holocaust*, p. 164.
76. Dean, 'Witnessing', p. 112; *Aversion and Erasure*, p. 142.
77. Dean, *Aversion and Erasure*, pp. 101–42.
78. LaCapra, *Writing History, Writing Trauma*, pp. 98–99, 86–87.
79. Dan Stone, 'Holocaust Testimony and the Challenge to the Philosophy of History', in *Social Theory after the Holocaust*, ed. by Charles Fine and Robert Turner (Liverpool: Liverpool University Press, 2000), pp. 219–34 (pp. 223, 227, 226).
80. Dori Laub, 'Bearing Witness or the Vicissitudes of Listening', in Felman and Laub, *Testimony*, pp. 57–74 (pp. 59, 61, 60).
81. Saul Friedländer, *Nazi Germany and the Jews: The Years of Persecution, 1939–1939* (London: Weidenfeld & Nicolson, 1997), p. 2.
82. James E. Young, 'Between History and Memory: The Uncanny Voices of Historian and Survivor', *History and Memory Journal*, 9.1–2 (Autumn 1997), 47–58 (p. 55).

83. LaCapra, *Writing History, Writing Trauma*, p. 88.
84. Appearing under their *noms de guerre* at the time, the two men have been identified subsequently as Leon Feiner of the General Jewish Labour Bund in Poland and either Menachem Kirschenbaum or Adolf Berman as representative of the Zionists.
85. Young, *Writing and Rewriting the Holocaust*, pp. 26, 30, 27. See also Zoë Waxman, 'Testimony and Representation', in *The Historiography of the Holocaust*, ed. by Stone, pp. 485–507 (p. 489).
86. Henry Greenspan, *On Listening to Holocaust Survivors: Recounting Life and History* (New York: Praeger, 1998), p. 167.
87. Régine Waintrater, *Sortir du génocide: témoignage et survivance* [2003] (Paris: Payot & Rivages, 2011), p. 217. Cf. Levi, *The Drowned and the Saved*, p. 8; LaCapra, *Writing History, Writing Trauma*, p. 91; Eaglestone, *The Holocaust and the Postmodern*, p. 35.
88. Young, *Writing and Rewriting the Holocaust*, pp. 160, 21, 165.
89. Lawrence Langer, *Holocaust Testimonies: The Ruins of Memory* (New Haven, CT: Yale University Press, 1991), p. 204.
90. Geoffrey Hartman, 'Tele-suffering and Testimony in the Dot Com Era', in *Visual Culture and the Holocaust*, ed. by Barbie Zelizer (London: Athlone Press, 2001), pp. 111–26 (p. 111). Cf. Young, *Writing and Rewriting the Holocaust*, p. 109.
91. Vice, 'Poland', p. 77. Rémy Besson quotes his email exchanges with Ziva Postec: 'The Karski Report: A Voice with the Ring of Truth', trans. by John Tittensor, *Études photographiques*, 27 (May 2011), 1–12 (p. 2).
92. Lanzmann, 'Le Lieu et la parole', pp. 417, 416. Cf. Neil Ascherson, 'The *Shoah* Controversy', *Soviet Jewish Affairs*, 16.1 (1986), 53–61 (p. 58).
93. Ascherson, 'The *Shoah* Controversy', p. 58.
94. Vice, 'Poland', p. 73.
95. Sue Vice states that 'the nature of the excluded testifiers and these moments that are re-enacted are ones that concern not the process of killing as they do in *Shoah*, but attempts at resistance and rescue': *Claude Lanzmann's 'Shoah' Outtakes: Holocaust Rescue and Resistance* (London: Bloomsbury, 2021), p. 2. Lanzmann reiterates this belief in his autobiography where he identifies the subject of *Shoah* as 'la mort même, la mort et non pas la survie' [death itself, death and not survival]: *Le Lièvre de Patagonie* (Paris: Gallimard, 2009), p. 437.
96. Lanzmann, 'Le Lieu et la parole', pp. 418, 423.
97. LaCapra, *Writing History, Writing Trauma*, p. 187. This view is shared by Ascherson, 'The *Shoah* Controversy', p. 58.
98. Young, *Writing and Rewriting the Holocaust*, p. 165.
99. Felman, 'The Return of the Voice', p. 205.
100. Eaglestone, *The Holocaust and the Postmodern*, pp. 31–33.
101. LaCapra, *Writing History, Writing Trauma*, p. 104.
102. Lawson, *Debates on the Holocaust*, p. 277; LaCapra, *Writing History, Writing Trauma*, pp. 98–99; Felman, 'The Return of the Voice', p. 214.
103. Laub, 'Bearing Witness or the Vissicitudes of Listening', p. 57; LaCapra, *History and Memory after Auschwitz*, p. 110.
104. Lanzmann, 'Le Lieu et la parole', pp. 418–19, 417. The bystanders themselves claimed to have wanted to warn the Jews, a claim that Lanzmann dismisses.
105. LaCapra, *Writing History, Writing Trauma*, p. 187.
106. Ascherson, 'The *Shoah* Controversy', p. 57. Ascherson deems Lanzmann's decision regrettable since Bartoszewski could have provided first-hand information on Żegota's rescue activities.
107. Dori Laub, 'An Event Without a Witness: Truth, Testimony and Survival', in Felman and Laub, *Testimony*, pp. 75–92 (p. 81).
108. LaCapra, *Writing History, Writing Trauma*, pp. 142–43.
109. By 'an event-without-a-witness' Laub also means that most Holocaust witnesses have perished and that the Holocaust experience has annihilated the self and with it the possibility of coherent testimony: 'An Event Without a Witness'.
110. Dean, 'Witnessing', pp. 113, 116.
111. Laub, 'An Event Without a Witness', p. 78.

112. Agamben, *Remnants of Auschwitz*, p. 26. Cf. Derrida, 'Poetics and Politics of Witnessing', pp. 73–76.
113. Dambre, 'Entretien avec Yannick Haenel', p. 235.
114. Young, *Writing and Rewriting the Holocaust*, pp. 15–16.
115. LaCapra, *Writing History, Writing Trauma*, p. 96.
116. Stone, 'Holocaust Testimony', pp. 227–29, 224.
117. LaCapra, *Writing History, Writing Trauma*, p. 90. Lanzmann, 'Le Lieu et la parole', p. 419.
118. Felman, 'The Return of the Voice', p. 241.
119. Neither Haenel's use of the present tense in Part II nor his choice to present his protagonist's monologue in Part III as a running narration without paragraphs have been carried through in the novel's English translation.
120. Laub, 'An Event Without a Witness', p. 69.
121. In her analysis of the German response to Jan Karski's story, Katrin Stoll quotes Micha Brumlik's remark concerning the contrast between the Pole's insistence on the connection between the past and the present, and the Germans' systematic distanciation from their Nazi past. Stoll therefore considers Karski as 'a model for ethical engagement with the past that Germans could never aspire to': 'The Lack of Conscious Engagement with the Reality of the Holocaust or: On the Non-reception of Jan Karski in the Federal Republic of Germany', *Holocaust Studies*, 20.1–2 (2014), 57–82 (pp. 69, 57).
122. Laub, 'An Event Without a Witness', p. 69.
123. Lyotard, *Le Différend*, p. 10; *The Differend*, p. xii.
124. Ball extends the concept of 'thick affect' from witnesses to historians and writers who do not practice restraint that is thought to be proper to accounts of the past. She exemplifies 'thickly affective narratives' with John-Paul Himka's impassioned review of Daniel Mendelsohn's *The Lost: The Search for Six Million* and Jan Paweł Gross's *Neighbours*: 'Tales of Affect, "Thick" and "Thin"', pp. 189–98.
125. Lyotard, *Le Différend*, p. 11; *The Differend*, p. xiii.
126. Karyn Ball, 'Ex/propriating Survivor Experience, or Auschwitz "after" Lyotard', in *Witness and Memory: The Discourse of Trauma*, ed. by Ana Douglass and Thomas A. Vogler (New York: Routledge, 2003), pp. 249–73 (p. 253).
127. Ball, *Disciplining the Holocaust*, p. 115.
128. For further examples of *négationnisme*, see ibid., p. 95.
129. Lyotard, *Le Différend*, p. 16; *The Differend*, p. xx.
130. Ibid., pp. 91, 92, 30; pp. 56–57, 13.
131. Golsan, 'The Poetics and Perils of Faction', p. 63; Jacques-Pierre Amette, 'Le Torchon brûle autour de Jan Karski', *Le Point*, 1 February 2010 <https://www.memoiresdeguerre.com/article-le-torchon-brule-autour-de-jan-karski-63797911.html> [accessed 11 August 2016]. Karski's critical view of Roosevelt is clearly discernible in the material Lanzmann released as *Le Rapport Karski* and in Grünberg's *Karski or the Lords of Humanity*.
132. The only contemporaneous document of whose existence historians are aware is Karski's own thirty-page report of the meeting, which he submitted to the Polish ambassador, Jan Ciechanowski (also present at the meeting), and which was later forwarded to the Polish government in London. The document has been mentioned by historians Engel ('Jan Karski's Mission to the West, 1942–1944', p. 375), Andrzej Żbikowski, and Wood and Jankowski. 'Notatka z rozmowy w Prezydentem F. D. Roosevelt'em' [Minutes of the Conversation with President F. D. Roosevelt], 28 July 1943, HIA-Karski, Box 1, File 7 <http://karski.muzhp.pl/misja_raporty_karskiego_rozmowa.html> [accessed 12 February 2020].
133. Meg Jensen, 'Testimony', in *The Routledge Companion to Literature and Trauma*, ed. by Davis and Meretoja, pp. 66–78 (p. 68).
134. See Karski, 'Jan Karski', p. 181. According to Engel, Karski gave two hundred lectures 'from coast to coast', and published countless articles in leading American newspapers and magazines, in which he advocated the Jewish cause: 'Jan Karski's Mission to the West, 1942–1944', p. 364.
135. Laub, 'An Event Without a Witness', p. 68.
136. Lyotard, *Le Différend*, p. 29; *The Differend*, p. 13.

137. Laub, 'Bearing Witness or the Vissicitudes of Listening', p. 68.
138. For a discussion of the manipulation of Karski's testimony in *Le Rapport Karski*, see Bragança, 'Faire parler les morts'.
139. Laub, 'Bearing Witness or the Vissicitudes of Listening', p. 57.
140. Quoted by Rothe, 'Irresponsible Nonsense', p. 189.
141. Janet Jacob, *Memorialising the Holocaust: Gender, Genocide and Collective Memory* (London: I. B. Tauris, 2010), p. xii.
142. Rothe, 'Irresponsible Nonsense', pp. 187–90.
143. LaCapra, *Writing History, Writing Trauma*, pp. 146, 97. Cf. Jenni Goldenberg, 'The Impact of the Interviewer of Holocaust Survivor Narratives: Vicarious Traumatisation or Transformation?', *Traumatology*, 8.4 (2002), 215–31.
144. Dean, *Aversion and Erasure*, p. 144.
145. Ball, *Disciplining the Holocaust*, pp. 2, 4.
146. Weissman, *Fantasies of Witnessing*.
147. Susan Gubar, *Poetry after Auschwitz: Remembering What One Never Knew* (Bloomington: Indiana University Press, 2003), pp. 149–50.
148. Diane I. Popescu, 'Post-witnessing the Concentration Camps: Paul Auster's and Angela Morgan Cutler's Investigative and Imaginative Encounters with Sites of Mass Murder', *Holocaust Studies*, 22.2–3 (2016), 274–88 (p. 274).
149. Felman, 'The Return of the Voice', p. 206.
150. Ibid., p. 213.
151. Dean, 'Witnessing', p. 114.
152. Jean-François Lyotard, 'Réponse à la question', p. 31; 'Appendix: Answering the Question: What Is Postmodernism', p. 81.
153. See, for example, White, 'Historical Emplotment and the Problem of Truth'.
154. Vice, *Holocaust Fiction*, p. 7.
155. Ball, 'Tales of Affect, "Thick" and "Thin"', pp. 181–82.
156. Ibid., p. 189.
157. Boswell, 'Beyond Autobiography', p. 144. Cf. Vice, *Holocaust Fiction*, pp. 1–7. Vice cites the frequent argument that Holocaust fiction 'is tantamount to making fiction of the Holocaust' and that it invariably brings about the unwelcome sense of catharsis and redemption, or that, in contrast to the 'agonised uncertainties of those who went through the camps', it is disturbingly self-assured and unambiguous (pp. 1, 6).
158. Young, *Writing and Rewriting the Holocaust*, pp. 18–22. Alan Rosen, 'The Holocaust Witness: Wartime and Postwar Voices', in *A Companion to the Holocaust*, ed. by Gigliotti and Earl, pp. 451–67 (pp. 462–63).
159. Young, *Writing and Rewriting the Holocaust*, p. 61.
160. Rosen, 'The Holocaust Witness', p. 463.
161. Shoshana Felman, 'Camus' *The Plague*, or a Monument to Witnessing', in *Testimony: Crises of Witnessing in Literature, Psychoanalysis and History* (New York: Routledge, 1992), pp. 93–111 (pp. 95–96).

CONCLUSION

Over the course of this study, I have demonstrated the presence of characteristically postmodern narrative techniques in six contemporary French novels about the Holocaust, and have discussed the cognitive, epistemological, and ethico-political implications of these techniques for our understanding of the Nazi genocide and of its legacies in the post-witness era. The core chapters addressed the six novels individually, focusing on their different aspects, yet systematically pointing to the intersections between their concerns and representational strategies. Chapter One posited Patrick Modiano's *Dora Bruder* as the inaugural text of the important turn in French literature, which the present study has recognised and examined. This turn consists, on the one hand, in the espousal of narrative devices found across postmodern fiction in the anglophone and other linguistic contexts, and, on the other, in a renewed confrontation with France's wartime past and with French memory politics regarding the Vichy period. Chapter One identified Modiano's narrative also as a beacon of the nascent scholarly interest in the geography and environmental impact of the Nazi genocide. It construed *Dora Bruder*'s relationship with Parisian topography as self-contradictory and therefore as postmodern, and probed the ideological agenda underpinning Modiano's simultaneous trust in the topographical approach and doubt in its efficacy. Chapter Two questioned the motivations behind Assouline's efforts to nuance the culpability of a wartime collaborator and his attendant attack on the binary conception of *les années noires*. My discussion focused on *La Cliente*'s postmodern indeterminacy, manifest in the novel's appropriation of Levi's concept of the 'Grey Zone' and in its own generic undecidability. It demonstrated the capacity of French historiographic metafiction to challenge Hutcheon's overwhelmingly positive evaluation of the genre, and in particular her almost unwavering conviction that postmodernism is aligned with progressive political agendas. Chapter Three examined Aaron's thematisation of the specificity of the female experience of Nazi persecution and of female survival strategies, and her emphasis on the Holocaust's protracted consequences which affect society both vertically and horizontally. The chapter's focal point was Aaron's interrogation of the viability and ethics of stable and cohesive identities in the post-Holocaust era, after the Nazis instrumentalised essentialist ethnic and gender categories for their murderous ends. Chapter Four approached the ethics of Littell's decision to focalise a Holocaust novel through a Nazi from the perspective of perpetrator trauma. Concentrating on the protagonist's habit of usurping images of Jewish suffering to convey his mental wounding, I argued that the trope of trauma enables Littell to control readerly engagement with the perpetrator and, by generating limited empathy, to provoke a reconsideration of our positionality in relation to evil, both past and present. It also helps to reinscribe Holocaust victims into the perpetrator's self-centred and self-serving monologue, creating a novel space for the articulation of the agony of these victims in an age marked by Holocaust fatigue. Chapter Five interpreted Claudel's postmodern parody of the fairy tale and the beast fable as a way of exposing the implications of the Enlightenment's liberal humanism for various subgroups of humanity, for animals, and for the environment. Claudel's critical engagement with popular genres that rely on anthropomorphic representations of animals and zoomorphic representations of humans foregrounds the shared sources of our persecution of human otherness and our centuries-long subjugation, exploitation, and mistreatment of nonhuman animals. Finally, Chapter Six analysed Haenel's inscription of the genre of testimony to bring to the fore the traumata produced by the Holocaust but obfuscated by conventional historiography. Correspondingly, Haenel's novel sets out to unsilence the wrongs that dominant political regimes and mainstream historiographies reflecting these regimes' interests, have inflicted on the Jews, on their Polish messenger, and on Poland itself. I demonstrated that, with his generically unstable narrative and concern with various differends, Haenel responds to Lyotard's recommendation that postmodern writers should attend to historical injustices by creating discursive means capable of articulating them. This assertion could be extended to all the other writers considered in this study except Assouline, whose problematic ideological agenda undermines the trust of Hutcheon and others in postmodernism's ethical stand through its commitment to marginalised or even persecuted alterity.

Irrespective of the different foci of the six chapters, my analyses have revealed a consistent presence in the examined novels of postmodern motifs and narrative techniques, such as self-reflexivity, explicit and parodic intertextuality, irony, discontinuity, and denial of closure. They have demonstrated that, contrary to the anxieties surrounding the conjunction of postmodern aesthetics and Holocaust thematics, these strategies mostly enhance the ethical investment of the studied novels. For example, the self-doubt characterising the six narratives opposes modernity's essentialist and universalist thinking which the Nazi ideology perniciously co-opted for its genocidal objectives. Likewise, their self-consciousness as fictional constructs destabilises the mimetic illusion that conventional fiction creates, and therefore attenuates, the misgivings about Holocaust fiction which has been accused of diminishing the genocide's factuality and of turning one person's pain into another's aesthetic pleasure. In the same vein, the self-reflexivity of historiographic metafiction provides an opportunity for voicing the aporias attached to Holocaust culture. That is to say, postmodern novels thematise the representational, epistemological, and moral conundrums posed by literature about the Nazi Judeocide, and by their authors' own sense of moral authority (or indeed its lack) to narrate events that lie beyond their experiential knowledge or even their familial biography. I have argued that, in the absence of direct knowledge of the narrativised historical realities, the six novels amply and overtly draw on textualisations of the Jewish tragedy, both historical and cultural. The texts they incorporate are then subjected to a parodic reading, while the narrative models that the six novels embrace are questioned with a view to exposing their impotence to render the disorientation experienced by the victims, the fragmentariness of their knowledge, and the traumatogenic and therefore reiterative and intrusive character of their memory. To rise to these challenges, the novels mix narrative genres and offer non-chronological, disjointed, and circular story lines. In this way, they deny their readers the comfort of the completeness, continuity, cause-and-effect logic, cohesion, and closure that belong to the realist repertoire, but that are at odds with the Holocaust experience.

The ethical position of the six novels manifests itself not only in their response to the difficulties posed by writing sensitively and responsibly about the Jewish tragedy from a considerable generational distance, but also through their concern with both marginal identities within Holocaust history and more recent instances of persecuted otherness. By mobilising the Auschwitz apocalypse to foreground injustices other than those arising from the Holocaust, the six novels reflect or even anticipate new disciplinary approaches to the Nazi genocide of Europe's Jews. Among these approaches is the effort to link Holocaust and postcolonial studies, and thus to yield analogies between wartime anti-Semitism and colonial violence. Another example is the intersection of Holocaust studies with feminism and gender theory, which shines light on the specificity of the female experience of Nazi persecution and on the repressions suffered by other than normative sexualities. Other fruitful methodologies encouraged by French postmodern fiction about the Nazi genocide derive from perpetrator studies, trauma studies, animal studies, ecocriticism, and posthumanism. The cross-disciplinary perspectives necessitated by the six novels addressed in this monograph testify to their potential to generate new knowledge about the Holocaust and a better understanding of more contemporary phenomena. The six novels also share the concerns and goals of postmodern historiography which, having abandoned positivist epistemologies, searches for representational means capable of tackling the specific cognitive and ethical problems posed by the Holocaust. Postmodern literature's complementary relationship with contemporary Holocaust history supports Hutcheon's confidence in closing the gap between two previously distinct discursive modes.

In the narrower context of France's tortured and vacillating relationship with its wartime past and of French literature's role in negotiating this relationship, I consider the six novels as an important intervention in the debates surrounding *les années noires* and French post-war memory politics. This intervention lies, as we have seen, in the efforts of the six writers to challenge dominant discourses and their counter-discourses, to nuance existing interpretations of the wartime years, and to give voice to little-discussed aspects of the Occupation. Some of the novels studied here insert the tragic fate of French Jews into the broader contexts of French history, of Hitler's pan-European aggression, and of the long tradition of anti-Jewish prejudice which goes beyond the borders not only of France but also of Europe. On the formal level, the six novels firmly implant the generic category of historiographic metafiction in the French literary landscape, where postmodernism has so far elicited limited interest from both writers and critics. Apart from bearing witness to the influence of anglophone theories and practices of postmodernism on French culture, they remind us that these theories and practices had been shaped by French post-war thought. This is evidenced by the applicability of Lyotard's philosophy, Derrida's deconstruction, and Levinasian ethics to the six texts. Finally, with their formally postmodern and contextually pan-European dimension, the novels analysed in this book point to future memorial and representational strategies regarding the Jewish tragedy. Namely, they designate literature as an important vector of Holocaust memory and of reflection about the Holocaust's lasting implications for our society, culture, philosophy, and politics.

BIBLIOGRAPHY OF WORKS CITED

Primary Sources

AARON, SOAZIG, *Le Non de Klara* (Paris: Maurice Nadeau, 2002)
——*Refusal*, trans. by Barbara Bray (London: Harvill Secker, 2007)
ASSOULINE, PIERRE, *La Cliente* (Paris: Gallimard, 1998)
CLAUDEL, PHILIPPE, *Le Rapport de Brodeck* (Paris: Stock, 2007)
——*Brodeck*, trans. by John Cullen (New York: Anchor Books, 2010)
HAENEL, YANNICK, *Jan Karski* (Paris: Gallimard, 2009)
——*The Messenger*, trans. by Ian Monk (Melbourne: Text Publishing, 2011)
LITTELL, JONATHAN, *Les Bienveillantes* (Paris: Gallimard, 2006)
——*The Kindly Ones*, trans. by by Charlotte Mendel (London: Vintage, 2010)
MODIANO, PATRICK, *Dora Bruder* [1997] (Paris: Gallimard Folio, 2000)
——*The Search Warrant*, trans. by Joanna Kilmartin (London: Harvill Secker, 2014)

Secondary Sources

ABBOTT, H. PORTER, 'Diary Fiction', *Orbis Litterarum*, 37 (1982), 21–31
——*Diary Fiction: Writing as Action* (Ithaca, NY: Cornell University Press, 1984)
ADAMCZYK-GARBOWSKA, MONIKA, 'Polish Literature on the Holocaust', in *Literature of the Holocaust*, ed. by Alan Rosen (Cambridge: Cambridge University Press, 2013), pp. 150–63
ADAMI, VALENTINA, *Trauma Studies and Literature: Martin Amis's 'Time's Arrow' as Trauma Fiction* (Frankfurt am Main: Peter Lang, 2008)
ADAMS, JENNI, *Magic Realism in Holocaust Literature: Troping the Traumatic Real* (Basingstoke: Palgrave Macmillan, 2011)
——'Reading (as) Violence in Jonathan Littell's *The Kindly Ones*', in *Representing Perpetrators in Holocaust Literature and Film*, ed. by Jenni Adams and Sue Vice (London: Vallentine Mitchell, 2013), pp. 25–46
——'Relationships to Realism in Post-Holocaust Fiction: Conflicted Realism and the Counterfactual Historical Novel', in *The Bloomsbury Companion to Holocaust Literature*, ed. by Jenni Adams (London: Bloomsbury, 2014), pp. 81–102
——'Traces, Dis/Continuities, Complicities: An Introduction to Holocaust Literature', in *The Bloomsbury Companion to Holocaust Literature*, ed. by Jenni Adams (London: Bloomsbury, 2014), pp. 1–24
ADAMS, JENNI, and SUE VICE (eds), *Representing Perpetrators in Holocaust Literature and Film* (London: Vallentine Mitchell, 2013)
ADORNO, THEODOR, 'Kulturkritik und Gesellschaft', in *Prismen: Kulturkritik und Gesellschaft* (Munich: Deutschen Taschenbuch Verlag, 1963), pp. 7–26
——*Minima Moralia: Reflections from Damaged Life*, trans. by E. F. N. Jephcott [1951] (London: Verso, 2005)
——'On Commitment [Continued]', trans. by Francis McDonagh, *Performing Arts Journal*, 3.3 (Winter, 1979), 57–67

AGAMBEN, GIORGIO, *Homo Sacer: Sovereign Power and Bare Life*, trans. by Daniel Heller-Roazen (Stanford, CA: Stanford University Press, 1989)
—— *Infancy and History: Essays on the Destruction of Experience*, trans. by Liz Heron (London: Verso, 1993)
—— *Remnants of Auschwitz: The Witness and the Archive*, trans. by Daniel Heller-Roazen (New York: Zone Books, 1999)
ALAIMO, STACY, *Bodily Natures: Science, Environment, and the Material Self* (Bloomington: Indiana University Press, 2010)
AMATO, JOSEPH A., *Victims and Values: A History and a Theory of Suffering* (New York: Greenwood Press, 1990)
AMESBERGER, HELGA, 'Reproduction under the Swastika: The Other Side of the Glorification of Motherhood', in *Sexual Violence against Jewish Women during the Holocaust*, ed. by Sonja Maria Hedgepeth and Rochelle G. Saidel (Lebanon, NH: Brandeis University Press, 2010), pp. 139–55
AMETTE, JACQUES-PIERRE, 'Le Torchon brûle autour de Jan Karski', *Le Point*, 1 February 2010 <https://www.memoiresdeguerre.com/article-le-torchon-brule-autour-de-jan-karski-63797911.html>
ANDERSON, MICHELLE E., 'Perpetrator Trauma, Empathic Unsettlement, and the Uncanny: Conceptualisations of Perpetrators in South Africa's *Truth Commission Special Report*', *Journal of Perpetrator Research*, 2.1 (2018), 95–118
APEL, DORA, *Memory Effects: The Holocaust and the Art of Secondary Witnessing* (New Brunswick, NJ: Rutgers University Press, 2002)
ARENDT, HANNAH, *Antisemitism: Part One of the Origins of Totalitarianism* (New York: Harcourt Brace, 1951)
—— *Eichmann in Jerusalem: A Report on the Banality of Evil* (New York: Penguin, 1994)
—— *The Origins of Totalitarianism* (San Diego: Harcourt Brace, 1979)
ARLOW, JAKOB A., 'Metaphor and the Psychanalytic Situation', *Psychanalytic Quarterly*, 43 (1979), 363–85
ARNDS, PETER, 'On the Awful German Fairy Tale: Breaking Taboos in Representations of Nazi Euthanasia and the Holocaust in Günter Grass's *Die Blechtrommel*, Edgar Hilsenrath's *Der Nazi & der Friseur*, and Anselm Kiefer's Visual Art', *German Quarterly*, 75.4 (Autumn 2002), 422–39
ASCHERSON, NEAL, 'The Shoah Controversy', *Soviet Jewish Affairs*, 16.1 (1986), 53–61
ASHLIMAN, D. L., *Folk and Fairy Tales: A Handbook* (Westport, CT: Greenwood Folklore Handbooks, 2004)
ASHOLT, WOLFGANG. 'A German Reading of the German Reception of *The Kindly Ones*', in *Writing the Holocaust Today: Critical Perspectives on Jonathan Littell's 'The Kindly Ones'*, ed. by Aurélie Barjonet and Liran Razinsky (Amsterdam: Rodopi, 2012), pp. 221–38
ASLANOV, CYRIL, 'Visibility and Iconicity of the German Language in *The Kindly Ones*', in *Writing the Holocaust Today: Critical Perspectives on Jonathan Littell's 'The Kindly Ones'*, ed. by Aurélie Barjonet and Liran Razinsky (Amsterdam: Rodopi, 2012), pp. 61–74
ASSOULINE, PIERRE, *L'Épuration des intellectuels 1944–1945* (Brussels: Édition Complexe, 1996)
—— *Le Fleuve Combelle* (Paris: Calmann-Levy, 1997)
—— *Hergé* (Paris: Plon, 1996)
—— *Jean Jardin: une éminence grise* (Paris: Gallimard, 1986)
—— *Lutetia* (Paris: Gallimard, 2002)
—— 'Modiano: lieux de mémoire', *Lire*, 176 (1990), 35–46
—— 'Rencontre avec Pierre Assouline à l'occasion de la parution de *La Cliente* (1998)' <http://www.gallimard.fr/catalog/entretiens/01035681.htm>
—— *Sigmaringen* (Paris: Gallimard, 2014)
—— *Simenon: biographie* (Paris: Julliard, 1992)

—— *Un demi-siècle d'édition française* (Paris: Balland, 1984)
ATTERTON, PETER, 'Dog and Philosophy: Does Bobby Have What It Takes to Be Moral?', in *Face to Face with Animals: Levinas and the Animal Question*, ed. by Peter Atterton and Tamra Wright (New York: State University of New York Press, 2019), pp. 63–92
AVNI, ORA, 'Patrick Modiano: A French Jew?', *Yale French Studies*, 85 (1994), 227–47
BACCHILEGA, CRISTINA, *Postmodern Fairy Tales: Gender and Narrative Strategies* (Philadelphia: University of Pennsylvania Press, 1997)
BAER, ELIZABETH R., 'A Postmodern Fairy Tale of the Holocaust: Jane Yolen's *Briar Rose*', *Studies in American Jewish Literature*, 24 (2005), 145–52
BAER, ELIZABETH R., and MYRNA GOLDBERG (eds), *Experience and Expression: Women, the Nazis, and the Holocaust* (Detroit: Wayne State University Press, 2003)
BAKER, STEVE, *Picturing the Beast: Animals, Identity and Representation* (Urbana: University of Illinois Press, 2001)
BALL, KARYN, *Disciplining the Holocaust* (New York: State University of New York Press, 2008)
—— 'Ex/propriating Survivor Experience, or Auschwitz "after" Lyotard', in *Witness and Memory: The Discourse of Trauma*, ed. by Ana Douglass and Thomas A. Vogler (New York: Routledge, 2003), pp. 249–73
—— 'Tales of Affect, "Thick" and "Thin": On Distantiation in Holocaust Historiography', *Holocaust Studies*, 20.1–2 (2014), 179–217
BARENBAUM, MICHAEL, 'Holocaust: European History', *Encyclopaedia Britannica* <https://www.britannica.com/event/Holocaust>
BAR ON, BAT-AMI, and ANN FERGUSON, *Daring to Be Good: Essays in Feminist Ethico-politics* (London: Routledge, 1998)
BARTHES, ROLAND, *Roland Barthes by Roland Barthes*, trans. by Richard Howard (Berkley: University of California Press, 1994)
BARTOV, OMER, 'Introduction', in *The Holocaust: Origins, Implementation, Aftermath*, ed. by Omer Bartov (London: Routledge, 2000), pp. 1–18
BASSI, GIULIA, 'Against Historical Positivism: Some Skeptical Reflections about the Archival Fetishism', *Mnemoscape*, 1 (2015) <https://www.mnemoscape.org/single-post/2014/09/08/Against-Historiographical-Positivism-Some-Skeptical-Reflections-about-the-Archival-Fetishism---by-Giulia-Bassi>
BAUER, YEHUDA, *Rethinking the Holocaust* (New Haven, CT: Yale University Press, 2001)
BAUMAN, ZYGMUNT, 'The Holocaust's Life as a Ghost', in *Social Theory after the Holocaust*, ed. by Robert Fine and Charles Turner (Liverpool: Liverpool University Press, 2000), pp. 7–18
—— *Modernity and the Holocaust* [1989] (London: Polity Press, 1993)
—— *Postmodern Ethics* (Oxford: Blackwell, 1993)
BAUMEL, JUDITH TYDOR, *Double Jeopardy: Gender and the Holocaust* (London: Vallentine Mitchell, 1998)
BBC, 'Obama Angers Poles with Death Camps', 30 May 2012 <https://www.bbc.com/news/world-europe-18264036>
BEAUVOIR, SIMONE DE, *Le Deuxième sexe. I* (Paris: Gallimard Folio, 1986)
BEM, JEANNE, 'Dora Bruder ou la biographie déplacée de Modiano', *Cahiers de l'Association Internationale des études françaises*, 52 (2000), 221–32
BENJAMIN, ANDREW, *Of Jews and Animals* (Edinburgh: Edinburgh University Press, 2010)
BENNETT, ANDREW, *Suicide Century: Literature and Suicide from James Joyce to David Foster Wallace* (Cambridge: Cambridge University Press, 2017)
BENSOUSSAN, GEORGES, 'Éditorial', in *La Shoah dans la littérature française*, ed. by Myriam Ruszniewski-Dahan and Georges Bensoussan (= special issue of *Revue d'histoire de la Shoah: le monde juif*, 176 (September–December 2002)), 4–13

Béon, Yves, *Planet Dora: A Memoir of the Holocaust and the Birth of the Space Age* (Boulder, CO: Westview Press, 1997)

Berberich, Christine, '"I think I'm beginning to understand. What I'm writing is an infranovel": Laurent Binet, *HHhH* and the Problem of "Writing History"', *Holocaust Studies*, 25.1–2 (2019), 74–87

Berger, James, 'Review: Trauma and Literary Theory', *Contemporary Literature*, 38.3 (Autumn 1997), 569–82

Berger, Joseph, 'The Peril of Vulgarisation', *Dimensions: A Journal of Holocaust Studies*, 5.1 (1989), 3–6

Bernard-Donals, Michael, 'Theory and the Ethics of Holocaust Representation', in *The Bloomsbury Companion to Holocaust Literature*, ed. by Jenni Adams (London: Bloomsbury, 2014), pp. 103–19

Besemeres, John, 'Jan Karski's Valiant Failures', in *A Difficult Neighbourhood: Essays on Russia and East-central Europe Since World War II* (Canberra: Australian National University Press, 2016), pp. 49–62

Besson, Rémy, 'The Karski Report: A Voice with the Ring of Truth', trans. by John Tittensor, *Études photographiques*, 27 (May 2011), 1–12

Bettelheim, Bruno, *The Uses of Enchantment: The Meaning and Importance of Fairy Tales* (London: Penguin, 1976)

Biasin, Gian Paolo, 'Till My Ghastly Tale Is Told: Levi's Moral Discourse from *Se questo è un uomo* to *I sommersi e I salvati*', in *Reason and Light: Essays on Primo Levi*, ed. by Susan Tarrow (Ithaca, NY: Cornell University Press, 1990), pp. 127–41

Bikont, Anna, *The Crime and the Silence: Confronting the Massacre of Jews in Wartime Jedwabne*, trans. by Alissa Valles (New York: Farrar, Straus & Giroux, 2004)

Bilik, Dorothy, *Immigrant-survivors: Post-Holocaust Consciousness in Recent Jewish American Fiction* (Middletown, CT: Wesleyan University Press, 1981)

Binder, Anne-Berenike, 'Soazig Aaron, *Le Non de Klara* — "paroles suffoquées" oder der Desakralisierung der Überlebenden', in *'Mon ombre est restée là-bas': literarische und mediale Formen des Erinnerns in Raum und Zeit* (Tübingen: Max Niemayer, 2008), pp. 117–69

Binet, Laurent, 'Exclusive: The Missing Pages of Laurent's *HHhH*', *The Millions*, 16 April 2012 <https://themillions.com/2012/04/exclusive-the-missing-pages-of-laurent-binets-hhhh.html>

—— *HHhH* (Paris: Grasset, 2009)

—— *HHhH*, trans. by Sam Taylor (London: Vintage)

Bird, Stephanie, 'Perpetrator and Perpetration in Literature', in *The Routledge International Handbook of Perpetrator Studies*, ed. by Susanne C. Knittel and Zachary J. Goldberg (London: Routledge, 2020), pp. 301–10

Birnbaum, Daniel, and Anders Olsson, 'An Interview with Jacques Derrida on the Limits of Digestion', *e-flux Journal*, 2 (January 2009) <https://www.e-flux.com/journal/02/68495/an-interview-with-jacques-derrida-on-the-limits-of-digestion/>

Blanckeman, Bruno, 'Droit de 6ari (un Paris de Patrick Modiano)', in *Lectures de Modiano*, ed. by Roger-Yves Roche (Nantes: Cécile Defaut, 2009), pp. 163–78

Blanrue, Paul-Éric, *Les Malveillantes: enquête sur le cas Jonathan Littell* (Paris: Scali, 2006)

Błoński, Jan, 'Biedni Polacy patrzą na getto', *Tygodnik Powszechny*, 2 (1987), 1, 4

—— 'The Poor Poles Look at the Ghetto', in *'My Brother's Keeper?': Recent Polish Debates on the Holocaust*, ed. by Antony Polonsky [1990] (Oxford: Routledge, 1998), pp. 34–53; [another edition], in *Jews and the Emerging Polish State*, ed. and trans. by Antony Polonsky (= special issue of *Polin: Studies in Polish Jewry*, 2 (2008)), 321–36

Bloxham, Donald, *Genocide on Trial: War Crimes Trials and the Formation of Holocaust History and Memory* (Oxford: Oxford University Press, 2001)

BOND, LUCY, and STEF CRAPS, *Trauma* (Abingdon: Routledge, 2020)
BORNAND, MARIE, *Témoignage et fiction: les récits de rescapés dans la littérature de la langue française* (Geneva: Droz, 2004)
BOSWELL, MATTHEW, 'Beyond Autobiography: Hybrid Testimony and the Art of Witness', in *The Future of Testimony: Interdisciplinary Perspectives on Witnessing*, ed. by Jane Kilby and Antony Rowland (New York: Routledge, 2014), pp. 144–59
BOUGNOUX, DANIEL, 'Max Aue, personage de roman', *Le Débat*, 144 (March-April 2007), 66–69
BOURIS, ERICA, *Complex Political Victims* (Bloomfield, CT: Kumarian Press, 2007)
BRAGANÇA, MANUEL, 'Faire parler les morts: sur *Jan Karski* et la controverse Lanzmann-Haenel', *Modern and Contemporary France*, 23 (2015), 35–46
BRAIDOTTI, ROSI, *Nomadic Subjects: Embodiment in Contemporary Feminist Theory* (New York: Columbia University Press, 1994)
BRANAMAN, ANN, 'Gender and Sexuality in Liquid Modernity', in *The Contemporary Bauman*, ed. by Anthony Elliott (London: Routledge, 2007), pp. 117–35
BRAUN, ROBERT, 'The Holocaust and Problems of Historical Representation', *History and Theory*, 33.2 (May 1994), 172–97
BRENNER, RACHEL F., 'Holocaust *Memories* and Polish Catholic Identity: Cultural Transmutations of Warsaw Ghetto Uprising', in *The Palgrave Handbook of Holocaust Literature and Culture*, ed. by Victoria Aarons and Phyllis Lassner (Basingstoke: Palgrave Macmillan, 2020), pp. 233–50
BRETT, LILY, *Auschwitz Poems: Gedichte Englisch und Deutsch* (Vienna: Suhrkamp, 2004)
BRITTON-JACKSON, LIVIA, *I Have Lived a Thousand Years* (New York: Simon & Schuster, 1997)
BROOKS, ANN, *Postfeminisms: Feminism, Cultural Theory and Cultural Forms* (London: Routledge, 1997)
BROSSAT, ALAIN, *Les Tondues: un carnaval moche* (Paris: Manya, 1992)
BROWN, ADAM, *Judging 'Privileged' Jews: Holocaust Ethics, Representation, and the 'Grey Zone'* (New York: Berghahn Books, 2013)
BROWNING, CHRISTOPHER R., '"Alleviation" and "Compliance": The Survival Strategies of the Jewish Leadership in the Wierzbnik Ghetto and Starachowice Factory Slave Labour Camps', in *Gray Zones: Ambiguities and Compromise in the Holocaust and Its Aftermath*, ed. by Jonathan Petropoulos and John K. Roth (New York: Berghahn Books, 2005), pp. 26–36
—— 'German Memory, Judicial Interrogation, Historical Reconstruction: Writing Perpetrator History from Postwar Testimony', in *Probing the Limits of Representation: Nazism and the 'Final Solution'*, ed. by Saul Friedländer (Cambridge, MA: Harvard University Press, 1992), pp. 22–36
—— *Ordinary Men: Reserve Police Battalion 101 and the Final Solution in Poland* (New York: HarperCollins 1992)
BRUMLIK, MICHA, 'Der zähe Schaum der Verdrängung', *Der Spiegel*, 8 (1986), <https://www.spiegel.de/spiegel/print/d-13518094.html>
BUETTNER, ANGI, *Holocaust Images and Picturing Catastrophe: The Cultural Politics of Seeing* (Farnham: Ashgate, 2011)
BUDICK, EMILY MILLER, *The Subject of Holocaust Fiction* (Bloomington: Indiana University Press, 2012)
BURGIN, VICTOR, *The End of Art Theory: Criticism and Postmodernity* (Basingstoke: Macmillan, 1986)
BURNET, RÉGIS, 'Du miroir au face-à-face: voir comme Dieu voit dans le Nouveau Testament', *Pallas: Revue d'Études Antiques*, 92 (2013) <https://journals.openedition.org/pallas/266>

BUTLER, CHRISTOPHER, *After the Wake: An Essay on the Contemporary Avant-garde* (Oxford: Oxford University Press, 1980)
BUTLER, JUDITH, *Gender Trouble: Feminism and the Subversion of Identity* [1990] (London: Routledge, 2014)
CAIRNS, LUCILLE, '"La Mémoire de la Shoah": The Contentious Case of Soazig Aaron's *Le Non de Klara*', *French Studies*, 64 (October 2010), 438–50 (p. 449)
CANETTI, ELIAS, *Crowds and Power*, trans. by Carol Stewart (New York: Seabury, 1978)
CARD, CLAUDIA, 'Groping Through Grey Zones', in *On Feminist Ethics and Politics*, ed. by Claudia Card (Lawrence: University Press of Kansas, 1999), pp. 3–26
CARPENTIER, MÉLANIE, 'Le Conteur humaniste: interview avec Philippe Claudel', *Le Figaro*, 10 March 2006 <http://www.evene.fr/livres/actualite/interview-philippe-claudel-petite-fille-monsieur-linh-295.php>
CARRARD, PHILIPPE, 'Historiographic Metafiction, French Style', *Style*, 48.2 (Summer 2014), 181–202
CARUTH, CATHY, 'Introduction to Part I: Trauma and Experience', in *Trauma: Explorations in Memory*, ed. by Cathy Caruth (Baltimore, MD: Johns Hopkins University Press, 1995), pp. 3–12
—— *Unclaimed Experience: Trauma, Narrative and History* (Baltimore, MD: Johns Hopkins University Press, 1996)
CHAOUAT, BRUNO, 'Antisemitism Redux: On Literary and Theoretical Perversions', in *Resurgent Antisemitism: Global Perspectives*, ed. by Alvin H. Rosenfeld (Bloomington: Indiana University Press, 2013), pp. 118–39
CHARLESWORTH, ANDREW, 'The Topography of Genocide', in *The Historiography of the Holocaust*, ed. by Dan Stone (Basingstoke: Palgrave Macmillan, 2004), pp. 216–52
CHRULEW, MATTHEW, and CHRIS DANTA, 'Fabled Thought: On Jacques Derrida's *The Beast & the Sovereign*', *SubStance*, 43.2 (2014), 3–9
CHANTER, TINA, 'Feminism and the Other', in *The Provocation of Levinas: Rethinking the Other*, ed. by Robert Bernasconi and David Wood (London: Routledge, 2002), pp. 32–54
—— *Time, Death and the Feminine* (Stanford, CA: Stanford University Press, 2011)
CLARK, DAVID L., 'On Being "The Last Kantian in Nazi Germany": Dwelling with Animals after Levinas', in *Configuring the Human in Western History*, ed. by Jennifer Ham and Matthew Senior (New York: Routledge, 1997), pp. 165–98
CLARK, TIMOTHY, *The Cambridge Introduction to Literature and the Environment* (Cambridge: Cambridge University Press, 2011)
CLAMMER, JOHN, 'Performing Ethnicity: Performance, Gender, Body and Belief in the Construction and Signalling of Identity', *Ethnic and Racial Studies*, 38.12 (2015), 2159–66
CLEMENTI, FEDERICA K., *Holocaust Mothers and Daughters: Family, History and Trauma* (Lebanon, NH: Brandeis University Press, 2013)
CLIFFORD, REBECCA, *Commemorating the Holocaust: The Dilemmas of Remembrance in France and Italy* (Oxford: Oxford University Press, 2013)
CODDE, PHILIPPE, 'Transmitted Holocaust Trauma: A Matter of Myth and Fairy Tales?', *European Judaism: A Journal for the New Europe*, 42.1 (Spring 2009), 62–75
COETZEE, J. M., *Elizabeth Costello* (New York: Viking, 2003)
COLE, TIM, 'Geographies of the Holocaust', in *A Companion to the Holocaust*, ed. by Simone Gigliotti and Hilary Earl (Hoboken, NJ: John Wiley, 2020), pp. 333–47
—— *Holocaust City: Making of a Jewish Ghetto* (New York: Routledge, 2003)
—— '"Nature Was Helping Us": Forests, Trees and Environmental Histories of the Holocaust', *Environmental History*, 19.4 (2019), 665–86
—— 'Review Essay: Landscapes of Holocaust Memory', *Journal of Jewish Identities*, 4.2 (2011), 71–75
—— *Traces of the Holocaust: Journeying In and Out of the Ghettos* (London: Bloomsbury, 2011)

COLES, GREGORY, 'Emerging Voices: The Exorcism of Language: Reclaimed Derogatory Terms and Their Limits', *College English*, 76.5 (May 2016), 424–46

COLVIN, KELLY RICCIARDI, *Gender and French Identity after the Second World War: Engendering Frenchness* (London: Bloomsbury, 2017)

COMPAGNON, ANTOINE, *Les Cinq Paradoxes de la modernité* (Paris: Seuil, 1990)

CONWAY, JILL KER, *When Memory Speaks: Reflections on Autobiography* (New York: Alfred A. Kopf, 1998)

COOKE, DERVILA, and COLIN NETTELBECK, 'Modiano in the Feminine: À nous deux, madame la vie', *Nottingham French Studies*, 45.2 (Summer 2006), 39–53

COQUIO, CATHERINE. *La Littérature en suspens. Écritures de la Shoah: le témoignage et les œuvres* (Paris: L'Arachnéen, 2015)

COSNARD, DENIS, 'Modiano-Klarsfeld: une correspondence autour de *Dora Bruder*' <http://lereseaumodiano.blogspot.com/2012/01/modiano-klarsfeld-une-correspondance.html>

COSTELLOE, TIMOTHY M., 'The Invisibility of Evil: Moral Progress and the "Animal Holocaust"', *Philosophical Papers*, 32.2 (2003), 109–31

CRAPS, STEF, 'Beyond Eurocentrism: Trauma Theory in the Global Age', in *The Future of Trauma Theory: Contemporary Literary and Cultural Criticism*, ed. by Sam Durrant and Robert Eaglestone (New York: Routledge, 2013), pp. 45–62

CRITCHLEY, SIMON, *The Ethics of Deconstruction: Derrida and Levinas* (Oxford: Blackwell, 1992)

CROSTHWAITE, PAUL, *Trauma, Postmodernism and the Aftermath of World War II* (Basingstoke: Palgrave Macmillan, 2009)

CROWNSHAW, RICHARD, 'Perpetrator Fictions and Transcultural Memory', *Parallax*, 17.4 (2011), 75–89

CURTHOYS, NED, 'Evaluating Risk in Perpetrator Narratives: Resituating Jonathan Littell's *The Kindly Ones* as Historical Fiction', *Textual Practice*, 31.3 (2017), 457–75

CUSHMAN, SARAH, 'The Auschwitz Women's Camp: An Overview and Reconsiderations', in *The Palgrave Handbook of Holocaust Literature and Culture*, ed. by Victoria Aarons and Phyllis Lassner (Basingstoke: Palgrave Macmillan, 2020), pp. 707–24

DAMAMME-GILBERT, BÉATRICE, 'The Question of Genre in Holocaust Narrative: The Case of Patrick Modiano's *Dora Bruder*', in *Genre Trajectories: Identifying, Mapping, Projecting*, ed. by Garin Dowd and Natalia Rulyova (Basingstoke: Palgrave Macmillan, 2015), pp. 45–65

DAMBRE, MARC, 'Entretien avec Yannick Haenel: précisions sur *Jan Karski*', in *Mémoires occupées: fictions françaises et Seconde Guerre mondiale*, ed. by Marc Dambre (Paris: Presses Sorbonne Nouvelle, 2013), pp. 233–42

DANEY DE MARCILLAC, MARIE, 'Fables philosophiques d'Emmanuel Levinas et de Michel Serres: Ulysse et les bêtes', *Littérature*, 4.168 (2012), 71–84

DANGY, ISABELLE, 'Hôtels, cafés et villas tristes: lieux privés et lieux publics dans les romans de Modiano', in *Lectures de Modiano*, ed. by Roger-Ives Roche (Nantes: Cécile Defaut, 2009), pp. 179–98

DANTA, CHRIS, '"Might Sovereignty Be Devouring?": Derrida and the Fable', *SubStance*, 43.2 (2014), 37–49

DASTON, LORRAINE, and GREGG MITMAN, 'Introduction', in *Thinking with Animals: New Perspectives on Anthropomorphism*, ed. by Lorraine Daston and Gregg Mitman (New York: Columbia University Press, 2005), pp. 1–14

DAUZAT, PIERRE-ÉMMANUEL, *Holocauste ordinaire: histoires d'usurpation. Extermination, littérature, théologie* (Paris: Bayard Centurion, 2007)

DAVIS, COLIN, 'Disenchanted Places: Patrick Modiano's *Quartier perdu* and Recent French Fiction', in *Il senso del nonsense: scritti in memoria di Lynn Salkin Sbiroli*, ed. by M. S. Moretti, R. R. Cappelletti, and O. Martinez (Naples: Edizioni Scientifiche Italiane, 1995), pp. 663–76

—— *Levinas: An Introduction* (Notre Dame, IN: University of Notre Dame Press, 1996)
DAVIS, KAREN, *The Holocaust and the Henmaid's Tale: A Case for Comparing Atrocities* (New York: Lantern Books, 2005)
DAWIDOWICZ, LUCY S., *The Holocaust and the Historians* (Cambridge, MA: Harvard University Press, 1981)
DAWN, KAREN, and PETER SINGER, 'Converging Convictions: Coetzee and His Characters on Animals', in *J. M. Coetzee and Ethics*, ed. by Anton Leist and Peter Singer (New York: Columbia University Press, 2010), pp. 109–18
DEAN, CAROLYN J., *Aversion and Erasure: The Fate of the Victim after the Holocaust* (Ithaca, NY: Cornell University Press, 2017)
—— *The Fragility of Empathy after the Holocaust* (Ithaca, NY: Cornell University Press, 2004)
—— 'Witnessing', in *The Routledge Companion to Literature and Trauma*, ed. by Colin Davis and Hanna Meretoja (New York: Routledge, 2020), pp. 109–20
DECOUT, MAXIME, 'Patrick Modiano's *Dora Bruder*: Wandering Down Memory Lane', in *Shadows in the City of Light: Paris in Postwar French Jewish Writing*, ed. by Sara R. Horowitz, Amira Bojadzija-Dan, and Julia Creet (New York: State University of New York Press, 2021), pp. 113–22
DELBO, CHARLOTTE, *Auschwitz, et après I* (Paris: Minuit, 1970)
—— *Auschwitz and After*, trans. by Rosette C. Lamont, 2nd edn (New Haven, CT: Yale University Press, 2013)
DELEUZE, GILLES, and FÉLIX GUATTARI, *Mille plateaux* (Paris: Minuit, 1980)
DERRIDA, JACQUES, 'L'Animal que donc je suis (À suivre)', in *L'Animal autobiographique*, ed. by Marie-Louise Mallet (Paris: Galilée, 1999), pp. 251–301
—— 'The Animal That Therefore I Am', trans. by David Wills, *Critical Inquiry*, 28.2 (Winter 2002), 369–418
—— *The Beast and the Sovereign. Volume 1*, trans. by Geoffrey Bennington (Chicago: University of Chicago Press, 2009)
—— 'Poetics and Politics of Witnessing', in *Sovereignties in Question: The Poetics of Paul Celan*, ed. by Thomas Dutoit and Outi Pasanen (New York: Fordham University Press, 2005), pp. 65–96
—— *Spectres de Marx* (Paris: Galilée, 1993)
—— *Spectres of Marx: The State of the Debt, the Work of Mourning and the New International*, trans. by Peggy Kamuf (New York: Routledge, 1994)
DESMARAIS, JULIE, *Femmes tondues: France-Libération. Coupables, amoureuses, victimes* (Montreal: Presses de l'Université Laval, 2010)
DES PRES, TERRENCE, *Survivor: An Anatomy of Life in the Death Camps* (Oxford: Oxford University Press, 1976)
DRISCOLL, KÁRI, 'Perpetrators, Animals, and Animality', in *The Routledge Handbook of Perpetrator Studies*, ed. by Susanne C. Knittel and Zachary J. Goldberg (New York: Routledge, 2020), pp. 192–205
DUFFY, HELENA, '"Les années noires avaient été grises": A Metaethical Analysis of Pierre Assouline's Appropriation of Primo Levi's "Grey Zone"', *French Forum*, 44.1 (Spring 2019), 29–44
—— 'La Bienveillance de la critique polonaise: An Analysis of the Polish Reception of *The Kindly Ones*', in *Writing the Holocaust Today: Critical Perspectives on Jonathan Littell's 'The Kindly Ones'*, ed. by Aurélie Barjonet and Liran Razinsky (Amsterdam: Rodopi, 2012), pp. 239–56
—— 'The Ethics of Metawitnessing in Yannick Haenel's *Jan Karski*', *Dapim*, 32.1 (2018), 1–21
—— 'Philippe Claudel's *Le Rapport de Brodeck* as a Parody of the Fable or the Holocaust Universalized', *Holocaust Studies*, 24.4 (2018), 503–26

—— 'Postmémoire culturelle, paramémoire ou complicité traumatique? Une enquête sur la Shoah dans *L'Origine de la violence* de Fabrice Humbert', in *Enquêter sur la Shoah aujourd'hui* (= special issue of *Europe* (forthcoming))

—— 'The Silence of the Mothers: Representation of Holocaust Motherhood in Art Spiegelman's *Maus* and Philippe Claudel's *Brodeck*', *Journal of Holocaust Research*, 34.2 (April 2020), 138–54

—— 'Space of Trauma/ Space of Freedom: The Forest as a Posttraumatic Landscape in Two Holocaust Narratives', in *Interpreting Violence: Narrative, Ethics and Hermeneutics*, ed. by Cassandra Falke, Victoria Fareld, and Hanna Meretoja (New York: Routledge, forthcoming)

—— 'Shit, Blood and Vomit: The Dreams of a Nazi in Jonathan Littell's *The Kindly Ones*', in *Dreams and Atrocity: The Oneiric in Representations of Trauma*, ed. by Emily-Rose Baker and Diane Otosaka (Manchester: Manchester University Press, forthcoming)

—— *World War II in Andreï Makine's Historiographic Metafiction: No One Is Forgotten, Nothing Is Forgotten* (Amsterdam: Brill, 2018)

EAGLETON, TERRY, 'Capitalism, Modernism and Postmodernism', in *Modern Criticism and Theory: A Reader*, ed. by David Lodge (London: Longman, 1988), pp. 385–98

EAGLESTONE, ROBERT, *The Broken Voice: Reading Post-Holocaust Literature* (Oxford: Oxford University Press, 2017)

—— *The Holocaust and the Postmodern* (Oxford: Oxford University Press, 2004)

—— 'Levinas and the Holocaust', in *The Oxford Handbook of Levinas*, ed. by Michael L. Morgan (Oxford: Oxford University Press, 2019), pp. 37–52

—— 'Postmodernism and Ethics against the Metaphysics of Comprehension', in *The Cambridge Companion to Postmodernism*, ed. by Steven Connor (Cambridge: University of Cambridge Press, 2005), pp. 182–95

—— *Postmodernism and Holocaust Denial* (Cambridge: Icon Books, 2001)

EARL, HILARY, 'Nazi Perpetrators and the Law: Postwar Trials, Courtroom Testimony, and Debates about the Motives of Nazi War Criminals', in *The Routledge International Handbook of Perpetrator Studies*, ed. by Susanne C. Knittel and Zachary J. Goldberg (London: Routledge, 2020), pp. 109–19

EDWARDS, NATHALIE, *Voicing Voluntary Childlessness: Narratives of Non-mothering in French* (Bern: Peter Lang, 2015)

ELLIOTT, ANTHONY, 'The Theory of Liquid Modernity: A Critique of Bauman's Recent Sociology', in *The Contemporary Bauman*, ed. by Anthony Elliott (London: Routledge, 2007), pp. 46–62

ELIAS, AMY J., *Sublime Desire: History and Post-1960s Fiction* (Baltimore, MD: Johns Hopkins University Press, 2001)

ELIAS, RUTH, 'Reproduction and Resistance during the Holocaust', in *Women and the Holocaust*, ed. by Esther Fuchs (Lanham, MD: University Press of America, 1999), pp. 19–32

ELLIS, MARK H., *Beyond Innocence and Redemption: Confronting the Holocaust and Israeli Power. Creating a Moral Future for the Jewish People* (Eugene, OR: Wipf & Stock, 1990)

ENGEL, DAVID, 'Jan Karski's Mission to the West, 1942–1944', *Holocaust and Genocide Studies*, 5.4 (1990), 363–80

ENGELKING, BARBARA, and JAN GRABOWSKI (eds), *Dalej jest noc: losy Żydów w wybranych powiatach okupowanej Polski* [*Night Without End: The Fate of Jews in Selected Counties of Occupied Poland*], 2 vols (Warsaw: Centrum Badań nad Zagładą Żydów, 2018)

EVERINGHAM, CHRISTINE, *Motherhood and Modernity: An Investigation into the Rational Dimension of Mothering* (Buckingham, PA: Open University Press, 1994)

EZRAHI, SIDRA DEKOVEN, 'Acts of Impersonation: Barbaric Spaces as Theatre', in *Mirroring Evil: Nazi Images/ Recent Art*, ed. by Norman L. Kleeblatt (New York: The Jewish Museum, 2001), pp. 17–38

———— *By Words Alone: The Holocaust in Literature* (Chicago: The University of Chicago Press, 1980)
———— 'Representing Auschwitz', *History and Memory*, 7.1 (1996), 121–54
FAKENHEIM, EMIL, *The Jewish Return into History: Reflections in the Age of Auschwitz and a New Jerusalem* (New York: Schokhen Books, 1978)
FANON, FRANZ, *Les Damnés de la terre* (Paris: François Maspero, 1961)
FARÍAS, VICTOR, *Heidegger and Nazism* (Philadelphia: Temple University Press, 1998)
FEIN, HELEN, *Accounting for Genocide: National Responses and Jewish Victimisation during the Holocaust* (New York: Free Press, 1979)
FELMAN, SHOSHANA, 'Camus' *The Plague*, or a Monument to Witnessing', in *Testimony: Crises of Witnessing in Literature, Psychoanalysis and History* (New York: Routledge, 1992), pp. 93–111
———— *The Juridical Unconscious: Trials and Traumas in the Twentieth Century* (Cambridge, MA: Harvard University Press, 2002)
———— 'The Return of the Voice: Claude Lanzmann's *Shoah*', in *Testimony: Crises of Witnessing in Literature, Psychoanalysis and History* (New York: Routledge, 1992), pp. 204–08
FELMAN, SHOSHANA, and DORI LAUB, *Testimony: Crises of Witnessing in Literature, Psychoanalysis and History* (New York: Routledge, 1992)
FELSKI, RITA, *Uses of Literature* (Oxford: Blackwell, 2008)
FELSTINER, MARY LOWENTHAL, *To Paint Her Life: Charlotte Salomon in the Nazi Era* (New York: Harper Perennial, 1994)
FINE, ELLEN S., 'Women and the Holocaust: Strategies for Survival', in *Reflections of the Holocaust in Art and Literature*, ed. by Randolph L. Braham (Boulder, CO: Csengeri Institute for Holocaust Studies, 1990), pp. 79–95
FISHER, JAMES, 'Péter Forgács's *Free Fall* into the Holocaust', in *Visualizing the Holocaust: Documents, Aesthetics, Memory*, ed. by David Bathrick, Brad Prager, and Michael D. Richardson (Rochester, NY: Camden House, 2008), pp. 239–60
FLASCHKA, MONIKA J., '"Only Pretty Women Were Raped": The Effects of Sexual Violence on Gender Identities in the Concentration Camps', in *Sexual Violence against Jewish Women during the Holocaust*, ed. by Sonja Maria Hedgepeth and Rochelle G. Saidel (Lebanon, NH: Brandeis University Press, 2010), pp. 77–93
———— 'Sexual Violence: Recovering a Suppressed History', in *A Companion to the Holocaust*, ed. by Simone Gigliotti and Hilary Earl (Hoboken, NJ: John Wiley, 2020), pp. 469–86
FOENKINOS, DAVID, *Charlotte* (Paris: Gallimard, 2014)
FOLEY, BARBARA, 'Fact. Fiction, Fascism: Testimony and Mimesis in Holocaust Narratives', *Comparative Literature*, 34.4 (1982), 330–60
FONTENAY DE, ÉLISABETH, *Le Silence des bêtes: la philosophie à l'épreuve de l'humanité* (Paris: Fayard, 1998)
———— *Sans offenser le genre humain: réflexion sur la cause animale* (Paris: Albin Michel, 2008)
———— *Without Offending Humans: A Critique of Animal Rights*, trans. by William Bishop (Minneapolis: University of Minnesota Press, 2012)
FORTI, SIMONA, *New Demons: Rethinking Power and Evil Today*, trans. by Zakiya Hanafi (Stanford, CA: Stanford University Press, 2015)
FOSTER, HAL, '(Post)Modern Polemics', *New German Critique*, 33 (Autumn 1984), 67–78
FOUCAULT, MICHEL, *Herculine Barbin*, trans. by Richard McDougall (London: Vintage, 2010)
———— 'Nietzsche, Genealogy, History', in *Language, Countermemory, Practice: Selected Essays and Interviews*, ed. by Donald F. Bouchard (Ithaca, NY: Cornell University Press, 1977), pp. 139–64
———— 'Omnes et singulatim: vers une critique de la raison politique', *Le Débat*, 4.41 (1986), 5–36

—— *Surveiller et punir: naissance de la prison* (Paris: Gallimard, 1975)
FREUD, SIGMUND, 'Beyond the Pleasure Principle', in *The Standard Edition of the Psychological Works of Sigmund Freud*, trans. by and ed. by James Strachey and others, 24 vols (London: Hogarth Press, 1953–74), XVIII, 1–60
—— 'From the History of Infantile Neurosis', in *The Standard Edition of the Complete Psychological Works of Sigmund Freud*, trans. by and ed. by James Strachey and others, 24 vols (London: Hogarth Press, 1954), XVII, 7–122
FRIED, GREGORY, '*Inhalt Unzulässig*: Late Mail from Łódź — A Meditation on Time and Truth', in *Postmodernism and the Holocaust*, ed. Alan Milchman and Alan Rosenberg (Amsterdam: Rodopi, 1998), pp. 23–52
FRIEDLÄNDER, SAUL, 'Introduction', in *Probing the Limits of Representation: Nazism and the 'Final Solution'*, ed. by Saul Friedländer (Cambridge, MA: Harvard University Press), pp. 1–21
—— *Nazi Germany and the Jews: The Years of Persecution, 1939–1939* (London: Weidenfeld & Nicolson, 1997)
FROST, LAURA, '"Every Woman Adores a Fascist": Marguerite Duras, Sylvia Plath, and Feminist Visions of Fascism', in *Sex Drives: Fantasies of Fascism in Literary Modernism* (Ithaca, NY: Cornell University Press, 2001), pp. 120–50
—— *Sex Drives: Fantasies of Fascism in Literary Modernism* (New York: Cornell University Press, 2002)
FRØLAND, CARL MÜLLER, *Understanding Nazi Ideology: The Genesis and Impact of Political Faith*, trans. by John Irons (Jefferson, NC: McFarland, 2020)
FUDGE, ERICA, *Animal* (London: Reaktion Books, 2002)
FULBROOK, MARY, 'The Making and Un-making of Perpetrators: Patterns of Involvement in Nazi Persecution', in *The Routledge Handbook of Perpetrator Studies*, ed. by Susanne C. Knittel and Zachary J. Goldberg (New York: Routledge, 2019), pp. 25–36
GEFFROY, LUCIE, 'Philippe Claudel: la guerre pour obsession', *L'Orient Littéraire*, 166 (April 2020) <http://www.lorientlitteraire.com/article_details.php?cid=33&nid=5808>
GELBIN, CATHY S., 'Between Persecution and Complicity: The Life Story of a Former "Jewish *Mischling*"', *Holocaust Studies*, 11.2 (2005), 74–93
GELLINGS, PAUL, *Poèsie et mythes dans l'œuvre de Patrick Modiano: le fardeau du nomade* (Paris: Minard, 2000)
GENZ, STÉPHANIE, and BENJAMIN A. BRABON, *Postfeminism: Cultural Texts and Theories* (Edinburgh: Edinburgh University Press, 2009)
GERHARDI, GERHARD, 'Topographie et histoire: Paris et l'Occupation dans l'œuvre de Patrick Modiano', in *Paris sous l'Occupation: Paris unter deutscher Besatzung*, ed. by Wolfgang Drost and others (Heidelberg: Universitätsverlag Carl Winter, 1995), pp. 114–21
GIBBS, ALAN, *Contemporary American Trauma Narratives* (Edinburgh: Edinburgh University Press, 2014)
GIESEN, BERNHARD, 'The Trauma of Perpetrators: The Holocaust as the Traumatic Reference of German National Identity', in *Cultural Trauma and Collective Identity*, ed. by Jeffrey C. Alexander and others (Berkley: University of California Press, 2004), pp. 112–54
GIGLIOTTI, SIMONE, *The Train Journey: Transit, Captivity and Witnessing in the Holocaust* (New York: Berghahn Books, 2009)
GILMORE, LEIGH, *The Limits of Autobiography: Trauma and Testimony* (Ithaca, NY: Cornell University Press, 2001)
GIORDANO, ALBERTO, ANNE KELLY KNOWLES, and TIM COLE, 'Geographies of the Holocaust', in *Geographies of the Holocaust*, ed. by Anne Kelly Knowles, Tim Coles, and Alberto Giordano (Bloomington: Indiana University Press, 2014), pp. 1–17

Głowacka, Dorota, 'The Shattered World: Writing of the Fragment and Holocaust Testimony', in *The Holocaust's Ghost: Writings on Art, Politics, Law and Education*, ed. by F. C. DeCoste and Bernard Schwartz (Edmonton: University of Alberta Press, 2000), pp. 37–54

Gold, Mark, *Animal Rights: Extending the Circle of Compassion* (Oxford: Jon Carpenter, 1995)

Goldberg, Zachary J., 'What's Moral Character Got to Do with It? Perpetrators and the Nature of Moral Evil', in *The Routledge International Handbook of Perpetrator Studies*, ed. by Susanne C. Knittel and Zachary J. Goldberg (London: Routledge, 2020), pp. 74–83

Goldenberg, Jenni, 'The Impact on the Interviewer of Holocaust Survivor Narratives: Vicarious Traumatisation or Transformation?', *Traumatology*, 8.4 (2002), 215–31

Goldenberg, Myrna, 'Different Horrors, Same Hell: Women Remembering the Holocaust', in *Thinking the Unthinkable: Meanings of the Holocaust*, ed. by Roger S. Gotlieb (Mahwah, NJ: Paulist Press, 1990), pp. 150–66

—— 'Memoirs of Auschwitz Survivors: The Burden of Gender', in *Women in the Holocaust*, ed. by Dalia Ofer and Lenore J. Weitzman (New Haven, CT: Yale University Press, 1998), pp. 327–39

Golsan, Richard J., 'L'"Affaire Jan Karski"': réflexions sur un scandale littéraire et historique', in *Mémoires occupées: Fictions françaises et Seconde Guerre mondiale*, ed. by Marc Dambre (Paris: Presses Sorbonne Nouvelle, 2013), pp. 183–90

—— 'The American Reception of Max Aue', *SubStance*, 39.1 (2010), 174–83

—— '*Les Bienveillantes* et sa réception critique : littérature, morale, histoire', *L'Exception et la France contemporaine: histoire, imaginaire et littérature*, ed. by Marc Dambre and Richard J. Golsan (Paris: Presses Sorbonne Nouvelle, 2010), pp. 45–56

—— 'History and the "Duty of Memory" in Postwar France: The Pitfalls of Remembrance', in *What Happens to History: The Renewal of Ethics in Contemporary Thought*, ed. by Howard Marchitello (New York: Routledge, 2001), pp. 23–40

—— 'Modiano historien', *Studies in 20th and 21st Century Literature*, 31.2 (2007), 415–33

—— 'The Poetics and Perils of Faction: Contemporary French Fiction and the Memory of World War II', *Romanic Review*, 105 (2014), 53–68

—— *Vichy's Afterlife: History and Counterhistory in Postwar France* (Lincoln: University of Nebraska Press, 2000)

Gontard, Marc, *Écrire la crise: l'esthétique postmoderne* (Rennes: Presses universitaires de Rennes, 2013)

Gourevitch, Philip, 'Among the Dead', in *Disturbing Remains: Memory, History, and Crisis in the Twentieth Century*, ed. by Michael S. Roth and Charles G. Salas (Los Angeles: Getty Research Institute, 2001), pp. 63–76

Grabes, Herbert, 'Ethics, Aesthetics, and Alterity', in *Ethics and Aesthetics: The Moral Turn of Postmodernism*, ed. by Gerhard Hoffman and Alfred Hornung (Heidelberg: Universitätsverlag Carl Winter, 1996), pp. 13–28

Gratton, Johnnie, 'Postmemory, Prememory, Paramemory: The Writing of Patrick Modiano', *French Studies*, 59.1 (2005), 39–45

—— 'Postmodern Fiction: Practice and Theory', in *The Cambridge Companion to the French Novel: From 1800 to the Present*, ed. by Timothy Unwin (Cambridge: Cambridge University Press, 1997), pp. 241–60

Green, Mary Jean, 'People Who Leave No Trace: *Dora Bruder* and the French Immigrant Community', *Studies in 20th and 21st Century Literature*, 31.2 (2007), 434–49

Greenhouse, Emily, 'Interview: Philippe Claudel', trans. by Emily Greenhouse, *Granta*, 111 (30 June 2010) <https://granta.com/interview-philippe-claudel/>

Greenspan, Henry, *On Listening to Holocaust Survivors: Recounting Life and History* (New York: Praeger, 1998)

GRENAUDIER-KLIJN, FRANCE, 'Landscapes Do Not Lie: War, Abjection and Memory in Philippe Claudel's *Le Rapport de Brodeck*', *Essays in French Literature and Culture*, 47 (November 2010), 87–107
—— 'Street Names in Patrick Modiano's Work: *La Place de l'étoile* and the case of rue Lauriston', *Neohelicon*, 44 (2017), 217–27
GRIERSON, KARLA, *Discours d'Auschwitz: littérature, représentation, symbolisation* (Paris: Honoré Champion, 2003)
GROSS, JAN T., *Sąsiedzi: Historia zagłady żydowskiego miasteczka* (Sejny: Pogranicze, 2000)
—— *Neighbours: The Destruction of the Jewish Community in Jedwabne, Poland* (Princeton, NJ: Princeton University Press, 2001)
GROSSBERG, LAWRENCE, *Bringing It All Back Home: Essays on Cultural Studies* (Durham, NC: Duke University Press, 1997)
GUBAR, SUSAN, *Poetry after Auschwitz: Remembering What One Never Knew* (Bloomington: Indiana University Press, 2003)
GUICHARNAUD, JACQUES, 'De la Rive gauche à l'au-delà de la Concorde: remarques sur la topographie parisienne de Patrick Modiano', in *Dilemmes du roman: Essays in Honour of Georges May*, ed. by Catherine Lafarge (Saratoga, CA: Anma Libri, 1990), pp. 341–52
GUREVITZ, DAVID. 'Literature as Trauma: The Postmodern Option — Franz Kafka and Cormac McCarthy', in *Interdisciplinary Handbook of Trauma and Culture*, ed. by Yochai Ataria and others (New York: Springer, 2016), pp. 3–26
HAAKEN, JANICE, *Pillar of Salt: Gender, Memory, and the Perils of Looking Back* (New Brunswick, NJ: Rutgers University Press, 1998)
HABERMAS, JÜRGEN, 'Modernity Versus Postmodernity', *New German Critique*, 22 (Winter 1981), 3–14
HALIMI, ANDRÉ, *La Délation sous l'Occupation* (Paris: Alain Moreau, 1983)
HANCOCK, IAN, 'Romanies and the Holocaust: Re-evaluation and Overview', in *The Historiography of the Holocaust*, ed. by Dan Stone (Basingstoke: Palgrave Macmillan, 2004), pp. 383–96
HARAWAY, DONNA, 'The Cyborg Manifesto and Fractured Identities', in *Reading Feminist Theory: Modernity to Postmodernity*, ed. by Susan Archer Mann and Ashly Suzanne Patterson (Oxford: Oxford University Press, 2015), pp. 212–17
HARDMAN, ANNA, *Women and the Holocaust* (London: Holocaust Education Trust, 2000)
HARRIES, MARTIN, *Forgetting Lot's Wife: On Destructive Spectatorship* (New York: Fordham University Press, 2007)
HARTMAN, GEOFFREY, 'Public Memory and its Discontents', *Raritan: A Quarterly Review*, 13.4 (Spring 1994), 24–40
—— 'Tele-Suffering and Testimony in the Dot Com Era', in *Visual Culture and the Holocaust*, ed. by Barbie Zelizer (London: Athlone Press, 2001), pp. 111–26
HARZEWSKI, STEPHANIE, *Chick Lit and Postfeminism* (Charlottesville: University of Virginia Press, 2011)
HASKINS, CASEY, 'Art, Morality, and the Holocaust: The Aesthetic Riddle of Benigni's *Life Is Beautiful*', *Journal of Aesthetics and Art Criticism*, 59.4 (Autumn, 2001), 373–84
HATT, CHERYL, 'Teaching the Holocaust through Geography', *Teaching Geography*, 36.3 (2011), 108–10
HEDGEPETH, SONJA MARIA, and ROCHELLE G. SAIDEL (eds), *Sexual Violence against Jewish Women during the Holocaust* (Lebanon, NH: Brandeis University Press, 2010)
HEINEMANN, MARLENE E., *Gender and Destiny: Women Writers and the Holocaust* (New York: Greenwood Press, 1986)
HENKE, SUZETTE A., *Shattered Subjects: Trauma and Testimony in Women's Life-writing* (Basingstoke: Palgrave Macmillan, 1998)

HENNIGFELD, URSULA, 'Le Mirroir brisé: Reassessing the Occupation (1940–44) in Novels by Modiano, Assouline and Rozier', *Anuari de Filologia: Literatures Contemporànies*, 8 (2018), 137–58
HERMANSSON, CASIE, *Reading Feminist Intertextuality through Bluebeard Stories* (New York: Edwin Mellen, 2001)
HERTZOG, ESTHER, 'Subjugated Motherhood and the Holocaust', *Dapim: Studies on the Holocaust*, 30.1 (2016), 16–34
HEWITT, LEAH D., 'Vichy's Female Icons: Chabrol's *Story of Women*', in *Gender and Fascism in Modern France*, ed. by Melanie Hawthorne and Richard J. Golsan (Hanover, NH: University of New England Press, 1997), pp. 156–74
HIGGINS, LYNN, 'Lieux de mémoire et géographie imaginaire dans *Dora Bruder*', in *Le Roman français au tournant du XXIe siècle*, ed. by Marc Dambre, Aline Mura-Brunel, and Bruno Blanckeman (Paris: Presses Sorbonne Nouvelle, 2004), pp. 394–405
—— 'Unfinished Business: Reflections on the Occupation and May '68', *L'Esprit Créateur*, 33.1 (Spring 1993), 105–10
HILBERG, RAUL, *The Destruction of European Jews* (Chicago: Quadrangle Books, 1961)
—— 'I Was Not There', in *Writing and the Holocaust*, ed. by Berel Lang (New York: Holmes & Meier, 1988), pp. 17–25
—— *Perpetrators, Victims, Bystanders: The Jewish Catastrophe 1933–1945* (New York: HarperCollins, 1992)
—— *The Politics of Memory: The Path of a Holocaust Historian* (Chicago: Ivan R. Dee, 1996)
HILLMAN, SUZANNE, ' "Not Living, but Going": Unheroic Survival, Trauma, Performance, and Video Testimony', *Holocaust Studies*, 21.4 (2015), 215–35
HILSUM, MIREILLE, 'L'Arrestation: poétique des transport chez Modiano', in *Lectures de Modiano*, ed. by Roger-Yves Roche (Nantes: Cécile Defaut, 2009), pp. 137–48
HIMMELFARB, GERTRUDE, *On Looking into the Abyss: Untimely Thoughts on Culture and Society* (New York: Alfred A. Knopf, 1994)
—— 'Telling It as You Like It: Post-modernist History and the Flight from Fact', in *The Postmodern History Reader*, ed. by Keith Jenkins (London: Routledge, 1997), pp. 157–74
HIRSCH, DAVID H., *The Deconstruction of Literature: Criticism after Auschwitz* (Hanover, NH: University Press of New England, 1991)
HIRSCH, MARIANNE, 'The Generation of Postmemory', *Poetics Today*, 29.1 (Spring 2008), 103–28
—— *The Generation of Postmemory: Writing and Visual Culture after the Holocaust* (New York: Columbia University Press, 2012)
HLADKI, PAWEL, ' "Qui témoigne pour le témoin?" Question de la liberté littéraire à l'exemple de *Jan Karski* de Yannick Haenel', *Études romanes de Brno*, 33 (2012), 57–67
HOESS, RUDOLPH, *Commandant of Auschwitz: The Autobiography of Rudolph Hoess*, trans. by Constantine Fitzgibbon (London: Weidenfeld & Nicolson, 1959)
HOGAN, REBECCA, 'Engendered Autobiographies: The Diary as a Feminine Form', *Prose Studies*, 14.2 (1991), 95–107
HOGUE, SÉBASTIEN, 'Oublier ou se souvenir? Culpabilité et mémoire dans *Le Rapport de Brodeck* de Philippe Claudel' (unpublished Masters dissertation, Université de Laval, 2015)
HOLM, HELGE VIDAR, 'Chronotopes in Patrick Modiano's Fictional Writing of History', *Bergen Language and Linguistics Studies*, 7 (2017), 103–12
HOROWITZ, NANCY, *Primo Levi and the Identity of a Survivor* (Toronto: University of Toronto Press, 2016)
HOROWITZ, SARA R., 'The Gender of Good and Evil: Women and Holocaust Memory', in *Gray Zones: Ambiguities and Compromise in the Holocaust and Its Aftermath*, ed. by Jonathan Petropoulos and John K. Roth (New York: Berghahn Books, 2005), pp. 165–78

—— 'Memory and Testimony of Women Survivors of Nazi Genocide', in *Women of the Word: Jewish Women, Jewish Writing*, ed. by Judith R. Baskin (Detroit: Wayne State University Press, 1994), pp. 258–82

—— 'Women in Holocaust Literature: Engendering Trauma Memory', in *Women in the Holocaust*, ed. by Dalia Ofer and Lenore J. Weitzman (New Haven, CT: Yale University Press, 1998), pp. 364–78

HOWE, IRVING, 'Writing and the Holocaust', in *A Voice Still Heard: Selected Essays of Irving Howe*, ed. by Nina Howe with Nicolas Howe Bukowski (New Haven, CT: Yale University Press, 2014), pp. 277–98

HOWELL, PHILIP, 'Animals, Agency and History', in *The Routledge Companion to Animal-Human History*, ed. by Hilda Kean and Philip Howell (London: Routledge, 2019), pp. 197–221

HUGGAN, GRAHAM, '"Greening" Postcolonialism: Ecocritical Perspectives', *Modern Fiction Studies*, 50.3 (Autumn, 2004), 701–33

HUNTER, ANNA CLARE, 'Tales from Over There: The Uses and Meanings of Fairy-tales in Contemporary Holocaust Narrative', *Modernism*, 20.1 (2013), 59–75

—— '"To Tell the Story": Cultural Trauma and Holocaust Metanarrative', *Holocaust Studies*, 25.1–2 (2019), 12–27

HUSSON, ÉDOUARD, 'La Vraie Histoire des *Bienveillantes*', *L'Histoire*, 320 (May 2007), 6–19

HUSSON, ÉDOUARD, and MICHEL TERESTCHENKO, *Les Complaisantes: Jonathan Littell et l'écriture du mal* (Paris: De Guibert, 2007)

HUTCHEON, LINDA, *A Poetics of Postmodernism: History, Theory, Fiction* (New York: Routledge, 1988)

—— *The Politics of Postmodernism* (London: Routledge, 1989)

—— *A Theory of Parody: The Teachings of Twentieth-Century Art Forms* (London: Routledge, 1985)

HUTTON, MARGARET-ANNE, *Testimony from Nazi Camps: French Women's Voices* (London: Routledge, 2005)

HUYSSEN, ANDREAS, 'Mapping the Postmodern', *New German Critique*, 33 (Autumn 1984), 5–52

—— *Present Pasts: Urban Palimpsests and the Politics of Memory* (Stanford, CA: Stanford University Press, 2003)

HYMAN, PAULA E., 'New Debate on the Holocaust', *The New York Times Magazine*, 14 September 1980 <https://www.nytimes.com/1980/09/14/archives/new-debate-on-the-holocaust-has-the-popularization-of-this-tragedy.html>

IMORT, MICHAEL, 'Wilhelmine Forestry and the Forest as a Symbol of Germandom', in *Germany's Nature: Cultural Landscapes and Environmental History*, ed. by Thomas Lekan and Thomas Zeller (New Brunswick, NJ: Rutgers University Press, 2005), pp. 55–80

IRIGARAY, LUCE, 'The Power of Discourse and the Subordination of the Feminine', in *The Irigaray Reader*, ed. by Margaret Whitford (Oxford: Blackwell, 1991), pp. 118–32

JACOB, JANET, *Memorialising the Holocaust: Gender, Genocide and Collective Memory* (London: I. B. Tauris, 2010)

JAMESON, FREDRIC, 'Postmodernism and Consumer Society', in *Postmodern Culture*, ed. by Hal Foster (London: Pluto, 1985), pp. 111–25

—— *Postmodernism, or the Cultural Logic of Late Capitalism* (Durham, NC: Duke University Press, 1991)

JARDIN, ALEXANDRE, 'The Cry of my Conscience about my Family's Collaboration', *Guardian*, 12 January 2011 <https://www.theguardian.com/commentisfree/2011/jan/12/french-crime-collaboration-nazi>

JEFFERSON, ANN, *Biography and the Question of Literature in France* (Oxford: Oxford University Press, 2007)

JENSEN, MEG, 'Testimony', in *The Routledge Companion to Literature and Trauma*, ed. by Colin Davis and Hanna Meretoja (New York: Routledge, 2020), pp. 66–78
JOLY, LAURENT, *Dénoncer les juifs sous l'Occupation* (Paris: CNRS, 2017)
—— 'Introduction', in *La Délation dans la France des années noires*, ed. by Laurent Joly (Paris: Perrin, 2012), pp. 17–69
JOLY, LAURENT (ed.), *La Délation dans la France des années noires* (Paris: Perrin, 2012)
JOLY, STÉPHANIE, 'Entretien avec Laurent Binet pour son ouvrage *HHhH*', *Le Site de Paris-ci la culture* <http://www.pariscilaculture.fr/2011/07/entretien-avec-laurent-binet/>
JUNE, PAMELA B., *The Fragmented Female Body: The Postmodern, Feminist and Multiethnic Writings of Toni Morison, Theresa Hak Kyung Cha, Phyllis Alexia Perry, Gayl Jones, Emma Pérez, Paula Gunn Allen, and Kathy Acker* (New York: Peter Lang, 2010)
JURT, JOSEPH, 'La Mémoire de la Shoah: *Dora Bruder*', in *Patrick Modiano*, ed. by John E. Flower (Amsterdam: Brill, 2007), pp. 89–108
KAKUTANI, MICHIKO, 'When History and Memory Are Casualties', *The New York Times*, 30 April 1993 <https://www.nytimes.com/1993/04/30/arts/critic-s-notebook-when-history-is-a-casualty.html>
KALECHOFSKY, ROBERTA, *Animal Suffering and the Holocaust: The Problem with Comparisons* (Marblehead, MA: Micah Publications, 2003)
KAPLAN, BRETT ASHLEY, *Landscapes of Holocaust Postmemory* (New York: Routledge, 2011)
—— *Unwanted Beauty: Aesthetic Pleasure in Holocaust Representation* (Urbana: University of Illinois Press, 2007)
KARSKI, JAN, *The Great Powers and Poland, 1919–1945: From Versailles to Yalta* (Washington, DC: University Press of America, 1985)
—— 'Jan Karski', in *The Liberation of the Nazi Concentration Camps 1945: Eyewitness Accounts of the Liberators*, ed. by Brewster S. Chamberlin and Marcia Feldman (Washington, DC: United States Holocaust Memorial Council, 1987), pp. 176–78
—— 'Notatka z rozmowy w Prezydentem F. D. Roosevelt'em' [Minutes of the Conversation with President F. D. Roosevelt], 28 July 1943, HIA-Karski, Box 1, File 7 <http://karski.muzhp.pl/misja_raporty_karskiego_rozmowa.html>
KASS, LEON R., 'The Wisdom of Repugnance', in *The Ethics of Human Cloning*, ed. by Leon R. Kass and James Q. Wilson (Washington, DC: AEI Press, 1998), pp. 3–60
KATZ, ERIC, *Anne Frank's Tree* (Cambridge: White Horse, 2015)
—— 'Nature's Healing Power, the Holocaust, and the Environment', *Judaism*, 46.1 (Winter 1997), 79–89
KAWAKAMI, AKANE, *A Self-conscious Art: Patrick Modiano's Postmodern Fictions* (Liverpool: Liverpool University Press, 2000)
—— *Patrick Modiano* (Oxford: Oxford University Press, 2016)
KEAN, HILDA, and PHILIP HOWELL, 'Writing in Animals in History', in *The Routledge Companion to Animal-human History*, ed. by Hilda Kean and Philip Howell (London: Routledge, 2019), pp. 3–28
KELLNER, HANS, '"Never Again" Is Now', *History and Theory*, 33.2 (May 1994), 127–44
KERMAN, JUDITH B., and John Edgar Borning (eds), *The Fantastic in Holocaust Literature and Film: Critical Perspectives* (Jefferson, NC: McFarland, 2015)
KERR, JUDITH, *When Hitler Stole Pink Rabbit* (London: HarperCollins, 2008)
KERSHEN, ANNE J., *Uniting the Tailors: Trade Unionism among the Tailors of London and Leeds, 1870–1939* (London: Routledge, 1995)
KERTZER, ADRIENNE, '"Don't You Know Anything?": Childhood and the Holocaust', in *The Bloomsbury Companion to Holocaust Literature*, ed. by Jenni Adams (London: Bloomsbury, 2014), pp. 121–38
KIELAR, WIESŁAW, *Anus Mundi: Five Years in Auschwitz*, trans. by Susanne Flatauer (London: Penguin, 1982)

KLEIN, WAYNE, 'Truth's Turning: History and the Holocaust', in *Postmodernism and the Holocaust*, ed. by Alan Milchman and Alan Rosenberg (Amsterdam: Rodopi, 1998), pp. 53–84

KNECHT, EDGAR, 'Le Juif errant: éléments d'un mythe populaire', *Romantisme*, 9 (1975), 84–96

KNITTEL, SUZANNE, *The Historical Uncanny: Disability, Ethnicity, and the Politics of Holocaust Memory* (New York: Fordham University Press, 2014)

KNITTEL, SUSANNE C., and ZACHARY J. GOLDBERG (eds), *The Routledge International Handbook of Perpetrator Studies* (London: Routledge, 2020)

KOLÁŘ, STANISLAV, *Seven Responses to the Holocaust in American Fiction* (Ostrava: Universum, 2004)

KOONZ, CLAUDIA, *Mothers in the Fatherland: Women, the Family and Nazi Politics* [1987] (New York: Routledge, 2013)

KOSTRO, ROBERT, 'Tradycja i otwartość' [Tradition and Opennenss], *Tygodnik Powrzechny*, 17, (21 April 2014) <https://www.tygodnikpowszechny.pl/tradycja-i-otwartosc-22632>

KOSTYRKO, WERONIKA, *Tancerka i Zagłada. Historia Poli Nireńskiej* [A Dancer and the Holocaust: A History of Pola Nireńska] (Warsaw: Czerwone i Czarne, 2019)

KOTTE, CHRISTINA, *Ethical Dimensions in British Historiographic Metafiction: Julian Barnes, Graham Swift, Penelope Lively* (Freiburg: Wissenschaftlicher Verlag Trier, 2001)

KRALL, HANNA, *The Woman from Hamburg and Other True Stories*, trans. by Madeline G. Levine (New York: Other Press, 2005)

KRAVITZ, ASHER, *The Jewish Dog*, trans. by Michal Kessler (New York: Penlight Publications, 2015)

KREMER, S. LILLIAN, 'Sexual Abuse in Holocaust Literature: Memoir and Fiction', in *Sexual Violence against Jewish Women during the Holocaust*, ed. by Sonja Maria Hedgepeth and Rochelle G. Saidel (Lebanon, NH: Brandeis University Press, 2010), pp. 177–99

—— *Women's Holocaust Writing: Memory and Imagination* (Lincoln: University of Nebraska Press, 1999)

KRISTEVA, JULIA, 'De l'abjection à la banalité du mal: conférence avec Jonathan Littell, Centre Roland Barthes, 24.04.2007' <http://www.kristeva.fr/abjection.html>

KRYSTAL, HENRY (ed.), *Massive Psychic Trauma* (New York: International University Press, 1968)

KUON, PETER, 'From "Kitsch" to "Splatter": The Aesthetics of Violence in *The Kindly Ones*', in *Writing the Holocaust Today: Critical Perspectives on Jonathan Littell's 'The Kindly Ones'*, ed. by Aurélie Barjonet and Liran Razinsky (Amsterdam: Rodopi, 2012), pp. 33–45

KUPFER-KOBERWITZ, EDGAR, *Die Tierbrüder: eine Betrachtung zum Ethischen Leben* (Hamburg: Höcker Verlag, 2010)

—— *Animal Brothers: Reflections on an Ethical Way of Life*, trans. by Ruth Mossner, in *Compassionate Spirit* <https://compassionatespirit.com/wpblog/books/animal-brothers/>

KURTZ, J. ROGER, 'Introduction', in *Trauma and Literature*, ed. by J. Roger Kurtz (Cambridge: Cambridge University Press, 2018), pp. 1–17

KUSHNER, TONY, 'Britain, the United States and the Holocaust', in *The Historiography of the Holocaust*, ed. by Dan Stone (Basingstoke: Palgrave Macmillan, 2004), pp. 253–75

—— 'Holocaust Testimony, Ethics, and the Problem of Representation', *Poetics Today*, 27 (Summer 2006), 275–96

LACAPRA, DOMINICK, 'Historical and Literary Approaches to the "Final Solution": Saul Friedländer and Jonathan Littell', in *History, Literature, Critical Theory* (Ithaca, NY: Cornell University Press, 2013), pp. 95–119

—— *History and its Limits: Human, Animal, Violence* (Ithaca, NY: Cornell University Press, 2009)

—— *History and Memory after Auschwitz* (Ithaca, NY: Cornell University Press, 1998)
—— *History in Transit: Experience, Identity, and Critical Theory* (Ithaca, NY: Cornell University Press, 2004)
—— 'Representing the Holocaust: Reflections on the Historians' Debate', in *Probing the Limits of Representation: Nazism and the 'Final Solution'*, ed. by Saul Friedländer (Cambridge, MA: Harvard University Press, 1992), pp.108–27
—— *Understanding Others: Peoples, Animals, Pasts* (Ithaca, NY: Cornell University Press, 2018)
—— *Writing History, Writing Trauma* (Baltimore, MD, & London: Johns Hopkins University Press, 2001)
LACOSTE, CHARLOTTE, 'L'Ère du bourreau', *Esprit*, 347.8–9 (August-September 2008), 254–57
—— 'La Fascination du mal: une nouvelle mode littéraire', *Cité*, 45 (2011), 168–74
—— *Séductions du bourreau* (Paris: Presses universitaires de France, 2010)
LAGROU, PIETER, 'Victims of Genocide and National Memory: Belgium, France and the Netherlands, 1945–1965', *Past and Present*, 154 (1997), 187–90
LANDWEHR, MARGARETE J. 'The Fairy Tale as Allegory for the Holocaust: Representing the Unrepresentable in Yolen's *Briar Rose* and Murphy's *Hansel and Gretel*', in *Fairy Tales Reimagined: Essays on New Retellings*, ed. by Susan Reddington Bobby (Jefferson, NC: McFarland, 2009), pp. 153–67
LANG, BEREL, *Holocaust Representation: Art within the Limits of History and Ethics* (Baltimore, MD: Johns Hopkins University Press, 2000)
—— *Primo Levi: The Matter of a Life* (New Haven, CT: Yale University Press, 2013)
—— 'The Representation of Limits', in *Probing the Limits of Representation: Nazism and the 'Final Solution'*, ed. by Saul Friedländer (Cambridge, MA: Harvard University Press, 1992), pp. 300–17
LANG, JOCHEN VON, *The Secretary: Martin Bromann, the Man Who Manipulated Hitler*, trans. by Christa Armstrong and Peter White (New York: Random House, 1979)
LANGER, LAWRENCE, 'The Dilemma of Choice in the Deathcamps', *Centerpoint*, 4 (Autumn 1980), 222–31
—— 'Gendered Suffering? Women in Holocaust Testimonies', in *Women in the Holocaust*, ed. by Dalia Ofer and Lenore J. Weitzman (New Haven, CT: Yale University Press, 1998), pp. 351–63
—— *Holocaust Testimonies: The Ruins of Memory* (New Haven, CT: Yale University Press, 1991)
—— *Versions of Survival: The Holocaust and the Human Spirit* (New York: State University of New York Press, 1982)
LANZMANN, CLAUDE, '*Les Bienveillantes*, vénéneuse fleur du Mal', *Le Journal du Dimanche*, 3114, 17 September 2006, p. 14
—— 'Jan Karski de Yannick Haenel: un faux roman', *Les Temps modernes*, 657 (January-March 2010) <https://www.cairn.info/revue-les-temps-modernes-2010-1-page-1.htm>
—— 'Le Lieu et la parole', in *Au sujet de 'Shoah'*, ed. by Michel Deguy (Paris: Belin, 1990), pp. 407–25
—— *Le Lièvre de Patagonie* (Paris: Gallimard, 2009)
—— 'Les Non-lieux de la mémoire', in *Au sujet de 'Shoah'*, ed. by Michel Deguy (Paris: Belin, 1990), pp. 385–406
—— *Shoah*, original typescript, United States Holocaust Memorial Museum <https://collections.ushmm.org/film_findingaids/RG-60.5006_01_trs_en.pdf>
—— 'Une documentation impeccable mais... Lanzmann juge *Les Bienveillantes*', *Le Nouvel Observateur*, 2185, 21–26 September 2006, p. 14
LARCENET, MANU, *Le Rapport de Brodeck*, 2 vols (Paris: Dargaud, 2015–16)

LASKA, VERA (ed.), *Women in the Resistance and in the Holocaust: Voices of Eyewitnesses* (Westport, CT: Greenwood, 1983)
LASKER-WALLFISH, ANITA, *Inherit the Truth* (New York: Thomas Dunn, 2000)
LAUB, DORI, 'An Event Without a Witness: Truth, Testimony and Survival', in Shoshana Felman and Dori Laub, *Testimony: Crises of Witnessing in Literature, Psychoanalysis and History* (New York: Routledge, 1992), pp. 75–92
—— 'Bearing Witness or the Vicissitudes of Listening', in Shoshana Felman and Dori Laub, *Testimony: Crises of Witnessing in Literature, Psychoanalysis and History* (New York: Routledge, 1992), pp. 57–74
LAWSON, TOM, *Debates on the Holocaust* (Manchester: Manchester University Press, 2010)
LEAKE, ERIC, 'Humanizing the Inhuman: The Value of Difficult Empathy', in *Rethinking Empathy through Literature*, ed. by Meghan Marie Hammond and Sue J. Kim (New York: Routledge, 2014), pp. 175–85
LEDOUX-BEAUGRAND, EVELYNE, 'Emprunt et bricolage: traces mémorielles de la Shoah dans *Drancy Avenir* et *Jan Karski*', *French Forum*, 39 (Winter 2014), 143–57
—— 'Les Restes d'Auschwitz: intertextualité et postmémoire dans *Jan Karski* de Yannick Haenel et *C'est maintenant du passé* de Marianne Rubinstein', *Études françaises*, 49 (2013), 145–62
LEE, SANDER H., 'Primo Levi's *Grey Zone*: Implications for Post-Holocaust Ethics', *Holocaust and Genocide Studies*, 30.2 (Autumn 2016), 276–97
LEITNER, ISABELLA, *Fragments of Isabella: A Memoir of Auschwitz* (New York: Thomas Y. Crowell, 1978)
LEMÉNAGER, GRÉGOIRE, 'Génération Littell', *Le Nouvel Observateur*, 5 July 2010 <https://bibliobs.nouvelobs.com/romans/20100705.BIB5425/generation-littell<.html>
LEVENKORN, NAOMI, 'Death and the Maidens: "Prostitution", Rape and Sexual Slavery during World War II', in *Sexual Violence against Jewish Women during the Holocaust*, ed. by Sonja Maria Hedgepeth and Rochelle G. Saidel (Lebanon, NH: Brandeis University Press, 2010), pp. 13–28
LEVI, PRIMO, *The Drowned and the Saved*, trans. by Raymond Rosenthal (London: Michael Joseph, 1988)
—— 'Primo Levi's Heartbreaking, Heroic Answers to the Most Common Questions He Was Asked about *Survival in Auschwitz*', trans. by Ruth Feldman, *The New Republic*, 17 February 1986 <https://newrepublic.com/article/119959/interview-primo-levi-survival-auschwitz>
—— *The Reawakening*, trans. by Stuart Woolf (New York: Simon & Schuster, 1965)
LEVI, PRIMO, and MARCO VIGEVALI, 'Words, Memory, Hope', in *The Voice of Memory: Interviews 1961–1987*, ed. by Marco Belpoliti and Robert Gordon, trans. by Robert Gordon (New York: Polity Press, 2001), pp. 250–57
LEVIN, MICHAEL DAVID, 'Cinders, Traces, Shadows on the Page: The Holocaust in Derrida's Writing', in *Postmodernism and the Holocaust*, ed. by Alan Milchman and Alan Rosenberg (Amsterdam: Rodopi, 1998), pp. 265–86
LEVINAS, EMMANUEL, 'Nom d'un chien ou le droit naturel', in *Difficile liberté: essais sur le judaïsme* (Paris: Albin Michel, 1976), pp. 199–202
—— 'The Name of a Dog, or Natural Rights', in *Difficult Freedom: Essays on Judaism*, trans. by Seán Hand (Baltimore, MD: Johns Hopkins University Press, 1990), pp. 151–53
—— 'La Signification et le sens', *Revue de métaphysique et de morale*, 2 (April-May, 1964), 126–56
—— 'Signification and Sense', in *Humanism of the Other*, trans. by Nidra Poller (Urbana: University of Illinois Press, 2003), pp. 9–44
—— *Totalité et infini: essai sur l'extériorité* (The Hague: Martinus Nijhoff, 1971)

―― 'La Trace de l'autre', *Tijdschrift voor Filosofie*, 3 (September 1963), 605–23
―― 'The Trace of the Other', trans. by A. Lingis, in *Deconstruction in Context: Literature and Philosophy*, ed. by Mark C. Taylor (Chicago: University of Chicago Press, 1986), pp. 345–59
LEVINE, MADELINE G., 'The Ambiguity of Moral Outrage in Jerzy Andrzejewski's "Wielki Tydzień"', *Polish Review*, 32.4 (1987), 385–99
LEVINE, PAUL A.,'On-lookers', in *The Oxford Handbook of Holocaust Studies*, ed. by Peter Hayes and John K. Roth (Oxford: Oxford University Press, 2002), pp. 156–69
LÉVY, CLARA, *Écriture de l'identité: les écrivains juifs après la Shoah* (Paris: Presses universitaires de France, 1998)
LEVY, DANIEL, and NATAN SZNAIDER, *The Holocaust and Memory in the Global Age*, trans. by Assenka Oksiloff (Philadelphia: Temple University Press, 2006)
LEWIS, INGRID, *Women in European Holocaust Films: Perpetrators, Victims and Resisters* (Basingstoke: Palgrave Macmillan, 2017)
LEWY, GUENTER, *Perpetrators: The World of Holocaust Killers* (Oxford: Oxford University Press, 2017)
LEYS, RUTH, *From Guilt to Shame: Auschwitz and After* (Princeton, NJ: Princeton University Press, 2007)
―― *Trauma: A Genealogy* (Chicago: University of Chicago Press, 2000)
LIFTON, ROBERT JAY, *The Nazi Doctors: Medical Killings and the Psychology of Genocide* (New York: Basic Books, 1986)
LIPSTADT, DEBORAH, *Beyond Belief: The American Press and the Coming of the Holocaust 1933–1945* (New York: Free Press, 1986)
―― *Denying the Holocaust: The Growing Assault on Truth and Memory* (New York: Free Press, 1993)
―― 'Invoking the Holocaust', *Judaism*, 30.3 (Summer 1981), 335–43
LITTELL, JONATHAN, *Le Sec et l'humide* (Paris: Gallimard, 2008)
LITTELL, JONATHAN, and SAMUEL BLUMENFELD, 'Il faudra du temps pour expliquer ce succès', *Le Monde*, 17 November 2006 <https://www.lemonde.fr/livres/article/2006/11/16/jonathan-littell-il-faudra-du-temps-pour-expliquer-ce-succes_835008_3260.html>
LITTELL, JONATHAN, and ASSAF UNI, 'The Executioner's Song', *Haaretz*, 29 May 2008 <https://www.haaretz.com/1.4985953>
LODGE, DAVID, *The Modes of Modern Writing: Metaphor, Metonymy, and the Typology of Modern Literature* (London: Edward Arnold, 1977)
LORENZ, HENDRIK, 'The Analysis of the Soul in Plato's *Republic*', in *The Blackwell Guide to Plato's 'Republic'*, ed. by Gerasimos Santas (Oxford: Blackwell, 2006), pp. 146–55
LOUWAGIE, FRANSISKA, *Témoignages et littérature d'après Auschwitz* (Amsterdam: Brill, 2020)
LOWER, WENDY, *Hitler's Furies: German Women in the Nazi Killing Fields* (New York: Vintage, 2014)
LUCKHURST, ROGER, *The Trauma Question* (New York: Routledge, 2008)
LYOTARD, JEAN-FRANÇOIS, 'Appendix: Answering the Question: What Is Postmodernism', in *The Postmodern Condition: A Report on Knowledge*, trans. by Geoff Bennington and Brian Massumi (Manchester: Manchester University Press, 1984), pp. 71–84
―― *Le Différend* (Paris: Minuit, 1983)
―― *The Differend: Phrases in Dispute*, trans. by Georges Van Den Abbeele (Manchester: Manchester University Press, 1988)
―― 'Réponse à la question: qu'est-ce que le postmoderne?', *Critique*, 419 (1982), 357–67
MACDONALD, DAVID B., 'Pushing the Limits of Humanity? Reinterpreting Animal Rights and "Personhood" through the Prism of the Holocaust', *Journal of Human Rights*, 5.4 (2006), 417–37

MACMILLAN, DAN, 'Dehumanization and the Achievement of *Schindler's List*', in *The Holocaust: Memories and History*, ed. by Victoria Khiterer (Newcastle: Cambridge Scholars Publishing, 2014), pp. 311–34

MACNAIR, RACHEL M., 'Perpetration-induced Stress in Combat Veterans', *Peace and Conflict: Journal of Peace Psychology*, 8.1 (2002), 63–72

—— *Perpetration-induced Traumatic Stress: The Psychological Consequences of Killing* (New York: Praeger, 2002)

—— 'Psychological Reverberations for the Killers: Preliminary Historical Evidence for Perpetration-induced Traumatic Stress', *Journal of Genocide Research*, 3.2 (2001), 273–78

MAGNAN, JEAN-MARIE, 'Un apatride nommé Modiano', *Sud*, 19 (1976), 120

MAGUEN, SHIRA, and OTHERS, 'The Impact of Killing in War on Mental Health Symptoms and Related Functioning', *Journal of Traumatic Stress*, 22.5 (2009), 435–43

MALGOUZOU, YANNICK, *Les Camps nazis: réflexions sur la réception littéraire française* (Paris: Classiques Garnier, 2012)

MAGYAR ISAACSON, JUDIT, *Seed of Sarah* (Chicago: University of Illinois Press)

MALKA, RUTH, '"Paris of Days Gone By": The Quest for Memory in the Postwar Haunted City — A Case Study of Georges Perec's and Patrick Modiano's Novels', in *Shadows in the City of Light: Paris in Postwar French Jewish Writing*, ed. by Sara R. Horowitz, Amira Bojadzija-Dan, and Julia Creet (New York: State University of New York Press, 2021), pp. 123–37

MAŁCZYŃSKI, JACEK. 'Jak drzewa świadczą? W stronę nie-ludzkich figuracji świadka' [How Do Trees Testify? Towards an Nonhuman Figuration of the Witness], *Teksty Drugie*, 3 (2018), 373–85

MAŁCZYŃSKI, JACEK, and OTHERS, 'The Environmental History of the Holocaust', *Journal of Genocide Studies*, 22.2 (2020), 183–96

MARIN, LOUIS, *Food for Thought*, trans. by Mette Hjort (Baltimore, MD: Johns Hopkins University Press, 1989)

MARKIEWICZ, HENRYK, 'On the Definitions of Literary Parody', in *To Honour Roman Jakobson: Essays on the Occasion of His 70th Birthday, 11 October 1966*, 3 vols (The Hague: Mouton, 1967), II, 1264–72

MARTÍNEZ-ALFARO, MARÍA JESÚS, 'The Estrangement Effect in Three Holocaust Narratives: Defamiliarising Victims, Perpetrators and the Fairy-tale Genre', *Journal of the Spanish Association of Anglo-American Studies*, 42.1 (June 2020), 37–56

—— 'Rewriting the Fairy Tale in Louis Murthy's and Lisa Goldstein's Holocaust Narratives', *European Journal of English Studies*, 20.1 (2016), 64–82

MARY-RABINE, LUC, 'Les Lieux de Modiano', in *Cahiers de l'Herne: Patrick Modiano*, ed. by Maryline Heck and Raphaëlle Guidée (Paris: L'Herne, 2012), pp. 101–04

MATHÉ, SYLVIE, 'The "Grey Zone" in William Styron's *Sophie's Choice*', *Études anglaises*, 4 (2004), 453–66

MATTHÄUS, JÜRGEN, 'Historiography and the Perpetrators of the Holocaust', in *The Historiography of the Holocaust*, ed. by Dan Stone (Basingstoke: Palgrave Macmillan, 2004), pp. 197–215

MAZIARCZYK, ANNA, 'Une inquiétante puissance du blanc: l'écriture lazaréenne dans *Dora Bruder* de Patrick Modiano', *Romanica Wratislaviensia*, 61 (2014), 109–20

MCARA, CATRIONA, and DAVID CALVIN (eds), *Anti-tales: The Uses of Disenchantment* (Newcastle upon Tyne: Cambridge Scholars Publishing, 2011)

MCGLOTHLIN, ERIN, 'Narrative Perspective and the Holocaust Perpetrator: Edgar Hilsenrath's *The Nazi and the Barber* and Jonathan Littell's *The Kindly Ones*', in *The Bloomsbury Companion to Holocaust Literature*, ed. by Jenni Adams (London: Bloomsbury, 2014), pp. 159–77

—— *Second-generation Holocaust Literature: Legacies of Survival and Perpetration* (New York: Camden House, 2006)
—— 'Theorizing the Perpetrator in Bernard Schlink's *The Reader* and Martin Amis's *Time's Arrow*', in *After Representation: Holocaust, Literature, and Culture*, ed. by R. Clifton Spargo and Robert M. Ehrenreich (New Brunswick, NJ: Rutgers University Press, 2008), pp. 210-21
McNally, Richard J., *Remembering Trauma* (Cambridge, MA: Harvard University Press, 2003)
McRobbie, Angela, *The Aftermath of Feminism: Gender, Culture and Social Change* (Los Angeles: Sage, 2009)
Mehlman, Jeffrey, 'French Literature and the Holocaust', in *Literature and the Holocaust*, ed. by Alan Rosen (Cambridge: Cambridge University Press, 2013), pp. 174-90
Melson, Robert, 'Choiceless Choices: Surviving on False Papers on the "Aryan" Side', in *Gray Zones: Ambiguities and Compromise in the Holocaust and Its Aftermath*, ed. by Jonathan Petropoulos and John K. Roth (New York: Berghahn Books, 2005), pp. 97-106
Meretoja, Hanna, 'Narrative Dynamics, Perspective Taking, and Engagement: Jonathan Littell's *Les Bienveillantes*', in *The Ethics of Storytelling: Narrative Hermeneutics, History and the Possible* (Oxford: Oxford University Press, 2018), pp. 217-54
Merin, Yehuda, and Jack Nusan Porter, 'Three Jewish Family Camps in the Forests of Volyn, Ukraine during the Holocaust', *Jewish Social Studies*, 46.1 (Winter 1984), 83-92
Meyers, Valerie, 'Animal Farm: An Allegory of Revolution', in *George Orwell's 'Animal Farm'*, ed. by Harold Bloom (New York: Infobase, 2009), pp. 23-34
Michael, Megali Cornier, *Feminism and the Postmodern Impulse: Post-World War II Fiction* (New York: State University of New York Press, 1996)
Milchman, Alan and Alan Rosenberg (eds), *Postmodernism and the Holocaust* (Amsterdam: Rodopi, 1998)
Miller, Nancy K., and Jason Tougaw, 'Introduction', in *Extremities: Trauma, Testimony and Community*, ed. by Nancy K. Miller and Jason Tougaw (Urbana: Illinois University Press, 2002), pp. 1-24
Milne, Anna-Louise, 'Introduction: The City as a Book', in *The Cambridge Companion to the Literature of Paris*, ed. by Anna-Louise Milne (Cambridge: Cambridge University Press, 2013), pp. 1-18
Miłosz, Czesław, *Selected Poems* (New York: Seabury Press, 1973)
Missler, Heike, *Cultural Politics of Chick Lit: Popular Fiction, Postfeminism and Representation* (London: Routledge, 2017)
Mitschke, Samantha, 'The Sacred, the Profane, and the Space in Between: Site-specific Performance at Auschwitz', *Holocaust Studies*, 22.2-3 (2016), 228-43
Modiano, Patrick, *Les Boulevards de ceinture* [1972] (Paris: Gallimard Folio, 1978)
—— *Ring Roads*, trans. by Frank Wynne, in *The Occupation Trilogy* (New York: Bloomsbury, 2015), pp. 218-324
—— *La Place de l'étoile* (Paris: Gallimard, 1968)
—— *La Place de l'étoile*, trans. by Caroline Hillier, in *The Occupation Trilogy* (New York: Bloomsbury, 2015), pp. 1-116
—— *Livret de famille* (Paris: Gallimard, 1977)
—— *Quartier perdu* (Paris: Gallimard, 1984)
—— *A Trace of Malice*, trans. by Anthea Bell (Henley-on-Thames: Aidan Ellis, 1988)
—— *Un cirque qui passe* (Paris: Gallimard, 1992)
—— *After the Circus*, trans. by Mark Polizzotti (New Haven, CT: Yale University Press, 2015)
Mohamed, Saira, 'The Contours and Controversies of Perpetrator Trauma', in *The*

Routledge Handbook of Perpetrator Studies, ed. by Susanne C. Knittel and Zachary J. Goldberg (New York: Routledge, 2019), pp. 265–75
—— 'On Monsters and Men: Perpetrator Trauma and Mass Atrocity', *Columbia Law Review*, 115 (2015), 1157–1216Moore, Alison M., 'History, Memory and Trauma in Photography of the *Tondues*: Visuality of the Vichy Past through the Silent Image of Women', *Gender and History*, 17.3 (2005), 657–81
MORINA, KRISTINA, and KRIJN THIJS, 'Introduction: Probing the Limits of Categorisation', in *Probing the Limits of Categorisation: The Bystander in Holocaust History*, ed. by Kristina Morina and Krijn Thijs (New York: Berghahn, 2019), pp. 1–14
MORAG, RAYA, 'Perpetrator Trauma and Current Israeli Documentary Cinema', *Camera Obscura*, 27.2 (2012), 93–132
—— *Waltzing with Bashir: Perpetrator Trauma in the Cinema* (London: I. B. Tauris, 2013)
MORGENSTERN, NAOMI, 'The Primal Scene in the Public Domain: E. L. Doctorow's *The Book of Daniel*', *Studies in the Novel*, 35.1 (Spring 2003), 68–88
MORRIS, ALAN, *Patrick Modiano* (Amsterdam: Rodopi, 2000)
MORSE, ARTHUR, *While Six Million Died: A Chronicle of American Apathy* (New York: Random House, 1968)
MOUCHARD, CLAUDE, *Qui si je criais...? Œuvres-témoignages dans les tourments du XXe siècle* (Paris: Lawrence Teper, 2007)
MOYN, SAMUEL, 'A Nazi Zelig: Jonathan Littell's *The Kindly Ones*', *Nation*, 3 December 2009 <https://www.thenation.com/article/nazi-zelig-jonathan-littells-kindly-ones/>
MUNCH-JURISIC, DITTE MARIE, 'Perpetrator Disgust: A Morally Destructive Emotion', in *Emotions and Mass Atrocity: Philosophical and Theoretical Explorations*, ed. by Thomas Brudholm and Johannes Lang (Cambridge: Cambridge University Press, 2018), pp. 142–61
NASH, RICHARD, *Animal Nomenclature: Facing Other Animals* (New York: Routledge, 2006)
NICK, I. M., *Personal Names, Hitler and the Holocaust: A Socio-onomastic Study of Genocide and Nazi Germany* (New York: Lexington Books, 2019)
NICOL, BRAN, *The Cambridge Introduction to Postmodern Fiction* (Cambridge: Cambridge University Press, 2009)
NIVAT, GEORGES, '*Les Bienveillantes* et les classiques russes', *Le Débat*, 144 (March-April 2007), 56–65
NORA, PIERRE, 'Between Memory and History: *Les Lieux de mémoire*', *Representations*, 26 (Spring 1989), 7–24
—— *Les Lieux de mémoire*, 7 vols (Paris: Gallimard, 1984–94)
NORA, PIERRE, and JONATHAN LITTELL, 'Conversation sur l'histoire et le roman', *Le Débat*, 144 (March-April 2007), 25–44
NOVAK, AMY, 'Who Speaks? Who Listens? The Problem of Address in Two Nigerian Trauma Novels', *Studies in the Novel*, 40.1–2 (2008), 31–51
NOVICK, PETER, *The Holocaust in American Life* [1991] (Boston: Houghton Mifflin, 2000)
NOVITCH, MYRIAM, *Le Génocide des Tsiganes sous le régime nazi* (Paris: AMIF and the Ghetto Fighters' House, Israel, 1968)
NÜNNING, VERA, 'Ethics and Aesthetics in British Novels at the Beginning of the Twenty-First Century', in *Ethics in Culture: The Dissemination of Values through Literature and Other Media*, ed. by Astrid Erll, Herbert Grabes, and Ansgar Nünning (Berlin: Walter de Gruyter, 2008), pp. 360–91
NUSSBAUM, MARTHA C., *Love's Knowledge: Essays on Philosophy and Literature* (Oxford: Oxford University Press, 1990)
OBERGÖKER, TIMO, 'Shoah et récit fictionnel, un champ de force délicat: *Le Non de Klara* de Soazig Aaron', in *Témoignages de l'après-Auschwitz dans la littérature juive-française*

d'aujourd'hui: enfants de survivants et survivans-enfants, ed. by Annelies Schulte Nordholt (Amsterdam: Rodopi, 2008), pp. 205–18

OFER, DALIA, and LENORE J. WEITZMAN (eds), *Women in the Holocaust* (New Haven, CT: Yale University Press, 1998)

O'KEEFE, CHARLES, 'Patrick Modiano's Raphaël Schlemilovitch and Homer's Odysseus Laertiades: Fit(ted) Companions', *Comparative Literature Studies*, 53.1 (2016), 28–56

—— *A Riffaterrean Reading of Patrick Modiano's 'La Place de l'étoile': Investigating the Family Crime* (Birmingham, AL: Summa Publications, 2005)

OLIN, MARGARET, 'Lanzmann's *Shoah* and the Topography of the Holocaust Film', *Representations*, 57 (Winter 1997), 1–23

O'REILLY, TERENCE, *Hitler's Irishmen* (Cork: Mercier Press, 2008)

OŚRODEK 'Brama Grodzka — Teatr NN', 'Czesław Miłosz (1911–2004)' <http://teatrnn.pl/leksykon/artykuly/czeslaw-milosz-19112004/>

PADFIELD, PETER, *Himmler: Reiseführer-SS* (London: Cassell, 2001)

PANNÉ, JEAN-LOUIS, *Jan Karski, le 'roman' et l'histoire* (Saint-Malo: Pascal Galodé, 2014)

PARRAU, ALAIN, *Écrire les camps* (Paris: Belin, 1995)

PAULSSON, GUNNAR S., *The Secret City: The Hidden Jews of Warsaw, 1940–1945* (New Haven, CT: Yale University Press, 2002)

PATAI, DAPHNE, 'Political Fiction and Patriarchal Fantasy', in *George Orwell's 'Animal Farm'*, ed. by Harold Bloom (New York: Infobase, 2009), pp. 3–22

PATTERSON, CHARLES, *Eternal Treblinka: Our Treatment of Animals and the Holocaust* (New York: Lantern Books, 2001)

PATTERSON, DAVID, *Anti-semitism and its Metaphysical Origins* (New York: Cambridge University Press, 2015)

—— 'The Moral Dilemma of Motherhood in the Nazi Death Camps', in *Problems Unique to the Holocaust*, ed. by Harry James Cargas (Lexington: University Press of Kentucky, 1999), pp. 7–24

PAXTON, ROBERT O., *Vichy France: Old Guard and New Order* (New York: Knopf, 1972)

—— *La France de Vichy, 1940–1944*, trans. by Claude Bertrand (Paris: Seuil, 1973)

PENKOWER, MONTY N., *The Jews Were Expendable: Free World Diplomacy and the Holocaust* (Chicago: University of Illinois, 1983)

PENTLIN, SUSAN L., 'Holocaust Victims of Privilege', in *Problems Unique to the Holocaust*, ed. by Harry James Cargas (Lexington: University Press of Kentucky, 1999), pp. 25–42

PERL, GISELLA, *I Was a Doctor in Auschwitz* (New York: International Universities Press, 1948)

PERRY, EDITH, 'Rêves et fantasmes dans *Les Bienveillantes*', in *'Les Bienveillantes' de Jonathan Littell*, ed. by Murielle Lucie Clément (Cambridge: OpenBook, 2010), pp. 103–24

PESCHANSKI, DENIS, '*Les Bienveillantes*, roman à controverse', *Libération*, 7 November 2006 <https://www.liberation.fr/evenement/2006/11/07/les-bienveillantes-roman-a-controverse_56610>

PETROPOULOS, JONATHAN, and JOHN K. ROTH, 'Prologue: The Gray Zones of the Holocaust', in *Gray Zones: Ambiguities and Compromise in the Holocaust and Its Aftermath*, ed. by Jonathan Petropoulos and John K. Roth (New York: Berghahn Books, 2005), pp. xv–xxii

PETTITT, JOANNE, *Perpetrators in Holocaust Narratives: Encountering the Nazi Beast* (Basingstoke: Palgrave Macmillan, 2017)

PEUKERT, DETLEV, *Volksgenossen und Gemeinschaftsfremde: Anpassung, Ausmerze und Aufbegehren unter dem Nationalsozialismus* (Cologne: Bund-Verlag, 1982)

PINCHEVSKI, AMIT, *Transmitted Wounds: Media and the Mediation of Trauma* (Oxford: Oxford University Press, 2019)

PIOTROWSKI, TADEUSZ, 'Assistance to the Jews', in *Poland's Holocaust: Ethnic Strife, Collaboration with Occupying Forces and Genocide in the Second Republic 1918–1947* (Jefferson, NC: McFarland, 1998), pp. 112–28

POHL, DIETER, 'War, Occupation and the Holocaust in Poland', in *The Historiography of the Holocaust*, ed. by Dan Stone (Basingstoke: Palgrave Macmillan, 2004), pp. 89–119

POPESCU, DIANE I., 'Post-witnessing the Concentration Camps: Paul Auster's and Angela Morgan Cutler's Investigative and Imaginative Encounters with Sites of Mass Murder', *Holocaust Studies*, 22.2–3 (2016), 274–88

POPKIN, JEREMY, 'A Historian's View of *The Kindly Ones*', in *Writing the Holocaust Today: Critical Perspectives on Jonathan Littell's 'The Kindly Ones'*, ed. by Aurélie Barjonet and Liran Razinsky (Amsterdam: Rodopi, 2012), pp. 187–200

POZNANSKI, RENÉE, 'French Apprehensions, Jewish Expectations: From a Social Imaginary to a Political Practice', in *The Jews Are Coming Back: The Return of the Jews to Their Countries of Origin after WWII*, ed. by David Bankier (New York: Berghahn Books, 2005), pp. 25–57

PRESCOTT, MATT, 'Letter to the Jewish Community', PETA, 3 December 2003

PRIEMEL, KIM CHRISTIAN, 'War Crimes Trials, the Holocaust, and Historiography, 1943–2011', in *A Companion to the Holocaust*, ed. by Simone Gigliotti and Hilary Earl (Hoboken, NJ: John Wiley and Sons, 2020), pp. 173–89

QUINT, DAVID, *Epic and Empire: Politics and Generic Form from Virgil to Milton* (Princeton, NJ: Princeton University Press, 1993)

RĂDULESCU, ANDA, 'Max Aue de Jonathan Littell: un marginal des plus controversés', *Analele Universității din Craiova*, 1 (2012), 263–70

RANK, OTTO, *The Trauma of Birth* [1924] (London: Routledge, 1999)

RAOUL, VALERIE, *The French Fictional Journal: Fictional Narcissism/ Narcissistic Fiction* (Toronto: University of Toronto Press, 1980)

RASSON, LUC, 'How Nazis Undermine Their Own Point of View', in *Writing the Holocaust Today: Critical Perspectives on Jonathan Littell's 'The Kindly Ones'*, ed. by Liran Razinsky and Aurélie Barjonet (Amsterdam: Rodopi, 2012), pp. 97–110

RAU, PETRA, *Our Nazis: Representations of Fascism in Contemporary Literature and Film* (Edinburgh: Edinburgh University Press, 2013)

RAVENHALL, HENRY, 'The Untimely Subject: Reporting Discourse and Bearing Witness in Villehardouin's *La Conquête de Constantinople* and Yannick Haenel's *Jan Karski*', *Interfaces*, 7 (2020), 1–28

RAY, LARRY, and SŁAWOMIR KAPRALSKI, 'Introduction to the Special Issue: Disputed Holocaust Memory in Poland', in *Disputed Holocaust Memory in Poland*, ed. by Larry Ray and Sławomir Kapralski (= special issue of *Holocaust Studies*, 25.3 (2019)), 209–19

RAZINSKY, LIRAN, 'History, Excess and Testimony in Jonathan Littell's *Les Bienveillantes*', *French Forum*, 33.3 (Fall 2008), 69–87

—— 'Not the Witness We Wished for: Testimony in Jonathan Littell's *Kindly Ones*', *Modern Language Quarterly*, 71.2 (June 2020), 175–96

—— 'The Similarity of Perpetrators', in *Writing the Holocaust Today: Critical Perspectives on Jonathan Littell's 'The Kindly Ones'*, ed. by Aurélie Barjonet and Liran Razinsky (Amsterdam: Rodopi, 2012), pp. 47–60

—— 'We Are All the Same: Max Aue, Interpreter of Evil', *Yale French Studies*, 121 (2012), 140–54

READING, ANNA, *The Social Inheritance of the Holocaust: Gender, Culture and Memory* (Basingstoke: Palgrave Macmillan, 2002)

REGAN, TOM, *The Case for Animal Rights* (Los Angeles: University of California Press, 1983)

REICHELT, KATRIN, *Der Wald war unser letzter Ausweg: Hilfe für verfolgte Juden im Deutsch besetzten Weißrussland 1941–1944* (Berlin: Lukas, 2017)

RICH, IAN, *Holocaust Perpetrators of the German Police Battalions: The Mass Murder of Jewish Civilians, 1940–1942* (London: Bloomsbury, 2018)

RING, JENNIFER, *The Political Consequences of Thinking: Judaism in the Work of Hannah Arendt* (New York: State University of New York Press, 1997)

RINGELHEIM, JOAN, 'The Split between Gender and the Holocaust', in *Women in the Holocaust*, ed. by Dalia Ofer and Lenore J. Weiztman (New Haven, CT: Yale University Press, 1998), pp. 340–50

—— 'The Unethical and the Unspeakable: Women and the Holocaust', in *The Holocaust: Theoretical Readings*, ed. by Neil Levi and Michael Rothberg (Edinburgh: Edinburgh University Press, 2010), pp. 169–77

—— 'Women in the Holocaust: A Reconsideration of Research', *Signs*, 10.4 (Summer 1985), 741–61

RITTNER, CAROL ANN, and JOHN K. ROTH (eds), *Different Voices: Women and the Holocaust* (St Paul, MN: Paragon House, 1993)

RITVO, HARRIET, *The Animal Estate: The English and Other Creatures in the Victorian Age* (Cambridge, MA: Harvard University Press, 1987)

ROBIN, RÉGINE, 'Le Paris toujours déjà perdu de Patrick Modiano', *Cahiers de l'Herne: Patrick Modiano*, ed. by Maryline Heck and Raphaëlle Guidée (Paris: L'Herne, 2012), 93–100

ROSE, GILLIAN, *Mourning Becomes the Law: Philosophy and Representation* (Cambridge: Cambridge University Press, 1996)

ROSE, JACQUELINE, *The Haunting of Sylvia Plath* (Cambridge, MA: Harvard University Press, 1992)

ROSEN, ALAN, 'The Holocaust Witness: Wartime and Postwar Voices', in *A Companion to the Holocaust*, ed. by Simone Gigliotti and Hilary Earl (Hoboken, NJ: John Wiley, 2020), pp. 451–67

ROSENFELD, ALVIN, 'The Holocaust According to William Styron', *Midstream* 25.10 (December 1979), 43–49

ROSENMAN, ANNY DAYAN, *Les Alphabets de la Shoah* (Paris: CNRS, 2007)

ROSKIES, DAVID G., and NAOMI DIAMANT, *A Holocaust Literature: A History and Guide* (Waltham, MA: Brandeis University Press, 2012)

ROTHBERG, MICHAEL, *Multidirectional Memory: Remembering the Holocaust in the Age of Decolonisation* (Stanford, CA: Stanford University Press, 2009)

—— *Traumatic Realism: The Demands of Holocaust Representation* (Minneapolis: University of Minnesota Press, 2000)

ROTHE, ANNE, 'Irresponsible Nonsense: An Epistemological and Ethical Critique of Postmodern Trauma Theory', in *Interdisciplinary Handbook of Trauma and Culture*, ed. by Yochai Ataria and others (New York: Springer, 2016), pp. 181–94

—— *Popular Trauma Culture: Selling the Pain of Others in the Mass Media* (New Brunswick, NJ: Rutgers University Press, 2011)

—— 'Popular Trauma Culture: The Pain of Others Between Holocaust Tropes and Kitsch-Sentimental Melodrama', in *Interdisciplinary Handbook of Trauma and Culture*, ed. by Yochai Ataria and others (Basel: Springer, 2016), pp. 51–66

ROUSSET, DAVID. *L'Univers concentrationnaire* (Paris: Pavois, 1947)

ROUSSO, HENRY, *Le Syndrome de Vichy: de 1944 à nos jours* (Paris: Seuil, 1987)

ROUSSO, HENRY, and ÉRIC CONAN, *Vichy: un passé qui ne passe pas* (Paris: Fayard, 1994)

ROUX, BAPTISTE, *Figures de l'Occupation dans l'œuvre de Patrick Modiano* (Paris: L'Harmattan, 1999)

ROZMARIN, MIRI, 'Staying Alive: Matricide and the Ethical-political Aspects of Mother-daughter Relations', *Studies in Gender and Sexuality*, 17.4 (2016), 242–53

Rubin, Gary E., 'The Film *Shoah*: Understanding Polish and Jewish Responses', *Shofar*, 4.2 (Winter 1986), 33–35
Ruszniewski-Dahan, Myriam, *Romanciers de la Shoah: si l'écho de leur voix faiblit* (Paris: L'Harmattan, 1999)
Ruszniewski-Dahan, Myriam, and Georges Bensoussan (eds), *La Shoah dans la littérature française* (= special issue of *Revue d'histoire de la Shoah*, 176 (September-December 2002))
Sabbah, Danièle, '"Il y a eu les retours solitaires [...] au cœur désaffecté de l'âme": *Le Non de Klara* de Soazig Aaron', in *Trauma et texte*, ed. by Peter Kuon (Frankfurt am Mein: Peter Lang, 2008), pp. 311–30
Sandberg, Eric, '"This Incomprehensible Thing": Jonathan Littell's *The Kindly Ones* and the Aesthetics of Access', *The Cambridge Quarterly*, 43.3 (2014), 231–55
Sanyal, Debarati, *Memory and Complicity: Migrations of Holocaust Remembrance* (New York: Fordham University Press, 2015)
Sax, Boria, *Animals in the Third Reich: Pets, Scapegoats, and the Holocaust* (New York: Continuum, 2000)
Seabra Neves, Márcia, 'La Néo-fable animalière: devenir-animal et métamorphose', in *Le Néo: sources, héritages et réécritures dans les cultures européennes*, ed. by Karine Martin-Cardini and Jocelyne Aubé-Bourligueux (Rennes: Presses universitaires de Rennes, 2016), pp. 279–93
Schaal, Susanne, and others, 'Mental Health 15 Years after the Killings in Rwanda: Imprisoned Perpetrators of the Genocide Against the Tutsi versus a Community Sample of Survivors', *Journal of Traumatic Stress*, 26.4 (2012), 446–53
Schama, Simon, *Landscape and Memory* (London: HarperCollins, 1995)
Schoenfeld, Gabriel, 'Auschwitz and the Professors', *Commentary*, 105–106 (June 1998), 42–46
Schönbeck, Sebastian, 'Return to the Fable: Rethinking a Genre Neglected in Animal Studies and Ecocriticism', in *Texts, Animals, Environments: Zoopoetics and Ecopoetics*, ed. by Frederike Middelhoff and others (Freiburg: Rombach, 2019), pp. 111–26
Schönfelder, Christa, *Wounds and Words: Childhood and Family Trauma in Romantic and Postmodern Fiction* (Bielefeld: Transcript, 2013)
Schreiber, Elizabeth, '*Car cela devient une histoire*: Representation of the Holocaust in the Imaginative and Collective Memoirs of Charlotte Delbo', in *Re-examining the Holocaust through Literature*, ed. by Aukje Kluge and Benn E. Williams (Cambridge: Cambridge Scholars Publishing, 2009), pp. 2–38
Schudrich, Michael Joseph, 'Rabin Schudrich: Jeśli nawet komuś się to nie podoba, w Polsce jestem u siebie [Wywiad] '[Rabbi Schudrich: Even if People Don't Like It, Poland is My Home [Interview], *Wirtualna Polska*, 1 March 2021 <https://wiadomosci.wp.pl/rabin-schudrich-nawet-jesli-komus-sie-to-nie-podoba-w-polsce-jestem-u-siebie-wywiad-6613058256014304a>
Schulte Nordholt, Annelies, '*Dora Bruder*: le témoignage par le biais de la fiction', in *Patrick Modiano*, ed. by John E. Flower (Amsterdam: Brill, 2007), pp. 75–87
—— *Perec, Modiano, Raczymow: la génération d'après et la mémoire de la Shoah* (Amsterdam: Rodopi, 2008)
Schulte Nordholt, Annelies (ed.), *Témoignages de l'après-Auschwitz dans la littérature juive-française d'aujourd'hui: enfants de survivants et survivants-enfants* (Amsterdam: Rodopi, 2008)
Schuppli, Susan, *Material Witness: Media, Forensics, Evidence* (Cambridge, MA: MIT Press, 2020)
Schuster, Joshua, *The Ecology of Modernism: American Environments and Avant-garde Poetics* (Tuscaloosa: University of Alabama Press, 2015)
Schwarz-Bart, André, *Le Dernier des Justes* (Paris: Seuil, 1959)

—— *The Last of the Just*, trans. by Stephen Baker (New York: Atheneum, 1961)
SEMPRÚN, JORGE, 'Ohne die Literatur Stirb die Erinnerung', *Frankfurter Allgemeine Zeitung*, 8 February 2008, p. 35
—— 'Un récit de Soazig Aaron: merci Klara!', *Le Nouvel Observateur*, 1951, 28 April 2002, p. 120
SENIAVSKAIA, ELENA L., 'Heroic Symbols: Reality and Mythology of the War', *Russian Studies in History*, 37.1 (Summer 1988), 61–87
SERENY, GITA, *Into the Darkness: An Examination of Conscience* (New York: Vintage, 1974)
SHANDLER, JEFFREY, *Holocaust Memory in the Digital Age: Survivors' Stories and New Media Practices* (Stanford, CA: Stanford University Press, 2017)
SICHER, EFRAIM, *Breaking Crystal: Writing and Memory after Auschwitz* (Urbana: University of Illinois Press, 1998)
—— *The Holocaust Novel* (London: Routledge, 2005)
SILVERMAN MAX, 'Introduction: Lazarus and the Modern World', in *Concentrationary Art: Jean Cayrol, the Lazarean and the Everyday in Post-war Film, Literature, Music and the Visual Arts*, ed. by Griselda Pollock and Max Silverman (New York: Berghahn Books, 2019), pp. 1–28
—— *Palimpsestic Memory: The Holocaust and Colonialism in French and Francophone Fiction and Film* (New York: Berghahn Books, 2013)
SILVERMAN, MAXIM, *Facing Postmodernity: Contemporary French Thought* (London: Routledge, 1999)
SIMONS, JOHN, *Animal Rights and the Politics of Literary Representation* (Basingstoke: Palgrave Macmillan, 2002)
SINGER, ISAAC BASHEVIS, 'The Letter Writer', in *The Séance and Other Stories* (New York: Farrar, Straus & Giroux, 1968)
—— *The Penitent* (New York: Farrar, Straus & Giroux, 1968)
SINGER, PETER, *Animal Liberation* (New York: Avon Books, 1990)
SMITH, KEVIN PAUL, *The Postmodern Fairy Tale: Folkloric Intertexts in Contemporary Fiction* (Basingstoke: Palgrave Macmillan, 2007)
SMYTH, EDMUND J., 'The *Nouveau Roman*: Modernity and Postmodernity', in *Postmodernism and Contemporary Fiction*, ed. by Edmund J. Smyth (London: Batsford, 1991), pp. 54–73
SOMMER, ROBERT, 'Sexual Exploitation of Women in Nazi Concentration Camp Brothels', in *Sexual Violence against Jewish Women during the Holocaust*, ed. by Sonja Maria Hedgepeth and Rochelle G. Saidel (Lebanon, NH: Brandeis University Press, 2010), pp. 45–60
SPIEGELMAN, ART, *The Complete Maus* [1986–91] (London: Penguin, 2003)
—— *Metamaus: A Look Inside a Modern Classic, Maus* (New York: Pantheon, 2011)
STEINER, JEAN-FRANÇOIS, *Treblinka*, trans. by Helena Weaver (New York: Simon & Schuster, 1967)
STEPHENS, CARMELLE, 'Saints and Martyrs: Popular Maternal Tropes in Holocaust Memoir', *Journal of Holocaust Research*, 34.2 (April 2020), 95–110
STIER, OREN BARUCH, *Holocaust Icons: Symbolizing the Shoah in History and Memory* (New Brunswick, NJ: Rutgers University Press, 2015)
STILL, JUDITH, *Derrida and Other Animals: The Boundaries of the Human* (Edinburgh: Edinburgh University Press, 2015)
STOLA, DARIUSZ, 'The Polish Government-in-exile and the Final Solution: What Conditioned its Actions and Inactions?', in *Contested Memories: Poles and Jews during the Holocaust and Its Aftermath*, ed. by Joshua D. Zimmerman (New Brunswick, NJ: Rutgers University Press, 2002), pp. 85–119
—— 'The Polish Government-in-exile: National Unity and Weakness', *Holocaust Studies*, 18.2–3 (Autumn/Winter 2012), 95–118

STONE, ALISON, 'Stealing Lot's Wife and Daughters from the Bible: A Response to Rozmarin's "Staying Alive"', *Studies in Gender and Sexuality*, 17.4 (2016), 254–61
STONE, DAN, *Constructing the Holocaust: A Study in Historiography* (London: Vallentine Mitchell, 2003)
—— *Histories of the Holocaust* (Oxford: Oxford University Press, 2010)
—— 'Holocaust Testimony and the Challenge to the Philosophy of History', in *Social Theory after the Holocaust*, ed. by Charles Fine and Robert Turner (Liverpool: Liverpool University Press, 2000), pp. 219–34
STOW, KENNETH, *Jewish Dogs: An Image and its Interpreters: Continuity in the Catholic-Jewish Encounter* (Stanford, CA: Stanford University Press, 2006)
STRANGEWAYS, AL, '"The Boot in the Face": The Problem of the Holocaust in the Poetry of Sylvia Plath', *Contemporary Literature*, 37.3 (Autumn 1996), 370–90
STOLL, KATRIN, 'The Lack of Conscious Engagement with the Reality of the Holocaust or: On the Non-reception of Jan Karski in the Federal Republic of Germany', *Holocaust Studies*, 20.1–2 (2014), 57–82
SULEIMAN, SUSAN RUBIN, '"Oneself as Another": Identification and Mourning in Patrick Modiano's *Dora Bruder*', *Studies in 20th and 21st Century Literature* 31.2 (2007), 1–26
—— 'Performing Perpetrator as Witness: Jonathan Littell's *Les Bienveillantes*', in *After Testimony: The Ethics and Aesthetics of Holocaust Narrative for the Future*, ed. by Jakob Lothe, Susan Rubin Suleiman, and James Phelan (Columbus: Ohio State University Press, 2012), pp. 99–119
—— 'When the Perpetrator Becomes a Reliable Witness: On Jonathan Littell's *Les Bienveillantes*', *New German Critique*, 106 (Winter 2009), 1–19
—— 'The 1.5 Generation: Thinking about Child Survivors and the Holocaust', *American Imago*, 59.3 (Autumn 2002), 277–95
SÜTTERLIN, NICOLE A., 'History of Trauma Theory', in *The Routledge Companion to Literature and Trauma*, ed. by Colin Davis and Hanna Meretoja (New York: Routledge, 2020), pp. 11–22
SZOPER, MICHAEL, 'Jan Karski: Personal Reflections on the Life of a Saint', *Polish Review*, 59.4 (2014), 73–80
SUNDQUIST, ERIC J., 'Mr. Styron's Planet', in *Shades of the Planet: American Literature as World Literature*, ed. by Wai Chee Dimock and Lawrence Buell (Princeton, NJ: Princeton University Press, 2007), pp. 103–40
SZTYBEL, DAVID, 'Can Treatment of Animals Be Compared to the Holocaust?', *Ethics & the Environment*, 11.1 (2006), 97–132
SZUREK, JEAN-CHARLES, 'Shoah: de la question juive à la question polonaise', in *Au sujet de 'Shoah'*, ed. by Michel Deguy (Paris: Belin, 1990), pp. 357–82
TAME, PETER, 'Isotopias in Invented Autobiography: Four Novels on the Occupation by Patrick Modiano', in *Isotopias: Places and Spaces in French War Fiction of the Twentieth and Twenty-First Centuries* (Oxford: Peter Lang, 2015), pp. 475–508
—— 'Lieux réels et lieux imaginaires dans *Les Bienveillantes*', in *'Les Bienveillantes' de Jonathan Littell*, ed. by Murielle Lucie Clément (Cambridge: OpenBook, 2010), pp. 213–30
TATAR, MARIA, 'Bluebeard', in *The Oxford Companion to Fairy Tales*, ed. by Jack Zipes (Oxford: Oxford University Press, 2000)
THEWELEIT, KLAUS, *Male Fantasies. I: Women, Floods, Bodies, History*, trans. by Stephen Conway (Cambridge: Polity Press, 1987)
—— 'On the German Reaction to Jonathan Littell's *Les Bienveillantes*', *New German Critique*, 36.1 (Winter 2009), 21–34
TODOROV, TZVETAN, *Facing the Extreme: Moral Life in Concentration Camps*, trans. by Arthur Denner and Abigail Pollack (New York: Metropolitan Books, 1995)

TORY, AVRAHAM, *Surviving the Holocaust: The Kovno Ghetto Diary*, ed. by Martin Gilbert, trans. by Jerzy Michałowicz (Cambridge, MA: Harvard University Press, 1990)

TSETI, ANGELIKI, 'In the Absence of Ruins: The "Non-sites of Memory" in Claude Lanzmann's *Shoah* and Daniel Mendelsohn's *Lost: A Search for Six of Six Million*', in *Ruins in the Literary and Cultural Imagination*, ed. by Efterpi Mitsi and others (Basingstoke: Palgrave Macmillan, 2019), pp. 213–28

UNGAR, STEVEN, 'Out of the Past: The Perpetrator Portrait as Literary and Historical Exercise', *Yale French Studies*, 121 (2012), 185–203

UNITED STATES HOLOCAUST MEMORIAL MUSEUM, HOLOCAUST ENCYCLOPEDIA, 'Lodz', <https://encyclopedia.ushmm.org/content/en/article/lodz>

—— 'Polish Victims', <https://encyclopedia.ushmm.org/content/en/article/polish-victims>

VAN DEN ABBEELE, GEORGES, 'Fable', *Historical Materialism*, 16.4 (2008), 233–38

VANDENBERG-DAVES, JODI, *Modern Motherhood: An American History* (New Brunswick, NJ: Rutgers University Press, 2014)

VAN DER KOLK, BESSEL A., and JOSE SAPORTA, 'Biological Response to Psychic Trauma', in *International Handbook of Traumatic Stress Syndromes*, ed. by John P. Wilson and Beverley Raphael (New York: Springer, 1993), pp. 28–48

VAN DER KOLK, BESSEL A., and ONNO VAN DER HART, 'The Intrusive Past: The Flexibility of Memory and the Engraving of Trauma', in *Trauma: Explorations in Memory*, ed. by Cathy Caruth (Baltimore, MD: Johns Hopkins University Press, 1995), pp. 158–82

VIARD, BRUNO, 'Les Silences des *Bienveillantes*', in *'Les Bienveillantes' de Jonathan Littell*, ed. by Murielle Lucie Clément (Cambridge: OpenBook, 2010), pp. 73–86

VIART, DOMINIQUE, 'Claude Simon: le travail de la mémoire', radio interview with Matthieu Garrigou-Lagrange, *La Compagnie des auteurs*, 27 February 2019 <https://www.franceculture.fr/emissions/la-compagnie-des-auteurs/claude-simon-34-le-travail-de-la-memoire>

—— 'Filiations littéraires', in *États du roman contemporain. Écritures contemporains 2: actes du colloque de Calaceite, Fondation Noésis, 6–13 juillet 1996*, ed. by Jan Baetens and Dominique Viart (Paris: Minard, 1999), pp. 115–39

—— 'Le Silence des pères au principe du "récit de filiation"', *Études françaises*, 45.3 (2009), 95–112

VICE, SUE, *Claude Lanzmann's 'Shoah' Outtakes: Holocaust Rescue and Resistance* (London: Bloomsbury, 2021)

—— *Holocaust Fiction* (London: Routledge, 2000)

—— 'Poland: The Ethics of Filming', in *Shoah* (Basingstoke: Palgrave Macmillan, 2011), pp. 73–79

VIDAL-NAQUET, PIERRE, 'L'Épreuve de l'historien: réflexions d'un généraliste', in *Au sujet de 'Shoah': le film de Claude Lanzmann*, ed. by Michel Deguy (Paris: Belin, 2011), pp. 270–88

—— 'Memory and History', trans. by David Ames Curtis, *Common Knowledge*, 5.2 (1966), 14–20

VIRGILI, FABRICE. *La France 'virile': les femmes tondues à la Libération* (Paris: Payot, 2000)

—— *Shorn Women: Gender and Punishment in Liberation France*, trans. by John Flower (Oxford: Berg, 2002)

WAINTRATER, RÉGINE, *Sortir du génocide: témoignage et survivance* [2003] (Paris: Payot & Rivages, 2011)

WAJCMAN, GÉRARD, *L'Object du siècle* (Paris: Verdier, 1998)

WARDI, CHARLOTTE, *Le Génocide dans la fiction romanesque* (Paris: Presses universitaires de France, 1986)

WEINER WEBER, SUZANNE, 'Shedding City Life: Survival Mechanisms of Forest Fugitives during the Holocaust', *Holocaust Studies*, 18.1 (2012), 1–28

WAUGH, PATRICIA, *Feminine Fictions: Revisiting the Postmodern* [1989] (London: Routledge, 2012)
—— *Metafiction: The Theory and Practice of Self-conscious Fiction* (London: Routledge, 1984)
WAXMAN, ZOË, 'Testimony and Representation', in *The Historiography of the Holocaust*, ed. by Dan Stone (Basingstoke: Palgrave Macmillan, 2004), pp. 485–507
—— *Women in the Holocaust: A Feminist History* (Oxford: Oxford University Press, 2017)
WEIGEL, SIGRID, 'The Symptomatology of the Universalised Concept of Trauma: On the Failing of Freud's Reading of Tasso in the Trauma of History', trans. by Georgina Paul, *New German Critique*, 90 (Autumn 2003), 85–94
WEISSMAN, GARY, *Fantasies of Witnessing: Postwar Efforts to Experience the Holocaust* (Ithaca, NY: Cornell University Press, 2004)
WEISS-WENDT, ANTON (ed.), *The Nazi Genocide of the Roma: Reassessment and Commemoration* (New York: Berghahn Books, 2013)
WELLER, JAMES, *Becoming Evil: How Ordinary People Commit Genocide and Mass Killing* (Oxford: Oxford University Press, 2007)
WESSELING, ELISABETH, *Writing History as a Prophet: Postmodernist Innovations in a Historical Novel* (Amsterdam: John Benjamin's Publishing Company, 1991)
WHITE, HAYDEN, 'Historical Emplotment and the Problem of Truth', in *Probing the Limits of Representation: Nazism and the 'Final Solution'*, ed. by Saul Friedländer (Cambridge, MA: Harvard University Press, 1992), pp. 37–54
—— *Metahistory: The Historical Imagination in 19th-Century Europe* [1973] (Baltimore, MD: Johns Hopkins University Press, 2014)
WHITEHEAD, ANNE, *Trauma Fiction* (Edinburgh: Edinburgh University Press, 2004)
WIESEL, ELIE, 'All Was Lost, Yet Something Was Preserved: A Review of the Chronicle of the Lodz Ghetto, 1941–1944', *The New York Times Books Review*, 19 August 1984, p. 1
—— 'Eichmann's Victims and the Unheard Testimony', *Commentary*, 32 (December 1961), 510–16
—— 'The Holocaust as Literary Inspiration', in *Dimensions of the Holocaust: A Series of Lectures Presented at Northwestern University*, ed. by Elie Wiesel and others (Evanston, IL: Northwestern University Press, 1977), pp. 5–19
WIEVIORKA, ANNETTE, *L'Ère du témoin* [1998] (Paris: Pluriel, 2013)
—— 'The Witness in History', trans. by Jared Stark, *Poetics Today*, 27.2 (Summer 2006), 385–97
—— 'Faux témoignage', *L'Histoire*, 349 (January 2010) <http://www.lhistoire.fr/faux-témoignage>
WILDE, ALAN, 'Shooting for Smallness: Limits and Values in Some Recent American Fiction', *Boundary 2*, 13.2–3 (1985), 343–69
WILLIAMS, BENN E., 'Varying Shades of Grey: Pierre Assouline at the Frontier of Fact and Fiction', in *Re-examining the Holocaust through Literature*, ed. by Aukje Kluge and Benn E. Williams (Cambridge: Cambridge Scholars Publishing, 2009), pp. 111–30
WILSON, JEFFREY K., *The German Forest: Nature, Identity, and the Contestation of a National Symbol 1871–1914* (Toronto: University of Toronto Press, 2012)
WINK, AMY L., 'Diaries', in *Encyclopaedia of Feminist Theories*, ed. by Loraine Code (London: Routledge, 2000), pp. 133–35
WINSTONE, MARTIN, *The Holocaust Sites of Europe: An Historical Guide* (London: I. B. Tauris, 2010)
WISE, STEVEN, *Rattling the Cage: Towards Legal Rights for Animals* (Cambridge, MA: Perseus Books, 2000
WOOD, THOMAS E., and STANISŁAW M. JANKOWSKI, *Karski: How One Man Tried to Stop the Holocaust* (New York: John Wiley, 1994)

WOLF, NELLY, 'Figures de la fuite chez Patrick Modiano', in *Patrick Modiano*, ed. by John E. Flower (Amsterdam: Brill, 2007), pp. 211–22
WYMAN, DAVID, *The Abandonment of the Jews: America and the Holocaust 1941–1945* (New York: Pantheon, 1984)
YEHOSHUA, A. B., *Between Right and Right* (Garden City, NY: Doubleday, 1981)
YOGEV, MICHAEL, 'The Fantastic in Holocaust Literature: Writing and Unwriting the Unbearable', *Journal of the Fantastic in the Arts*, 5.2 (1993), 32–49
YOSEF, RAZ, *The Politics of Loss and Trauma in Israeli Cinema* (New York: Routledge, 2011)
YOUNG, JAMES E., 'Between History and Memory: The Uncanny Voices of Historian and Survivor', *History and Memory Journal*, 9.1–2 (Autumn 1997), 47–58
—— 'Holocaust Documentary Fiction: The Novelist as Eyewitness', in *Writing and the Holocaust*, ed. by Berel Lang (New York: Holmes & Meier, 1988), pp. 200–15
—— *Writing and Rewriting the Holocaust: Narrative and the Consequences of Interpretation* (Bloomington: Indiana University Press, 1988)
YUDKIN, LEON, 'Is Aharon Appelfeld a Holocaust Writer?', in *The Holocaust and the Text: Speaking the Unspeakable*, ed. by Andrew N. Leak and George Paizis (Basingstoke: Macmillan, 2000), pp. 142–58
ZALEWSKI, MARYSIA, *Feminism after Postmodernism? Theorising through Practice* (London: Routledge, 2003)
ZELIZER, BARBIE, *Remembering to Forget: Holocaust Memory through the Camera's Eye* (Chicago: University of Chicago Press, 1999)
ZIMMERMAN, JOSHUA D., 'Changing Perception in the Historiography of Polish-Jewish Relations during the Second World War', in *Contested Memories: Poles and Jews during the Holocaust and Its Aftermath*, ed. by Joshua D. Zimmerman (New Brunswick, NJ: Rutgers University Press, 2002), pp. 1–16
ZIPES, JACK, *The Brothers Grimm: From Enchanted Forests to the Modern World* (Basingstoke: Palgrave Macmillan, 2002)
—— 'The Contamination of the Fairy Tale, or the Changing Nature of the Grimms' Fairy Tales', *Journal of the Fantastic in the Arts*, 11.1 (2000), 77–93
—— *Grimm Legacies: The Magic Spell of the Grimm Folk and Fairy Tales* (Princeton, NJ: Princeton University Press, 2014)
—— *Spells of Enchantment: Wondrous Fairy Tales of Western Culture* (New York: Penguin, 1991)

Filmography

Avant l'hiver, dir. by Philippe Claudel (2013)
Cabaret, dir. by Bob Fosse (1972)
Le Chagrin et la pitié, dir. by Marcel Ophüls (1971)
The 81st Blow, dir. by Haim Gouri (1974)
Ilsa: She-wolf of the S.S., dir. by Don Edmonds (1974)
Il y a longtemps que je t'aime, dir. by Philippe Claudel (2008)
Karski or the Lords of Humanity, dir. by Sławomir Grünberg (2015)
Lacombe Lucien, dir. by Louis Malle (1974)
Nuit et brouillard, dir. by Alain Resnais (1955)
Le Rapport Karski, dir. By Claude Lanzmann (2010)
Schindler's List, dir. by Steven Spielberg (1993)
Shoah, dir. by Claude Lanzmann (1985)
La vita è bella, dir. by Roberto Benigni (1997)
Wielki Tydzień [Holy Week], dir. by Andrzej Wajda (1945)

INDEX

Aaron, Soazig 77, 95, 103 n. 2
  Le Non de Klara 2, 16, 73 n. 17, 77–110, 219
  La Sentinelle tranquille sous la lune 103 n. 3
abortion 82, 87
Adams, Jenni 139, 155
Adorno, Theodor 7, 168
Aesop 151, 161, 162, 165
Agamben, Giorgio 4, 60, 61, 98, 162, 195, 201
Albarahi, David 114
Algerian War 34–36, 119, 144 n. 74
allegory 98, 151, 152, 162, 164, 168, 173, 174
Allies 17, 88, 100, 166, 183, 186, 188, 189, 190, 192–94, 197, 207, 208, 212 n. 41
Amato, Joseph 99
amenorrhea 82, 86
America 75 n. 51, 78, 102, 183, 186, 188, 190, 196, 199, 203
Améry, Jean 82, 178 n. 86
Amesberger, Helga 89, 107 n. 64
Amis, Martin 114
anachronism 55, 78, 81, 99, 101, 112, 116, 128, 132, 189, 193, 205, 209
Andersen, Hans Christian 165
Andrzejewski, Jerzy, *Wielki Tydzień* 184
animals 151, 153, 154, 159, 161–67, 171, 172–74, 178 n. 89, 182 n. 145, 220
  agency of 166–67
  holocaust of 17, 168–71, 180 n. 116, 179 n. 111, 181 n. 120
  rights of 6, 17, 168
Antelme, Robert 5, 82
anti-Semitism 4, 22 n. 95, 31, 33, 37, 50 n. 50, 66, 68, 71, 72, 78, 82, 91, 93, 95–96, 101, 193, 164, 192, 194, 198
  in Vichy France 34, 36, 38, 41, 43, 46, 57, 64–65, 69, 90, 210 n. 14, 221
  of Polish society 67, 97, 184, 186, 189, 192, 202, 208
anthropocentrism 161, 171, 174, 167, 179 n. 102
Antti, Arne 157
Apel, Dora 31
Arendt, Hannah 37, 131, 141 n. 26, 196
Arnds, Peter 155, 157
Ascherson, Neal 198, 200, 215 n. 97, 215 n. 106
Assouline, Pierre, 111, 220
  La Cliente 15, 56–72
  L'Épuration des intellectuel 76 n. 68

Le Fleuve Combelle 57
Lutetia 57
Sigmaringen 57
Auschwitz:
  the camp of 8, 25, 26, 27, 33, 44, 59, 60–61, 66, 74 n. 38, 78, 82, 85, 86, 87, 90, 91, 92, 96, 97, 131, 135, 137, 152, 177 n. 65, 179 m 93, 181 n. 125, 192, 196–97
  synecdoche for the Holocaust 4, 60, 95, 114, 204, 208, 221
  museum 33, 199

Babi Yar 112, 124, 125, 131, 140 n. 12
Baer, Elizabeth 155, 156
Ball, Karyn 138, 185, 187, 206, 208–09, 214 n. 68, 216 n. 124
barracks 27, 34–36, 39, 43, 45
Barthes, Roland 8
  and the 'effet de réel' 27
Bartoszewski, Władysław 200, 215 n. 106, 108 n. 81
Bartov, Omer 60
Bassi, Giulia 70
Bauer, Yehuda 81
Bauman, Zygmunt 99, 102, 173
  and 'liquid identity' 91, 95, 102, 108 n. 81
Baumel, Judith Tydor 87, 106 n. 58
Beauvoir, Simone de 84
Benigni, Roberto 155
Benjamin, Andrew 166
Bettelheim, Bruno 162
Binet, Laurent, *HHhH* 3, 113–14
Birkenau (women's camp of) 82, 86, 88, 96, 177 n. 65
Blanrue, Paul-Éric 111
Błoński, Jan 185
Bornand, Marie 6, 7
Borowski, Tadeusz 82, 176 n. 76
Boswell, Matthew 11
Bougnoux, Daniel 112
Bouris, Erica 100
Brabon, Benjamin 81
Braidotti, Rosi 93
Brooks, Ann 80, 81
Brossat, Alain 58
Brown, Adam 60–61, 66
Browning, Christopher 41 n. 75, 120
Budnitz, Judy 155

Buettner, Angi 124, 146 n. 112
Burgin, Victor 91
Butler, Judith 95–96
bystanders 12, 17, 26, 40, 57, 60, 61, 98, 122, 123, 125, 135, 184, 188, 192–93, 200, 202, 214 n. 68, 215 n. 104

Cairns, Lucille 78, 95, 103 n. 2, 109 n. 104
camp sisters 82, 83, 87, 106 n. 58
Camus, Albert 209
Canetti, Elias 158
carnophallogocentrism 160, 162, 163, 171
Caruth, Cathy 16, 116–20, 122, 126–27, 129, 133, 136, 145 n. 82, 145 n. 84, 195
Catholicism 67, 71
Cayrol, Jean 5, 19 n. 33, 36
Celan, Paul 30, 82, 127, 178 n. 86, 147 n. 126, 186
Céline 57, 72, 93
Chanter, Tina 45, 49 n. 32
Chaouat, Bruno 77, 99
Charlesworth, Andrew 26
Chełmno (Kulmhof) Castle 40, 154, 157
Churchill, Winston 193
Cixous, Hélène 168, 169
Clammer, John 80, 95
Claudel, Philippe, *Le Rapport de Brodeck* 2, 16, 48 n. 13, 100, 151–82
Clifford, Rebecca 84
Codde, Philippe 156
Coetzee, J.M. 168, 169, 182 n. 137
Cole, Tim 26
collaboration 1, 4, 36, 39, 40, 55, 57, 58, 60, 62–65, 69, 71, 75 n. 57, 160, 162, 169, 173
  feminine (*la collaboration horizontale*) 56, 58, 71, 85
  of 'privileged' Jews 66, 100, 152
  of prominent intellectuals 13, 22 n. 94, 57, 75 n. 51
colonialism 35–36, 50 n. 50, 92, 172, 221
Conan, Éric 55
Cooke, Dervila 42
Coquio, Catherine 6–8
Costelloe, Timothy 169, 179 n. 111
Crosthwaite, Paul 22 n. 103, 118
Czechoslovakia 3, 113

Dauzat, Pierre-Émmanuel 111
Davis, Colin 29, 45
Davis, Karen 168
Dawidowicz, Lucy 195–96
Dean, Carolyn 124, 143 n. 54, 196, 200, 206
deconstruction 6, 13, 35, 79–80, 98, 118, 126, 173, 222
Delbo, Charlotte 5, 26, 77, 82, 111
Deleuze, Gilles and Félix Guattari 2, 153, 167, 174
denunciation (*la délation*) 42, 56–58, 62–65, 67–72, 80, 152, 157
Derrida, Jacques 2, 6, 13, 14, 19 n. 33, 23 n. 106, 30, 34, 79, 98, 147 n. 126, 153, 160, 162, 163, 165, 167, 168, 170–74, 178 n. 95, 180 n. 117, 186, 222

Des Pres, Terrence 86, 135
le devoir de mémoire 44, 55, 62
différend (*le différend*) 17, 153, 183, 187, 197, 203–04, 206
discontinuity 1, 2, 81, 92, 93, 201, 202, 208, 220, 221
Dostoevsky, Fyodor, *The Brothers Karamazov* 60
Drancy 27, 38, 42, 88, 161
Driscoll, Kári 154, 169

Eaglestone, Robert 6, 12–15, 29, 49 n. 36, 137, 199
Eagleton, Terry 11
ecocriticism 26, 171, 221
Eichmann, Adolf 100, 114, 146 n. 105, 195, 200
Einsatzgruppen 112, 136
Elliach, Yaffa 154
empathic unsettlement 115, 139
empathy 115, 44, 115, 123, 126, 129, 134, 136, 138, 139, 142 n. 45, 156, 162, 189, 205, 206, 220
empathy fatigue 10, 116, 125
Engel, David 190, 212 n. 41, 216 n. 32, 216 n. 34
épuration (purges) 15
ethics 2, 3, 4, 6, 13, 15, 17, 29–30, 45, 46, 47, 58, 60, 72, 101, 119, 166, 173, 199, 109, 209, 219, 220, 222
Ezrahi, Sidra DeKoven 48, 154, 231 n. 43
'ex-centricity' 2, 12, 58, 113
excremental assault 86, 135

fable 9, 16, 151–53, 154, 155, 157, 161–67, 169, 171–73, 182 n. 134, 220
Fackenheim, Emil 93
fairy tale 16, 151, 153, 156, 159–61, 163, 164–65, 172, 173, 175 n. 22, 176 n. 45, 176 n. 50, 220
  and the Holocaust 153–56
Faurisson, Robert 14–15, 204, 206, 208
Federman, Raymond 5, 19 n. 29
Felman, Shoshana 51 n. 72, 117, 195, 199, 207, 209
Felski, Rita 115
feminism 16, 79, 80–81, 92, 104 n. 17, 221
Fink, Ida 82
Foer, Jonathan Safran 154
Fontenay, Élisabeth de 168, 174
forest 26, 48 n. 13, 129–30, 137, 152, 158–59, 169, 176 n. 53
Foucault, Michel 2, 13, 22 n. 95, 80, 95–96, 102, 163
Frank, Anne 100
Frank, Hans 113
Frankfurter, Felix 205
Freud, Sigmund 117, 126, 133, 134, 136, 143 n. 55, 148 n. 148, 148 n. 160, 200
Fried, Gregory 13–14
Friedländer, Saul 197, 202
Fulbrook, Mary 193

Gallimard, Gaston 57
Gary, Romain 5
Gelbin, Cathy 81
Genz, Stéphanie 81

Gestapo 33, 63, 188, 193
Gibbs, Alan 113, 114, 118, 119, 138, 141
Głowacka, Dorota 93
Goebbels, Joseph 169
Goldberg, Myrna 81
Goldberg, Zachary 114, 146 n. 105
Golsan, Richard 35, 42, 73 n. 6
Gouri, Haim, *The 81ˢᵗ Blow* 206
Grabes, Herbert 12
Grass, Günter 155
Gratton, Johnnie 3, 35, 52 n. 88
Green, Mary Jean 32, 50 n. 45, 51 n. 68
Grey Zone 16, 55, 58, 59–62, 65–67, 70–72, 74 n. 32, 75 n. 41, 98, 131, 170, 219
Grierson, Karla 5–6
Grimm Brothers 157, 158, 176 n. 50, 176 n. 53
Gross, Jan Paweł 185
Grossberg, Lawrence 91
Gubar, Susan 207
Guicharnaud, Jacques 28
Guitry, Sacha 64

Haenel, Yannick, *Jan Karski* 2, 3, 17, 183–217
Haraway, Donna 92, 102
Hardman, Anna 82
Hartman, Geoffrey 125, 198
Heidegger, Martin 13, 170
Heine, Heinrich 164
Hennigfeld, Ursula 68, 73 n. 6
Hergé 57
Heydrich, Reinhard 3, 113
Hilberg, Raul 78, 145 n. 89, 179 n. 111, 183, 192, 195, 196
Hilsenrath, Edgar, *Der Nazi und der Friseur* 132, 155
Hilsum, Mireille 41
Himmelfarb, Gertrude 13, 11 n. 97
Himmler, Heinrich 113, 131, 136, 145 n. 88, 151, 169
Hirsch, Marianne 10, 89
historiographic metafiction ix, 1–3, 4, 6–7, 8, 9–12, 13, 16, 18 n. 6, 35, 38, 46, 56, 58, 71, 72, 81, 98, 113, 118, 138, 139, 186, 219–21
Hitler, Adolf 57, 87, 91, 93, 96, 112, 125, 126, 152, 141 n. 16, 162, 178 n. 76, 178 n. 89, 181 n. 122, 188, 193, 221
Holocaust:
  de-Judaisation of 71, 82, 95
  denial of 4, 11, 13–15, 112, 204, 208, 216 n. 128
  fatigue 10, 16, 125, 139, 147 n. 116, 220
  metanarrative 138, 156
  piety 139
  universalisation of 78, 115, 123
  women's experience of 12, 67, 77, 79, 81–83, 85–91, 104 n. 27, 105 n. 31, 105 n. 33, 105 n. 36, 106 n. 48, 132, 135, 160, 219, 221
homosexuality 96, 112, 113, 118, 134, 137, 180 n. 117
Horowitz, Nancy 88
Horowitz, Sara 83, 89

Höss, Rudolph 105 n. 36, 131, 136, 137, 181 n. 125
Howell, Philip 165, 179 n. 102
Hugo, Victor, *Les Misérables* 35
Humbert, Fabrice, *L'Origine de la violence* 3, 114
Hunter, Anna 139, 156
Husson, Édouard 112
Hutcheon, Linda 1, 2–3, 7, 10, 11, 18 n. 5, 27, 34, 38, 46, 71, 72, 81, 113, 153, 173, 211, 220
Hutton, Margaret Anne 95
Huyssen, Andrew 35, 81

identification 11, 15, 29, 42–44, 52 n. 88, 52 n. 89, 98, 115–16, 120, 122, 123, 128, 130, 132, 135, 136, 138, 142 n. 45, 156, 167, 187, 203, 206
Ikor, Roger 5
infanticide 82
intertextuality 1, 2, 7, 10, 27, 42, 46, 56, 60, 78, 81, 93, 98, 124, 127, 128, 132, 151, 152, 156, 159, 205, 220–21
irony 2, 3, 4, 7, 10, 29, 13, 26, 32, 36, 63, 65, 98, 123, 130, 132, 133, 137, 139, 153, 164, 199, 220
Israel 75 n. 57, 78, 99, 100, 120, 132, 190, 196, 210 n. 6, 211 n. 16
Izbica Lubelska 188, 191, 197, 203, 211 n. 26

Jacobs, Janet 206
Jameson, Fredric 11, 18 n. 10, 94
Jardin, Jean 57, 73 n. 8
Jensen, Meg 205
Judaism 85, 92, 95, 96, 122, 138
Judenräte (Jewish Councils) 66, 115
June, Pamela 81, 93
Jurt, Joseph 46

Kafka, Franz 194
Kakutani, Michiko 13, 14, 23 n. 106
Kaplan, Brett Ashley 36
Karmel, Ilona 82
Karski, Jan, *Story of the Secret State* 183, 185, 187, 194, 197, 205
Kass, Leon 111, 131
Kasztner, Rudolf 66, 75 n. 57
Katz, Eric 26
Katyń 186, 194
Kawakami, Akane 27, 28, 45
Kean, Hilda 165
Kerman, Judith 155
Kertész, Imre 7, 8
Klüger, Ruth, *weiter leben* 155, 202
Knittel, Susanne 114
Koonz, Claudia 91
Kosinski, Jerzy 82, 154, 178 n. 86
  The Painted Bird 161–62
Kosmodemyanskaya, Zoya 126–27, 147 n. 120
Krall, Hanna, 'The Woman from Hamburg' 77
Kremer, Lillian 87
Krilov, Ivan 161

Kristallnacht 152, 156, 157, 174 n. 6
Kristeva, Julia 111, 172
Kushner, Tony 193, 195

Lacan, Jacques 107 n. 76, 126
LaCapra, Dominick 8, 9, 11, 44, 74 n. 32, 79, 98, 99, 100, 111, 112, 115, 116, 120, 138, 165, 168, 174, 194–95, 196, 197, 198, 199, 200, 202, 206
Lacoste, Charlotte 114
La Fontaine, Jean de 161, 171, 172
Landwehr, Margarete 155
Lang, Berel 8, 13, 75
Langer, Lawrence 66, 71, 104 n. 27, 107 n. 26, 198
Langfus, Anna 26, 82
Lanzmann, Claude 11, 21 n. 75, 26, 39, 40, 111, 140 n. 5, 187, 212 n. 41, 214 n. 59, 215 n. 95, 215 n. 104
   Le Rapport Karski 198, 206, 216 n. 131
   Shoah 26, 39–40, 51 n. 72, 114, 132, 157, 184, 185, 187, 188, 189, 190, 194, 195, 198, 199, 200, 202, 206, 207, 208–09, 210 n. 7, 215 n. 95
Laub, Dori 117, 196–97, 199– 201, 203, 206, 207, 216 n. 109
Laval, Pierre 57
Lawson, Tom 195
Leake, Eric 115
Lee, Sander 61, 72, 75 n. 41
Leitner, Isabella 82, 106 n. 53
Lengyel, Olga, *Five Chimneys* 66, 75 n. 61, 82
Levi, Primo 82, 128, 163, 164, 166, 178n 86, 179 n. 93
   'The Grey Zone' 16, 58, 59–62, 65, 66, 71, 74 n. 25, 74 n. 32, 74 n. 33, 74 n. 36, 98, 100, 219
   La tregua 88
Levinas, Emmanuel 2, 6, 15, 29–30, 45, 49 n. 32, 126, 131, 153, 164, 170, 179 n. 106, 222
Lévy, Clara 6
Levy, Daniel 190
Leys, Ruth 119–21, 126
lieux de mémoire 39, 51 n. 68
Lipstadt, Deborah 13, 146 n. 116, 192
Littell, Jonathan, *Les Bienveillantes* 2, 3, 16, 47 n. 13, 100, 111–49, 188
Lot's wife 127–28
Lutetia (hotel) 57, 83, 87
Lyotard, Jean-François 2, 6, 14, 15, 17, 19 n. 33, 151, 153, 187, 195, 199, 203–04, 206, 208, 220, 222

McGlothlin, Erin 114, 116
MacNair, Rachel 119, 144 n. 77
Małczyński, Jacek 26
Malgouzou, Yannik 6, 8
Malle, Louis 5, 17 n. 1, 57
de Man, Paul 13, 22 n. 94, 22 n. 98
Manon Lescaut 42
Manouchian, Missak 30, 42
Manzoni, Alessandro 60

Marin, Louis 172
material witness 26, 38, 40
Meretoja, Hanna 123, 141 n. 20
Merle, Robert, *La Mort est mon métier* 114
metafiction 1, 2, 4, 11, 16, 27, 46, 78, 113, 119, 121, 156, 186, 198, 205
   historiographic ix, 1–2, 4, 6–7, 8, 9–12, 13, 16, 18 n. 6, 35, 38, 46, 56, 58, 71, 72, 81, 98, 113, 118, 138, 139, 186, 219–21
   traumatic 16, 111, 113, 118–19
Milchman, Alan 13
milieux de mémoire 39
Milne, Anna-Louise 28
Miłosz, Czesław 183–84, 189, 210 n. 6
Mischlinge 12, 81, 101
la mode rétro 1
modernity 9, 13, 21 n. 62, 22 n. 103, 37, 79, 81, 108 n. 81, 118, 139, 144 n. 70, 173, 204
Modiano, Albert 33, 40–43, 46, 49 n. 40
Modiano, Patrick, *Dora Bruder* 1, 2, 3, 15, 25–53, 55, 62, 111, 219
   Les Boulevards de ceinture 19 n. 29, 28, 32, 42
   Un cirque qui passe 46
   Lacombe Lucien 17 n. 1, 57
   Livret de famille 52
   La Place de l'étoile 1, 19 n. 29, 31–32, 43, 49
   Quartier perdu 28, 30
   Rue des Boutiques obscures 19 n. 29, 51 n. 61
Mohamed, Saira 116, 119, 121, 123
Morag, Raya 119, 120
Morgenstern, Naomi 118
Morina, Kristina 193
Morris, Alan 35, 43
Morse, Arthur 192
motherhood 16, 77, 79, 83, 87–90, 97, 102, 130, 160
Muhsfeldt, Erich 59, 60, 61
multidirectional memory 17, 50 n. 50
Munch-Jurisic, Ditte-Marie 131
Murphy, Louise 155

négationnisme 4, 11, 13–15, 112, 204, 208, 216 n. 128
Nettelbeck, Colin 42
Nireńska, Pola 190
Nivat, Georges 111
NKVD (Soviet People's Commissariat for Internal Affairs) 123, 129
non-places of memory 36, 39–40
Nora, Pierre 39, 51 n. 67, 111, 117
le nouveau roman 3
Nünning, Vera 12
Nuremberg trials 12, 186, 193, 208
Nussbaum, Martha 115

Olin, Margaret 40, 51 n. 72
Ophüls, Marcel, *Le Chagrin et la pitié* 5, 17 n. 1
Orwell, George, *Animal Farm* 161

Ozick, Cynthia 82, 104 n. 27

palimpsest 34, 36, 63, 102
palimpsestic memory 35, 64
Papon, Maurice 36
Paris 27–33, 36–42, 50 n. 52, 51 n. 61, 56, 66, 78, 90, 137, 183
  as a palimpsest 34–36
parody 1, 2, 9, 10, 16, 17, 27, 28, 83, 98, 102, 127, 151, 153, 160, 162, 172–73, 220, 221
patriarchy 69, 74 n. 33, 79, 80, 81, 86, 91–92, 101–02, 108 n. 66, 128
Patterson, Charles 168, 178 n. 90, 178 n. 111, 181 n. 125
Patterson, David 13
St Paul 65, 68–72, 76 n. 65, 69, 71–72
Pentlin, Susan 55, 57
Perec, Georges 5, 19 n. 33, 202
perpetrator 41, 56, 58, 79, 97, 98, 99, 116, 120, 123, 126, 128, 132, 142 n. 43, 178 n. 91
  disgust 129–32
  as a marginal figure 114–15
  novels about 114, 142 n. 35
  trauma 16, 48 n. 13, 116, 119–22, 130, 134, 138, 139, 144 n. 77, 219
Perry, Edith 134, 137
PETA 168, 180 n. 119
Pétain, Philippe 64
Petropoulos, Jonathan 59
Picoult, Jodi 114
Plath, Sylvia 96, 98
Plato, 123–24, 127, 128, 163
Poe, Edgar Allan 39
Poland x, 17, 39, 40, 67, 69, 113, 169, 183–85, 188–92, 194, 197, 198, 205, 208, 210 n. 7, 210 n. 15, 211 n. 16, 211 n. 26, 212 n. 41, 312 n. 43, 215 n. 84, 220
Poliakov, Léon 195
politics 6, 12, 17, 26, 81, 92, 101, 118, 124, 173, 174, 195, 208, 219, 221, 222
Popescu, Diana 207
Porajmos 12, 88, 100–01, 107 n. 65, 129, 157
postcolonialism 80, 171, 221
postfeminism 6, 16, 79, 80–81, 85, 92, 93, 102, 103 n. 13
posthumanism 221
postmemory 10
postmodern topography 28
postmodernism 2, 4, 6, 7, 10, 11, 13, 16, 27, 72, 79, 85, 91, 94, 117, 153, 173, 186, 219
  and ethics 12, 220
  and feminism 80–81, 104 n. 17
  and France 2–3, 6, 18 n. 10, 221–22
  and Holocaust denial 13–15
  and trauma 117–18, 144 n. 69, 144 n. 70
Post-Traumatic Stress Disorder (PTSD) 117, 119, 120
Prager, Eve, *Eve's Tattoo* 44

Prescott, Matt 168
'privileged' Jews 58–59, 62, 65, 66, 71, 86, 110
prostitution 42, 82, 86, 106 n. 52

racism 13, 36, 79, 91, 145 n. 84, 85, 101, 165, 168
Raczymow, Henry 5, 11, 52 n. 89, 115
Rank, Otto 133
rape 82, 164, 169
Rasson, Luc 134
Razinsky, Liran 129, 146 n. 100
realism 1, 3, 8–9, 11, 14, 20 n. 62, 27–28, 70, 95, 104 n. 17, 144 n. 70, 151, 154, 155, 202, 221
récit de filiation 41
résistancialisme 68, 84
Resnais, Alan, *Nuit et brouillard* 4
Ricœur, Paul 44
Ringelheim, Joan 81, 104 n. 27
La Rochelle, Drieu 57, 64
Roosevelt, Franklin 188, 193, 192, 193, 199, 203, 204–05, 216 n. 131
Rose, Gillian 99, 124
Rosen, Alan 209
Rosenberg, Alan 13
Rosenfarb, Chava 82, 155
Roth, John 59
Rothberg, Michael 8, 9, 17, 50, 118, 144 n. 70, 145 n. 84
Rothe, Anne 99, 100, 117, 119, 120, 121, 138, 206
Rousset, David 61
Rousso, Henry 15, 55, 68
Roux, Baptiste 30
Rozmarin, Miri 128
Rumkowski, Chaim 59, 60, 66
Ruszniewski-Dahan, Myriam 6, 7, 8

Sandberg, Eric 129
Sanyal, Debarati 50 n. 50, 61, 74 n. 32, 114, 123, 127, 131, 141 n. 17
Sax, Boria 165, 178 n. 89
Schama, Simon 25
Schwarz-Bart, André 164, 177 n. 69
Sciaky, Albert (François Vernet) 42
self-reflexivity 10, 11, 56, 81, 83, 186, 220
Semprún, Jorge 5, 26, 78, 111
Schlink, Berhard 114
Schönbeck, Sebastian 171, 181 n. 133
Schreiber, Elizabeth 154
Schuppli, Susan 26, 38
Shlonsky, Avraham 172
Sicher, Efraim 11
Silverman, Max 5, 35, 36, 50 n. 50, 64
Simenon, Georges 56, 57, 75 n. 51
Singer, Isaac Bashevis 168
Singer, Peter 168, 182 n. 137
Smith, Kevin Paul 154, 156, 160
Sonderkommando 59, 60, 78, 196, 197

spatial turn 25
Spiegelman, Art, *Maus* 79, 82, 154, 161, 178 n. 74, 184
Spielberg, Steven, *Schindler's List* 11, 115, 178 n. 89
Stalin, Joseph 188, 194
Still, Judith 165, 172
Stone, Dan ix, 6, 9, 14, 20 n. 60, 195, 196, 202
Styron, William, *Sophie's Choice* 66–67
suicide 68, 120, 130, 163, 164, 188, 190
Suleiman, Susan Rubin 5, 44–45, 52 n. 89
Sznaider, Natan 190
Sztybel, David 168, 170, 181 n. 128

Tame, Peter 32
Tasso, Torquato, *Gerusalemme Liberata* 16, 119, 122, 129, 145 n. 84
Terestchenko, Michel 112
testimony 6, 7, 9, 11, 14, 17, 78, 89, 114, 117, 120, 126, 153, 186–89, 194–209, 215 n. 109, 220
Theweleit, Klaus 112, 134
Thijs, Krijn 193
Thompson, Stith 157
Todorov, Tzvetan 60
la tonte 16, 56, 58, 65, 67–69, 71, 73 n. 17, 85, 97
Tournier, Michel, *Le Roi des Aulnes* 18 n. 12, 114
trace 28–31, 34, 43–44, 49 n. 32, 49 n. 36, 201, 202
trauma 6, 10, 11, 16, 111, 113, 114, 116, 117, 120–22, 123, 126, 129, 130, 143 n. 58, 144 n. 69, 144 n. 70, 145 n. 84, 154, 155, 195, 196, 199–203, 207, 219, 221
  culture 97, 117
  of birth 133, 148 n. 146
  envy 132
  perpetrator 16, 113, 116, 119, 122, 123, 125–26, 128–34, 137–39, 144 n. 74, 144 n. 77, 219
  secondary 79, 97, 120, 125, 146 n. 114
  transgenerational 79, 88, 97, 101
traumatic metafiction 16, 111, 113, 118–19
traumatic realism 9, 113, 141 n. 20, 144 n. 69
Treblinka 20 n. 45, 40, 132, 141 n. 26, 157, 169, 178 n. 90, 178 n. 111, 181 n. 125, 200, 202

Tseti, Angeliki 15

Ukraine 122, 126, 129, 197, 136

Viard, Bruno 122
Viart, Dominique 2, 41, 51 n. 73
Vice, Sue 11, 198, 214 n. 57, 215 n. 95, 217 n. 157
Vichy syndrome 15, 55
Vidal-Naquet, Pierre 196

Wajcman, Gérard 5, 181 n. 128
Wajda Andrzej, *Wielki Tydzień* 185
Wandering Jew (Rootless Jew) 31–33
Wardi, Charlotte 6, 8
Warsaw Ghetto 8, 184–85, 187, 188, 191, 194, 200, 202, 210 n. 6
Waugh, Patricia 11, 70, 81, 94
Waxman, Zoë 82, 86
Weber, Florian 157
Weissman, Gary 207
Wesseling, Elisabeth 12
White, Hayden 14, 20 n. 56
Whitehead, Anne 118
Wiesel, Elie 7, 11, 25, 26, 82, 146 n. 116, 190, 206, 213 n. 46, 213 n. 50
Wievorka, Annette 114, 187–89, 193, 195, 196, 211 n. 21
Wilkomirski, Benjamin 44, 189, 206

Yolen, Jane, *Briar Rose* 154, 157
  Devil's Arithmetic 155
Young, James 9, 93, 142 n. 43, 196–99
Yourcenar, Margarete 168

Zipes, Jack 155, 158
zoomorphism 16, 154, 163, 172, 220
Zygielbojm, Szmul 188
Żegota 189, 215 n. 106

www.ingramcontent.com/pod-product-compliance
Lightning Source LLC
Chambersburg PA
CBHW080223170426

43192CB00015B/2729